Cracking the

AP®

SPANISH LANGUAGE & CULTURE EXAM WITH AUDIO CD

2020 Edition

By the Staff of The Princeton Review

PrincetonReview.com

Penguin
Random
House

The Princeton Review
110 East 42nd St, 7th Floor
New York, NY 10017
Email: editorialsupport@review.com

Published in the United States by Penguin Random House
LLC, New York, and in Canada by Random House of
Canada, a division of Penguin Random House Ltd., Toronto.

Special thanks to VeinteMundos.com for permission
to use their articles in this book. Thanks also to Drake
Turrentino for use of the name *Special Olympics*.

Every effort has been made to trace and acknowledge
copyright material. The author and publisher would
welcome any information from the people who believe
they own copyrights to material in this book.

ISBN: 978-0-525-56834-6
ISSN: 2330-8451

Editor: Sarah Litt
Production Editor: Ali Landreau
Production Artist: Jennifer Chapman

Printed in the United States of America.

10 9 8 7 6 5 4 3 2 1

2020 Edition

Editorial

Rob Franek, Editor-in-Chief
David Soto, Director of Content Development
Stephen Koch, Survey Manager
Deborah Weber, Director of Production
Gabriel Berlin, Production Design Manager
Selena Coppock, Managing Editor
Aaron Riccio, Senior Editor
Meave Shelton, Senior Editor
Chris Chimera, Editor
Sarah Litt, Editor
Orion McBean, Editor
Brian Saladino, Editor
Eleanor Green, Editorial Assistant

Penguin Random House Publishing Team

Tom Russell, VP, Publisher
Alison Stoltzfus, Publishing Director
Amanda Yee, Associate Managing Editor
Ellen Reed, Production Manager
Suzanne Lee, Designer

Acknowledgments

The Princeton Review would like to thank Anne Goldberg-Baldwin, Ali Landreau, and Jennifer Chapman for their invaluable contributions to the 2020 edition of this book.

Audio Track List

Contents

Get More (Free) Content

at **PrincetonReview.com/cracking**

As easy as **1•2•3**

1 Go to PrincetonReview.com/cracking and enter the following ISBN for your book:

9780525568346

2 Answer a few simple questions to set up an exclusive Princeton Review account. *(If you already have one, you can just log in.)*

3 Enjoy access to your **FREE** content!

Once you've registered, you can...

- Get our take on any recent or pending updates to the Spanish Language & Culture Exam with Audio CD

- Take a full-length practice PSAT, SAT, and/or ACT

- Get valuable advice about the college application process, including tips for writing a great essay and where to apply for financial aid

- If you're still choosing between colleges, use our searchable rankings of *The Best 385 Colleges* to find out more information about your dream school

- Access comprehensive study guides and a variety of printable resources

- Check to see if there have been any corrections or updates to this edition

Need to report a potential **content** issue?

Contact **EditorialSupport@review.com** and include:

- full title of the book
- ISBN
- page number

Need to report a **technical** issue?

Contact **TPRStudentTech@review.com** and provide:

- your full name
- email address used to register the book
- full book title and ISBN
- Operating system (Mac/PC) and browser (Firefox, Safari, etc.)

Look For These Icons Throughout The Book

 ONLINE ARTICLES

 ONLINE AUDIO

 PROVEN TECHNIQUES

 APPLIED STRATEGIES

 MORE GREAT BOOKS

 STUDY BREAK

Part I
Using This Book to Improve Your AP Score

- Preview: Your Knowledge, Your Expectations
- Your Guide to Using This Book
- How to Begin

PREVIEW: YOUR KNOWLEDGE, YOUR EXPECTATIONS

Welcome to your *Cracking the AP Spanish Language and Culture Exam, 2020 Edition*. Your route to a high score on the AP Spanish Language and Culture Exam depends a lot on how you plan to use this book. Respond to the following questions.

1. Rate your level of confidence about your knowledge of the content tested by the AP Spanish Language and Culture Exam:

   A. Very confident—I know it all.
   B. I'm pretty confident, but there are topics for which I could use help.
   C. Not confident—I need quite a bit of support.
   D. I'm not sure.

2. Circle your goal score for the Exam:

   5   4   3   2   1   I'm not sure yet

3. What do you expect to learn from this book? Circle all that apply to you.

   A. A general overview of the test and what to expect
   B. Strategies for how to approach the test
   C. The content tested by this exam
   D. I'm not sure yet

YOUR GUIDE TO USING THIS BOOK

Cracking the AP Spanish Language and Culture Exam, 2020 Edition is organized to provide as much—or as little—support as you need, so you can use this book in whatever way will be most helpful to improving your score on the AP Spanish Language and Culture Exam.

- The remainder of **Part I** will provide guidance on how to use this book and help you determine your strengths and weaknesses.

- **Part II** of this book will
  o provide information about the structure, scoring, and content of the AP Spanish Language and Culture Exam
  o help you to make a study plan
  o point you towards additional resources

- **Part III** of this book will explore various strategies, such as
  o how to attack multiple choice questions
  o how to manage your time to maximize the number of points available to you

Online Audio

When you register your book online, you can download and/or stream all audio tracks that accompany the listening and speaking sections.

- how to write effective essays and responses
- how to synthesize and interpret integrative listening and reading tasks
- how to answer effectively in the speaking portions of the exam

- **Part IV** of this book is a review of the grammar topics you should master to do well on the test.

- **Part V** of this book contains contains two full-length practice tests, answers and explanations, sample student responses with scored evaluations, and translations for all test passages and questions. (Bubble sheets can be found in the very back of the book for easy tear-out.)

You may choose to use some parts of this book over others, or you may work through the entire book. This will depend on your needs and how much time you have. Let's now look at how to make this distinction.

Once you register your book online, you can print out the bubble sheets for both practice tests!

HOW TO BEGIN

1. **Take a Test**

   Before you can decide how to use this book, you need to take a practice test. Doing so will give you insight into your strengths and weaknesses, and the test will also help you make an effective study plan. If you're feeling test-phobic, remind yourself that a practice test is a tool for diagnosing yourself—it's not how well you do that matters, but how you use the information gleaned from your performance to guide your preparation.

   So, before you read further, take Practice Test 1, which is found in Part V of this book. Be sure to do so in one sitting, following the instructions that appear before the test.

2. **Check Your Answers**

   Using the answer key on page 236, count how many multiple-choice questions you got right and how many you missed. Don't worry about the explanations for now, and don't worry about why you missed questions. We'll get to that soon.

3. **Reflect on the Test**

After you take your first test, respond to the following questions:

- How much time did you spend on the multiple-choice questions?

- How many multiple-choice questions did you miss?

- How many multiple-choice questions did you guess on?

- How much time did you spend on the email response?

- How much time did you spend on the essay?

- Do you feel you had the knowledge and vocabulary needed to address the subject matter of the written portion?

- Do you feel you wrote a well-organized, thoughtful email and essay?

- How fluid and comfortable did you feel on the conversation?

- How fluid and comfortable did you feel on the presentation speech?

- Did you feel like you froze at any point in time when answering the speaking prompts?

- Did you have the knowledge and vocabulary needed for your spoken responses?

- Circle the content areas that were most challenging for you and draw a line through the ones in which you felt confident/did well.

main purpose questions
infer/suggest questions
understanding the passages
interpreting humor and irony in the passages and listening sections
retaining information from listening sections
relating listening and reading passages to one another
organizing your email response and persuasive essay
addressing the speaker appropriately in conversation
pronouncing your words clearly and with a good accent

How about grammar?

prepositions	personal *a*
por vs. *para*	irregular verbs
vocabulary	preterite vs. imperfect tenses
subjunctive/conditional	pronouns

4. **Read Part II of this Book and Complete the Self-Evaluation**
    Part II will provide information on how the test is structured and scored.

    As you read Part II, re-evaluate your answers to the questions above. At the end of Part II, you will revisit and refine the questions you answered above. You will then be able to make a study plan, based on your needs and time available, that will allow you to use this book most effectively.

5. **Engage with Parts III and IV**
    Notice the word *engage*. You'll get more out of this book if you use it intentionally than if you read it passively and hope for an improved score through osmosis.

    Strategy chapters will help you think about your approach to the question types on this exam. Part III will open with a reminder to think about how you approach questions now and then close with a reflection section asking you to think about how/whether you will change your approach in the future.

    The Part IV grammar review is designed to provide an overview of the verbs and grammar forms you should have mastered by test day. You will have the opportunity to assess your mastery of this content through several drills and a reflection section.

6. **Take Practice Test 2 and Assess Your Performance**
    Once you feel you have developed the strategies you need and gained the knowledge you lacked, take Practice Test 2. You should do so in one sitting, following the instructions at the beginning of the test.

    When you are done, check your answers to the multiple-choice sections. See whether a teacher will read your responses to the free-response questions and provide feedback.

    Once you have taken the test, reflect on what areas you still need to work on, and revisit the chapters in this book that address those deficiencies. Through this type of reflection and engagement, you will continue to improve.

7. **Keep Working**
    As we will discuss in Part II, there are other resources available to you, including a wealth of information on the AP Students website. You can continue to explore areas in which you can stand to improve and engage in those areas right up to the day of the test.

Part II
About the AP Spanish Language and Culture Exam

- The Structure of the AP Spanish Language and Culture Exam
- How the AP Spanish Language and Culture Exam Is Scored
- Overview of Skills Tested
- How AP Exams Are Used
- Other Resources
- Designing Your Study Plan

THE STRUCTURE OF THE AP SPANISH LANGUAGE AND CULTURE EXAM

The AP Spanish Language and Culture Exam consists of the following two sections:

Notice something different?
At the time this book went to press, The College Board was making some changes to your AP course. Make sure to check on the College Board website for any updates!

- **Section I** is the multiple-choice section, which tests *reading* and *listening* skills.
- **Section II** is the free-response section, which tests *writing*, *listening*, and *speaking* skills.

The College Board provides a breakdown of the types of questions covered on the exam. This breakdown will *not* appear in your test booklet: It comes from the preparatory material the College Board publishes. The chart below summarizes exactly what you need to know for the exam.

Section		Number of Questions	Percent of Final Score	Time
Section I: Multiple Choice				Approx. 95 minutes
Part A	Interpretive Communication: Print Texts	30 questions	50%	Approx. 40 minutes
Part B	Interpretive Communication: Print and Audio Texts (combined)	35 questions		Approx. 55 minutes
	Interpretive Communication: Audio Texts			
Section II: Free Response				Approx. 85 minutes
Interpersonal Writing: Email Reply		1 prompt	12.5%	15 minutes
Presentational Writing: Persuasive Essay		1 prompt	12.5%	Approx. 55 minutes (15 minutes to read; 40 minutes to write)
Interpersonal Speaking: Conversation		5 prompts	12.5%	20 seconds for each response
Presentational Speaking: Cultural Comparison		1 prompt	12.5%	2 minutes to respond (4 minutes to prepare)

The exam is approximately 3 hours long and has two parts—multiple choice and free response. Each section of the exam is worth 50 percent of the final exam grade.

Section I: Multiple Choice—65 questions; 1 hour and 35 minutes (50% of grade)

Part A—30 questions; 40 minutes

- Interpretive Communication: Print Texts. Reading comprehension questions are based on a variety of authentic print materials, including prose fiction, journalistic articles, advertisements, letters, maps, and tables. Some of the written texts may include a visual component or a web page. Questions will ask you to identify the main points and significant details, and make inferences and predictions from the written texts. Some questions may require making cultural inferences or inserting an additional sentence in the appropriate place in the reading passage.

> ## A Note on Directions
> All directions in the examination booklet will be printed in English and in Spanish. Familiarize yourself with the directions in this book so that you will not have to spend more time on them than necessary. On test day, choose the language you are more comfortable with and skim only that set of the directions. Don't waste time reading both sets of directions, or worse yet, comparing the translations for accuracy. Use that time to jot down notes and organize your responses if possible.

Part B—35 questions; 55 minutes

- Interpretive Communication: Print and Audio Texts (combined). The first of the two listening subsections pairs print texts with audio selections representing a variety of sources (interviews, podcasts, conversations, public service announcements, etc.).
- Interpretive Communication: Audio Texts. The second of the two subsections consists solely of audio selections representing the same types of sources described above. All audio selections will be played twice, and you will have time to preview the questions before answering them.

You are encouraged to take notes during this part of the exam and are given writing space for that purpose. Your notes will not affect your scores. Total scores on the multiple-choice section are based on the number of questions answered correctly. Points are not deducted for incorrect answers, and no points are awarded for unanswered questions.

Section II: Free Response—4 tasks; 1 hour and 25 minutes (50% of grade)

Writing

- Interpersonal Writing: Email Reply. You'll be asked to read and then write a formal response to an email message. For example, you may be prompted to reply to a job or scholarship offer. (15 minutes; 12.5% of final exam grade)

- Presentational Writing: Persuasive Essay. This prompt requires you to synthesize information from a variety of print and audio sources, present the different viewpoints, indicate your own viewpoint, and defend it thoroughly. You'll be given an essay prompt and several minutes to read and listen to the materials before you start writing. (15 minutes to review materials plus 40 minutes to write; 12.5% of final exam grade)

Speaking

- Interpersonal Speaking: Conversation. This section requires you to verbally respond to a series of recorded cues. Your responses will be guided by an outline of a short conversation, which will be provided. You will be assigned one side of the conversation, and the recording will supply the other. Your responses will be recorded. (20 seconds per response; 12.5% of final exam grade)
- Presentational Speaking: Cultural Comparison. You'll be asked to make a 2-minute presentation on a given cultural topic. Your assignment is to compare cultural features of your own community with those found in an area of the Spanish-speaking world with which you are familiar. You're encouraged to cite examples from materials you've read, viewed, or listened to, as well as from personal experiences and observations. (12.5% of final exam grade)

HOW THE AP SPANISH LANGUAGE AND CULTURE EXAM IS SCORED

Your Multiple-Choice Score

At the time this book went to press, The College Board was making some changes to your AP course. Make sure to check on the College Board website for any updates!

In the multiple-choice section of the test, you are awarded one point for each question that you answer correctly, and you receive no points for each question that you leave blank or answer incorrectly. That is, the famous "guessing penalty" on the SAT and SAT Subject Tests does not apply to this test. So, even if you are completely unsure, guess. In Part III, we'll show you how to narrow down your choices and make educated guesses.

Your Free-Response Score

Each AP essay and spoken response question is scored on a scale from 0 to 5, with 5 being the best score. Essay readers (who are high school or university Spanish instructors) will grade your essays and spoken responses, and the score for each section will be worth roughly 12.5% of your total score.

In general, an essay that receives a "5" answers all facets of the question completely, making good use of specific examples to support its points, and is "well-written," which is a catch-all phrase that means its sentences are complete, properly punctuated, clear in meaning, and varied (that is, they exhibit a variety of structure and use a large academic vocabulary). Graders are looking for you to have an ease of expression in the Spanish language, utilizing idiomatic phrases where appropriate and correct vocabulary and grammar. Can you accurately convey your point and go into detail on the essays? on the spoken responses? This knowledge of vocabulary, grammar, and idioms will garner you a high score on Part B of the test. Lower-scoring essays are considered to be deficient in these qualities to a greater or lesser degree, and students who receive a "0" have basically written gibberish or "I don't know." If you write an essay that is not on the topic, you will receive a blank ("—"). This is equivalent to a zero.

Detailed scoring guidelines for each of the four free-response prompts are available for download at the College Board's AP Spanish Language and Culture Exam Information page (see page 14 for a link).

Your Final Score

Your final score of 1 to 5 is a combination of your scores from the two sections. Remember that the multiple-choice section counts for 50 percent of the total and the essay/spoken response section counts for 50 percent. This makes them equal, so you must concentrate on doing your best on both parts. If you can get a score of 44 (number correct) on a multiple-choice section with 65 questions, you have about a 99 percent chance of getting at least a score of 3 on the exam.

What Your Final Score Will Mean

After taking the test in early May, you will receive your scores sometime around the first week of July, which is probably when you'll have just started to forget about the entire harrowing experience. Your score will be, simply enough, a single number that will either be a 1, 2, 3, 4, or 5. Here is what those numbers mean.

Score Meaning	Approximate percentage of all test takers receiving this score	Roughly equivalent first-year college course grade	Will a student with this score receive credit?
5—Extremely qualified	23.7%	A	Usually
4—Well qualified	34.7%	A–, B+, B	Usually
3—Qualified	29.9%	B–, C+, C	Maybe
2—Possibly qualified	10.3%	N/A	Very Rarely
1—Not qualified	1.4%	N/A	No

OVERVIEW OF SKILLS TESTED

The AP Spanish Language and Composition Exam tests the following skills and knowledge:

Grammar. Section I will mostly test the following categories:

- Vocabulary
- Verb tenses
- Pronouns
- Idioms

Writing and Speaking. In Section II, you will:

- Integrate text and audio sources, identifying similarities and differences.
- Form opinions and support those opinions with evidence and examples.
- Use a variety of relevant vocabulary.
- Self-monitor and adjust responses to the prompts. If needed, circumlocution and paraphrasing can be helpful to keep yourself on track for answering questions. This may help you, in a pinch, to familiarize yourself with new terms or still convey your point if that vocabulary word you need escapes you.
- Focus on building vocabulary related to the following categories: current events, family, the arts, politics, history, and social issues.

Hey! What's going on here? If some of the material in this book looks different than what you see on the test, it's because at the time this book went to press, The College Board was making some changes to your AP course. Make sure to check on the College Board website for any updates!

HOW AP EXAMS ARE USED

Different colleges use AP exam scores in different ways, so it is important that you go to a particular college's website to determine how it uses AP exam scores. The three items below represent the main ways in which AP exam scores can be used.

More Great Books
Check out The Princeton Review's college guidebooks, including *The Best 385 Colleges, The Complete Book of Colleges, Paying for College,* and many more!

- **College Credit.** Some colleges will give you college credit if you score well on an AP exam. These credits count towards your graduation requirements, meaning that you can take fewer courses while in college. Given the cost of college, this could be quite a benefit, indeed.

- **Satisfy Requirements.** Some colleges will allow you to "place out" of certain requirements if you do well on an AP exam, even if they do not give you actual college credits. For example, you might not need to take an introductory-level course, or perhaps you might not need to take a class in a certain discipline at all.

- **Admissions Plus.** Even if your AP exam will not result in college credit or even allow you to place out of certain courses, most colleges will respect your decision to push yourself by taking an AP course or even an AP exam outside of a course. A high score on an AP exam shows mastery of more difficult content than is taught in many high school courses, and colleges may take that into account during the admissions process.

OTHER RESOURCES

There are many resources available to help you improve your score on the AP Spanish Language and Culture Exam, not the least of which are your teachers. If you are taking an AP class, you may be able to get extra attention from your teacher, such as obtaining feedback on your essays. If you are not in an AP course, reach out to a teacher who teaches AP Spanish Language and Culture, and ask whether the teacher will review your essays or otherwise help you with content.

AP Students

Another wonderful resource is AP Students, the official site of the AP exams. The scope of the information at this site is quite broad and includes

- The *AP Spanish Language and Culture Exam Course and Exam Description* (Effective Fall 2013), which includes details on what content is covered and sample questions
- Released free-response questions from the 2015 exam, including audio prompts
- Exam practice tips
- Full rubrics for the written and spoken portions of the test
- Sample activities to help you improve your Spanish and prepare for the exam

The AP Students home page address is: http://apcentral.collegeboard.com/home

The AP Spanish Language and Culture Exam Course home page address is: http://apcentral.collegeboard.com/apc/public/courses/teachers_corner/3499.html

The AP Spanish Language and Culture Exam Information page (where you can find those scoring guidelines mentioned earlier) is: http://apcentral.collegeboard.com/apc/public/exam/exam_information/4554.html

Finally, The Princeton Review offers in-person and online tutoring for the AP Spanish Language and Culture Exam. Our expert instructors can help you refine your strategic approach and add to your content knowledge. For more information, call 1-800-2REVIEW.

Break up your review into manageable portions. Download our helpful study guide for this book, once you register online.

DESIGNING YOUR STUDY PLAN

In Part I, you identified some areas of potential improvement. Let's now delve further into your performance on Practice Test 1, with the goal of developing a study plan appropriate to your needs and time commitment.

Read the answers and explanations associated with the multiple-choice questions (starting at page 236). After you have done so, respond to the following questions:

- Review the Overview of Skills Tested on page 12 and, next to each one, indicate your rank of the topic as follows: "1" means "I need a lot of work on this," "2" means "I need to beef up my knowledge," and "3" means "I know this topic well."
- How many days/weeks/months away is your AP Spanish Language and Culture Exam?
- What time of day is your best, most focused study time?
- How much time per day/week/month will you devote to preparing for your AP Spanish Language and Culture Exam?
- When will you do this preparation? (Be as specific as possible: Mondays and Wednesdays from 3:00 to 4:00 P.M., for example.)
- What are your overall goals in using this book?

Part III
Test-Taking Strategies for the AP Spanish Language and Culture Exam

PREVIEW

Review your responses to the first three questions on page 4 of Part I and then respond to the following questions:

- How many multiple-choice questions did you miss even though you knew the answers?
- On how many multiple-choice questions did you guess blindly?
- How many multiple-choice questions did you miss after eliminating some answers and guessing based on the remaining answers?
- Did you create an outline before you wrote each essay?
- Did you find any of the essays easier/harder than the others—and, if so, why?
- What was your plan of attack with the spoken portions of the exam?
- Did you have phrases at the ready as templates to answer the questions?
- Was the spoken portion difficult? If so, which part? How so?

HOW TO USE THE CHAPTERS IN THIS PART

Before you read the following Strategy chapters, take a moment to think about how you approach each question type. As you read and engage in the directed practice, be sure to appreciate the ways in which you can improve. At the end of Part III, you will have the opportunity to reflect on how you will change your approach.

Chapter 1
How to
Approach the
Multiple-Choice
Section

THE STRUCTURE OF THE MULTIPLE CHOICE SECTION

The multiple choice section on the exam breaks down into reading and listening selections. Part A consists entirely of reading comprehension passages while Part B contains integrated reading and listening passages and interpretive communication, or dual listening passages. These different combinations of reading and listening require varying ways of interfacing with the material, which we will break down below.

INTERPRETIVE COMMUNICATION: PRINT TEXTS

Strategy for all Parts of the Multiple Choice

Reading Passages

Since the test makers design the test with a serious time crunch, it is important to have a strategy to tackle the passage, and this might not include reading the entire passage. Remember that this is an open-book test, so there is no reason to read and remember the entire passage. Usually, this sort of approach leads to re-reading, which wastes valuable time on the test. Instead, know what the questions ask for; this will direct and guide your reading to help you find the answers as opposed to retaining information that you may or may not need.

> Basic approach:
>
> 1. Read the introduction
> 2. Work the questions
> 3. Work the passage and answers

Step 1: Read the Introduction

Always read the short introduction that gives a little bit of information about the subject *(tema)*, when the piece was written, who is speaking or writing, and where the passage appeared. While this information might seem like a waste of time when there is so much to read in the passages, it gives a bit of context that will make the rest of the passage more digestible. Besides, it actually might help lead to the answers to the general questions!

If it seems like a difficult passage, find an easier passage to tackle first and then come back to it. By knowing some context right away, you may be able to enter into the text more easily, which will lead to less rereading and therefore saved time on the text.

Step 2: Work the Questions

The key to being efficient on this test is to know what the questions are asking ahead of time. That way, you are primed to know what to read or listen for. Many test takers waste valuable time on the test by reading the entire passage or listening through the entire conversation, and then going back to reread what they partially remember. There is no need to try to retain the entire passage, so why try? Instead, work the questions.

There are a couple of things to note when working the questions: one is whether questions are general or specific. Take a look at the questions below:

> *¿Quién narra este pasaje?*
> Who is narrating the passage?

> *¿De qué se trata este pasaje?*
> What is this passage about?

> *¿Cuál es el propósito del artículo?*
> What is the purpose of the article?

> *¿Cuál de las siguientes afirmaciones resume mejor el artículo?*
> Which of the following statements best summarizes the article?

> *¿Cuál es una conclusión lógica que se puede hacer sobre este contenido?*
> What is a logical conclusion based on the content?

Note that none of these questions contains specific information from any particular passage, nor are there any line references to point you in the right direction. Therefore, they must be general questions. Mark them as general questions with a "G" or any other mark of your choice and save them for last. Oftentimes, the test makers place these types of questions at the beginning of the question bank, but there is no rule saying you have to do these questions in order. Instead, work some questions that do have line references or key words easily found in the text first, and then you will have more information with which to answer those general questions afterwards.

Take a look at these specific questions and notice what they contain in contrast to the general questions:

> *Según el autor en el primer párrafo, ¿por qué hay una crisis contemporánea de salud mundial?*
> According to the author in the first paragraph, why is there a contemporary world health crisis?

> *En el segundo párrafo, David Soler espera que*
> According to the second paragraph, David Soler hopes that

> *Se menciona* Un chien andalou *para*
> Un chien andalou is mentioned in order to

¿Cómo llegó Vera a la rumba?
How did Vera come to know rumba?

¿A que se refiere "no aborda la dimensión política" (línea 54)?
What does "he does not address the political dimension" refer to (line 54)?

Notice a few things here: line references, such as *línea 54*, are always wonderful ways to know where to look in a passage for the answers. While line references are not always available, other indicators such as *el segundo párrafo* can lead to the correct window of the text. Other useful tools are key words that are specific to the passage or listening track. Capitalized names and places are great key words to locate in a passage because they are often easier to spot. Titles, words in italics, quotations, and other easily recognizable words or symbols are great key words to scan the text or listen for.

Finally, know what the question is asking. Most questions are "what" or "why" questions, and knowing which one a question is will frame how you work to answer them. The "what" questions generally begin with *Cuál, De qué,* or other similar phrases that are simply asking what the passage says, and the answer will be a paraphrase of information found directly in the passage or introduction. Questions that contain language such as *por qué* or *se menciona...para* require a bit more analysis of not only what the author says, but also why he or she says it. The "why" the question is asking for, however, is always something that can be found in the passage. Unlike more speculative, creative responses you might dream up in English or Spanish literature class, there is always an objectively right response based on the text here.

Is it a *what* question or a *why* question?

Step 3: Work the Passage & Answers

Now that you know what you are looking for, go to the passage and read what is necessary to answer the questions. For listening comprehension, listen for the key words to appear in the context of the lecture or conversation and jot down quick notes about what the characters say. Remember, the answers are always written explicitly in the text or said explicitly in the audio. From there, compare what you know the answer to be with what is given in the answer choices.

The Power of POE

The wonderful thing about multiple-choice questions is that the wrong answers are there for you to identify and eliminate. The test makers write answer choices with common types of wrong answers that, with a bit of practice, will become easily recognizable. Here are some common traps that you might come across:

- Extreme answers: avoid words like *todos, siempre, nunca,* etc., which often turn the statement into something beyond what the passage stated.
- Words taken out of context: sometimes you see words in the passage that show up in the answer choices, but they are used differently or taken out of context to make the choice too literal.
- Right information, wrong question: a true statement that does not answer the question is a wrong answer.
- Outside knowledge: limit yourself to only things you can point to within the passage or quote from listening. Outside knowledge, even if true, will never be a correct response.

Proven Techniques
Use POE to help boost your score.

Pacing

Pacing is how much time you spend on each passage and even each question. Thinking about pacing requires thinking about ordering your approach in terms of level of difficulty. Remember, questions have varying levels of difficulty, and you don't get extra credit for harder questions. So: take the easy test first! Find the passages that will be easier to answer and complete them before you move on to the more difficult ones. That way, you guarantee yourself points before you tackle the harder questions, and you can take the time you'll need to work on those without worrying about sacrificing any easy points.

Final Advice on the Reading Passages

There are a variety of approaches to tackling the passages, depending on comfort level and reading speed. For some, a general skim is comfortable. For others, reading the first line of each paragraph to see the structure of the passage is helpful. Others search for a key word by reading until they find it. Still others search for the key word and only read the window around the key word or line reference, about 5 lines before and after. This depends on individual comfort, so try a couple of different ways of engaging with the passage to find what works best for you. Consider how much time you have left in the test as well: if you are running out of time, perhaps finding those key words and getting those last couple of points is more efficient than trying to read for the main idea or analysis questions. Let's try a sample passage and apply these strategies:

Sample Passage

SOURCE: https://www.veintemundos.com/magazines/207-en/

(Translation on page 27)

El siguiente artículo sobre una mujer quien descubrió una manera de crear materiales sostenibles para joyería apareció en una revista latinoamericana en 2018.

Celina Brizuela es doctora en química y farmacia, emprendedora y luchadora. Después de trabajar 18 años en una firma de investigación, decidió comprar un taller de joyería. En 2010 empezó a crear materiales con la apariencia de oro y plata tomando como base desechos sólidos (llaves, tuberías, latas) para dar vida a la denominada "ecojoyería". En 2017, Celina ganó el premio a la mejor diseñadora de joyas de Honduras. Sus creaciones llegan hoy a Guatemala, Nicaragua y EE.UU.; a futuro piensa exportarlas a Europa.

Honduras es un país que refleja un fuerte ascenso en las oportunidades laborales femeninas. El Instituto Nacional de Estadísticas confirma que más de 900 000 madres aportan a la economía del país. Los sectores donde hay mayor participación de mujeres son comercio, salud, educación, industria manufactura y microempresas. En la economía informal está todo el aporte femenino de las emprendedoras. A su vez, el núcleo de gran parte de los pequeños emprendimientos es de carácter familiar.

No obstante, la informalidad, la falta de historia crediticia y los altos costos son los principales obstáculos que enfrentan estas empresas. Cabe mencionar que ahora las mujeres están incursionando en otros espacios que tradicionalmente habían sido dominados por los hombres, como el cuidado de los recursos naturales, el medio ambiente y la participación política. Sin embargo, las féminas ganan menos en comparación con los varones.

Una mujer emprendedora enfocada al medio ambiente y el arte es Celina Brizuela. Madre de dos hijas y originaria de Tegucigalpa. Su interés por hacer cosas nuevas surgió en la compañía de investigación norteamericana donde trabajó. Siempre le ha gustado salirse de lo que todo el mundo está haciendo, así que un día decidió seguir su sueño: alquiló un taller de joyería para crear sus propias piezas en base a desechos sólidos metálicos disponibles a nivel local.

Por si fuera poco, por medio de una aleación, Celina logró transformar esos metales de modo que tuvieran las mismas características del oro y la plata. En 2017 fue premiada como la mejor diseñadora de joyas de Honduras por el "Consejo Hondureño de la Empresa Privada y la Cámara de Comercio e Industrias de Tegucigalpa".

"Me gusta observar las tendencias, actualizarme y ver qué es lo que está pasando y qué hacen otros grandes diseñadores de joyas". En 2014 Piso Diez Diseño invitó a Celina a ser parte de su grupo de diseñadores y fue ahí cuando tuvo su primera pasarela con ellos. En 2017 participó en Fashion Week Honduras donde mostró una línea única, romántica, que llevaba por nombre Celeste, su color predilecto y el nombre de su empresa, puesto en honor a su madre, una mujer artista. "Me sentí muy honrada por participar y fue mi primera vez".

Actualmente son nueve personas que trabajan directamente en el taller de Celina. "Somos los únicos que estamos haciendo esa aleación en Honduras. Hay algunas empresas que se dedican a hacer cosas con metales, pero Corporación Celeste es la única firma que saca una aleación para hacer oro y plata", resalta la diseñadora.

Hay mucha gente que la invitó a ir a las universidades para contar su historia. "Mi sueño para el futuro es que la ecojoyería se posicione como una marca hondureña, que podamos mostrar a la gente que en Honduras no solamente hay violencia y corrupción; que vean y aprecien la creatividad y el talento de los emprendedores así como la belleza de nuestro país. Deseo que trascienda lo que estamos haciendo. Hay tantas cosas interesantes en Honduras", concluye Celina.

1. ¿Cuál es el propósito del pasaje?

   (A) mostrar el poder del oro y de la plata en la economía

   (B) contar la historia de una emprendedora que ha cambiado la manera en que hace joyería

   (C) ilustrar como hay un crecimiento de empresarias feministas en Honduras

   (D) advertir de que la falta de crédito destruye los emprendimientos familiares

2. ¿Cuál de las conclusiones sobre la "ecojoyería" es verdad?

   (A) La aleación transforma los materiales sostenibles al oro y la plata.

   (B) La manera de hacer joyería con materiales reciclados es la invención de Celina.

   (C) Los materiales reciclados son más duros que el oro y la plata.

   (D) Celeste es el único color que se puede crear con el proceso de aleación.

3. Se menciona la falta de historia crediticia en el tercer párrafo para

   (A) comparar algunos tipos de interés para los emprendedores.

   (B) notar que Celina tiene mal crédito.

   (C) mostrar que las féminas reciben préstamos más pequeños que los varones.

   (D) demostrar algunas dificultades que enfrenten a los emprendedores Hondureños.

4. ¿Por qué Celina nombra su negocio Celeste?

   (A) Es en honor de los artistas femeninas.

   (B) Es el color natural que resulta por el proceso de aleación.

   (C) Es el color favorito de su mamá.

   (D) Es su color favorito y en honor de su madre.

5. Podemos inferir que

   (A) Fashion Week Honduras fue el primer pasarela para Celina.

   (B) El proceso de aleación convierte los metales sostenibles al oro y a la plata.

   (C) Honduras es un país afligido por la corrupción y violencia.

   (D) Se puede encontrar la joyería de Celina en los estados unidos.

6. Un título apropiado para este artículo sería

(A) "Emprendedoras feministas"

(B) "Obstáculos financieros para los emprendedores"

(C) "Joyería recién descubierta: aleación sostenible"

(D) "Fashion Week y la 'ecojoyería'"

Here's How to Crack It

First, look at the introduction: the magazine article is about a woman who discovered new ways of making jewelry with sustainable materials instead of traditional gold and silver. Next, look below to the questions before diving into the passage to see which questions are easiest to tackle first.

Questions 1, 5, and 6 are general questions, so save them for later: there is no need to read the whole passage from start to finish to try to answer these first. Rather, find more specific questions to work on first, and then you will most likely have enough information to answer the other questions. Remember also that the introduction can sometimes provide information on the general questions.

2. ¿Cuál de las conclusiones sobre la "ecojoyería" es verdad?

(A) La aleación transforma los materiales sostenibles al oro y la plata.

(B) La manera de hacer joyería con materiales reciclados es la invención de Celina.

(C) Los materiales reciclados son más duros que el oro y la plata.

(D) Celeste es el único color que se puede crear con el proceso de aleación.

Ok, this question has a clear key word *ecojoyería* so find it in the passage to find the answer. The passage states, *En 2010 empezó a crear materiales con la apariencia de oro y plata tomando como base desechos sólidos (llaves, tuberías, latas) para dar vida a la denominada "ecojoyería".* The sentence refers to Celina, who started to create materials with the appearance of gold and silver. Eliminate (A) because the alloy does not transform the materials *into* gold and silver, but rather to have the *appearance of* gold and silver. Keep (B) because this is a paraphrase of what the passage says, that she started to create materials. While this may not be enough to prove invention, keep it. Eliminate (C) because it does not say that the materials are stronger than gold or silver. Eliminate (D) as well because it does not say the only color that can be created is pale blue. There is further proof in the passage: *Corporación Celeste es la única firma que saca una aleación para hacer oro y plata",* meaning that the only company to do so is Celina's company. The correct answer is (B).

3. Se menciona la falta de historia crediticia en el tercer párrafo para

(A) comparar algunos tipos de interés para los emprendedores.

(B) notar que Celina tiene mal crédito.

(C) mostrar que las féminas reciben préstamos más pequeños que los varones.

(D) demostrar algunas dificultades que enfrenten a los emprendedores Hondureños.

This question has the key phrase *la falta de historia crediticia* as well as a paragraph reference, making this information doubly easy to find in the passage. *Se menciona…para* is essentially a "why" question, so read for why the author mentions the lack of credit history in the passage. The passage states that *la falta de historia crediticia y los altos costos son los principales obstáculos que enfrentan estas empresas.* Therefore, this is an obstacle that entrepreneurs may encounter. The passage does not compare interest rates, so eliminate (A). The passage does not explicitly say that Celina is one of the entrepreneurs who has a lack of credit, so eliminate (B) as well. While the passage mentions women making less money than men, it does not mention them receiving smaller loans as well. Eliminate (C). The information found in the passage does show proof of some difficulties that Honduran entrepreneurs encounter. The correct answer is (D).

4. ¿Por qué Celina nombra su negocio Celeste?
   (A) Es en honor de los artistas femeninas.
   (B) Es el color natural que resulta por el proceso de aleación.
   (C) Es el color favorito de su mamá.
   (D) Es su color favorito y en honor de su madre.

This question contains the key words Celina and Celeste. It is usually easy to locate capital letters in the passage, and Celeste specifically appears in the 6th and 7th paragraphs. The passage states that the business *llevaba por nombre Celeste, su color predilecto y el nombre de su empresa, puesto en honor a su madre, una mujer artista.* This quote tells you it's Celina's favorite color and that she also chose the name in honor of her mother, a female artist. Choice (A) is too broad, referring to female artists in general, so eliminate it. Choice (B) is not stated in the passage, and does not match the proof that pertains to Celeste, so eliminate this choice as well. While (C) may seem tempting, it does not say that pale blue is her mother's favorite color, but rather Celina's favorite color; eliminate (C). Finally, (D) matches the quote from the passage, so it must be the answer.

Now, go back and tackle that questions that asked about the passage as a whole or that do not have clear line references and key words:

1. ¿Cuál es el propósito del pasaje?
   (A) mostrar el poder del oro y de la plata en la economía
   (B) contar la historia de una emprendedora que ha cambiado la manera en que hace joyería
   (C) ilustrar como hay un crecimiento de empresarias feministas en Honduras
   (D) advertir de que la falta de crédito destruye los emprendimientos familiares

Since you have worked the other questions first, you have now read enough to be able to tackle this one. Remember that the introduction talks about a woman who discovered a way of creating jewelry with sustainable materials. Use POE to eliminate answer choices that do not match. Eliminate (A) because, while gold and silver are mentioned in the passage, they don't represent the main idea. Choice (B) is a paraphrase of the introduction as well as the main idea introduced in the first paragraph, so keep this choice. While (C) may seem tempting, it is a bit too broad and does not mention Celina, the "who" the article is about. Eliminate (D) as well because the passage is not a warning about bad credit, but rather mentions it as a challenge faced by some family businesses. Notice also how the word *destruye* is a bit too strong. The test makers generally do not use harsh or extreme language. The correct answer is (B).

POE tip:
Avoid extreme language in the answer choices

5. Podemos inferir que

    (A) Fashion Week Honduras fue el primer pasarela para Celina.

    (B) El proceso de aleación convierte los metales sostenibles al oro y a la plata.

    (C) Honduras es un país afligido por la corrupción y violencia.

    (D) **Se puede encontrar la joyería de Celina en los estados unidos.**

With an inference question like this one, let the answer choices help. Unlike in English or Spanish classes, on this test inferences are merely true statements that can be found in the passage. Use the answer choices to find the right windows within the passage. Use *Fashion Week* to locate the right window for (A), reading a few lines before and a few lines after the words, which appear in paragraph 6. The passage states in the sentence before the mention of Fashion Week, *En 2014 Piso Diez Diseño invitó a Celina a ser parte de su grupo de diseñadores y fue ahí cuando tuvo su primera pasarela con ellos*. This quote disproves (A), so eliminate it. For (B), look for key words such as *oro* and *plata* or *metales sostenibles* in the passage. The passage states that *En 2010 empezó a crear materiales con la apariencia de oro y plata tomando como base desechos sólidos*. This means the materials she creates have the "appearance" of silver and gold, but they are not actually silver and gold. Eliminate this choice. Now look for Honduras in the passage: it appears in the 2nd and 8th paragraphs. While the second paragraph does not mention violence and corruption, there is mention in the 8th paragraph: *que podamos mostrar a la gente que en Honduras no solamente hay violencia y corrupción; que vean y aprecien la creatividad y el talento de los emprendedores así como la belleza de nuestro país*. Choice (C) is too strong, so eliminate it as well. Now evaluate (D). The passage mentions the United States in the form of *los EE.UU.* in the first paragraph: *Sus creaciones llegan hoy a Guatemala, Nicaragua y EE.UU*. Since they can be found today in the United States, it's definitely possible to find them in the U.S. The correct answer is (D).

POE tip:
Only choose answers that are explicitly in the passage.

6. Un título apropiado para este artículo sería

    (A) "Emprendedoras feministas"

    (B) "Obstáculos financieros para los emprendedores"

    (C) **"Joyería recién descubierta: aleación sostenible"**

    (D) "Fashion Week y la 'ecojoyería'"

With a question that asks you to choose a title for the passage, it is best to save it for last since you will have a better sense of the passage as a whole after tackling others first. Use POE heavily on questions like this, comparing the main idea of the passage with the offerings in the answer choices. Consider the first choice, "*Emprendedoras feministas*": this title is too broad and goes beyond the scope of the text, since the passage talks about female entrepreneurs, not necessarily feminists. Eliminate (A). Evaluate (B): *obstáculos finanieros* is certainly something the passage talks about for entrepreneurs, but is it the main point of the passage? The main point is Celina's creation of sustainable jewelry, so eliminate (B). Choice (C), *joyería recién descubierta: aleación sostenible,* talks about a recently discovered way of creating a sustainable alloy for jewelry, so keep this choice since this is what Celina has done. Choice (D) mentions only details of the passage, not the main point, when it combines Fashion Week with ecojewelry. The correct answer is (C).

Only a detail? Not the main point? Eliminate it!

Translation:

The following article appeared in a Latin American magazine in 2018 about a woman who discovered a way of creating sustainable materials for jewelry.

Celina Brizuela is a doctor of chemistry and pharmacy, entrepreneur, and fighter. After working for 18 years in an investigative firm, she decided to buy a jewelry shop. In 2010 she started to create materials with the appearance of gold or silver taken from solid waste (keys, pipelines, cans) in order to give life to the so-called "ecojewelry." In 2017, Celina won the prize for best jewelry designer in Honduras. Her creations can be found today in Guatemala, Nicaragua, and the United States; in the future she is thinking about exporting them to Europe.

Honduras is a country that reflects a strong increase in work opportunities for women. The National Institute of Statistics confirms that more than 900,000 mothers contribute to the country's economy. The sectors where there is the greatest participation from women are commerce, health, education, industry manufacturing, and microbusinesses. In the informal economy, there is a very high degree of feminine support for entrepreneurs. At the same time, the nucleus of most of the small enterprises is a family one.

However, the informality, the lack of credit history, and the high costs are the principal obstacles that confront these businesses. It is fitting to mention that now the women are dabbling in other spaces that have traditionally been dominated by men, such as the preservation of natural resources, the environment, and political participation. Nevertheless, women earn less in comparison to men.

A female entrepreneur focused on the environment and art is Celina Brizuela, mother of two daughters and originally from Tegucigalpa. Her interest in creating new things surfaced while she was working at the North American investigative company. She always had enjoyed escaping what everyone else was doing, so one day she decided to follow her dream: she rented a jewelry shop to create her own pieces from discarded solid metals available on a local level.

As if that were not enough, through means of creating an alloy, Celina was able to transform those metals in such a way that they had the same characteristics as gold and silver. In 2017 she was recognized as the best jewelry designer in Honduras by the Honduran Counsel of Private Business and the Chamber of Commerce and Industry of Tegucigalpa.

"It pleases me to observe the trends, update myself, and see what is happening and what the other great jewelry designers are doing." In 2014, Tenth Floor Designs invited Celina to be part of a group of designers and was there when she had her first runway fashion show with them. In 2017, she participated in Honduras Fashion week where she showed her unique, romantic line called Celeste, her favorite color and the name of her business—named in honor of her mother, a female artist. "I felt very honored to participate and it was my first time."

Nowadays there are nine people who work directly for Celina in her shop. "We are the only ones who are making this alloy in Honduras. There are some businesses that are dedicated to doing things with metals, but Celeste Corporation is the only firm that extracts an alloy to make gold and silver," notes the designer.

There are a lot of people who invited her to go to universities to tell her story. "My dream for the future is that ecojewelry is positioned as a Honduran brand, that we can show people that in Honduras there is not only violence and corruption; I hope that they can see and appreciate the creativity and talent of entrepreneurs as well as the beauty of our country. "I want it to transcend what we are doing. There are so many interesting things in Honduras," concludes Celina.

1. What is the purpose of the passage?
    (A) show the power of gold and silver in the economy
    (B) tell the story of an entrepreneur who has changed the way in which jewelry is made
    (C) illustrate that there are a growing number of feminist entrepreneurs in Honduras
    (D) warn that lack of credit destroys family enterprises

2. Which of the following conclusions about "ecojewelry" is true?
    (A) The alloy process transforms sustainable materials into gold and silver.
    (B) The method of making jewelry with recycled materials is Celina's invention.
    (C) The recycled materials are harder than gold and silver.
    (D) Pale blue is the only color that can be made with the alloy process.

3. Lack of credit history is mentioned in the third paragraph in order to
    (A) compare some interest rates for entrepreneurs.
    (B) note that Celina has bad credit.
    (C) show that women receive smaller loans than do men.
    (D) demonstrate some difficulties that Honduran entrepreneurs may face.

4. Why does Celina call her business Celeste?
    (A) It is in honor of female artists.
    (B) It is the natural color that results from the alloy process.
    (C) It is the favorite color of her mother.
    (D) It is her favorite color and is in honor of her mother.

5. We can infer that

   (A) Fashion Week Honduras was Celina's first runway show.

   (B) The alloy process converts sustainable metals into gold and silver.

   (C) Honduras is a country afflicted by corruption and violence.

   (D) It is possible to find Celina's jewelry in the United States.

6. An appropriate title for this article would be

   (A) "Feminist Entrepreneurs"

   (B) "Financial Obstacles for Entrepreneurs"

   (C) "Recently Discovered Jewelry: Sustainable Alloy Practices

   (D) "Fashion Week and 'Ecojewelry'"

PRACTICE PASSAGE 1

Sample Print Texts Selection

You will read several selections. Each selection is accompanied by a number of questions. For each question, choose the response that is best according to the selection and mark your answer on your answer sheet.	Vas a leer varios textos. Cada texto va acompañado de varias preguntas. Para cada pregunta, elige la mejor respuesta según el texto e indícala en la hoja de respuestas.

Introducción

El siguiente artículo apareció en 1996 en el periódico *La Jornada de Lima*.

LIMA, PERÚ: "No hubo ningún otro remedio", explicó el presidente peruano Alberto Fujimori al hablar con Eduardo Taboada, corresponsal extranjero de la emisora
Línea Univisión, durante una entrevista realizada en la capital
5 peruana. Fujimori habló pocos minutos después del ataque militar contra el grupo terrorista Tupac Amaru, que se había apoderado de la embajada japonesa hacía 4 meses. El grupo, integrado por 22 guerrilleros y sus cuatro líderes, secuestró a 72 rehenes, la mayoría de ellos diplomáticos
10 extranjeros, quienes habían sido cautivos dentro del recinto japonés por 130 días.

Los soldados peruanos iniciaron el ataque a las tres de la tarde, según el periodista Taboada, quien presenció el evento tan inesperado. A pesar de que el ataque empleara
15 muchas estrategias, apenas duró cuarenta minutos. Un grupo de soldados se dirigió por la parte delantera de la embajada y otro grupo se abalanzó a la parte posterior. Utilizaron armas con láser y rifles que hasta pudieron ubicar a los terroristas adentro, gracias a la ayuda de una com-
20 putadora especial. Ninguno de los terroristas salió con vida de la residencia, de acuerdo con los informes del noticiero Univisión de Miami. La emisora nacional de Perú, Noti-Uno, interrumpió su programación para transmitir en vivo escenas de la crisis. Pocos detalles fueron divulgados por la
25 censura de la prensa para proteger a los rehenes.

Fujimori proclamó orgullosamente que habían acabado de una vez con el terrorismo y nunca negociaría con terroristas, lo cual sigue siendo la política oficial del Perú. Sin embargo, Fujimori se vio obligado a iniciar conversaciones
30 con los rebeldes fuertemente armados después de que varios gobiernos extranjeros, cuyos ciudadanos se encontraban dentro de la embajada, presionaron para evitar un ataque militar. Fujimori sí dialogó con los rebeldes, pero al mismo tiempo iba planeando clandestinamente un asalto militar.

35 Mucha gente de la comunidad mundial opinó que las acciones del gobierno peruano eran innecesarias. Un sacerdote conocido en el Perú, el Padre Xavier Venancio, reiterando la opinión de la iglesia peruana, pensó que la situación podría haberse resuelto a través de una manera
40 pacífica. El presidente Fujimori reafirmó que no había otra manera de resolver la crisis, ya que "se nos acababa el tiempo y nuestro compromiso principal fue garantizar la seguridad y bienestar de los rehenes. Esperar más no nos convenía". El presidente japonés Hashimoto dijo pocos
45 minutos después de la exitosa liberación de los rehenes que "no debe haber nadie que pueda criticar al presidente". La prensa peruana confirmó esto, a través de unas encuestas realizadas en todo el territorio nacional en las cuales el noventa por ciento (90%) de la población peruana estuvo
50 a favor de la acción militar de Fujimori. Con esta nueva derrota de otro grupo subversivo, Fujimori ya marca su segunda victoria militar contra el terrorismo. En 1992, Fujimori arrasó con el grupo terrorista más temido del país, El Sendero Luminoso, tras el arresto de su enigmático
55 líder, Abimael Guzmán. Sendero Luminoso fue el grupo terrorista de mayor involucramiento y hegemonía al nivel nacional, habiendo aterrorizado el país por más de 25 años; un periodo sumamente violento que ocasionó la muerte de más de 35.000 peruanos. En su auge el grupo se apoderó
60 de casi el 40% del territorio peruano. Ese grupo maoísta inspiró a su vez a otros grupos tales como Tupac Amaru que se desafiaran del gobierno peruano a través del conflicto armado. Con estos gloriosos éxitos, el gobierno peruano pretende restaurar, según Fujimori, "el progreso, la paz y la
65 prosperidad" en la nación andina.

Por ahora reinará la estabilidad en el Perú, pero como nos ha narrado la historia, la tranquilidad es un deleite que se saborea por unos cortos momentos, y sabremos cuándo surgirá otro movimiento subversivo que busque desalojar la
70 tan deseada paz que tanto anhela el pueblo peruano.

La Jornada de Lima, 1996

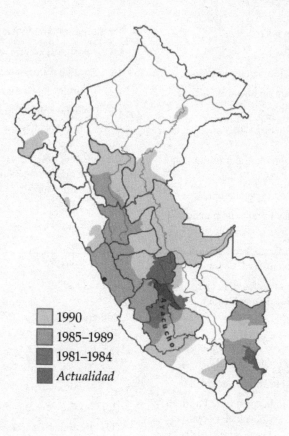

1990
1985–1989
1981–1984
Actualidad

Víctimas de Ataques Terroristas en el Perú

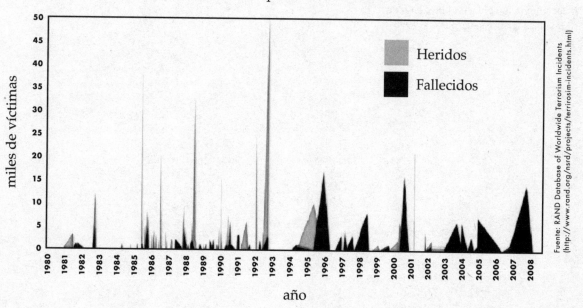

Heridos

Fallecidos

miles de víctimas

año

Fuente: RAND Database of Worldwide Terrorism Incidents (http://www.rand.org/nsrd/projects/terrirosim-incidents.html)

1. ¿Por qué negoció Fujimori con los rebeldes?

    (A) Porque era su política oficial.

    (B) Porque había sentido presión de otros países.

    (C) Porque le daba tiempo para organizar un ataque militar simultáneamente.

    (D) Todas estas respuestas son correctas.

2. ¿Cuál de estas conclusiones sobre el asalto militar a la embajada es falsa?

    (A) El ataque había sido planeado detalladamente.

    (B) El ataque ocasionó el fallecimiento de muchos terroristas.

    (C) El ataque marcó la segunda vez que Fujimori había derrotado a un enemigo del Estado.

    (D) Si se hubiera utilizado la tecnología, la crisis habría podido resolverse de una forma más eficaz y pacífica.

3. Podemos inferir que

    (A) después de la intervención militar de 1996, no se irrumpió más actividad terrorista semejante

    (B) el gobierno peruano siguió las pautas de Fujimori y continuó su política de no negociar con los rebeldes

    (C) al partir de 1996, terrorismo volvió a surgir después de un declive de 5 años

    (D) la tecnología fue el factor clave en reducir la amenaza terrorista después de 1996

4. Un titular apropiado para este artículo sería

    (A) "Fujimori en un jaque mate con los terroristas"

    (B) "Salvajes invaden embajada, perecen muchos"

    (C) "Fujimori deja que los terroristas lo pisoteen"

    (D) "Negociaciones logran defraudar a los terroristas, militares triunfan"

5. La siguiente oración se puede añadir al texto: "Se sabe que la violencia no resuelve nada, y a su vez, perpetúa aún más violencia". ¿Dónde serviría mejor la oración?

    (A) Línea 34

    (B) Línea 36

    (C) Línea 40

    (D) Línea 50

6. Podemos inferir que 1992 fue un año de mucha actividad terrorista en el Perú ya que

    (A) quedó cautivo el líder del grupo subversivo

    (B) otros grupos habían cometido actos violentos como respuesta a la captura del líder terrorista

    (C) hubo elecciones presidenciales en el Perú ese año

    (D) los terroristas aumentaron el territorio bajo su control

Translated Text and Questions, with Explanations

The following article appeared in 1996 in the newspaper *La Jornada de Lima*.

LIMA, PERU: "There was no other solution," explained Peruvian president Alberto Fujimori while speaking with Eduardo Taboada, foreign correspondent for the broadcast station Univisión, during an interview in the Peruvian capital. Fujimori spoke several minutes after the military attack against the terrorist group Tupac Amaru, who had taken control of the Japanese embassy four months earlier. The group, comprised of 22 guerillas and their four leaders, had kidnapped 72 hostages—the majority of whom were foreign diplomats—and who were held captive inside the Japanese residence for 130 days.

The Peruvian soldiers began the attack at 3 P.M., according to the journalist Taboada, who witnessed the unexpected event. Yesterday's attack lasted only 40 minutes despite the fact that it involved many strategies. One group of soldiers rushed through the front part of the embassy, while the other group rushed the back. They utilized weapons with lasers and rifles that were even able to locate the terrorists inside, thanks to the use of a special computer. None of the terrorists left the residence alive, according to reports from the news station Univisión in Miami. The national broadcast station of Peru, NotiUno, interrupted its programming to transmit live scenes of the crisis. Few details were divulged by the press in order to protect the hostages.

Fujimori proudly proclaimed that he had eliminated terrorism once and for all, and would never negotiate with terrorists, which continues to be the official policy of Peru. However, Fujimori was obliged to begin conversations with the heavily armed rebels, after various foreign governments, whose citizens were inside the embassy, pressured him to avoid a military assault. Fujimori did indeed speak with the rebels, but at the same time was secretly planning a military attack.

Many people of the global community felt that the actions of the Peruvian government were unnecessary. A well-known priest in Peru, Father Xavier Venancio, reiterating the opinion of the Peruvian church, felt that the situation could have been resolved through peaceful means. President Fujimori reaffirmed that there wasn't any other way to resolve the crisis, given that "time was running out for us, and our main goal was to guarantee the safety and well-being of the hostages. To wait any longer wouldn't have been beneficial." The Japanese president Hashimoto said a few minutes after the successful liberation of the hostages that "no one should be criticizing the president." The Peruvian press confirmed this, through interviews carried out throughout the nation in which ninety percent (90%) of Peruvians were in favor of Fujimori's military action. With this recent defeat of yet another subversive group, Fujimori marks his second victory against terrorism. In 1992, Fujimori obliterated the most feared terrorist group in the country, The Shining Path, with the arrest of its enigmatic leader, Abimael Guzman. The Shining Path was the most active and dangerous terrorist group in the nation, having terrorized the country for more than 25 years, an extremely violent period that saw the deaths of more than 35,000 Peruvians. At its peak, the group controlled almost 40% of the country. This Maoist group inspired other groups like Tupac Amaru to challenge the Peruvian government through armed conflict. With these glorious successes, the Peruvian government intends to restore, according to Fujimori, "progress, peace, and prosperity" to the Andean nation.

For now, all is calm in Peru, but as history has shown us, peace is a delicacy that can be savored for only a few short moments, and who knows when another subversive group will appear and attempt to destroy the much desired peace the Peruvian people hope for.

Here's How to Crack It

1. Why did Fujimori negotiate with the rebels?

    (A) Because it was his official policy.

    (B) Because he received pressure from other countries.

    (C) Because it gave him time to organize a military attack at the same time.

    (D) All of these answers are correct.

Choice (B) is the correct answer because the article states that he began dialogue with the rebels because the foreign governments wanted him to avoid a military attack. While (C) may be correct, the article doesn't state that Fujimori used the negotiations to "buy time." Choice (A) is incorrect, because Fujimori is quoted as saying he would never negotiate with terrorists. As a result, (D) is also incorrect.

2. Which of the following conclusions concerning the military assault on the embassy is false?

    (A) The attack was planned with great detail.

    (B) The attack caused the deaths of many terrorists.

    (C) The attack marked the second time that Fujimori had defeated an enemy of the state.

    (D) If technology had been used, the crisis could have been solved in a more efficient and peaceful manner.

This type of question is sometimes included to trip up the fast reader. Be sure to focus on the qualifying word "false" in the question. Thus, this question is looking for a false statement. The article states that the attack employed many strategies, which would suggest that (A) is a true statement. Likewise, (B) is also true, as the article stated that there were 26 terrorists and none escaped. Choice (C) is a true statement, as the article at the end discusses Fujimori's past successes. Choice (D) is a false statement, as technology (lasers and computers) was indeed used to end the crisis quickly. Thus, (D) is the correct answer.

3. We can infer that

    (A) after the military intervention of 1996, there wasn't any more similar terrorist activity

    (B) the Peruvian government followed Fujimori's lead and continued its policy of not negotiating with rebels

    (C) after 1996, terrorism resurged after a decline over 5 years

    (D) technology was a key factor in reducing the terrorist threat after 1996

Choice (C) is the correct answer, as the graph shows that terrorism declined for five years after 1996, but then had a sharp increase in 2001. This is a direct contradiction of (A). Choices (B) and (D) may be true, but there isn't any data to support those inferences.

4. An appropriate headline for this article would be

(A) "Fujimori in a checkmate with the terrorists"

(B) "Savages invade embassy, many perish"

(C) "Fujimori lets terrorists step all over him"

(D) "Negotiations manage to mislead terrorists, military triumphs"

The best answer is (D), as it captures the overall main idea of the article. While (A) does show that Fujimori has the upper hand, it doesn't give the detail of (D). Choice (B) refers to savages, which would not be used to describe the military in this article. Choice (C) is also incorrect, as it clearly is the opposite of the outcome of the standoff between the president and the terrorists.

5. The following sentence can be added to the text: **"It is known that violence doesn't resolve anything, and in turn, perpetuates even more violence."** Where would this fit best?

(A) Line 34

(B) Line 36

(C) Line 40

(D) Line 50

The correct answer is (C), as it would be a logical quote by the nonviolent priest mentioned in the article. In this position it advances the flow and meaning of the paragraph. Choice (A), line 34, does follow some text that reinforces the idea of a nonviolent solution, but as our inserted sentence is an opinion, it wouldn't fit here since the previous sentence is about planning a military intervention. Choice (D) is incorrect, as the previous sentence in the article speaks of the nation's overwhelming approval of the attack. While (B) could also accommodate the sentence, a clearly better fit would be (C) given the preceding and subsequent sentences. These types of questions test your ability to accommodate sentences in a paragraph where they would have the best flow and impact; be sure to read the surrounding sentences to get a better idea of where to put them.

6. We can infer that 1992 was a year of much terrorist activity in Peru since

(A) the leader of a subversive group was captured

(B) there were other violent acts by other groups as a response to the capture of the terrorist leader

(C) there were elections in Peru that year

(D) the terrorists increased the territory under their control

Choice (D) is the correct answer as shown by the map. There are no references to (C) anywhere so it can be eliminated. Choices (A) and (B) are too similar for one of them to be the right answer, and the graph does not show which groups are responsible for the terrorist acts so it isn't possible to determine. In addition, the terrorist leader was captured in December, so the year had already ended: another reason (B) is incorrect.

PRACTICE PASSAGE 2

Introducción

El siguiente artículo apareció en 2015 en una revista electrónica de cultura latinoamericana.

Cuba ¿País de Emprendedores?

Hombres y mujeres cubanos que crean nuevos negocios poco o nada tienen que ver con los emprendedores a nivel mundial. En esta isla del Caribe la economía es muy diferente al resto cuando se habla de iniciativas, startup y emprendimiento.

Linea
5

En Cuba, cuando se va a comenzar un negocio innovador, en lo primero que se piensa es en la familia: "Mi tío me prestará una parte del dinero; mi hermano trabajará conmigo; mi primo buscará la materia prima, y mi esposa y yo seremos los vendedores. Después repartimos toda la ganancia según los aportes de cada cual". Así piensan los cubanos cuando van a crear un nuevo negocio, desde una simple guarapera hasta un hostal. Orelvys Bormey Torres, un joven ingeniero industrial, altamente especializado en su área, que crea un negocio junto a su familia, asumen los riesgos económicos y tiene éxito.

10

15

Por supuesto que este emprendedor de Villa Clara no tiene un pelo de tonto: lo primero que hizo fue inscribir su marca en el Registro Cubano de la Propiedad Industrial. Además, organizó el negocio de tal forma que toda familia pudiese participar. El objetivo es que el negocio fuese más fácil de administrar al tener que pagar menos por empleados externos contratados, entre otras ventajas de trabajar con la parentela.

20

¿Y por qué el maní? Sencillamente encontraron que había poca diversidad de productos hechos con base en este alimento y los que existían eran muy caros. Así crearon una gama de productos que pueden competir con los del mercado "oficial", pero a menores precios.

25

Un detalle interesante en este negocio es que partieron con materias primas y prácticas tecno productivas que estaban en la familia desde hacía varias generaciones: sus abuelos y sus padres siempre cosecharon el maní en esas tierras. O sea, tenían herramientas, conocimientos y materia prima garantizados. Orelvys solo requirió de un pequeño crédito bancario y de sus ahorros, pues en Cuba nadie opta por el crowdfunding, ya que son opciones alejadas por la poca penetración digital que tiene el país.

30

35

Sus resultados fueron tan exitosos que fue la primera, y hasta ahora única iniciativa particular cubana que ha obtenido el Premio 2014 de la Oficina Cubana de la Propiedad Industrial a la "Creatividad y la Innovación Tecnológica en la categoría de Signos Distintivos".

40

Uno de los más rentables es la recarga doble del saldo de telefonía móvil desde el extranjero. ¿Y qué es esto? Un sistema que representa una gran entrada de dinero a la empresa en poco tiempo y a la que solo acceden aquellos que tienen familiares y amigos en el extranjero.

45

Ese es uno de los nichos interesantes que han descubierto los emprendedores cubanos, creado sitios en Internet desde donde hacer estas recargas y servicios físicos en Cuba. ¿Cómo opera? A nivel local se paga 23 o 25 CUC y desde el extranjero te recargan 20 dólares, que aquí en Cuba se te convierten en 40 CUC.

50

Como en Cuba todo es diferente al resto del mundo, aquí ningún emprendedor usa KickStarter o Indiegogo. En Cuba la financiación de proyectos emprendedores muchas veces cuenta con ayuda de familiares y en otras ocasiones con "inversiones extranjeras" de parientes y amigos que residen en otros países. Eso sí, los encargados del negocio en Cuba nunca reconocen que recibieron ayuda económica desde el extranjero, ya que es algo todavía "gris" en la legislación cubana.

55

60

Otra de las opciones que tienen los aventureros y emprendedores cubanos es pedir un crédito bancario. Pero al parecer no es una oferta muy masificada entre los cubanos, pues recientes informes del Banco Central de Cuba dan a conocer que durante el año 2014 solo 658 de los llamados "cuentapropistas" pidieron créditos a las entidades bancarias estatales. Fueron 75 en la capital y 583 en el resto del país; esto representa el 0,1% de los más de 347.000 trabajadores privados registrados, que son lo que se considera emprendedores en Cuba.

65

70

Todos estos son emprendedores cubanos que han sabido sacar adelante sus pequeños negocios privados en medio de una economía estatal compleja y marcada por el burocratismo. Pero sobre todo han demostrado que los cubanos pueden encontrar nichos comerciales y posibilidades de negocios donde otros solo verían problemas, pues como dice la frase popular: "El cubano es capaz de venderle hielo a un esquimal".

75

80

1. ¿Cuál es el propósito del artículo?

   (A) Para mostrar que Cuba ha tenido éxito a nivel mundial con iniciativas y emprendimientos

   (B) Para describir los negocios innovadores en Cuba y cómo han creado negocios con pocos recursos

   (C) Para ilustrar las idiosincrasias de los emprendedores

   (D) Para introducir un cambio fiscal para los emprendedores cubanos

2. ¿Por qué se menciona Orelvys Bormey Torres?

   (A) Para sugerir que todos los negocios como los de él van a tener éxito

   (B) Porque es ingeniero y también emprendedor

   (C) Para ilustrar los riesgos de crear un negocio innovador

   (D) Para dar un ejemplo de un emprendedor que involucra a su familia en su negocio

3. El impacto del gobierno cubano es uno de

   (A) apoyo

   (B) creatividad

   (C) destrucción

   (D) aislamiento

4. ¿Qué significa el título "Cuba ¿País de Emprendedores?"

   (A) Cuba es un país improbable para crear negocios privados.

   (B) Los emprendedores no son legítimos.

   (C) Los emprendedores solamente tienen negocios que involucran sus parientes.

   (D) Es un país único y compuesto de emprendedores influyentes.

5. Se menciona "¿Y por qué el maní?" para

   (A) ilustrar que hay pocos recursos en Cuba

   (B) describir algunos legumbres que existen naturalmente en Cuba

   (C) mostrar como se involucra la familia en el negocio

   (D) comentar sobre los productos caros que existen en el mercado cubano

6. La última frase "El cubano es capaz de venderle hielo a un esquimal" significa que

   (A) todos los negocios cubanos tienen problemas a causa del burocratismo

   (B) los cubanos son los mejores emprendedores al nivel mundial

   (C) el emprendedor cubano es sabio y usa los recursos que tiene para crear su negocio

   (D) los cubanos y los esquimales hacen negocios a menudo

Translated Text and Questions, with Explanations

Introduction

The following article appeared in 2015 in an electronic magazine of Latin American culture.

Cuba: Country of Entrepreneurs?

Cuban men and women who create new businesses have little, if anything, to do with entrepreneurs at the world level. On this island in the Caribbean, the economy is very different from the rest of the world when speaking of initiatives, startups, and entrepreneurship.

In Cuba, when one is going to start an innovative business, the first thing to think about is the family: "My uncle will lend me part of the money; my brother will work with me; my cousin will look for the raw material, and my wife and I will be the vendors. Then, we will distribute all of the profit according to each person's contributions." This is how Cubans think when they are going to create a new business, from a simple guarapo stand to an inn. Orelvys Bormey Torres, a young industrial engineer, highly specialized in his field, who created a business together with his family, assumes the economic risks and is successful.

Of course this entrepreneur from Villa Clara is not a fool: the first thing that he did was register his brand with the Cuban Registry of Industrial Property. In addition, he organized the business in such a way that the whole family could participate. The objective is that the business would be easier to manage, having to pay less for externally contracted employees, among other advantages of working with relatives.

And why the peanut? They simply found that there was little product diversity made with this food base and those that existed were very expensive. Thus they made a gamut of products that can compete with those on the "official" market, but at lower prices.

An interesting detail in this business is that they shared in raw materials and technological productive practices that existed in the family for several generations: his grandparents and his parents always harvested the peanut on these grounds. That is, that they had the tools, know-how, and guaranteed raw material. Orelvys only needed a small bank credit and his savings, because in Cuba no one opts for crowdfunding, as those options are cut off because of the low level of digital penetration the country has.

Their results were so successful that it was the first, and until now the only, private Cuban initiative that won the 2014 Prize from the Cuban Office of Industrial Property for "Creativity and Technological Innovation in the category of Distinctive Signs."

One of the most profitable businesses is the double cell-phone balance refill from abroad. And what is this? It's a system that represents a grand influx of money to the business in little time and which only those who have family and friends abroad access.

This is one of the interesting niches that Cuban entrepreneurs have discovered, having created Internet sites from which to make these refills and physical services in Cuba. How does it work? At the local level one pays 23 or 25 CUC and from abroad they recharge you 20 dollars, which here in Cuba converts to 40 CUC.

Since Cuba is different from the rest of the world, here no entrepreneur uses Kickstarter or Indiegogo. In Cuba the financing of entrepreneurial projects many times counts on help from family members, and other times on "foreign investments" from relatives and friends who reside in other countries. Yes, the managers of businesses in Cuba never recognize they received financial help from abroad, since it is still a "grey area" in Cuban law.

Another of the options that Cuban adventurers and entrepreneurs have is to ask for a bank loan. But it appears not to be widely used among Cubans, as recent reports of the Central Bank of Cuba have revealed that during the year 2014 only 658 of the so-called "self-employed" asked for loans from state banks. There were 75 in the capital and 583 in the rest of the country; this represents 0.1% of the more than 347,000 registered private workers, which are those considered to be entrepreneurs in Cuba.

All these are Cuban entrepreneurs who have managed develop their small private businesses in the middle of a complex and highly bureaucratic state economy. But above all, they have demonstrated that Cubans can find commercial niches and business possibilities where others only would see problems, as goes the popular phrase: "The Cuban is capable of selling ice to an Inuit."

Here's How to Crack It

1. What is the main point of the article?

    (A) To show that Cuba has had success on the global level with entrepreneurial initiatives

    (B) To describe innovative businesses in Cuba and how people have created businesses with few resources

    (C) To illustrate the idiosyncrasies of entrepreneurs

    (D) To introduce a fiscal change for Cuban entrepreneurs

The main point of the article is to show some of the creativity and resourcefulness needed to grow a business in Cuba. It says the opposite of (A), and does not mention either (C) or (D). Therefore, (B) is the best response.

2. Why is Orelyvs Bormey Torres mentioned?

    (A) To suggest that all busineses like his are going to be successful

    (B) Because he is an engineer as well as an entrepreneur

    (C) To illustrate the risks when one creates an innovative business

    (D) To give an example of an entrepreneur who involves his family in his business

Orelvys Bormey Torres is an engineer as well as an entrepreneur, but that is not why he is mentioned, eliminating (B). Choice (A) is too broad, as is (C). The real reason he is mentioned is to show how he built his business and involves his family members in the business.

3. The impact of the Cuban government is one of

    (A) support

    (B) creativity

    (C) destruction

    (D) isolation

The Cuban government is isolating, hence the limited resources available to entrepreneurs. They struggle to compete on the global stage as a result. There certainly are many creative entrepreneurs in Cuba, but the question asks about the government, not the entrepreneurs. Therefore, (D) is the correct response.

4. What does the title "Cuba: Country of Entrepreneurs?" signify?

    (A) Cuba is an improbable country to create private businesses.

    (B) The entrepreneurs are not legitimate.

    (C) The entrepreneurs only have businesses that involve their relatives.

    (D) It is a unique country that is comprised of influential entrepreneurs.

The question mark in the title suggests that Cuba is an unlikely place for private businesses to grow and flourish, as (A) suggests. Choice (B) is not mentioned in the passage, and (C) is too extreme. Choice (D) is tempting, but goes too far by suggesting the whole country is made up of entrepreneurs. Therefore, (A) is the best response.

5. "And why the peanut?" is mentioned to
   (A) illustrate that there are few resources in Cuba
   (B) describe some legumes that exist naturally in Cuba
   (C) show how the family is involved in the business
   (D) comment on the expensive products that exist in the Cuban market

Choice (B) is too literal, and (D) recycles words that are in the passage, but that is not why the peanut is mentioned. Choice (C) best encapsulates *why* the peanut is mentioned, and that is to show how Torres's family works together on different aspects of the business.

6. The last phrase, "The Cuban is capable of selling ice to an Inuit" means that
   (A) all Cuban businesses have problems because of the bureaucracy
   (B) Cubans are the best entrepreneurs on the world stage
   (C) the Cuban entrepreneur is wise and uses the resources he or she has to create a business
   (D) Cubans and Inuits frequently do business together

Choice (C) is the best response because it best ties together the main idea of the passage. Choice (A) is too extreme, (B) is false according to the passage, and (D) is just silly.

PRACTICE PASSAGE 3

Introducción

El siguiente artículo fue escrito por Catalina Marzorati-Strauß en 2015.

Laguna Garzón: obra de arte en la naturaleza

Dos amantes del arte y de la arquitectura reconocidos internacionalmente se unieron para construir en Uruguay una obra prácticamente única en el mundo: un puente circular sobre la Laguna Garzón, ubicado a no más de 100 metros de distancia del mar. El lugar se caracteriza por una belleza inigualable, lo agreste de su paisaje y sus famosos crepúsculos dorados en la época veraniega. Una verdadera obra maestra que cuando esté culminada pasará a ser parte del paisaje natural, pero que no ha estado exenta de polémica especialmente de parte de grupos ecologistas.

Uruguay destaca por su arquitectura y puentes extravagantes como el ondular de Leonel Viera, el de Las Américas en Montevideo o incluso el aeropuerto de Carrasco. Hoy, el país da paso a un nuevo y singular proyecto: un desafío contra las fuerzas naturales, de alta modernidad y control ecológico. Un puente circular, apoyado en una línea única de 28 columnas de 25 metros de altura.

El puente unirá los dos palmos de la Ruta 10 entre Maldonado y Rocha. Por el lado de adentro de la rotonda se transitará con vehículos y por fuera por una terraza "volada", que tendrá una senda peatonal para los transeúntes. Incluso los pescadores tendrán su espacio con zonas para poder sentarse cómodamente y observar los crepúsculos dorados y la variedad de aves de la zona, dos cosas que caracterizan a la laguna.

Según la crítica que se escucha en la zona, sí. La franja que divide el mar de la laguna no tiene más de 500 mt en su zona más ancha y está en este momento completamente loteada para ser vendida a inversores extranjeros.

Se debe reconocer que más allá de todo posible interés económico, se unieron dos amantes del arte con una visión en común: hacer una obra maestra que fluya en y con la naturaleza. Por un lado está el inversor, Costantini, de ojo artístico y director del Museo de Arte Malba de Argentina, uno de los más famosos en Sudamérica. Por el otro está Rafael Vinoly, el arquitecto uruguayo que hizo el diseño del puente.

Vinoly se caracteriza por sus obras innovadoras a nivel internacional y según comenta, "el gran precio profesional de un arquitecto es justamente el péndulo constante de verse a uno mismo como artista y al mismo tiempo tener que respetar los adelantos técnicos de cada obra."

El Ministerio de Transporte, luego de años de tratativas e intentos por lograr un paso sobre la Laguna Garzón, aceptó el proyecto de este puente circular, como los hay pocos en el mundo.

Sin embargo, como toda nueva creación artística, aún no plasmada y difícil de imaginar, no está ausente de crítica. Es más, este puente vivió grandes temporales antes de ser construido. Estos no fueron causados por los conocidos vientos de la zona, debido a la cercanía al mar, sino que provinieron de críticas de los lugareños y de la sociedad.

La mayoría de ellas están basadas en los temores ante la posible destrucción y contaminación del medio ambiente. La Laguna Garzón fue declarada "Área de importancia para la conservación de aves", por la presencia de más de 700 variedades de pájaros de 32 especies diferentes. Entre ellas se encuentran especies amenazadas como el playerito canela y el bellísimo y elegante flamenco austral, así como peces y crustáceos poco comunes.

Hoy la laguna tiene una población de 77 personas, según la intendencia local. Hasta el año 2035 se proyecta una población de 11.200. Hoy existen solo 17 casas y para 2035 se esperan 2089 casas.

Para esta última fecha, se tiene previsto la construcción de una docena de proyectos de urbanización para personas acaudaladas, en su mayoría extranjeros. Antes de la planificación del puente, los precios por hectárea no sobrepasaban los U.S. $3000; hoy van desde U.S. $30.000 hasta U.S. $1.000.000 por ha.

1. Los dos amantes del arte y de la arquitectura

    (A) son destinados a tener éxito con el puente sobre la laguna

    (B) tienen las facultades necesarias para construir la obra prósperamente

    (C) tienen más recursos financieros que El Ministerio de Transporte

    (D) van a destruir el medio ambiente a causa de su obra maestra

2. Se menciona "el ondular de Leonel Viera, el de Las Américas en Montevideo o incluso el aeropuerto de Carrasco" en líneas 12–13 para

    (A) dar ejemplos de otras obras únicas de la arquitectura en Uruguay

    (B) inferir que los puentes en Uruguay son los mejores de Sudamérica

    (C) ilustrar las diferencias entre los puentes que ya existen

    (D) sugerir que el puente sobre la laguna debe ser como los otros diseños

3. Según la crítica, las siguientes consecuencias puedan pasar SALVO:

    (A) la urbanización de la zona

    (B) precios inflados para comprar lotes

    (C) los extranjeros controlarán la municipalidad

    (D) unas especies amenazadas estarán en peligro

4. Podemos inferir que

    (A) acabarán el puente en el año 2035

    (B) el puente puede poner en riesgo el medio ambiente

    (C) Costantini y Vinoly trabajaron con El Ministerio de Transporte para diseñar el puente

    (D) hoy en día un hectárea cuesta más de $30.000 dólares

5. ¿Por qué se menciona que la laguna tiene una población de 77 personas hoy en día?

    (A) Para introducir retórica en contra de la construcción del puente

    (B) Para cambiar el sujeto del párrafo

    (C) Para dar un ejemplo

    (D) Para demostrar un contraste

6. ¿Cuál es la idea principal de esta selección?

    (A) El puente está destinado a destruir la naturaleza con urbanización y contaminación.

    (B) La destrucción y la contaminación del medio ambiente son a causa de Costantini y Vinoly.

    (C) La Laguna Garzón fue declarada un área de importancia para la conservación de aves, y no se debe construir el puente.

    (D) El puente será una obra de arte significativa, pero hay riesgos ambientales y comerciales a la laguna.

Translated Text and Questions, with Explanations

Introduction

The following article was written by Catalina Marzorati-Strauß in 2015.

Garzón Laguna: Work of Art in Nature

Two internationally recognized art and architecture lovers united to construct a work in Uruguay that is practically one-of-a-kind in the world: a circular bridge over the Garzón Laguna, located no more than 100 meters from the sea. The location is characterized by an unequalled beauty, the wildness of its landscape, and its famous golden sunsets in the summer season. A true masterwork that when it is finished will become part of the natural landscape, but which has not been exempt from controversy, especially among ecological groups.

Uruguay stands out for its architecture and extravagant bridges like Leonel Viera's stressed ribbon bridge, the Bridge of The Americas in Mondevideo, or even the Carrasco airport. Today, the country gives rise to a new and singular project: a challenge against the natural forces, very modern and involving ecological control. A circular bridge, supported on a single line of 28 columns 25 meters high.

The bridge will unite the two spans of route 10 between Maldonado and Rocha. The inside of the rotunda will circulate vehicle traffic and on the outside the "flying" terrace will have a pedestrian pathway for passers-by. Even fishermen will have their space, with zones where they can sit comfortably and observe the golden sunsets and the variety of birds in the area, two things that characterize the laguna.

According to the criticism that one hears about the area, yes. The band that divides the sea from the laguna is not more than 500 meters in its widest place, and is at this moment completely divided into lots to be sold to foreign investors.

It should be recognized that beyond all the possible economic interest, the two art lovers united with a common vision to make a masterwork that flows in and with the nature around it. On one side is the investor, Costantini, with an artistic eye: the director of the Arte Malba Museum in Argentina, one of the most famous in South America. On the other side is Rafael Vinoly, the Uruguayan architect who designed the bridge.

Vinoly is known for his innovative works on an international level and according to his comment, "the great price, professionally, of being an architect is precisely the constant pendulum of seeing yourself as an artist and at the same time having to respect the technical specifications of each work."

The Ministry of Transportation, after years of negotiations and attempts to build a path over the Garzón Laguna, accepted this circular bridge project, as there are few in the world.

Nevertheless, as with all new artistic creations, even ones still unrealized and difficult to imagine, it's not free from criticism. Furthermore, this bridge lived through great storms before being constructed. Those were not caused by the well-known winds in the area, which are due to the close proximity to the sea, but rather by criticism from locals and from society.

The majority of critiques are based on fears of possible destruction and contamination of the environment. The Garzón Laguna was declared "an area of importance for bird conservation," because of the presence of over 700 varieties of birds from 32 different species. Among these, one encounters endangered species like the buff-breasted sandpiper and the beautiful and elegant Chilean flamingo, as well as uncommon fish and crustaceans.

Today the laguna has a population of 77 people, according to local administration. It is projected that by the year 2035 the population will be 11,200. Today there exist only 17 houses and by 2035 they expect 2089 houses.

By this latter date, the construction of a dozen urbanization projects have been planned for the wealthy, the majority of whom are foreigners. Before the planning of the bridge, prices per hectare weren't over 3,000 U.S. dollars; today they range from $30,000 up to $1,000,000.

Here's How to Crack It

1. The two art and architecture lovers

   (A) are destined to have success with the bridge over the laguna

   (B) have the necessary resources to successfully construct the work

   (C) have more financial resources than the Ministry of Transportation

   (D) are going to destroy the environment with their masterwork

Choice (B) is correct because they have made a deal with the Ministry of Transportation to fund the project. The bridge is not "destined" for anything, eliminating (A) and (D). Choice (C) is unsupported by the passage.

2. The phrase "Leonel Viera's stressed ribbon bridge, the Bridge of The Americas in Mondevideo, or even the Carrasco airport" is mentioned in lines 12–13 in order to

   (A) give examples of other unique architectural works in Uruguay

   (B) imply that the bridges in Uruguay are the best in South America

   (C) illustrate the differences among the bridges that already exist

   (D) suggest that the bridge over the laguna should be like the other designs

The phrase mentions other interesting architectural projects in Uruguay, as in (A). It does not say that the bridges are the best in South America or what the differences are among them, eliminating (B) and (C). It does not suggest anything about designs, eliminating (D) as well. Therefore, (A) is the correct response.

3. According to the critics, any of the following consequences could happen EXCEPT:

   (A) the urbanization of the area

   (B) inflated prices to buy land lots

   (C) foreigners will control the local government

   (D) some endangered species could be in danger

In the ninth paragraph, the article mentions risks to the environment and to the wildlife, and the last paragraph mentions the rapidly increasing prices for land in the area. Nowhere does the article say that foreigners will control the government, though they most likely will own land or businesses in the area once the commercial lots are developed. Therefore, (C) is correct.

4. We can infer that

   (A) the bridge will be completed en the year 2035

   (B) the bridge could put the environment at risk

   (C) Costantini and Vinoly worked with the Ministry of Transportation to design the bridge

   (D) today a hectare of land costs more than $30,000 dollars

Choice (B) is the only choice that can be supported by the text. Be careful to eliminate answer choices that are not written in the passage!

5. Why is it mentioned that the laguna has a population of 77 people today?

   (A) To introduce rhetoric against the construction of the bridge

   (B) To change the subject of the paragraph

   (C) To give an example

   (D) To demonstrate a contrast

The mention of the current population is to contrast with the possible increase to 11,200 people by 2035. It is not an example of a previous idea, nor does it change the subject of the paragraph, eliminating (B) and (C). It is a possible argument against the construction of the bridge, but it is not a rhetorical device in an argument, eliminating (A). Therefore, (D) is correct.

6. What is the main idea of the selection?

   (A) The bridge is destined to destroy the environment with urbanization and pollution.

   (B) The destruction and contamination of the environment are because of Costantini and Vinoly.

   (C) The Garzón Laguna was declared an area of importance for bird conservation and so the bridge should not be constructed.

   (D) The bridge will be a significant artwork, but there are environmental and commercial risks to the laguna.

Choice (A) predicts the future and is too extreme. Choice (B) attributes all of the bridge's potential destruction to the two art lovers, making it incorrect. Choice (C) contains a true statement and an unsupported opinion; regardless, it is not the main point of the passage. Only (D) is broad enough to encapsulate the main idea of the passage.

PRACTICE PASSAGE 4

Interpretive Communication: Print Texts

Introducción

El siguiente artículo apareció en 1993 en el periódico *La Cultura Latina*.

Panamá: el misterio de las calles sin nombre

Panamá es actualmente uno de los destinos turísticos más populares del continente y una de las economías más fuertes de la región. Sin embargo, el caos es parte natural de su hermosa ciudad capital. Casi no existe planificación urbana y tanto los propios panameños como los turistas sufren a diario tratando de encontrar una simple calle. Describir de forma visual la ubicación de un lugar puede ser complicado, algunos sin duda forma parte de la vida cotidiana de sus habitantes. Si te atreves, acompaña a nuestra periodista en esta misteriosa aventura a través de la ciudad, tratando de descifrar "el misterio de las calles sin nombre"…

A pesar de todos los avances logrados durante poco más de un siglo de vida republicana, los panameños todavía tenemos que convivir con algunos legados de nuestro pasado, como el no tener un sistema bien planificado y señalizado de calles. Hablar de cuadras, avenidas con nombres propios y edificios con numeración es muy extraño.

Después de la independencia, Panamá tuvo un gran crecimiento económico. Esto generó migraciones masivas desde áreas rurales del país y del extranjero, que obligaron a la ciudad a expandirse. De la noche a la mañana, esta urbe comenzó a crecer desordenadamente, sobrepasando la capacidad de planificación de las autoridades.

El crecimiento no se detuvo, incluso aumentó. La apertura del Canal y otros sucesos del siglo XX nos dejaron como herencia una ciudad no solamente llena de rincones, sino de calles que se quedaron sin nombre.

"Aquí cada quién hizo lo que le dio la gana, y no hubo autoridad interesada en poner orden", recuerda Carmen, docente retirada de 76 años de edad. "Hay unas calles que no tienen nombre, y otras que tienen hasta dos y tres", asegura.

Para Maru, argentina y miembro del cuerpo diplomático, este problema obedece a aspectos culturales arraigados en la mentalidad de los panameños. "La primera vez que intenté salir sola me aprendí la dirección y llamé un taxi. Cuando le di el nombre de la calle y el número de la embajada, el conductor no sabía de qué le estaba hablando. El hombre insistía en preguntarme sobre algún lugar de referencia que quedara cerca. Ningún taxista me pudo llevar."

Una cosa que le llama muchísimo la atención es que la gente utilice como puntos de referencia cosas que ya no existen y que dejaron incluso de existir mucho antes de que ellos nacieran, como "la Lechería", el Teatro Bella Vista, "el Casino", la estatua de Roosevelt o el antiguo Club de Golf, entre otros.

¿Solución?

Hace cerca de 15 años, la autoridad trató de señalizar casi todas las calles residenciales de la ciudad, asignándoles nombres de flores y plantas. Poco a poco los letreros fueron desapareciendo y con ellos, los nombres que se suponía que serían más fáciles de recordar. La fórmula de número, letra y punto cardinal ha vuelto a ser el sistema oficial utilizado por el Municipio de Panamá. Sin embargo, esto no parece haber hecho efecto en los habitantes de la ciudad, que están acostumbrados a su constante crecimiento y cambios.

Used by permission of VeinteMundos.com

1. ¿Cuál es el propósito del artículo?

   (A) Los habitantes de Panamá deben usar nombres para distinguir las calles.

   (B) La planificación urbana es un desafío para Panamá, que sigue cambiando con el crecimiento de la ciudad.

   (C) El nombramiento de las avenidas y calles es uno de los proyectos más importantes de la planificación urbana en Panamá.

   (D) Las personas entrevistadas tienen las soluciones para mejorar el sistema de nombrar las calles.

2. ¿Cuál es una explicación para las calles sin nombres?

   (A) Hay calles que no tienen nombre, y otras que tienen hasta dos y tres.

   (B) Es un destino turístico, y por lo tanto las calles no necesitan nombres.

   (C) Los extranjeros tenían sus propios nombres para ciertas calles, mientras que los panameños tenían otros para las mismas.

   (D) La ciudad creció desordenadamente, sobrepasando la capacidad de planificación de las autoridades.

3. Después de la independencia, todos los siguientes eventos sucedieron EXCEPTO:

   (A) Panamá tuvo un gran crecimiento económico.

   (B) Hubo una gran cantidad de migraciones a la ciudad desde áreas rurales del país.

   (C) La planificación urbana nombró las cuadras, avenidas, y calles con nombres propios.

   (D) Se abrió el Canal poco tiempo después.

4. Según la entrevista de Maru, ¿por qué se menciona el taxi?

   (A) Era difícil comunicar su destino al taxista con solamente el nombre de calle.

   (B) El taxista no podía comprender el acento argentino de Maru.

   (C) Los lugares de referencia se convertían en distracciones para el taxista.

   (D) Maru debe obedecer las tradiciones y la mentalidad de los panameños.

5. Se menciona «"la Lechería"… entre otros» para

   (A) nombrar unos lugares donde muchas personas nacieron

   (B) mostrar que muchos de los lugares de referencia son antiguos

   (C) sugerir nombres para las calles en estos lugares

   (D) dar ejemplos de lugares de referencia que ya no existen

6. Según el último párrafo, ¿qué podemos inferir de los cambios que ha implementado el Municipio de Panamá?

   (A) Los cambios fueron un fracaso porque nadie usa los nombres propios de las calles.

   (B) El Municipio de Panamá ordenó a los panameños que usen los nombres propios de las calles.

   (C) No parecen haber hecho mucho efecto.

   (D) La fórmula de número, letra, y punto cardinal mejorará la organización urbana de la ciudad.

Translated Text and Questions, with Explanations

Introduction

The following article appeared in 1993 in the periodical *The Latino Culture.*

Panama: The Mystery of the Nameless Streets

Nowadays Panama is one of the most popular tourist destinations on the continent and one of the strongest economies in the region. Nevertheless, chaos is a natural part of its beautiful capital city. Urban planning hardly exists, and just as many native Panamanians as tourists suffer daily trying to find a simple street. Describing the visual aspects of the whereabouts of a location can be complicated; this without a doubt is already part of the daily lives of its inhabitants. If you dare, accompany our journalist on this mysterious adventure through the city, trying to decipher "the mystery of the nameless streets"….

Despite all the successful advances over more than a century of republican life, we Panamanians still have to live with some legacies of our past, such as not having a well-planned system of naming the streets. Referring to districts and avenues with proper names and buildings with numbers is very strange.

After its independence, Panama underwent great economic growth. This generated large migrations to the city from rural areas of the country and abroad, which forced the city to expand. Overnight, this metropolis began to grow in a disorganized fashion, surpassing the planning capacity of the authorities.

The growth did not stop or slow, but rather increased. The opening of the Canal and other events of the 20th century left us with the legacy of a city not only full of nooks and corners, but also streets without names.

"Here, everyone did what he or she felt like, and there was no authority interested in creating order," remembers Carmen, a 76-year-old retired teacher. "There are some streets that do not have a name, and others that have two or three," she maintains.

For Maru, an Argentinian and member of the diplomatic corps, this problem lies in aspects of culture rooted in the mentality of the Panamanians. "The first time I tried to go out by myself, I found the address and called a taxi. When I gave him the name of the street and number of the embassy, the driver did not know what I was talking about. The man insisted on asking me for some landmarks that were around there. No taxi driver could get me there."

One thing that is very noticeable is that people use points of reference that do not exist anymore, including many from before they were born, like "the Dairy," "the Bella Vista theater," "the Casino," the statue of Roosevelt, or the old Golf Club, among others.

Solutions?

About 15 years ago, the authorities tried to post signs naming almost all the residential streets of the city, assigning them names of flowers and plants. Little by little, the signs disappeared, and, with them, the names that were supposed to be easier to remember. The formula of number, letter, and geographic point has become the official system utilized by the Panama Municipality. Nevertheless, this does not appear to have had an effect on the inhabitants of the city, who are accustomed to its constant growth and change.

Here's How to Crack It

1. What is the purpose of the article?

   (A) The inhabitants of Panama should use names to distinguish their streets.

   (B) Urban planning is a challenge for Panama, which continues to change and grow.

   (C) The classification of avenues and streets is one of the most important urban planning projects in Panama.

   (D) The interviewees have solutions to better the system of naming the streets.

Choice (B) is the correct answer. The main purpose of the article is to explain, through interviews, the phenomenon of Panama's unmarked streets, and the ways in which residents have substituted using landmarks as a means of coping with the problem. The urban planning system has had many challenges in naming and organizing the streets, due to the city's constant growth and change. The passage never mentions what Panamanians should or should not do (A), nor that the interviewees have solutions for the problem of naming the streets (D). Choice (C) is a trap because it is extreme.

2. What is one explanation for the streets without names?

   (A) There are some streets without names, while others have two or three.

   (B) It is a tourist destination, and, for the most part, it is not necessary to name the streets.

   (C) The foreigners had their own names for certain streets, while Panamanians had other names for the same ones.

   (D) The city grew in a disorderly fashion, surpassing the planning capacity of the authorities.

Choice (D) is the correct answer. After independence, the city grew at a rapid pace, a pace that the urban planners could not match. Therefore, the city expanded without adequate city planning, and developed without official street names. While (A) is mentioned during an interview, it is merely an observation, and not a real explanation for the nameless streets. Neither (B) nor (C) is true.

3. After independence, all of the following happened EXCEPT:

   (A) Panama experienced great economic growth.

   (B) There were many people who migrated to the city from rural areas of the country.

   (C) The urban planning department named the blocks, avenues, and streets with proper names.

   (D) The Canal opened shortly thereafter.

After independence, the city expanded economically (A), and attracted a lot of citizens from rural areas of the country (B). The Canal opened shortly after as well (D), but there is no mention that the urban planners named the streets, blocks, and avenues during that time. Therefore, (C) is correct.

4. According to Maru's interview, why is the taxi mentioned?

   (A) It was difficult to communicate her destination to the taxi driver using the name of the street.

   (B) The taxi driver couldn't understand Maru's Argentinian accent.

   (C) The landmarks became distractions for the taxi driver.

   (D) Maru should abide by the traditions and mentality of the Panamanians.

Maru recounts her experience of trying to take a taxi in Panama to illustrate how difficult it was to communicate her destination with only a street address. The taxi driver did not seem to understand this type of address, but rather asked for landmarks around the destination. Choice (B) recycles phrases, and the text never says that the taxi driver cannot understand Maru's accent. Choice (D) is not mentioned anywhere in the text. Therefore, (A) is correct.

5. "'The Dairy,'...among others" is mentioned to

   (A) name some locations where many people were born

   (B) show that many of the landmarks are old

   (C) suggest names for the streets in those locations

   (D) give some examples of landmarks that do not exist anymore

The Dairy, the Casino, the Bella Vista theater, and others are examples of landmarks that no longer exist, yet native residents still refer to them. In fact, these landmarks disappeared before many residents were born. Though these landmarks are or were old (C), that is not the main reason for their mention here. They are certainly not locations in which residents were born, as in (A). Therefore, (D) is correct, as they are merely landmarks that residents refer to.

6. According to the last paragraph, what can we infer about the changes that have been implemented by the Municipality of Panama?

   (A) The changes were a failure because no one uses the proper names of the streets.

   (B) The Municipality of Panama mandated that the Panamanians use the proper names of the streets.

   (C) The changes do not appear to have had much effect.

   (D) The formula of number, letter, and geographic coordinate will improve the city's urban planning.

Choice (C) is the correct answer. Many changes implemented in the last 15 years in Panama have not been of much use, as some of the street signs have disappeared, and Panamanians still refer to landmarks instead of street names for directions. Choice (A) is too extreme, and (D) predicts the future. Choice (B) is not mentioned in the passage, so (C) must be correct.

PRACTICE PASSAGE 5

Introducción

El siguiente panfleto apareció en 2008 del Ministerio de Salud de la Universidad de Puerto Rico.

INFLUENZA A (H1N1)
Información, precauciones y acciones a tomar.

¿Qué es la Influenza A(H1N1)?
Se trata de un nuevo virus de influenza capaz de producir la enfermedad en el ser humano, originado en el cerdo por el intercambio genético entre los virus porcinos, aviarios y humanos.

¿Cómo se transmite la influenza A(H1N1)?
De persona a persona (el virus entra al organismo por la boca, la nariz y los ojos), principalmente cuando las personas enfermas o portadoras de influenza A(H1N1) expulsan gotitas de saliva al estornudar o toser frente a otra sin cubrirse la boca y la nariz, al compartir utensilios o alimentos con una persona enferma, o al saludar de mano, beso o abrazo a una persona enferma. También se puede transmitir a través del contacto con superficies previamente contaminadas con gotitas de saliva de una persona enferma de influenza A(H1N1), tales como las manos, mesas, teclados de computadora, manijas, barandales, pañuelos desechables y telas.

¿Cuáles son los síntomas de la Influenza A(H1N1)?
Fiebre de 38 °C o más, tos y dolor de cabeza, acompañados de uno o más de los siguientes síntomas: escurrimiento nasal, congestión nasal, dolor de articulaciones, dolor muscular, decaimiento, dolor al tragar, dolor de pecho, dolor de estómago y diarrea.

¿Cuál es la gravedad de la enfermedad?
No se conoce hasta el momento la verdadera mortalidad de la enfermedad. Resulta importante hacer notar que la Influenza estacional también puede producir manifestaciones severas en pacientes que integran alguno grupos de riesgo (mayores de 65 y menores de 5 años, personas afectadas por enfermedades cardiorrespiratorias crónicas, inmunosuprimidos, y diabéticos).

¿Por cuánto tiempo puede una persona infectada propagar la influenza a otras?
Las personas infectadas por el virus de la Influenza AH1N1 pueden transmitir la enfermedad mientras tengan los síntomas y posiblemente hasta siete días después del inicio de la enfermedad. Los niños, especialmente los más pequeños, podrían ser contagiosos durante períodos más largos.

¿Existe un tratamiento efectivo?
El tratamiento con Tamaflu es efectivo especialmente si se administra en los primeros dos días de iniciados los síntomas y está recomendado en casos sospechosos o confirmados. Esta medicación será provista por el Ministerio de Salud con unas instrucciones que el médico comunicará al paciente.

¿Es útil la vacuna antigripal (Influenza estacional)?
La vacuna antigripal no incluye al virus Influenza AH1N1 por lo que no es útil para prevenir esta enfermedad. Sin embargo, es importante cumplir con la vacunación anual en los grupos de riesgo.

¿Qué debe hacer una persona que presente síntomas?

Acudir a la unidad de salud que le corresponda para que el médico le realice el diagnóstico clínico y de laboratorio. Sólo el médico deberá indicar la administración de medicamentos antivirales para el tratamiento. NO AUTOMEDICARSE.

¿Cuáles son los signos de alarma que deben motivar una consulta urgente?

Además de los síntomas ya descritos debe realizarse una consulta de urgencia en caso de presentar los siguientes síntomas.

- Dificultad para respirar
- Color azul o gris de la piel (cianosis)
- Dolor de pecho o abdomen
- Desorientación
- Vómito

Medidas De Prevención

Para reducir la probabilidad de exposición y transmisión del virus es muy importante que TODOS realicemos las medidas de higiene personal y del entorno. Por eso es muy importante que adoptemos como hábitos las siguientes medidas:

- Lavarse las manos frecuentemente con agua y jabón o utilizar gel a base de alcohol al llegar de la calle, antes de comer o después de estar en contacto con espacios contaminados.
- Al toser o estornudar, cubrirse la nariz y boca con un pañuelo desechable o con el ángulo interno del brazo.
- No escupir. Si es necesario hacerlo, utilizar un pañuelo desechable, meterlo en una bolsa de plástico, cerrarla con un nudo y tirarla a la basura.
- No tocarse la cara con las manos sucias, sobre todo la nariz, la boca y los ojos.
- Limpiar y desinfectar superficies y objetos de uso común en casa, oficinas y escuelas, además de ventilar y permitir la entrada de luz solar.
- No compartir bebidas ni utensilios que pueden transmitir los virus y otros gérmenes.

1. ¿Cuál es el tono del panfleto?

   (A) Miedo

   (B) Entusiasmo

   (C) Curiosidad

   (D) Aviso

2. Se puede trasmitir la Influenza H1N1 a través de

   (A) cubrirse la nariz y boca con un pañuelo desechable o con el ángulo interno del brazo

   (B) estar en contacto con los cerdos, el origen del virus

   (C) el contacto con superficies previamente contaminadas

   (D) ser mayor de 65 años o menor de 5 años, o ser de un grupo de riesgo elevado

3. Se menciona "mayores de 65… diabéticos" para

 (A) identificar unos grupos de riesgo elevado para las manifestaciones severas

 (B) recomendar que ellos tomen Tamaflu

 (C) identificar a personas que sienten fiebre de 38 °C o más, tos y dolor de cabeza, acompañados de otros síntomas

 (D) nombrar los grupos de personas que contraerán la influenza

4. Según el panfleto, ¿es útil la vacuna antigripal para prevenir la influenza H1N1?

 (A) Es una vacunación anual que los grupos de riesgo deben tomar para evitarse la influenza H1N1.

 (B) La vacuna no tiene ningún beneficio para nadie.

 (C) Es importante cumplir con la vacunación anual para evitar la influenza.

 (D) Aunque la vacuna anual previene la influenza regular, no incluye el H1N1.

5. Desorientación, vómitos, y otros síntomas similares son ejemplos de

 (A) los que se presentan en los grupos de riesgo

 (B) síntomas normales de la influenza, que se presentan durante solamente tres días

 (C) los que deben ocasionar una consulta de urgencia

 (D) los que resultan de las medidas de prevención

6. Todas las siguientes son medidas de prevención de la influenza SALVO

 (A) lavarse las manos frecuentemente con agua y jabón o utilizar gel a base de alcohol

 (B) al toser o estornudar, abrir la boca al aire libre

 (C) limpiar y desinfectar superficies y objetos de uso común

 (D) ventilar y permitir la entrada de luz solar

Translated Text and Questions, with Explanations

Introduction

The following pamphlet appeared in 2008 from the Ministry of Health of The University of Puerto Rico.

INFLUENZA A (H1N1)
Information, Precautions, and Actions to Take

What is Influenza A(H1N1)?

It is a new flu virus capable of making humans sick, originating from pigs in a genetic exchange between the porcine, avian, and human viruses.

How is Influenza A(H1N1) transmitted?

It is transmitted from person to person (the virus enters an organism through the mouth, nose, or eyes), primarily when sick persons or carriers of the Influenza A(H1N1) expel droplets of saliva from sneezing or coughing in front of another without covering the mouth or nose, when one shares utensils or food with a sick person, or when shaking hands, kissing, or hugging a sick person. Also, it can be transmitted through contact with surfaces previously contaminated by droplets of saliva from a person sick with Influenza A(H1N1) such as hands, tables, keyboards, handles, banisters, tissues, and fabrics.

What are the symptoms of Influenza A(H1N1)?

Fever of 38 °C or higher, cough, and headache, accompanied by one or more of the following symptoms: runny nose, nasal congestion, joint pain, muscular soreness, lack of energy, painful swallowing, chest pain, stomach pain, and diarrhea.

How serious is it?

At this point, the real severity of the disease is not known. It is important to note that the seasonal flu can also produce severe cases in patients in higher-risk groups (older than 65 and younger than 5 years of age, those affected by diseases such as chronic cardiorespiratory conditions, the immunosuppressed, and diabetics).

For how long can an infected person spread the flu to others?

Persons infected with the Influenza A(H1N1) virus can spread the sickness while they have symptoms, and possibly up to seven days after its start. Children, especially the youngest, can be contagious for longer durations of time.

Is there an effective treatment?

The treatment Tamaflu is effective, especially if administered in the first two days after the onset of symptoms, and is recommended in suspected or confirmed cases. The Health Ministry will provide this medication with instructions that the doctor will communicate to the patient.

Is the flu vaccine useful (seasonal Influenza)?

The flu vaccine does not include the Influenza A(H1N1) virus, and therefore is not useful in preventing this disease. Nevertheless, it is important for groups at higher risk to get the annual vaccination.

What should a person do if he/she presents symptoms?

Attend a heath clinic in which a doctor can carry out clinical and laboratory diagnostics. Only a doctor can prescribe and administer antiviral medications for treatment. DO NOT TREAT YOURSELF.

What are some warning signs that should prompt you to seek urgent care?

In addition to the symptoms already described, one should seek urgent care if the following symptoms are present:
- Difficulty breathing
- Blue- or grey-colored skin (cyanosis)
- Chest or abdominal pain
- Disorientation
- Vomiting

MEASURES FOR PREVENTION

To reduce the probability of exposure and transmission of the virus, it is important that EVERYONE carry out measures regarding personal hygiene and their surroundings. For this reason, it is very important that we adopt the following habits:

- Wash your hands frequently with soap and water or use alcohol-based gel upon arriving home, before eating, or after contact with contaminated spaces.
- When coughing or sneezing, cover your nose and mouth with a disposable tissue or the inside of your elbow.
- Do not spit. If it is necessary to do so, use a disposable tissue and put it in a plastic bag, tie it closed with a knot, and throw it in the trash.
- Do not touch your face with dirty hands: above all your nose, mouth, and eyes.
- Clean and disinfect commonly used surfaces and objects at homes, offices, and schools, along with ventilating and allowing in sunlight.
- Do not share beverages or utensils that can transmit viruses and other germs.

Here's How to Crack It

1. What is the tone of the pamphlet?

   (A) Fear

   (B) Enthusiasm

   (C) Curiosity

   (D) Advice

Choice (D) is correct. The tone of the pamphlet is one of advice and warning to college students about the seriousness of the flu. Though fear (A) might be tempting, it is too extreme, and the others, enthusiasm (B), and curiosity (C), do not make sense.

2. One can transmit the H1N1 virus by

   (A) covering the nose and mouth with a disposable tissue or with the inside of the elbow

   (B) being in contact with pigs, the origin of the virus

   (C) being in contact with previously contaminated surfaces

   (D) being older than 65 years old, younger than 5 years old, or in a group of increased risk

Choice (C) is correct. Covering your nose and mouth with a tissue or elbow is supposed to help stop the spread of the flu (A). However, having contact with previously contaminated surfaces that have bits of saliva from a sick person can contribute to the spread of the disease (C). Being in a group with elevated risk does not mean that one will get the flu, so it has nothing to do with transmitting the disease (D), and the pamphlet never mentions being around pigs as a means of transfer either (B).

3. "Those over 65…diabetics" are mentioned in order to

   (A) identify some groups at increased risk for severe cases

   (B) recommend that they take Tamaflu

   (C) identify some people who experience fevers of 38 °C and higher, cough, and headache, along with other symptoms

   (D) name the groups of people who will get the flu

Persons over 65, diabetics, and the others mentioned are various groups with elevated risk for getting the flu, not those who already have the flu. Tamaflu is the drug one takes when one already has the flu (B), and one also would already have the flu if one were presenting with fevers and other symptoms (C). Choice (D) predicts the future as to who will get the flu, so (A) is correct.

4. According to the pamphlet, is the flu vaccine useful in preventing the H1N1 virus?

    (A) It is an annual vaccination that at-risk groups should get to avoid the H1N1 virus.

    (B) The vaccine does not have any benefits for anyone.

    (C) It is important to get the annual vaccination to avoid influenza.

    (D) Even though the annual vaccine prevents the regular flu, it does not include the H1N1 virus.

Choice (D) is correct. The flu vaccine, while useful in protecting against seasonal Influenza, does not protect against the Influenza A(H1N1) virus. Choice (A) contains recycled words that suggest that at-risk groups should get the vaccine; however, the passage states that it does not protect against the H1N1 virus, and (B) is extreme. Choice (C) is contained in the passage, but does not answer the question of whether or not the vaccine protects against Influenza A(H1N1).

5. Disorientation, vomiting, and other similar symptoms are examples of

    (A) those which are present in high-risk groups

    (B) normal symptoms of the flu, which present themselves and only last three days

    (C) those which should result in emergency care

    (D) those which are the result of preventative measures

Choice (C) is correct. Disorientation, vomiting, and others are examples of symptoms that need urgent medical care. They are not normal symptoms that only last for three days, as in (B). These symptoms will not necessarily be present in at-risk groups (A), and they are certainly not the result of preventative measures (D).

6. All of the following are preventative measures for the flu EXCEPT

    (A) washing your hands frequently with soap and water or using alcohol-based gel

    (B) while coughing or sneezing, opening your mouth to the open air

    (C) cleaning and disinfecting commonly used surfaces and objects

    (D) ventilating areas and allowing in sunlight

Choice (B) is correct. Opening your nose and mouth to the open air while sneezing or coughing is exactly the opposite of what the pamphlet advises. All other choices are in the "preventative measures" portion of the pamphlet.

PRACTICE PASSAGE 6

Introducción

El siguiente artículo apareció en 1989 en una revista de literatura juvenil.

La Aventura de don Quijote en la escuela

En este Año del Quijote, el autor aprovecha para hablar de la lectura del clásico en la escuela y para analizar la gran cantidad de adaptaciones y recreaciones de la obra de Cervantes que están ‹colonizado› actualmente el mercado.

Como casi todo el mundo sabe, el 2005 es el año del *Quijote* ya que se coincide con los 400 años de su primera edición.
También coinciden —aunque ya no todo el mundo sabe— los

Línea
5   doscientos años de nacimiento de Hans Christian Andersen, el inmortal autor de cuentos tan universales como *El patito feo*, o los cien años de la muerte de Jules Verne, además los 50 años de la muerte de Albert Einstein, el de la teoría de la relatividad.

Es por ello que este año fue declarado oficialmente Año de la Lectura y del Libro. Hay muchos eventos conmemorativos que
10   celebrarán la historia del experto autor de la obra cervantina y muchos otros autores.

Versiones, adaptaciones, recreaciones del clásico

Lo primero que nos sorprende es la proliferación de diferentes versiones que lanzan las editoriales, con un esfuerzo evidente de ocupar el mercado. Adaptaciones en las que hay
15   supresión de partes o capítulos, o nuevas reescrituras intentando cambiar la historia, son las más fastidiosas.

Otra cosa son las versiones que llamamos ‹recreaciones o inclusiones libres›. Estas me parecen más honestas ya que no
20   hay interrupción en el personaje cervantino. Cuando se cambia el personaje, metido en otro mundo que no es el suyo, resulta demasiado esperpéntico y se le ‹infantiliza› demasiado, lo que a mi juicio, no es positivo para ganarse a corto plazo más lectores de la novela.

25   ### Darlo a conocer, sin imponerlo

Vistos todos estos argumentos, la pregunta clave es: ¿cómo se debe entonces proceder? ¿Cuál es la metodología adecuada? Es cierto que no hay soluciones fáciles porque el camino para consolidar hábitos de lectura está lleno de obstáculos.

30   Pero, dicho esto, lo que en primer lugar se debe hacer es educar, sin prisas pero sin pausas. La mejor medicina es extender el conocimiento de los buenos libros infantiles, de la buena literatura infantil o juvenil. Una vez puestos estos cimientos, el camino estará mejor preparado. Solo queda dar prioridad a
35   la lectura placentera, darles la oportunidad de leer y de elegir, declarar la lectura patrimonio común de los escolares. Incluso depararles la oportunidad de hojearlo o de no leerlo.

No sea el caso que el exceso de celo produzca los efectos contrarios a los que proponemos: «La sombra del *Quijote*
40   —dice Ana María Matute— planeaba sobre nuestras vidas de escolares nacientes como una amenaza. Para decirlo claramente: nos hicieron odiarlo».

En fin: un *Quijote* en verso, otro expurgado, otro adaptado, otro modernizado. ¿Qué queda del verdadero *Quijote*?

Adapted from "La aventura de don Quijote en la escuela," by Juan José Lage Fernández, Biblioteca Virtual de Prensa Histórica. http://prensahistorica.mcu.es

1. ¿Cuál de las siguientes afirmaciones resume mejor el artículo?

   (A) Las recreaciones y inclusiones libres son las mejores adaptaciones.

   (B) Cervantes es el autor más celebrado por los críticos de la literatura.

   (C) Hay dificultades para crear una adaptación destinada a los jóvenes, pero se les puede dar a conocer los libros clásicos.

   (D) Las versiones reescritas del *Quijote* resultaron en más lectores de corto plazo para la novela.

2. Se menciona "adaptaciones en las que hay supresión... nuevas reescrituras" para

   (A) describir las adaptaciones desconcertantes que intentan cambiar la historia

   (B) ganarse a corto plazo lectores de la novela por sus dibujos vibrantes

   (C) ilustrar una metodología adecuada de hacer las adaptaciones

   (D) promover la lectura placentera

3. Podemos inferir que las adaptaciones y libros condensados

   (A) producen los efectos contrarios, que hace los niños odiar los libros clásicos

   (B) son ridículos e inmaduros

   (C) pueden cultivar un agradecimiento de los libros clásicos

   (D) no pueden contener el "verdadero *Quijote*"

4. La imagen en el principio del artículo es uno que

   (A) ilustra el realismo de la historia del *Quijote*

   (B) muestra la sombra del *Quijote*

   (C) muestra un esfuerzo evidente de ocupar el mercado

   (D) puede acompañar las recreaciones o inclusiones libres

5. La siguiente frase se puede añadir al texto: "Los dibujos que acompañan estas ediciones también me parecen honestas por sus hermosos detalles que representan los personajes de una manera auténtica." ¿Dónde serviría mejor esta frase?

   (A) Después de las líneas 16–17: "nuevas reescrituras intentando cambiar la historia, son las más fastidiosas"

   (B) Después de la línea 20: "... interrupción en el personaje cervantino"

   (C) Después de las líneas 23–24: "... ganarse a corto plazo más lectores de la novela"

   (D) Después de las líneas 43–44: "en verso, otro expurgado, otro adaptado, otro modernizado"

6. ¿Cuál es el significado de la frase "la sombra del *Quijote*"?

   (A) El *Quijote* es una amenaza a los escolares nacientes.

   (B) Los niños obligados a leer el *Quijote* habían empezado a resentir el libro.

   (C) La sombra oscurece las palabras, que lo hace más difícil a leer.

   (D) *Don Quijote*, celebrando su aniversario de 400 años, es un libro monumental de la literatura clásica.

7. Podemos inferir que

   (A) al principio, el autor encontró las adaptaciones demasiado ‹infantiles›, pero al final concede que hay aspectos beneficiosos de estos libros

   (B) no hay solamente una manera de adaptar o condensar un libro de literatura clásica

   (C) los escolares deben leer los libros clásicos para ser más cultos

   (D) la literatura clásica no se debe ser adaptada porque se disminuye la importancia del texto

Translated Text and Questions, with Explanations

Introduction

The following article appeared in 1989 in a journal of youth literature.

The Adventure of Don Quijote in Schools

In this Year of Don Quixote, the author uses the opportunity to talk about classic literature in schools to analyze the great quantity of adaptions and recreations of Cervantes's work, which are "colonizing" the market.

As almost all the world knows, 2005 is the year of Don Quixote, coinciding with the 400-year anniversary of the book's first edition. Also coinciding—even though not all the world knows—is the 200th anniversary of the birth of Hans Christian Andersen, the immortal author of such universal stories as the *The Ugly Duckling*, and the 100th anniversary of the death of Jules Verne, in addition to the 50th anniversary of Albert Einstein's death (he of the Theory of Relativity).

For these reasons, this year was officially declared The Year of Reading and Books. There are many commemorative events that will praise the expert author of this work along with many other authors.

Versions, Adaptations, and Recreations of the Classic

The first thing that surprises us is the proliferation of different versions that publishers issue, with an evident effort to occupy the market. Adaptations which eliminate parts or chapters, or which rewrite them, intending to change the story, are the most bothersome.

Others are the versions that we call "recreations or free inclusions." They seem more honest to me, since they do not seem to be a departure from the Cervantine character. When one changes the character, involving it in another world that is not its own, it becomes too absurd and "infantilized," which, in my judgment, is not good as it only gains short-term readers for the novel.

Allow the Book to be Encountered, not Imposed

Seeing all these arguments, the key question is this: how should we now proceed? What is the appropriate method? Certainly, there are no easy solutions because the road to strengthen reading habits is full of obstacles.

But, that said, the first thing we should do is educate, without hurry or pause. The best medicine is to extend a knowledge of good children's books, of good children's and youth literature. Once these foundations are in place, the road will be more or less carved out ahead. All that remains is to give priority to reading for pleasure, giving schoolchildren the opportunity to read, choose, and claim the common wealth and heritage of reading. This includes allowing them the opportunity to leaf through a book and choose not to read it.

It may be the case that an excess of enthusiasm produces the opposite effect that we intend: "the shadow of *Don Quixote*," says Ana María Matute "soared over our lives as budding schoolchildren like a menace. To put it clearly, we were made to loathe it."

Anyhow, a *Don Quixote* in verse, another expurgated, another adapted, and another modernized: what remains of the real *Quixote*?

Here's How to Crack It

1. Which of the following statements best summarizes the article?

   (A) Recreations and "inclusive" editions are the best editions.

   (B) Cervantes is the author most celebrated by literary critics.

   (C) There are difficulties in creating adaptations for young people, though these can introduce them to classic literature.

   (D) The rewritten versions of *Don Quixote* have cultivated short-term readers of the novel.

The article focuses on the many adaptations and recreations of *Don Quixote* and the difficulties that come with making such editions. While some editions are better than others, they allow children to experience the classics at a young age. Choice (A) is a superlative, and though the author likes these editions, we cannot choose this answer choice because of its language. Choice (B) contains a superlative as well, and we do not have proof that Cervantes is the author most celebrated amongst literary critics. Choice (D) is true according to the article, but is not a summary of its main points. Therefore, (C) is correct.

2. "Adaptations which eliminate…which rewrite them" are mentioned in order to

   (A) describe the disconcerting adaptations which intend to change the story

   (B) gain short-term readers of the novel through their vibrant pictures

   (C) illustrate an adequate methodology for making adaptations

   (D) promote reading for pleasure

Choice (A) is correct. The author explicitly says that he finds these types of adaptations to be the most bothersome because they leave out parts of the story and change other parts. There is no proof of pictures in these editions, though many children's books contain illustrations (B). Since these adaptations are not seen as satisfactory by the author, they would not be an adequate method of creating an adaptation (C), nor do these examples necessarily promote reading for pleasure (D).

3. We can infer that the adaptations and condensed books

   (A) produce contrary effects that make children hate classic literature

   (B) are ridiculous and immature

   (C) can cultivate an appreciation of classic books

   (D) cannot encompass the "real *Quixote*"

We can only infer that adaptations can cultivate an appreciation of classic books. We cannot prove that these editions will produce adverse effects (A), or that they will necessarily be ridiculous or immature (B). In addition, these adaptations do not always miss the true spirit of the "real *Quixote*" (D). Therefore, (C) is correct.

4. The illustration at the start of the article is one that

(A) shows the realism of the story of *Don Quixote*

(B) shows the shadow of *Don Quixote*

(C) shows an evident effort to occupy the market

(D) can accompany recreations and "inclusive" editions

The illustration characterizes *Don Quixote*'s charming madness, which remains true to the original book, and therefore the most authentic adaptations might contain these same sentiments, i.e., the recreations and inclusive editions. Choice (A) does not work because the illustration does not depict realism, nor does it show the "shadow of *Don Quixote*" (B), as this phrase is taken out of context and is not related to the illustration. The illustration does not show evidence of occupying the market (C), so (D) must be correct.

5. The following sentence may be added to the text: "The pictures that accompany these editions also appear to me to be honest in their beautiful details that represent the characters with authenticity." Where would this fit best?

(A) After lines 16–17: "which rewrite them, intending to change the story, are the most bothersome"

(B) After line 20: "…departure from the Cervantine character"

(C) After lines 23–24: "gains short-term readers for the novel"

(D) After lines 43–44: "in verse, another expurgated, another adapted, another modernized"

The insertion of a sentence about illustrations that seem "honest as well" should be paired with the recreations and "inclusive" editions because those are described in a similar manner, and seem in line with the protagonist's character. Choice (A) would be the opposite of the correct answer, describing the more irksome adaptations that change the story of *Don Quixote*. Choice (C) may seem tempting, but the illustration is described in a positive light, opposite of the "short-term" readers. Choice (D) would not create good flow or continuity for the inserted sentence, so (B) is correct.

6. What is the meaning of the phrase "the shadow of *Don Quixote*"?

(A) *Don Quixote* is a menace to schoolchildren.

(B) The schoolchildren who were obliged to read *Don Quixote* had started to resent it.

(C) The shadow obscures the words, and makes it difficult to read.

(D) *Don Quixote,* celebrating its 400-year anniversary, is a great book of classic literature.

Choice (B) is correct. Schoolchildren felt the "shadow of *Don Quixote*" because schools placed so much emphasis on the book that the students began to dread it, as Ana María Matute stated in her quote. Choice (D) is contained in the passage but does not answer the question about the given phrase, and (A) recycles the words from the text, making it too literal. Choice (C) takes the word "shadow" too literally, so (B) must be true, as the meaning of the phrase is metaphorical.

7. It can be inferred that

    (A) in the beginning, the author found the adaptations too "infantile," but later he concedes that there are some beneficial aspects to them

    (B) **there is no one single way to adapt or condense a book of classic literature**

    (C) schoolchildren should read classic books in order to be cultured

    (D) classic literature should not be adapted because it belittles the importance of the text

Choice (B) is correct. Choice (A) contains recycled words, which, placed next to one another, change the meaning of the phrases as they are taken out of context. Choice (C) is offensive to the schoolchildren. Choice (D) is extreme, and does not go along with the main point of the article. Therefore, (B) is correct, as there is no one method of creating adaptations or condensations for pieces of classic literature.

PRACTICE PASSAGE 7

Introducción

El siguiente sitio de Internet trata de El Sistema, el programa nacional de Venezuela que comparte la música con niños desfavorecidos. El sitio apareció en mayo de 2003.

Tocar, Cantar y Luchar

Fundado en 1975 por maestro Dr. José Antonio Abreu, El Sistema Nacional de Orquestas y Coros Juveniles e Infantiles de Venezuela empezó en un garaje con 11 niños. Hoy en día, el programa, afectuosamente llamado "El Sistema", sirve a más que 500 mil estudiantes desfavorecidos en Venezuela y continúa crecer. Además, más de 42 países habían creado programas inspirados por El Sistema, entre ellos Argentina, Australia, Austria, Bolivia, Brasil, Canadá, Chile, Colombia, Corea del Sur, Costa Rica, Cuba, Ecuador, El Salvador, Escocia, los Estados Unidos, Francia, Guatemala, Honduras, India, Inglaterra, Italia, Jamaica, Japón, México, Nicaragua, Panamá, Paraguay, Perú, Portugal, Puerto Rico, la República Dominicana, Trinidad y Tobago, y Uruguay.

El Sistema en Venezuela enseña la música a través de instrucción individual y colectiva a niños tan jóvenes como 2 y 3 años de edad, y combina estas lecciones con participación en orquestas o coros infantiles y juveniles. En cada programa, las orquestas tienen más importancia que solamente compartir la música clásica: son dedicadas a la prevención de deserción escolar y la reducción del crimen en las ciudades. En un estudio, la tasa de abandono escolar ha disminuido desde 6,9% en estudiantes involucrados en El Sistema, comparado al 26,4% del grupo de control. También, se puede ver el gran impacto de El Sistema en las tasas reducidas de analfabetismo, marginalidad y exclusión en la población joven e infantil en Venezuela.

Los niños y sus padres son parte de la comunidad social en El Sistema que enfatiza la importancia del desarrollo del ser humano. Esta población de 500 mil niños y jóvenes venezolanos se distribuye en aproximadamente 285 orquestas pre-infantiles (entre 4 y 6 años), 220 orquestas infantiles (entre 7 y 16 años), 180 orquestas juveniles (entre 16 y 22 años), 30 orquestas profesionales, 360 agrupaciones corales, 1.355 agrupaciones corales afiliadas y más de 15.000 profesores en todas partes del país. Los profesores les enseñan a los niños a "tocar, cantar y luchar" para vencer los obstáculos de la pobreza y perseguir la educación formal.

Aquí en los Estados Unidos, hay muchos programas extracurriculares inspirados por El Sistema en Venezuela que promueven el cambio social en lugares con pocos recursos. El NAESIP (National Alliance of El Sistema-Inspired Programs) da a los niños en estas comunidades las herramientas para superar los obstáculos de la pobreza y para descubrir la importancia de educación. "He pensado siempre que la enseñanza de la música desde la más tierna infancia es una tarea hermosísima y crucial de toda sociedad. Esto es un ideal de la educación desde hace muchísimos siglos: la música forma parte del desarrollo espiritual y la conciencia y la formación estética del hombre", dice el maestro Abreu.

1. ¿Qué significa el título "Tocar, Cantar y Luchar"?

   (A) El Sistema enseña a los niños a luchar por su derecho a la educación y para superar la pobreza.

   (B) El Sistema enseña a los niños a luchar entre sí.

   (C) "Tocar y cantar" es una metáfora de la lucha en los países latinoamericanos.

   (D) Muchas veces los niños se pelean con sus padres.

2. ¿De qué se trata este artículo?

   (A) Hay un gran problema del analfabetismo, la pobreza y la marginalidad en Venezuela y en otras partes del mundo.

   (B) El Sistema ha creado un ambiente positivo para los niños involucrados, y otros países han creado programas de afiliados con el fin de mejorar las vidas de los niños desfavorecidos.

   (C) Todos los niños que participan en El Sistema tienen éxito con los estudios de música.

   (D) El NAESIP es la extensión de El Sistema en los Estados Unidos, también fundado por Maestro Abreu.

3. ¿Cómo ha cambiado la tasa de deserción escolar en Venezuela?

   (A) La tasa de deserción escolar ha aumentado en los estudiantes que no participan en El Sistema.

   (B) La tasa de abandono escolar ha crecido mientras la tasa de analfabeto ha disminuido.

   (C) La tasa de deserción escolar ha disminuido mientras la tasa de criminalidad ha aumentado en las zonas urbanas.

   (D) La tasa de deserción escolar ha disminuido, en comparación con los estudiantes que no están involucrados en El Sistema.

4. Se menciona las 285 orquestas pre-infantiles, 200 orquestas infantiles, 180 orquestas juveniles y otras para

   (A) demostrar cómo El Sistema ha crecido en Venezuela con más de 500 mil participantes

   (B) enfatizar que los estudiantes les gustan a las orquestas y los coros

   (C) ilustrar que los programas en otros países han crecido muchísimo como resultado de su inspiración de El Sistema

   (D) contrastar cómo El Sistema comenzó en un garaje y explicar cómo sus orquestas han reducido las tasas del analfabetismo

5. En el último párrafo, incluye la cita de Abreu para

   (A) demostrar que Dr. Abreu fue el maestro del año en 2013 porque ha dado oportunidades a muchos niños en Venezuela

   (B) probar que los niños de *El Sistema* han cambiado el mundo

   (C) ilustrar la importancia de la educación a través de música

   (D) dar un ejemplo de una tarea hermosísima que es parte de la educación espiritual

Translated Text and Questions, with Explanations

Introduction

The following Internet site is about El Sistema, the national program of Venezuela that shares music with disadvantaged children. The site appeared in May 2003.

To Play, Sing, and Struggle

Founded in 1975 by teacher Dr. José Antonio Abreu, the National System of Children's and Youth Orchestras and Choruses of Venezuela started in a garage with 11 young children. Today, the program, affectionately known as *El Sistema* (The System), serves more than 500 thousand disadvantaged students in Venezuela and continues to grow. Additionally, more than 42 countries have created programs inspired by El Sistema, among them Argentina, Australia, Austria, Bolivia, Brazil, Canada, Chile, Colombia, Costa Rica, Cuba, the Dominican Republic, Ecuador, El Salvador, England, France, Guatemala, Honduras, India, Italy, Jamaica, Japan, Mexico, Nicaragua, Panama, Paraguay, Peru, Portugal, Puerto Rico, Scotland, South Korea, Trinidad and Tobago, the United States, and Uruguay.

El Sistema in Venezuela teaches music through individual and group instruction to children as young as 2 or 3 years old, combining these lessons with participation in children's and youth orchestras and choruses. In every program, the orchestras have more significance than merely that of sharing classical music: they are dedicated to preventing school dropouts rates and reducing crime in the cities. In one study, the school dropout rate diminished to 6.9% amongst students participating in *El Sistema*, as compared to 26.4% in a control group. One can also see the great impact of *El Sistema* in reduced rates of illiteracy, marginality, and exclusion among the young population in Venezuela.

The children and their parents are part of the social communities of *El Sistema*, which emphasizes the importance of developing the human being. This population of 500,000 young Venezuelans is distributed across approximately 285 young children's orchestras (between 4 and 6 years old), 220 children's orchestras (7 to 16 years), 180 youth orchestras (16 through 22 years), 30 professional orchestras, 360 choral groups, 1,355 associated choral groups, and more than 15,000 teachers in all parts of the country. The teachers teach the students to "play, sing, and struggle" in order to overcome the obstacles of poverty and pursue formal education.

Here in the United States, there are multitudes of extracurricular programs inspired by *El Sistema* in Venezuela, which encourage social change in areas with limited resources. The NAESIP (National Alliance of *El Sistema*-Inspired Programs) gives children in these communities the tools to overcome the obstacles of poverty and discover the importance of education. "I've always thought that music education, from the most tender infancy, is a most beautiful task and is crucial to all society. It is an ideal of education that has existed for many centuries: music forms part of the spiritual development, conscience, and aesthetic formation of mankind," says Maestro Abreu.

Here's How to Crack It

1. What is the meaning of the title, "To Play, Sing, and Struggle"?

   (A) *El Sistema* teaches children to fight for their right to education and to overcome poverty.

   (B) *El Sistema* teaches children to fight with each other.

   (C) "To play and sing" is a metaphor for fighting in Latin American countries.

   (D) Many times, children fight with their parents.

Choice (A) is the correct answer. *El Sistema* teaches the children through music to fight for their rights to education and opportunity, and hopefully to overcome the obstacles they face with regard to illiteracy, lack of resources, and marginality. Choice (B) is way too literal; the program does not teach the children to fight with each other, nor does the passage say that children often fight with their parents, though that is a common occurrence (D). Choice (C) is not true and misinterprets the phrase "to play, sing, and struggle."

2. What is the article about?

   (A) There is a large problem of illiteracy, poverty, and marginality in Venezuela and in other parts of the world.

   (B) *El Sistema* has created a positive environment for involved students, and other countries have created affiliated programs in order to better the lives of disadvantaged children.

   (C) All the children who participate in *El Sistema* have success in music studies.

   (D) The NAESIP is the extension of *El Sistema* in the United States, also founded by Maestro Abreu.

Choice (B) is the correct answer. *El Sistema* is a program that creates a positive environment for disadvantaged children in Venezuela, and the programs it has inspired do the same in all parts of the world. Though (A) is true and is one of the main reasons for Dr. Abreu founding *El Sistema*, it is not the main focus of the article. Choice (C) is too extreme and goes beyond the scope of the passage. Choice (D) is not true, though Maestro Abreu is involved to some extent in the growth of these programs in the United States.

3. How has the school dropout rate changed in Venezuela?

   (A) The school dropout rate has risen in students who do not participate in *El Sistema*.

   (B) The school dropout rate has grown while the illiteracy rate has declined.

   (C) The school dropout rate has declined while the crime rate has risen in urban areas.

   (D) The school dropout rate has declined, compared to the students who are not involved in *El Sistema*.

Choice (D) is the correct answer. The school dropout rate has declined in students involved with *El Sistema*, as compared to those outside the program. We cannot know from the passage that dropout rates have risen among students who do not participate in the program (A). Choices (B) and (C) are both half-right: we expect that the illiteracy rate has declined, as (B) states, but this correct information is paired with growth in the dropout rate. Similarly, the decline in the dropout rate is paired with a rise in crime rates in urban areas, a statistic not mentioned in the passage (C).

4. The 285 young children's orchestras, 200 children's orchestras, 180 youth orchestras, and others are mentioned in order to

   (A) **demonstrate how *El Sistema* has grown in Venezuela with more than 500,000 participants**

   (B) emphasize that the students enjoy the orchestras and choruses

   (C) illustrate that the programs in other countries have grown a lot as a result of inspiration from *El Sistema*

   (D) contrast how *El Sistema* started in a garage and explain how its orchestras have lowered illiteracy rates

Choice (A) is the correct answer. Listing the number of the orchestras and choruses in Venezuela adds weight to how much *El Sistema* has grown since its humble beginnings. Choice (D) is a trap answer, as the orchestras are contrasted with *El Sistema*'s beginnings in a garage, but they do not explain lowered illiteracy rates in the country. The orchestras and choruses are specific to Venezuela, and do not have anything to do with the programs in other countries (C). Lastly, the passage does not mention whether the students enjoy the groups or not (B).

5. In the last paragraph, Abreu's quote is included in order to

   (A) demonstrate that Dr. Abreu was the teacher of the year in 2013 because he has given opportunities to many children in Venezuela

   (B) prove that the children in *El Sistema* have changed the world

   (C) **illustrate the importance of education through music**

   (D) give an example of a beautiful task that is part of a spiritual education

Choice (C) is the correct answer. Dr. Abreu calls music one of the most important and beautiful gifts one can teach children. It combines life lessons needed to help them out of poverty and to pursue their educations. While (A) is true because Dr. Abreu was named teacher of the year in 2013 by multiple organizations, it is never mentioned in the passage, nor is it the reason for his quote at the end of the article. The quote does not prove anything as (B) states, and (D) extracts words, changing the meaning from that in the passage.

Interpretive Communication: Print Texts Tips

- Choose the order in which you want to do the passages. Read a couple of sentences to see whether the writing style is easy to follow and the vocabulary is manageable. If so, go for it. If not, look ahead for something you find easier.

- Read the passage for topic and structure only. Don't read for detail, and don't try to memorize the whole thing. The first read is for you to get a sense of the general idea and the overall structure—that's all.

- Go straight to the general questions. Mark them as general questions with a "G" or any other mark of your choice and save them for last.

- Now, do the specific questions in order. For these, you're going to let the key terms in the question tell you where to look in the passage. Then, read the area that the question pertains to slowly and carefully. Find an answer choice that basically says the same thing. Answer choices are often paraphrases of the passage.

1. General Questions
2. Specific Questions

- Once you are finished with the specific questions, use your knowledge of the passage to answer the general questions. Ideally, you should be able to answer them without looking back at the passage. Most passages contain only a few general questions.

- Avoid specific answers on general questions, and on specific questions, avoid answers that are reasonable but go beyond the scope of the passage.

- Don't be afraid to use your LOTD if there are questions that stump you. You're done with a passage whenever you've answered all the questions that you can answer. Instead of wasting time trying to answer the last remaining question on a passage after all other techniques have failed to indicate the correct answer, go on to the next passage.

> Limit your knowledge only to the info in the passage. If you know more about the topic, leave that knowledge at the door.
>
> Beware of recycled words from the passage. Often, they are used out of context in these answer choices.

- Don't pick an answer choice just because you recall reading the word in the passage. Frequently that is a trick; correct answers will often use synonyms rather than the word originally used in the passage.

INTERPRETIVE COMMUNICATION: AUDIO TEXTS

The Audio Texts portion of the exam consists of audio recordings accompanied by multiple-choice questions. Your task is to listen to the audio carefully and answer the questions that are printed in your examination booklet. Each selection will be approximately three minutes in length and will be played twice. You will be given a designated amount of time to read a preview of the selection and skim the accompanying questions.

For each of the Audio Text samples in this section, you will find a translation of the selection with the answers and explanations that follow. Resist any urge you might have to sneak a peak while listening to the audio tracks. You'll get the most out of your practice just by listening carefully and taking notes. You can either play the audio CD included with this book or go online to PrincetonReview.com, where you may either download or stream the audio after registering your book (step-by-step instructions on how to do this are on page vi).

Here are the general directions for Part B, which also includes the Print and Audio Text (combined) questions. You will see these printed in your test booklet on test day, in both English and Spanish.

You will listen to several audio selections. The first two audio selections are accompanied by reading selections. When there is a reading selection, you will have a designated amount of time to read it.	Vas a escuchar varias grabaciones. Las dos primeras grabaciones van acompañadas de lecturas. Cuando haya una lectura, vas a tener un tiempo determinado para leerla.
For each audio selection, first you will have a designated amount of time to read a preview of the selection as well as to skim the questions that you will be asked. Each selection will be played twice. As you listen to each selection, you may take notes. Your notes will not be scored.	Para cada grabación, primero vas a tener un tiempo determinado para leer la introducción y prever las preguntas. Vas a escuchar cada grabación dos veces. Mientras escuchas, puedes tomar apuntes. Tus apuntes no van a ser calificados.
After listening to each selection the first time, you will have 1 minute to begin answering the questions; after listening to each selection the second time, you will have 15 seconds per question to finish answering the questions. For each question, choose the response that is best according to the audio and/or reading selection and mark your answer on your answer sheet.	Después de escuchar cada selección por primera vez, vas a tener un minuto para empezar a contestar las preguntas; después de escuchar por segunda vez, vas a tener 15 segundos por pregunta para terminarlas. Para cada pregunta, elige la mejor respuesta según la grabación o el texto e indícala en la hoja de respuestas.

Interpretive Communication: Audio Texts

Basic approach:

1. Preview the Questions
2. Take notes as you Listen
3. POE

There are two main types of listening passages: lecture passages and informal passages or conversations. For both of these types, preview your questions to know what to listen for. Avoid previewing the answer choices too closely, as they may actually lead you astray. The test makers often recycle words from the lectures and dialogues to throw you off, so just know which questions you need to listen for. When you listen, jot down notes in your scratch, noting the speaker, the subject matter, any transition words such as *sin embargo, pero, además, por otro lado*, etc. to discover how different points fit together in the lecture. Get your pencil in hand and be ready to write down a few quick words as you listen. Usually, there will be 2–3 key points that the lecturer tries to make, and he or she will lay out the overall argument at the beginning of the lecture as well as the end to wrap up the important ideas.

Give it a try:

Ready? Here we go! Listen carefully to the recordings in the following three listening samples and answer the questions as best as you can. Try jotting down notes as you listen. Even if it is just a word or a phrase, active listening will help you significantly here.

Sample Audio Text Selection 1

Primero tienes un minuto para prever las preguntas.

(1 minute)

Ahora escucha la selección.

PLAY AUDIO: Track 1

Ahora tienes un minuto para empezar a responder a las preguntas para esta selección. Después de un minuto, vas a escuchar la grabación de nuevo.

(1 minute)

Ahora escucha de nuevo.

PLAY AUDIO: Track 1

Ahora termina de responder a las preguntas para esta selección.

1. ¿Que es AeroEspaña?
   (A) Es la línea aérea.
   (B) Es la compañía de abogados.
   (C) Es el nombre del aeropuerto.
   (D) Es el nombre de la señora.

2. ¿Que trabajo tiene la Señora?
   (A) Es azafata.
   (B) Trabaja en el mostrador de la línea aérea.
   (C) Es abogada.
   (D) Es la jefa de administración.

3. ¿A dónde viaja la Señora?
   (A) Viaja a Londres.
   (B) Viaja a Barcelona.
   (C) Viaja a Burgos.
   (D) Viaja al mostrador de la línea aérea.

Apply Strategy!
Preview the questions and underline or circle any key terms to be listening for!

Remember the 5 W's here as well. What is happening? Who are the people? How did the conversation conclude?

Basic approach:

1. Preview the Questions
2. Take notes as you Listen
3. POE

What key words did you notice in the questions? If you noticed *AeroEspaña, trabajo, viaje,* and *la Señora,* great job! Your notes should be organized in a way that makes sense to you, and try to listen for the questions you previewed. From there, POE away!

Selection 1: Translated Text and Questions, with Explanations

(NARRATOR) In the airport

(MAN) Excuse me madam, but would you know where the ticket counter for AeroEspaña is?

(WOMAN) Where are you going?

(MAN) I am going to Barcelona, and I am in a big hurry because I believe the plane leaves within twenty minutes.

(WOMAN) That's right. There is a plane that leaves for Barcelona this morning. The ticket counter for AeroEspaña is at the end of this hallway on your right.

(MAN) Do you have the time?

(WOMAN) Yes, it is nine o'clock. I will accompany you to the counter if you wish. I am also going to Barcelona this morning.

(MAN) Well yes, of course, it would be my pleasure. I am Ricardo Herrero.

(WOMAN) Delighted to meet you. I am Teresa Vara.

(MAN) Are you by chance the attorney for the Arturo Águila Company?

(WOMAN) Yes, I am. And you are the chief financial officer. We have met before, haven't we?

(MAN) Yes, I think we met at the annual meeting last year in London. What a coincidence!

(WOMAN) I suppose that you are going to the meeting in Barcelona with the president of the company?

(MAN) Of course; what a small world!

1. What is AeroEspaña?

   (A) It is the airline.

   (B) It is the law firm.

   (C) It is the name of the airport.

   (D) It is the woman's name.

AeroEspaña is the name of the airline, (A). We know this because once inside the airport, the man asks the woman where the ticket counter is for the airline he is taking to Barcelona.

2. What work does the woman do?

   (A) She is a flight attendant.

   (B) She works at the ticket counter.

   (C) She is an attorney.

   (D) She is the head of administration.

Choice (C) is the correct answer. The woman is an attorney for the Arturo Águila Company.

3. Where is the woman going?

   (A) She is going to London.

   (B) She is going to Barcelona.

   (C) She is going to Burgos.

   (D) She is going to the ticket counter.

Barcelona is mentioned several times in the dialogue, so if you picked (B), you had your ears open! London is mentioned in the dialogue as well, but only in reference to the fact that the two had met there last year.

Sample Audio Text Selection 2

Primero tienes un minuto para prever las preguntas.

(1 minute)

Ahora escucha la selección.

PLAY AUDIO: Track 2

Ahora tienes un minuto para empezar a responder a las preguntas para esta selección. Después de un minuto, vas a escuchar la grabación de nuevo.

(1 minute)

Ahora escucha de nuevo.

PLAY AUDIO: Track 2

Ahora termina de responder a las preguntas para esta selección.

4. ¿Qué tienen en común las ciudades de Nueva York, Los Angeles, Chicago, Dallas, San Antonio y San Francisco?

    (A) Tienen una gran población de personas que hablan español.

    (B) Los nombres son de origen hispano.

    (C) Son ciudades crecientes.

    (D) Son ciudades con grandes compañías.

5. ¿Qué están haciendo con respecto al mercado hispano las compañías grandes como los productores de refrescos y zapatillas deportivas?

    (A) Están comprando más productos.

    (B) Están creciendo más y más.

    (C) Están comprando publicidad para el mercado hispano.

    (D) Están comprando productos hechos por hispanos.

6. ¿Cómo es el típico consumidor hispano?

    (A) Joven

    (B) Mayor

    (C) Liberal

    (D) Conservador

7. ¿Con cuáles marcas se identifica el consumidor hispano?

    (A) Marcas hispanas

    (B) Marcas de buena calidad

    (C) Marcas de mala calidad

    (D) Marcas que cuestan menos

Basic approach:

1. Preview the Questions
2. Take notes as you Listen
3. POE

Since this is a lecture instead of a dialogue, use transitional words to help identify the structure of the passage and therefore the key points. Words like *sin embargo*, *además*, and the like can help you to organize the passage and take good notes.

What key words did you notice in the questions? There were certainly a lot more than the previous passage. Underline these key words in the questions so you are on alert. You should have noticed words such as the cities in question 1, *zapatillos deportivos*, *típico consumidor*, and *marca*, among a couple others that are specific to this passage. Your notes should be reflective of the structure of the passage, using transitional words to notice new points and paragraphs. Try to listen for the questions you previewed. From there, POE away!

When taking notes, note the structure of the speech. If you hear a pause, this might be a clue that you have a new paragraph, and thus a new example, a contrast, or something similar, will come next.

Selection 2: Translated Text and Questions, with Explanations

The Hispanic Market in the United States

The U.S. Hispanic market is a source of opportunity for many large companies. The U.S. Hispanic market is a market that is growing daily. There are Spanish speakers in almost all of the major U.S. cities, especially in New York, Los Angeles, Chicago, Dallas, San Antonio, and San Francisco, just to name a few. All of the large companies have seen the value of the Hispanic consumer in today's marketplace.

Many of these companies, such as beverage producers, fast-food restaurants, and athletic shoe producers, spend a lot of money on advertising directed at the Hispanic consumer. The typical Hispanic consumer is very traditional; he likes the family. He also likes traditional values. The Hispanic consumer is also one who is loyal to the brand names that he considers of good quality. He identifies very easily with the brands that he likes. It doesn't matter to him to spend more money on a product if it is of better quality. The Hispanic market will continue to grow. Companies that ignore the importance of the Hispanic market do so at their own risk. The Hispanic consumer is a strong force in the marketplace of the future.

4. What do the cities New York, Los Angeles, Chicago, Dallas, San Antonio, and San Francisco have in common?

(A) They have large populations of Spanish speakers.

(B) Their names are of Hispanic origin.

(C) They are growing cities.

(D) They are cities with large companies.

Choices (B), (C), and (D) may or may not be true, but they have nothing to do with the short narrative. Therefore, the correct answer is (A); each of those cities has a large Spanish-speaking population.

5. What are the large companies, such as beverage producers and sports-shoe producers, doing with respect to the Hispanic market?
   (A) They are buying more products.
   (B) They are growing more and more.
   (C) They are buying advertising for the Hispanic market.
   (D) They are buying products made by Hispanics.

The word for advertising is *publicidad*. The large companies are, in fact, buying advertising directed at the Hispanic market. Notice that incorrect choices (A) and (D) also include the verb *comprando* to see whether you can be easily fooled; don't fall into this trap.

6. What is the typical Hispanic consumer like?
   (A) Young
   (B) Old
   (C) Liberal
   (D) Conservative

The typical Hispanic consumer is *tradicional*, which is closest to *conservador*. If this isn't immediately apparent, you may use POE to rule out the other answer choices. The age range (*joven* or *mayor*) of the typical Hispanic consumer is impossible to identify without detailed demographic information, which is not discussed in the short narrative. *Liberal* doesn't really make any sense, so it is an obvious wrong answer.

7. With which brand names does the Hispanic consumer identify?
   (A) Hispanic brand names
   (B) Good-quality brand names
   (C) Bad-quality brand names
   (D) Economical brand names

Hispanic consumers identify with good-quality brands. In fact, we are told that they do not mind paying more for an item if it is of better quality. Therefore, you should use POE to rule out (C) and (D). Nothing in the narrative indicates that the Hispanic market identifies with only Hispanic brand names, so you can say *adiós* to (A) as well.

Sample Audio Text Selection 3

Primero tienes un minuto para prever las preguntas.

(1 minute)

Ahora escucha la selección.

PLAY AUDIO: Track 3

Ahora tienes un minuto para empezar a responder a las preguntas para esta selección. Después de un minuto, vas a escuchar la grabación de nuevo.

(1 minute)

Ahora escucha de nuevo.

PLAY AUDIO: Track 3

Ahora termina de responder a las preguntas para esta selección.

8. ¿A quién va dirigida la revista *Mujer Moderna*?

   (A) Las mujeres del mundo interior de la moda

   (B) Las mujeres que trabajan

   (C) La mujer que se ocupa de la familia y la casa

   (D) La mujer contemporánea del mundo actual

9. ¿Cómo se distingue *Mujer Moderna* de las otras revistas de moda?

   (A) Es una revista de muñecas.

   (B) Es una revista de fantasía.

   (C) Se dedica a cómo la moda forma parte de la vida en el mundo actual.

   (D) Se dedica exclusivamente al mundo interior de la moda.

10. ¿Por qué está metida la revista *Mujer Moderna* en la causa social de los niños que nacen con el virus del SIDA?

    (A) Quiere dar ejemplo de responsabilidad hacia los desafortunados.

    (B) Quiere ser más contemporánea.

    (C) Era la causa de la Princesa Diana.

    (D) Está de moda ayudar a los menesterosos.

11. ¿Qué hay de interés para el hombre moderno en *Mujer Moderna*?

    (A) Puede aprender de la moda para hombres.

    (B) Puede aprender de la moda para su madre, hermana, novia o esposa.

    (C) Puede aprender sobre la Princesa Diana.

    (D) Puede aprender sobre si mismo.

12. ¿Qué relación hay entre la moda y el deporte, según la entrevista?

    (A) Muchos deportes tienen una moda desarrollada a su alrededor.

    (B) Muchos deportistas son modelos.

    (C) Todos los deportistas tienen mucho estilo.

    (D) La moda y el deporte son sinónimos.

Remember, active listening is your best friend here! Jot down key terms and main ideas.

Basic approach:

1. Preview the Questions
2. Take notes as you Listen
3. POE

This is a longer dialogue, so note transitions as well as you listen for key words and phrases. What key words did you notice as you previewed the questions? Hopefully, you noticed *Mujer Moderna, dirigido, distingue*, the entire phrase *niños que nacen con el virus del SIDA, hombre moderno*, and *la moda y el deporte*. Your notes should be organized in a way that shows changes in topic as well as cues from the questions you previewed. Use POE aggressively to eliminate answer choices.

Listening comprehension tests just that: listening comprehension! Most answers will not be terribly difficult conceptually.

Now let's take a look at the answers and explanations for Selection 3.

Selection 3: Translated Text and Questions, with Explanations

(NARRATOR) Now we are going to listen to an interview with someone very informed in the world of fashion, Ms. Luz Hurtado, editor of the magazine *Modern Woman*.

(MAN) Luz, to begin, can you describe for us the typical reader of *Modern Woman*? In other words, who is your target audience?

(WOMAN) Our magazine is directed at the woman of today, primarily between the ages of twenty and thirty-five years of age. Many of our readers work, but others devote themselves to caring for their family and home. Almost all of them have in common a deep interest in fashion. They are not necessarily those who work in the fashion industry, although many women in the fashion world do read our magazine. Let's say that our magazine brings the insider world of fashion to the contemporary woman.

(MAN) How is *Modern Woman* different from other fashion magazines?

(WOMAN) That is a very important question. When they offered me the job of editor at this magazine, I asked myself, "Do I really want to work for another fashion magazine?" I had worked in the past as a reporter for other fashion magazines, and I was no longer interested in working for another magazine like all of the others. But *Modern Woman* is different because it is directed at the woman who lives in the real world of today. It is not about silly dolls in a protected world or fantasy world. Our readers live in the real world, they work in the real world, and they care for their families in the real world. We don't devote ourselves exclusively to fashion but rather to the role of fashion in the complicated modern world.

(MAN) I have read that *Modern Woman* is very involved in various social causes, above all, children who are born with the AIDS virus. Can you explain to us the relationship between fashion and this very important social cause?

(WOMAN) Although it may be a bit out of the ordinary in the world of fashion, I think it is extremely important that we help those who are less fortunate. Is there a more innocent victim than a poor child who has been born contaminated with the AIDS virus? *Modern Woman* tries to foster a relationship with social causes to show our readers that it is the responsibility of each and every one of us to contribute to the improvement of society. Furthermore, there have been others who have cultivated a relationship between fashion and social causes; for example, let's remember the image of Princess Diana.

(MAN) That's true. Princess Diana was a symbol of fashion and of dedication to social causes. She was a very admirable person, don't you think so?

(WOMAN) Of course she was admirable. She was a very good person. The public figure was only a part of Diana. I met her on various occasions and was impressed by her sincerity and her genuine concern for those who suffer.

(MAN) Changing the topic a bit if I may, is your magazine valuable for the modern man?

(WOMAN) I think that there is a lot of value for the modern man who is interested in social causes that affect us all. Of course, it will also be interesting to the man who wants to find out about the latest fashion trends for his female friends, his girlfriend, his wife, his mother, his sister, etc. In short, it is a magazine directed primarily at those interested in feminine fashion, based on a philanthropic philosophy. For that reason, it can also be interesting to many men. However, we also have a very good sports section. (She laughs.)

(MAN)   What relationship is there, if any, between fashion and sports?

(WOMAN)   Of course there is a relationship between them. Fashion could be considered an attitude toward life. Fashion can be seen in everything that we do. We either do things with style or without style. It all depends on the mentality and the level of interest of the individual. For example, there is an entire fashion that has evolved precisely around sports. Tennis and golf are two very clear examples. They have a very determined fashion requirement that allows for individual styles as well. For example, the American tennis players Andre Agassi and the Williams sisters show their individuality with the unique clothing that they wear and their hairstyles. Whether or not we care for the styles they wear, we must admire their individualistic styles.

(MAN)   Of course, all three are very original. But tell us Luz, how did you get started in the world of fashion?

(WOMAN)   Always, ever since I was young, men's and women's fashions have interested me. My father worked in the Spanish Diplomatic Service, so we spent a lot of time abroad. We lived in Milan, Paris, Singapore, and New York. Perhaps because of the differences I observed between the styles of clothing of the various cultures, I leaned toward the field of fashion. I have also, since I was young, always felt a sense of responsibility for the less fortunate. My mother always dedicated herself to social causes. I learned a great deal from her.

(MAN)   Well, Ms. Luz Hurtado, we've run out of time. Thank you very much for being here with us.

8. Who is the target audience of *Modern Woman*?

    (A) Women from the inside world of fashion

    (B) Women who work

    (C) Women who care for their homes and families

    (D) The contemporary women of the real world

The correct answer is (D). The target audience of the magazine *Modern Woman* is the contemporary woman of today. Luz Hurtado says that the magazine is directed at those women who work and those who stay home and take care of the family. It tries to appeal to as many groups as possible. Use POE to eliminate (A), (B), and (C).

9. How is the magazine *Modern Woman* different from other fashion magazines?

    (A) It is a magazine about dolls.

    (B) It is a fantasy magazine.

    (C) It is devoted to the role of fashion in the real world today.

    (D) It is devoted exclusively to the inside world of fashion.

Modern Woman is different from other magazines because, according to the interview, it tries to explore the relationship between fashion and life in the modern world of today. It is not a magazine about dolls (A), nor of fantasy (B), nor an insider fashion magazine (D). Choices (C) and (D) may seem close, but the word *exclusivamente* in (D) should clue you in to the correct answer, (C), since you already know that the magazine tries to encompass a wide audience.

10. Why is *Modern Woman* involved with children born with the AIDS virus?

    (A) It wants to provide an example of responsibility to the needy.

    (B) It wants to be more contemporary.

    (C) It was Princess Diana's cause.

    (D) It is fashionable to help the needy.

Even if you didn't know that SIDA means AIDS in Spanish, you should be able to identify the one reasonable response among these four choices. If you use POE, you would quickly eliminate (C) and (D): The magazine would not be involved with a social cause just because Princess Diana had been involved without talking in greater detail about her. To say that it is fashionable to help those in need is just plain silly. Choice (B) is more reasonable, but once you compare it with (A), you'll find the correct answer.

11. What is of interest to the modern man in *Modern Woman*?

   (A) He can learn about men's fashions.

   (B) He can learn of the fashion trends affecting his mother, sister, girlfriend, or wife.

   (C) He can learn about Princess Diana.

   (D) He can learn about himself.

Choice (B) is the correct answer. According to the interview, the modern man can learn about the fashion interests of his sister, female friends, mother, girlfriend, or wife by reading *Modern Woman*. You can rule out (A), since men's fashion is never discussed in the interview except for a mention of Andre Agassi's individuality on the tennis court. Choices (C) and (D) simply refer to topics mentioned in the interview but not thoroughly discussed.

12. What relationship exists between fashion and sports, according to the interview?

   (A) Many sports have a fashion developed around them.

   (B) Many sports figures are models.

   (C) All sports figures have a lot of style.

   (D) Fashion and sports are synonymous.

According to what is said in the interview, the relationship between sports and fashion is that many sports figures, such as those in golf and tennis, develop their own styles within the sport. Choice (D) is completely wrong; fashion and sports are not synonymous. Choices (B) and (C) may be true but are not discussed in the interview. POE eliminates these right away. Therefore, (A) is the correct answer.

INTERPRETIVE COMMUNICATION: PRINT AND AUDIO TEXTS (COMBINED)

Now that you've practiced with Print Texts and Audio Texts, it's time to combine them! Note that on the test itself, you'll encounter the Print and Audio Texts (combined) section *before* the Audio Texts in Part B. For our purposes here, however, it makes more sense to familiarize you with the other sections first. As you might expect, this section combines an authentic print text (e.g., journalistic or literary text, ad, letter, or table) with a real-world audio source (e.g., interview, podcast, public service announcement, or presentation).

You will have time to read a preview of the selection and skim the questions before listening to the audio. The questions will pertain to both the print and audio texts. The audio selection is approximately 3 minutes in length and will be played twice. As with the Audio Text samples, you can listen to this audio selection either on the audio CD included with this book or online at PrincetonReview.com.

1. Read the Introduction
2. Preview the Passage Questions
3. Work the Passage and Answers
4. Rinse and Repeat for the Listening Text
5. Take Notes
6. POE

Ready? Here we go again! Listen carefully to the recording and read with care. Answer the questions to the best of your ability.

Sample Print and Audio Texts (Combined) Selection

Here are the general directions for the Print and Audio Texts (combined) section. You will see these instructions printed in your test booklet on test day in English and Spanish.

You will listen to several audio selections. The first two audio selections are accompanied by reading selections. When there is a reading selection, you will have a designated amount of time to read it.	Vas a escuchar varias grabaciones. Las dos primeras grabaciones van acompañadas de lecturas. Cuando haya una lectura, vas a tener un tiempo determinado para leerla.
For each audio selection, first you will have a designated amount of time to read a preview of the selection as well as to skim the questions that you will be asked. Each selection will be played twice. As you listen to each selection, you may take notes. Your notes will not be scored.	Para cada grabación, primero vas a tener un tiempo determinado para leer la introducción y prever las preguntas. Vas a escuchar cada grabación dos veces. Mientras escuchas, puedes tomar apuntes. Tus apuntes no van a ser calificados.
After listening to each selection the first time, you will have 1 minute to begin answering the questions; after listening to each selection the second time, you will have 15 seconds per question to finish answering the questions. For each question, choose the response that is best according to the audio and/ or reading selection and mark your answer on the answer sheet.	Después de escuchar cada selección por primera vez, vas a tener un minuto para empezar a contestar las preguntas; después de escuchar por la segunda vez, vas a tener 15 segundos por pregunta para terminarlas. Para cada pregunta, elige la mejor respuesta según la grabación o el texto e indícala en la hoja de respuestas.

Fuente número 1

Primero tienes 4 minutos para leer la fuente número 1.

Introducción

Este texto se trata de dos personajes e iconos de la cultura pop de Latinoamérica. El artículo original fue escrito por Joaquín Bode.

Condorito Y Mafalda—Iconos de la Cultura Pop

Hace más de 63 y 48 años, "Pepo" y "Quino" crearon Condorito y Mafalda, respectivamente, "para dar humor y reflexión al mundo; dos personajes universales de la cultura *Línea* pop", tal como se señala en la página Web "Culturacomic 5 .com".

Mientras que los dos son protagonistas muy representativos de la cultura latina, también es cierto que ambos son muy diferentes entre sí: Condorito es inocente y hasta torpe; Mafalda es inteligente e irónica. El primero vive feliz 10 la vida, disfrutando los pequeños placeres; mientras que la segunda establece una crítica social constante, casi con un afán revolucionario.

Eso sí: los dos tienen una gran personalidad, única y llamativa. Mafalda es auténtica, inteligente, analítica, liberal 15 y revolucionaria. Por su parte, Condorito es muy alegre, divertido, ingenioso, ladino y trata de sobrevivir con el menor esfuerzo posible. Le gustan mucho a sus amigos y aunque a veces es pendenciero y vengativo, en el fondo, tiene un gran corazón.

El mundo según Mafalda
20 Mafalda es la tira cómica por excelencia de Argentina. Esta niña de 6 años se impone a sí misma una gran misión: cambiar al mundo. Acompañada de amigos, y enloqueciendo a sus padres, siempre reflexiona acerca de cómo mejorar el 25 planeta y cómo cambiarlo desde los pequeños detalles. Se puede decir, incluso, que fue una de las primeras ecologistas latinoamericanas.

Nacida en el seno de una familia argentina de clase media, Mafalda cuenta con un variado y ecléctico grupo de amigos. 30 Además de su pequeño hermano Guille, el inocente, también están: Miguelito, el ingenuo; Susanita, cuyo mayor deseo en la vida es casarse con un hombre guapo y rico; Manolito, el conservador de ideas capitalistas; y la pequeña Libertad, una gran filósofa. Cada uno de los personajes representa 35 un elemento propio de la realidad argentina. Esta historieta aporta fuertemente a la reflexión. Siempre queda un mensaje que puede ser aplicado a cualquier realidad.

María Paz Castillo, coordinadora en Chile de la exposición "El Mundo de Mafalda", sostiene que el éxito de 40 esta pequeña se basa en que pese a ser una historia con casi 40 años de antigüedad, sigue siendo muy actual. "El mundo sigue teniendo los mismos problemas que antes", asegura. "Queremos acercar esta historieta a los niños y educarlos respecto al mundo. Hoy viven en una especie de burbuja, por 45 eso resulta importante que sepan cómo pensaba Mafalda", añade.

Un pájaro humorístico
Condorito es otro personaje que ha ganado popularidad en muchos lados. Creado en 1949 por el chileno René Ríos 50 ("Pepo"), está inspirado en el ave nacional de ese país: el cóndor. Aunque al inicio su aspecto era predominantemente animal, con el paso de los años se volvió más "humano".

Una de las características más llamativas de esta historieta es que no aborda la dimensión política de su entorno, sino 55 que más bien describe el esfuerzo, la picardía, el ingenio y las aventureras de personajes populares.

Junto a Condorito aparecen diferentes personajes siendo los más típicos el astuto sobrino "Coné"; la eterna y atractiva novia "Yayita"; el torpe enemigo "Pepe Cortisona"; su com- 60 padre "Don Chuma"; el alcohólico "Garganta de Lata"; y el simpático "Huevoduro".

Su humor es siempre blanco y su sátira inofensiva. A través de historias sencillas, se representa la vida cotidiana de los sectores populares de América Latina. De esta mane- 65 ra, se logra generar una cercanía cultural con los lectores.

"Condorito rescata lo popular; por eso a la gente le gusta y se identifica con él", afirma Juan Plaza, dibujante de cómics y quien desde hace 25 años se dedica a hacer las viñetas de Condorito. "Si bien es un chileno típico, también es pro- 70 fundamente universal, porque los demás miembros de la comunidad latinoamericana lo ven como un igual", agrega. "Este personaje fue capaz de quedarse grabado en el subconsciente de la gente. El hecho de que sea gracioso y que a las personas les guste sus chistes, permite que muchos quieran 75 seguir leyéndolo", concluye Plaza.

Used by permission of VeinteMundos.com

Fuente número 2

Tienes dos minutos para leer la introducción y prever las preguntas.

Introducción

Esta grabación se trata de un dibujante, Joaquin Salvador Lavado, y su famosa tira cómica *Mafalda*. La grabación dura aproximadamente tres minutos.

Ahora escucha la fuente número dos.

PLAY AUDIO: Track 4

Ahora tienes un minuto para empezar a responder a las preguntas para esta selección. Después de un minuto, vas a escuchar la grabación de nuevo.

(1 minute)

Ahora escucha de nuevo.

PLAY AUDIO: Track 4

Ahora termina de responder a las preguntas para esta selección.

1. ¿Cuál es el propósito de este artículo?

   (A) De convencer al lector que Condorito es más popular que Mafalda

   (B) De convencer al lector que Mafalda es más popular que Condorito

   (C) Informar al lector de dos personajes en la cultura Latina que son populares

   (D) Informar al lector la razón por qué estas tiras cómicas son controversiales en Latinoamérica

2. Según la fuente auditiva, ¿cómo reaccionan los Argentinos a Mafalda?

   (A) A algunos le gusta, y a otros no.

   (B) Piensan que es espectacular.

   (C) Es una historieta vieja e irrelevante.

   (D) No la conocen.

3. Según la fuente auditiva, ¿qué tipo de humor tiene Mafalda?

   (A) Chismosa

   (B) Inteligente

   (C) Satírico

   (D) Irónico e inofensivo

4. Según el artículo, ¿que se puede deducir sobre los amigos de Mafalda?

   (A) Es un grupo de amigos iguales.

   (B) Es un grupo de amigos variados, pero piensan en la misma manera que piensa Mafalda.

   (C) Es un grupo de amigos eclécticos que representan las ideas o realidades del público Argentino.

   (D) Es un grupo de amigos iguales que se llevan bien.

5. Según la fuente auditiva, ¿que piensa Cristóbal Navarro de Mafalda?

   (A) Ella es un personaje muy intelectual, pero a la misma vez muy idealista.

   (B) No se merece tanta atención.

   (C) Es popular pero complicada.

   (D) Es muy chiquita para tener opiniones tan adultas.

6. ¿A que se refiere "no aborda la dimensión política" (línea 54)?

   (A) Condorito no se preocupa por los temas políticos.

   (B) La política no impacta a Chile.

   (C) La política es importante en las tiras cómicas.

   (D) Es la dimensión más importante de este personaje.

7. Según el texto, ¿qué representa Condorito?

(A) Un personaje querido

(B) La única manera de que los lectores se acerquen culturalmente

(C) Las historietas simples y ejemplares de la vida cotidiana

(D) El ave nacional de Argentina

8. Según el artículo, ¿cómo es la actitud de Juan Plaza sobre Condorito?

(A) Desprecio

(B) Informativo

(C) Sarcástico

(D) Juguetona

9. Según la fuente auditiva, ¿qué es "El Mundo de Mafalda"?

(A) Una revista de tiras cómicas

(B) Una película

(C) Una juguetería

(D) Una exhibición interactiva

10. Según la fuente auditiva, ¿que representa Mafalda?

(A) La idiosincrasía del latinoamericano

(B) La cultura Argentina

(C) La cultura Chilena

(D) Los puntos de vista en la cultura latina

Read the introductions here to get a bit of context. What is the passage about? What is the recording about? Next, preview the questions for the passage and tackle those first. Find the window in the passage and work the answers just as you would in the other reading passages. Similarly, treat the audio passages exactly as you would the other listening passages, previewing the questions, taking notes, and using POE aggressively. Remember, listening passages are not going to ask terribly complicated questions!

Let's read the translation and take a look at each question more closely.

Preview, take notes, and attack the answer choices.

Sample Print and Audio Selection: Translated Texts and Questions, with Explanations

Source 1

Introduction

This text has to do with two iconic characters of Latin American pop culture. The original article was written by Joaquin Bode.

Condorito and Mafalda—Pop Culture Icons

More than 63 and 48 years ago, "Pepo" and "Quino" created Condorito and Mafalda, respectively, "to give humor and reflection to the world; two universal characters of pop culture," as stated on the website Culturacomic.com.

While the two protagonists are very representative of Latino culture, it is also true that both are very different from each other: Condorito is innocent and even clumsy; Mafalda is clever and ironic. The first lives a happy life, enjoying the simple pleasures, while the second establishes a constant social criticism, with an almost revolutionary zeal.

It's true: they both have great personality, unique and striking. Mafalda is genuine, intelligent, analytical, liberal, and revolutionary. Meanwhile, Condorito is very cheerful, funny, witty, and sly and tries to survive with the least possible effort. Condorito is very fond of his friends and although he is sometimes quarrelsome and vindictive, in reality, he has a big heart.

The World According to Mafalda

Mafalda is the quintessential comic strip from Argentina. This 6-year-old girl imposes on herself a grand mission: to change the world. Accompanied by her friends, and driving her parents crazy, she always reflects on how to improve the planet and how to change it, starting from the smallest details. You can even say that Mafalda was one of the first Latin American environmentalists.

Born into a middle class family in Argentina, Mafalda counts on her varied and eclectic group of friends. In addition to her little brother Guille, the innocent one, there are also: Miguelito, the naïve one; Susanita, whose greatest desire in life is to marry a handsome and rich man; Manolito, the conservative capitalist; and the small Libertad, a great philosopher. Each of these characters represents an element of truth in Argentina's own reality. This cartoon brings forth strong reflection. There is always a message that can be applied to any reality.

María Paz Castillo, coordinator of the "The World of Mafalda" exhibition in Chile, maintains that the success of this little girl is based on a story that, despite being almost 40 years old, is still very current. "The world still has the same problems as before," she says. "We want to bring this story to the children and educate them about the world. Today they live in a kind of bubble, so it is important for them to know how Mafalda thought," she adds.

A Humorous Bird

Condorito is another character that has gained popularity in many places. Created in 1949 by the Chilean René Ríos ("Pepo"), Condorito is inspired by the national bird of Chile: the condor. Although at first his appearance was predominantly animal, over the years he became more "human."

One of the most striking features of this cartoon is that it does not address the political dimension of its environment, but rather describes the effort, mischief, ingenuity, and adventures of popular characters.

Alongside Condorito, different typical characters appear: the astute nephew "Coné"; the eternal and attractive girlfriend "Yayita"; the clumsy enemy "Pepe Cortisone"; his friend "Don Chuma"; the alcoholic "Garganta de Lata (tin throat)"; and the friendly "Huevoduro (hard boiled egg)".

His humor is always simple and his satire is harmless. Through simple stories, the daily life of the popular sectors in Latin America is represented. In this manner, it is possible to generate a cultural closeness among readers.

"Condorito appeals to the general populace; this is why people like and identify with him," said Juan Plaza, cartoonist and the person who has dedicated 25 years to making Condorito vignettes. "While Condorito is a typical Chilean, he is also profoundly universal because the other members of the Latin American community see him as an equal," he adds. "This character was able to stay engraved in the people's subconscious. The fact that he is funny and that people like his jokes, means that people want to continue reading this comic," concludes Plaza.

Source 2

Introduction

This recording is about a cartoonist, Joaquin Salvador Lavado, and his famous comic strip, *Mafalda*.

(REPORTER) Joaquín Salvador Lavado, better known worldwide as Quino, was the creator of Mafalda. Mafalda appeared in the newspaper as a weekly comic strip from 1964 to 1973. Surely she was the queen of the world of cartoons, translated into different languages, including Japanese. Vignettes of Mafalda were published in books in South America and Europe.

If one finds an Argentinian and asks him about Mafalda, the reaction is always spectacular. Mafalda represents more than a great comic character; she represents the Latin American idiosyncrasy. This little girl, awake and observant, has made—and still makes—people of all ages, whether grandparents, adults, or children, laugh. Her humor—naïve, harmless, and full of irony—is the highlight of this cartoon. Her creator was able to perfectly capture the essence of Latino culture across borders and time barriers. In social networks and Internet blogs, many speak about the famous Mafalda. Besides being loved by the Argentine public, she is very funny. Mafalda has won the hearts and affection of many people over the years.

Why was it, and does it continue to be, one of the most famous cartoons? Mafalda has a great personality. She is genuine, intelligent, mature, liberal, revolutionary, a lover of justice and world peace, and above all, she hates soup. Apparently, as many say, Mafalda is a faithful copy of her creator.

Cristóbal Navarro is a guide in the exhibition "The World of Mafalda." This interactive exhibit can be seen today throughout South America.

(NAVARRO) What catches people's attention about this character is how such a little girl can have that type of worldview. This character also represents the Argentine people very well, with the picaresque nature they possess.

(REPORTER) Cristóbal says that Mafalda transcends genres and manages to keep its critical spirit over time. In that sense, he adds that Quino created Mafalda at the right time.

(NAVARRO) What people have told me during this exhibition, and what I also believe, is that Mafalda is a very idealistic, critical, and intellectual character.

(REPORTER)   During the most difficult times in Argentina's economy and social life, Mafalda was always present in the
perception of the great Argentine public. With humor
and truth, Mafalda was able to go further than Quino
ever could have imagined.

1. What is the purpose of this article?

   (A) To convince the reader that Condorito is more popular than Mafalda

   (B) To convince the reader that Mafalda is more popular than Condorito

   **(C) To inform the reader about two characters in Latin culture that are very
   popular**

   (D) To inform the reader of the reason these comic strips are controversial in Latin
   America

This article focuses on two pop culture icons that have been around for over 40
years. Each of these characters represents an important part of Latin American
culture, and the article describes why both characters are so relatable and loved
by the public. The purpose of the article is not to convince the reader that one
character is better than the other, thus (A) and (B) are incorrect. Choice (D) is not
mentioned in the article. Choice (C) is the correct answer.

2. According to the audio source, how do Argentinians react to Mafalda?

   (A) Some like her, some don't.

   (B) They think she is spectacular.

   (C) It's an old comic strip and not relevant anymore.

   (D) They don't know her.

The recording does not state that people don't know her or that some like her and
some don't. Choices (A) and (D) can be eliminated. It is, in fact, an old comic
strip, though it is still relevant to this day. Choice (C) is incorrect. The audio portion states that Argentinians have a spectacular reaction to Mafalda. Choice (B) is
the correct answer.

3. According to the audio source, what type of humor does Mafalda have?

   (A) Gossipy

   (B) Intelligent

   (C) Satirical

   (D) Ironic and not offensive

Mafalda is described as an intelligent character, but her sense of humor is not
described in the same way. She is not satirical or gossipy in nature, thus the only
plausible answer is (D), stated directly in the recording.

4. According to the article, what can be inferred about Mafalda's friends?

   (A) They are a group of friends that are the same.

   (B) They are a group of friends that are varied, but that think in the same manner as Mafalda.

   (C) They are a group of eclectic friends that represent the ideas or realities of the Argentine public.

   (D) They are a group of friends that are the same and that get along well.

The article describes both Mafalda's and Condorito's friends in detail. The article states that Mafalda counts on her varied and eclectic group of friends. Choices (A) and (D) can be eliminated. In that same paragraph, the author states that each of these characters represents an element of truth in the Argentine reality. Choice (B) is not stated anywhere in the article; thus (C) is the correct answer.

5. According to the audio source, what does Cristóbal Navarro think of Mafalda?

   (A) She is a very intellectual character, but at the same time very idealistic.

   (B) She doesn't deserve such attention.

   (C) She is popular, but complicated.

   (D) She is too little to have adult opinions.

According to the interview with Cristóbal Navarro, he states that the main reason Mafalda is well-liked by all is due to her precocious nature. Choice (D) should be eliminated. Navarro does not state (B) or (C), so they should be eliminated as well. Navarro states that many people who visit the exhibition tell him that she is very intellectual, but idealistic. He agrees with that statement. Choice (A) is the correct answer.

6. What does "it does not address the political dimension of its environment" refer to in line 54?

   (A) Condorito does not preoccupy himself with political topics.

   (B) Politics do not impact Chile.

   (C) Politics is important in comic strips.

   (D) It is the most important dimension of this character.

The comparison that the article is trying to make is that, although both Mafalda and Condorito are popular characters, they are very different from each other. Mafalda focuses more on the socio-economic aspect of life, and Condorito is concerned with the simpler things and representing daily life. Choice (B) is incorrect, and is talking about politics in a nation rather than the political view of Condorito. The article makes no mention of how politics impact comics, thus (C) should be eliminated. Choice (D) doesn't make sense. Choice (A) is the correct answer.

7. According to the text, what does Condorito represent?

(A) A loved character

(B) The only way that readers can become culturally close

(C) **Simple comic strips exemplary of daily life**

(D) The national bird of Argentina

The article states directly that Condorito is a comic strip that is full of simplicity and satire. The stories of Condorito represent the daily life of certain sectors in Latin America. The National bird of Chile inspired his character, but Condorito does not represent that. Choice (D) is incorrect. Although (A) is true, again this is not what Condorito represents in Latin American culture. Choice (B) is not correct; Condorito does not represent the only way that readers can be culturally close. Choice (C) is the correct answer.

8. According to the article, what is Juan Plaza's attitude towards Condorito?

(A) Contempt

(B) **Informative**

(C) Sarcastic

(D) Playful

The overall tone of the article is informative and positive. In Plaza's interview, he describes why the public relates to Condorito, and so well. Choices (A) and (C) can be eliminated. Choice (D) is not applicable since he is not making any joking remarks. Choice (B) is the correct answer.

9. According to the audio source, what is "The World of Mafalda" ?

(A) A comic strip magazine

(B) A movie

(C) A toy store

(D) **An interactive exhibition**

The reporter introduces Cristóbal Navarro as a guide in the exhibition "The World of Mafalda." This interactive exhibit can be seen today throughout South America. Choice (D) is the correct answer.

10. According to the audio source, what does Mafalda represent?

(A) **The idiosyncrasies of Latin Americans**

(B) Argentinian culture

(C) Chilean culture

(D) The viewpoints in Latin American culture

Mafalda represents more than a funny character or famous comic strip. Choices (B), (C), and (D) are not mentioned specifically. According to the recording, she represents the idiosyncrasies of the Latin American person. Choice (A) is correct.

Chapter 2
How to
Approach the Free-
Response Section

THE BASICS

The free-response section (Section II) of the AP Spanish Language and Culture Exam tests three important skills: writing, speaking, and listening. The Writing portion consists of two samples of writing: Interpersonal and Presentational. The Speaking portion consists of Interpersonal Speaking in the form of a simulated conversation, as well as a Presentational Speaking sample, in which an integration of reading and listening skills will yield an oral presentation. On the speaking part, you will be paced and prompted by a master recording for a total of 20 minutes.

At the time this book went to press, The College Board was making some changes to your AP course. Make sure to check on the College Board website for any updates!

WRITING

The Writing portion of the free-response section consists of two compositions. The first part tests your ability to write in the interpersonal mode. You will have 15 minutes to read a prompt and reply with your response. Some samples of this could be an email, postcard, or letter to a friend, as well as a journal, diary, or blog entry. The second part examines your ability to write in the presentational mode. Here, you will have 10 minutes to read a few printed sources and listen to an audio prompt. After this, you will have about 5 minutes to formulate your ideas and plan your response. Then, you will have 40 minutes to write your essay for a total time allotment of 55 minutes.

Interpersonal Writing: Email Reply

Let's take a look at a sample question for the interpersonal writing section. Typically, a response prompt will be an email from a professional offering you a study opportunity, a scholarship, a job, or an internship. It might also be a response to your request for a letter of recommendation. When presented with one of these situations, try to immerse yourself in the situation. Maybe you have never worked or traveled overseas before. It doesn't matter—you can make up things! Graders are looking to see how convincing you are in your writing piece. That's all.

Use your note-taking skills to make a quick outline for yourself. If you get stuck, make something up!

The key to this limited-time assignment is to read the prompt quickly, touching upon all the points required and expanding upon them as much as possible, with a grammatically correct and stylistically advanced manner. Spend less than 5 minutes reading the prompt and planning your answer, and begin writing your answer directly after having done so.

As you write, be sure to vary your vocabulary and your grammar. Graders don't want to see you use "bueno" and "malo" throughout your writing, and they definitely don't want to see you use only the present tense. Think about your speaking pattern in English. You don't speak only in present tense. You use a variety of tenses. Try to use some idiomatic expressions as well, to show that you are familiar with the intricacies of the language. Remember to use original ways to open and close your letter. Use appropriate structural indicators and transitional words like *por lo tanto*, *sin embargo*, *en primer lugar*, *para concluir*, *finalmente*, and *adicionalmente*. Also, because this writing sample is so short, do not repeat yourself. Some final tips are to avoid Anglicism and never, under any circumstance, use English in your writing. If you don't know the word for something, find a way to describe it.

This section is also testing your ability to write a formal letter using correct register, possessive pronouns, appropriate vocabulary, and correct openings and closings. Remember, a basic and grammatically correct essay will score no more than a 3. An essay with dynamism, upper-level structures, and depth will score much higher.

> Know who you are writing to! It is often best to err on the side of formality by using *usted* instead of *tú* on these responses.

Basic Approach:

1. Read Carefully
2. Brainstorm Vocab & Plan your Points
3. Write!

Try the following sample email reply question on your own.

Sample Question

You will write a reply to an email message. You have 15 minutes to read the message and write your reply.	Vas a escribir una respuesta a un mensaje electrónico. Vas a tener 15 minutos para leer el mensaje y escribir tu respuesta.
Your reply should include a greeting and a closing and should respond to all the questions and requests in the message. In your reply, you should also ask for more details about something mentioned in the message. Also, you should use a formal form of address.	Tu respuesta debe incluir un saludo y una despedida, y debe responder a todas las preguntas y peticiones del mensaje. En tu respuesta, debes pedir más información sobre algo mencionado en el mensaje. También debes responder de una manera formal.

Introducción

El siguiente correo electrónico le llegó de parte de la Señorita Ciara Duran de la Universidad Interamericana de Puerto Rico. Es una invitación para asistir a un Congreso juvenil durante el verano.

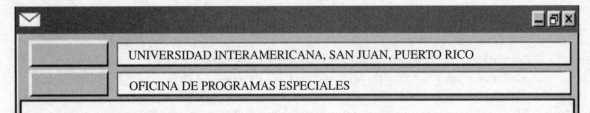

UNIVERSIDAD INTERAMERICANA, SAN JUAN, PUERTO RICO

OFICINA DE PROGRAMAS ESPECIALES

Estimado/a candidato/a:

Muchas gracias por haber expresado su interés en participar en nuestro Congreso Interamericano Juvenil que tendrá lugar el 14 de junio hasta el 5 de julio de este año en La Universidad Interamericana en San Juan, Puerto Rico. Me es muy grato ofrecerle un puesto como delegado representante este año.

Cada verano, nuestra universidad acoge a estudiantes visitantes de varios rincones del mundo hispano-hablante, lo cual nos aporta una perspectiva verdaderamente internacional ante los problemas que confrontan al joven de hoy. Como ya sabe, nuestra meta es alentar diálogo entre los jóvenes para definir cuáles son los problemas más contundentes que abarcan al joven. Y es de esperar que después de un intercambio de ideas, consigamos un mayor enfoque de cómo resolver la problemática regional que afecta a tantos jóvenes hoy en día.

Nosotros contamos con el esfuerzo y dedicación de los delegados voluntarios, ya que brindan una energía y espíritu servicial perspectiva única a las situaciones contundentes que confronta a nuestros países.

Para proveerle una experiencia de lo más agradable, además de confirmar su asistencia al Congreso, sería necesario que nos clarificara alguna información preliminar:

- Por favor díganos cuáles son algunos de los problemas actuales que confrontan a los jóvenes para que se incluyan en la agenda del Congreso. ¿Por qué le son importantes estos problemas?

- Durante su estadía aquí, puede optar por su alojamiento en un hotel o con una familia puertorriqueña. ¿Cuál sería su preferencia, y por qué?

- En el tiempo libre, habrá excursiones y oportunidades para intercambiar con la gente de Puerto Rico. ¿Qué actividades le interesarían a usted, y por qué?

Le pedimos que nos mande esta información de inmediato, ya que se aproxima la fecha límite para inscribirse en el programa.

Le saluda cordialmente,

Ciara Duran
Directora de Programas Estudiantes
Universidad Interamericana

Here's How to Crack It

Quickly brainstorm the vocabulary necessary for the task *(intercambiar, lograr, meta, en cuanto a, en cambio, por otra parte)*. Also, as it is a formal communication, have some of your generic lines in your back pocket that can be used for the opening and ending parts, for example: *Me dirijo a Usted* (I am writing to you); *Si fuera posible* (If it were possible); *Le doy las gracias de antemano por haberme atendido* (I thank you in advance for your attention). And of course, don't forget all that great grammar: subjunctive, indirect object pronouns, transitional words, variety of tenses, and idiomatic expressions. Try to have several in each category prepared beforehand so you can refer to them and use them readily. It's almost like having your clothes picked out the night before school; it makes things a lot easier when you are under pressure. Also, don't forget the inverted exclamation points and question marks. Don't overdo commas and semicolons; Spanish uses them much more sparingly than English.

> Have some canned transitional phrases ready to go!

> A quick brainstorm before you write helps you organize your thoughts and avoid getting stuck mid-response.

Translation of the Question

Introduction

You received the following email from Ms. Ciara Duran of Inter-American University in Puerto Rico; it's an invitation to attend a Youth Congress during the summer.

INTER-AMERICAN UNIVERSITY, SAN JUAN, PUERTO RICO
SPECIAL PROGRAMS OFFICE

Dear candidate:

Many thanks for having expressed your interest in participating in our Inter-American Youth Congress that will take place from the 14th of June to the 5th of July of this year at the Inter-American University in San Juan, Puerto Rico. It is my great pleasure to offer you a position as representative delegate this year.

Each summer, our university welcomes visiting students from various corners of the Spanish-speaking world, which provides us a truly international perspective on the problems confronting today's youth. As you already know, our goal is to encourage dialogue between young people in order to define which are the toughest problems the youth are facing. It is the hope that after an interchange of ideas, we will achieve a better focus on how to resolve the regional problems that affect so many youth today.

We count on the spirit and dedication of the volunteer delegates, as they bring energy and the unique perspective of the spirit of service to the tough problems confronting our nations.

To ensure your experience is as pleasant as possible, along with confirming your attendance to the Congress, we need to clarify some preliminary information:

- Please tell us some of the current problems confronting youth so that they can be included in the agenda for the Congress. Why are these problems important to you?
- During your stay here, you can choose lodging in a hotel or with a Puerto Rican family. Which would be your preference, and why?
- In your free time, there will be excursions and opportunities for interchange with the people of Puerto Rico. What activities would interest you, and why?

We ask that you send us this information immediately, since the deadline to register for the program is approaching.

Warm regards,

Ciara Duran
Director of Student Programs
Inter-American University

Sample Student Response

Estimada Señorita Duran:

Me dirijo a usted con el propósito de informarle sobre mi deseo de participar en el Congreso. Siempre he soñado con participar en un evento así de importante, y espero con ganas la oportunidad de intercambiar ideas con diferentes jóvenes del mundo hispano. Ojalá podamos lograr nuestra meta de definir y lidiar con los problemas que afectan a los jóvenes de hoy. Con el esfuerzo y el positivismo, ¡todo es posible!

Usted me preguntó sobre mis ideas acerca de los temas más contundentes que afectan a los jóvenes del mundo hispanohablante. Yo diría que entre estos problemas se encuentran el desempleo, la falta de alfabetismo en las zonas rurales y el daño al medioambiente. Son problemas muy globales en el sentido que afectan a toda la sociedad, y creo que si podemos progresar en la lucha contra sus efectos, podemos desarrollar un mundo mejor para futuras generaciones. Estos problemas me son importantes ya que estoy al punto de emprender mi carrera universitaria, y la crisis global de muchas maneras me limita las oportunidades profesionales. En cuanto al alfabetismo, gracias a la tecnología, vivimos en un mundo donde nadie tiene que aislarse. La educación ayuda no solo a que la gente pueda participar en la sociedad, sino también les da una voz para votar y ayudar a los demás, así creando el sentido de igualdad entre todos los ciudadanos. Y finalmente, vivimos en un mundo comprometido por la industrialización, la deforestación, y la explotación de los recursos naturales. Los ríos y lagos se ven cada día más contaminados, y el agua es tal vital a nuestra vida de tantas maneras. Espero poder informarles a mis compañeros la importancia de considerar estos problemas, pero al mismo tiempo, tengo muchas ganas de escuchar sus ideas también.

En cuanto al alojamiento, me gusta experimentar toda la cultura nativa, así que me encantaría vivir con una familia puertorriqueña. Es la mejor forma de entender y apreciar las perspectivas de otras culturas—¡ver el mundo a través de sus ojos!

Sé que Puerto Rico cuenta con muchos lugares turísticos. Si fuera posible, sería excelente visitar las zonas agrícolas de café y piñas para ver cómo se cosechan estos productos. También sé que la zona colonial de San Juan es muy histórica y pintoresca; y como soy fanática de la historia, tengo que visitar esa parte de la capital. Y claro está, ¡pasar un rato en sus lindas playas no vendría mal tampoco!

Nuevamente, le doy las gracias por esta oportunidad y espero mayor información sobre el evento. Si necesita más información de mi parte, sírvase de comunicarse conmigo a su conveniencia.

Un saludo cordial,

Victoria Hirsch

Translation of the Sample Student Response

Dear Ms. Duran:

I am writing to you to inform you of my desire to participate in the Congress. I have always dreamed of participating in an event of this importance, and I am looking forward to the opportunity to share ideas with different young people from the Hispanic world. I hope we can reach our goal of defining and dealing with the problems that affect the young people of today. With effort and positive thinking, anything is possible!

You asked me to share my ideas about the most pressing issues facing the youth of the Spanish speaking world. I would say that among these problems we find unemployment, illiteracy in rural areas, and damage to the environment. These are worldwide problems in the sense that they affect all levels of society, and I think that if we can progress in fighting their effects, we can create a better world for future generations. These problems are important to me because I am at the beginning of my university career, and the global crisis in many ways has limited my professional opportunities. In terms of literacy, thanks to technology, we live in a world where no one has to be isolated. Education not only helps people participate in society, but also it gives them a voice to vote and help others, thus creating a sense of equality among all citizens. And finally, the world we live in is one compromised by industrialization, deforestation, and the exploitation of natural resources. The rivers and lakes are becoming more contaminated each day, and water is vital to our lives in so many ways. I hope to have the chance to inform my colleagues about the importance of considering these problems, but at the same time I am interested in hearing their ideas as well.

In terms of lodging, I enjoy experiencing everything about the native culture, so I would love to live with a Puerto Rican family. That is the best way to understand and appreciate the perspectives of another culture—seeing the world through their eyes!

I know Puerto Rico has many tourist attractions. If it were at all possible, it would be wonderful to visit the agricultural zones of coffee and pineapples to see how these products are harvested. I also know that the colonial zone of San Juan is very historical and picturesque, and since I am a history fanatic, I have to visit that part of the capital. And of course, spending time on Puerto Rico's beautiful beaches would not be a bad idea either!

Once again, I thank you for this opportunity and I await further information about the event. If you need any more information from me, feel free to contact me at your convenience.

With cordial greetings,

Victoria Hirsch

Evaluation

This essay was organized, appropriate, and detailed; it would score a 5. The first paragraph clearly defined the writer's intention (to accept the invitation), the second paragraph talks about the topics that interest her, and the third and fourth paragraphs address specific questions from the prompt email. The closing makes the response even more cohesive. Notice also the breadth of vocabulary *(me dirijo a, contundentes, lidiar, cuenta con, fanática, claro está, sírvase de)* and grammar (subjunctive, *si* clauses, formal commands, preterite, conditional). This is also an important part that graders examine. The response is well presented and not repetitive. Notice also that the writer showed she knew information about the country (coffee and pineapples, the beach, the colonial district). This is very important to demonstrate here and in the presentational speaking section. In order to write a native-sounding letter, you might want to view examples of formal writing online, and try to incorporate several elements you observe in them that are not in your repertoire. Don't worry if you can't produce this lengthy a response. If you can duplicate parts of it, and mimic some of the grammar and style, you will be in good shape.

> Check out how this student used some idioms and the subjunctive. Steal some phrases and use them in your own writing!

Presentational Writing: Persuasive Essay

The second composition in the free-response section is a formal presentational writing sample. In this section, you will be required to read two sources and hear one audio piece and then respond to a written prompt. All resources will be related and must be referred to when you write your formal composition. You will have 6 minutes to read the scripts, and you will hear the audio selection twice. You should take notes while you listen. Finally, you will have 40 minutes to write your formal piece for a total of 55 minutes.

> Basic Approach:
>
> 1. Read and Take Notes
> 2. Brainstorm Vocab and Plan your Points
> 3. Write!

This section of the exam requires more extensive preparation than the Inter-personal Writing prompt, because we tend to have more experience with that form of communication in daily life. To do well on the Persuasive Essay, take plenty of time before the exam to expose yourself to a variety of media. Think of social and cultural topics that may appear in an exam. There could be questions on poverty, global warming, social unrest, or literacy implications across Latin America and Spain, or there could be questions based on music, food, and clothing trends. Making yourself as well rounded as possible and actively seeking Spanish printed and audio material will greatly help your score on this part.

Keep it formal in the per-suasive essay! Have some of those canned transition-al phrases ready to go.

So how do you plan for topics that are apparently limitless? Take the time to read newspapers from different areas of Latin America and Spain. Surely, you know how to use the Internet. Just do searches for *noticias latinoamericanas* or *periódicos chilenos* (*argentinos/españoles/peruanos*, and so on) and choose an article that is more challenging for you, grasping its message the best you can. It's not expected that you understand every word in an article, but if you can read the article's title, skim over it, and then read through it, you'll certainly be able to deduce its mean-ing. Read several articles and follow this procedure as you plan for the exam.

In order to train yourself for the audio prompt of this section, you will need to practice with dialects and search for meaning in a message. A fantastic and fun way to practice with dialects would be to turn on a Spanish soap opera (telenovela) or a movie in Spanish, lie back, and just listen. Some students choose an hour to watch television in Spanish and keep a notebook nearby. They jot down words they don't know or even full sentences they would like to include in their reper-toire. Another way you can practice for this section is to download some podcasts. Set your Internet browser to Spanish so you can see and read what is happening in the Spanish-speaking world. Listen to Spanish-speaking radio stations; music is an amazing way to learn vocabulary and improve comprehension. Listen to speeches or interviews in Spanish—start somewhere in the middle of the selection and pay close attention to detail. Take notes as you listen. Be sure to get materials from both Spain and Latin America, as the AP loves to include listening passages with a Spanish accent, which can be a little difficult to understand if you are not used to hearing it.

If you were learning vocabulary in English, you wouldn't gloss over words you don't know. Same idea here: Write them down, look them up, and learn to use them in context.

By reading various selections and listening to diverse audio samples, you begin to build vocabulary and you enhance your ability to make connections to meaning. These are essential tools to write a thorough formal composition. When you write the essay, be sure to make references to all three resources. Making references to the resources does not mean repeating something written or said in the selections; rather, you make an assertion or connection and use the materials to support your point of view. In your introduction you will explain your goal or position in reference to the topic question. In the paragraphs that follow, be sure to have a topic sentence in each to guide your thoughts and support your ideas with information from the sources. In your conclusion, do not repeat what you said in your introduction; rather, let it serve as a summation of your ideas throughout the essay. If you have time, proofread your composition and make sure you place accents where necessary and check your spelling. If you need to change a thought or idea, do not use correction fluid or try to erase what you wrote; just cross it out. You will not be penalized for doing this. Of course, this may sound silly, but try to be as neat as possible, as a well-presented essay is viewed favorably by graders.

Here's a sample persuasive essay prompt to try on your own.

Sample Question

You will write a persuasive essay to submit to a Spanish writing contest. The essay topic is based on three accompanying sources, which present different viewpoints on the topic and include both print and audio material. First, you will have 6 minutes to read the essay topic and the printed material. Afterward, you will hear the audio material twice; you should take notes while you listen. Then, you will have 40 minutes to prepare and write your essay. In your persuasive essay, you should present the sources' different viewpoints on the topic, clearly indicate your own viewpoint and defend it thoroughly. Use information from all of the sources to support your essay. As you refer to the sources, identify them appropriately. Also, organize your essay into clear paragraphs.	Vas a escribir un ensayo persuasivo para un concurso de redacción en español. El tema del ensayo se basa en las tres fuentes adjuntas, que presentan diferentes puntos de vista sobre el tema e incluyen material escrito y grabado. Primero, vas a tener 6 minutos para leer el tema del ensayo y los textos. Después, vas a escuchar la grabación dos veces; debes tomar apuntes mientras escuchas. Luego vas a tener 40 minutos para preparar y escribir tu ensayo. En un ensayo persuasivo, debes presentar los diferentes puntos de vista de las fuentes sobre el tema, expresar tu propio punto de vista y apoyarlo. Usa información de todas las fuentes para apoyar tu punto de vista. Al referirte a las fuentes, identifícalas apropiadamente. Organiza también el ensayo en distintos párrafos bien desarrollados.

Tema del ensayo:

¿Por qué nos urge mejorar las condiciones de vivir de los niños latinoamericanos?

Fuente número 1

Introducción

Este artículo apareció en la revista mexicana *Auge* en 2009.

A través del continente americano, a pesar de los enormes avances tanto en la tecnología agrícola como en las mismas técnicas de arar la tierra, los niveles de nutrición de varios países siguen estancados a niveles tan reducidos que se ven comprometidas la estatura física, la habilidad de poder trabajar una jornada completa y, peor aún, las capacidades intelectuales de sus ciudadanos. La Organización de Desarrollo y Fomento Internacional reporta que, según cifras de los gobiernos latinoamericanos, el consumo de calorías de la región alcanza un promedio de unas 2680 por día (comparado con unas 3450 en los Estados Unidos), y peor aún en los países centroamericanos apenas sobrepasa las 2250 calorías diarias. En los países de mayor actividad económica, como Argentina, Brasil y México, las diferencias regionales han dejado a ciertas zonas marginadas en condiciones similares. La malnutrición se empeora por la falta de servicios de salud, el desempleo y la alta tasa de enfermedad que resulta de la escasez de debido a los escasos servicios sanitarios adecuados.

Los efectos de la modernización y la caída económica mundial requieren una mano de obra de tiempo completo listo para trabajar horas extensas, y a los niveles de nutrición actuales muchos adultos apenas contarán con la energía necesaria para trabajar las 40 o más horas necesarias semanalmente. Entre el 40% de la población adulta clasificada como "pobre" (con un ingreso diario equivalente a unos $2,50 estadounidenses), la falta de nutrición es un factor constante que les aqueja muy a menudo.

No faltan de los esfuerzos para aliviar el problema, sino que lo que ha variado es la magnitud de su alcance y su eficacia en condiciones sociales y económicas sumamente inhóspitas. Se han registrado victorias en algunas áreas (como el programa Salta de Vitarte en Perú, que se concentró en las personas más pobres y les facilitó 3 servicios básicos) pero el obstáculo más formidable es la irremediable realidad económica en la que vive la población. Los programas de bienestar público intentan repartir certificados a las familias de bajo ingreso—parecido al programa de Cupones de Alimentos en los Estados Unidos—pero no existen ni los recursos ni la infraestructura para sostener el programa a largo plazo. Otros programas tienen como meta enfatizar la educación de salud y nutrición, pero los esfuerzos se hacen en balde ya que los ingresos familiares no generan lo suficiente para sostener dietas mejor balanceadas. Ningún esfuerzo ha logrado tener el impacto necesario para lidiar con el problema en toda su magnitud.

Fuente número 2

Introducción

Este artículo apareció en *Páginas Escolares,* una revista juvenil colombiana.

EL CÍRCULO DE AMOR

Cuando uno piensa en Guatemala, tal vez le llegue a la mente la imagen de un país pobre donde predomina la agricultura, o tal vez recuerde a la famosa Rigoberta Menchú, ganadora del Premio Nobel de La Paz en 1992 y con ella la gran tradición indígena que por siglos ha representado un papel omnipresente en la historia guatemalteca. Pero si conoce a Maria Giammarino, de Mahwah, Nueva Jersey, entonces lo primero que sabrá de Guatemala es sobre El Círculo de Amor.

El Círculo de Amor fue fundado por Giammarino en 2001, pero su interés en los guatemaltecos proviene desde los años 90, cuando visitaba el país por su trabajo de aeromoza en una línea aérea americana. Así nos cuenta su experiencia: "Durante unas cuantas estadías en el país, tuve la oportunidad de recorrer muchas de las zonas rurales más pobres. Una vez hicimos una excursión en canoa cerca de Livingston, que nos llevó a una aldea prácticamente olvidada por el mundo. Vimos una pobreza que me partió el alma. Llegamos a un pueblo retirado, y de repente vi a unas niñas de edad escolar vendiendo caramelos y cigarrillos en el muelle. ¡Les correspondía estar en la escuela! Una me llamó la atención: llevaba su ropita harapienta y andaba pata pelada, pero me ofreció una sonrisa dulce e inocente. Una mirada hacia el pueblo me confirmó lo peor: unas covachas con techo de estaño, y el desagüe en la calle cuyo olor perduraba y perduraba. Ni Dante hubiera vislumbrado un mundo así".

Después de cultivar una amistad, Giammarino empezó por enseñarle a tejer a la niña. Le obsequió el material y pronto la novata creó chompas de algodón no sólo para su familia, sino también para la venta. Giammarino le alquiló un pequeño puesto donde vendían la mercancía. Y así se inició El Círculo de Amor. Su aerolínea también le dio la mano, lanzando el programa "Quédate con el vuelto", que les pide a pasajeros norteamericanos que vuelven a su tierra que donen los quetzales sobrantes de su estudía en Guatemala. La campaña ha recaudado más de 10.000 dólares desde su inicio. Ahora hay talleres de tejer, los cuales les ayudan a las mujeres a aprender un oficio ya que juegan éstas un papel esencial en la estrategia de la sobrevivencia de las familias. Hay una pequeña cantina que sirve almuerzos a los residentes del pueblo. Y este año, gracias a la bondadosa ayuda de varios auspiciadores, se presenció la apertura de un pequeño consultorio médico que otorga un servicio de salud básico a los 1200 habitantes del pueblo.

El Círculo de Amor tiene como meta principal procurar el bienestar de las niñas guatemaltecas, muchas veces las más explotadas y marginadas de la sociedad. Las contribuciones también se destinan a la educación femenina, porque según Giammarino "a la gente sin acceso a la educación básica se les priva la voz". Por sólo 30 dólares mensuales, un patrocinador puede mandar a una niña a la escuela. El Círculo de Amor pone atención especial en reclutar a las niñas más pequeñas de una familia para que asistan a la escuela, lo cual es un privilegio reservado mayormente para los niños varones. La estrategia de elegir a la niña menor viene de la perspectiva de que mientras más joven sea ella al iniciar los estudios, más probabilidad tendrá de continuarlos en el futuro.

Fuente número 3

Tienes 30 segundos para leer la introducción.

Introducción

El siguiente discurso lo ofreció Alesandro Dávila, decano de la escuela de Economía de la Pontificia Universidad Católica del Perú en La X Asamblea del Pacto Andino, celebrado en Cajamarca, Perú el año pasado. Se titula "Declive de inversiones gubernamentales con la crisis económica andina".

Ahora escucha la fuente número tres.

PLAY AUDIO: Track 5

Ahora escucha de nuevo.

PLAY AUDIO: Track 5

Ahora tienes cuarenta minutos para preparar y escribir un ensayo persuasivo.

(40 minutes)

Translation of the Question

Essay topic:

Why is improving the living conditions of Latin American children an urgent need?

Source #1

Introduction

This article appeared in the Mexican magazine *Auge* in 2009.

Throughout the American continents, despite enormous advances in agricultural technology and plowing techniques, the levels of nutrition in various countries continue to stagnate at levels so low that citizens are left compromised in terms of physical stature, ability to work full-time, and (even worse) intellectual capacity. The International Development and Promotion Organization reports that, according to figures from Latin American governments, the average calorie consumption for the region reaches around 2680 per day (compared to about 3450 in the United States); it's even worse in the Central American countries, where it barely exceeds 2250 calories per day. In countries with more economic activity, such as Argentina, Brazil, and Mexico, regional differences have left certain marginalized areas in similar conditions. Malnutrition is exacerbated by the lack of health services, unemployment, and the high rate of sickness due to the scarcity of adequate sanitation services.

The effects of modernization and the global economic recession require a labor force ready to work extensive hours, and at current levels of nutrition many adults can barely count on getting the energy necessary to work the required 40 or more hours per week. Among the 40% of the adult population classified as "poor," (with a daily income equivalent to $2.50 in American dollars), lack of nutrition is a constant affliction.

Efforts to alleviate the problem are not lacking, but vary in the magnitude of their scope and their efficacy in extremely inhospitable social and economic conditions. Victories have been recorded in some areas (such as the Salta de Vitarte program in Peru, which concentrated on the poorest people and facilitated three basic services), but the most formidable obstacle is the irremediable economic reality in which the population lives. Public health programs try to distribute certificates to low-income families—similar to Food Stamp programs in the United States—but neither the resources nor the infrastructure exist to sustain the programs in the long run. Other programs aim to emphasize health and nutrition education, but their efforts are in vain since family incomes don't generate enough to sustain better-balanced diets. No endeavor has been successful in having the necessary impact to fight the problem in its whole magnitude.

Source #2

Introduction

This article appeared in *Páginas Escolares,* a Colombian youth magazine.

THE CIRCLE OF LOVE

When you think of Guatemala, maybe what comes to mind is an image of a poor country where agriculture predominates, or maybe you remember the famous Rigoberta Menchú, winner of the Nobel Peace Prize in 1992, and with her the great indigenous tradition that for centuries has played an omnipresent role in Guatemalan history. But if you know Maria Giammarino, of Mahwah, New Jersey, then the first thing you'll know about Guatemala is the Circle of Love.

The Circle of Love was founded by Giammarino in 2001, but her interest in Guatemalans began in the 90s, when she visited the country while working as a flight attendant for an American airline. She recounts her experience like this: "During a few stays in the country, I had the opportunity to travel through many of the poorest rural areas. Once we took a canoe excursion near Livingston, which brought us to a village practically forgotten by the world. We saw poverty that split open my soul. We came to a remote town, and suddenly I saw some school-age girls selling candy and cigarettes on a wharf. They should have been in school! One attracted my attention: She wore little ragged clothes and walked barefoot, but offered me a sweet and innocent smile. A look at the town confirmed the worst: a few hovels with tin roofs, and a drainage ditch in the street the smell of which lasted and lasted. Not even Dante would have imagined a world like that."

After cultivating a friendship, Giammarino began to teach the girl to knit. She gave her the materials and soon the novice was creating cotton sweaters not only for her family but also to sell. Giammarino rented her a tiny stall from which she sold the merchandise. And so began the Circle of Love. Her airline also lent a hand, launching the program "Keep the Change," which asked North American passengers returning home to donate the leftover *quetzales* (Guatemalan currency) from their stays in Guatemala. The campaign has collected more than 10,000 dollars since it began. Now there are knitting workshops, which help women learn a trade and so play an essential role in their families' survival. There is a small café that serves lunch to residents of the town. And this year, thanks to the kind-hearted help of various sponsors, witnessed the opening of a small doctor's office granting basic health services to the 1200 residents of the town.

The Circle of Love's principal goal is the well-being of Guatemala's young girls, often the most exploited and marginalized members of society. Contributions also go to education for females, because according to Giammarino, "people without access to basic education are deprived of their voice." For only 30 dollars per month, a sponsor can send a girl to school. The Circle of Love places special attention on recruiting families' youngest daughters for school, a privilege for the most part reserved for male children. The strategy of choosing the youngest daughter comes from the perspective that the younger a girl is upon beginning her studies, the more likely she is to continue them into the future.

Source #3

Introduction

The following discourse was offered by Alessandro Dávila, dean of the School of Economics of the Papal Catholic University of Peru in the 10th Assembly of the Andean Pact, celebrated in Cajamarca, Peru, last year. It is titled "Decline of Governmental Investments in the Andean Economic Crisis."

Audio Track 5

What I can predict with certainty is that the only thing that will change in Latin America is the climate. Our national problems have lots of ups and downs, but in the end come out the same: we are a poor country, and our most marginalized become more and more trapped in this vicious cycle that is poverty. The reality we are living is that our external debt suffocates us and almost robs us of the will to keep progressing. Almost 50% of our gross national product goes to satisfy payments to our European and North American creditors. Our problems are strongly rooted in our foreign relations, which leave a paltry amount for family planning, education, and vaccine programs. Our national budget is not enough for everything, and our children are suffering the worst. Investment in education has diminished 50%, and some precincts already in disrepair cannot even provide the minimum necessary for their classrooms, books, blackboards, floors, and potable water. And when it comes to survival, many choose to work rather than study. As a result, we as a region have one of the highest rates of illiteracy on the continent. One of the most sensitive problems the populations of our countries in general and specifically those most marginalized groups are going through right now is plummeting incomes. In Lima, the family shopping basket: basic necessities support less but cost more, and now the Milk League will suspend its deliveries of this valuable food to daycares due to exorbitant costs, and free lunches are already an endangered species. Ten years ago, every child in the Andean provinces received vaccines, dental exams, and school snacks. Now they are lucky to get one of the three. The data shows the sad reality. In Bolivia, the national budget for education programs diminished by 33% even though the student population grew by 8%. In Chile, falling income from exports resulted in the elimination of nutrition and family planning programs, scholarships, and four free clinics in the areas of greatest need. The conclusion we can extract reliably is that inequality and absolute poverty have grown with the economic crisis. Unfortunately, the world is blind to the problem. The "bailout," a first-world luxury, is not an option for us. In the future, based on what I see now, it's probable that the South American continent will experience negative growth, like the runaway inflation of the 80s, which will exacerbate the nutritional deficiencies, productivity problems, and sadly, the potential for growth and development for the future.

Sample Student Response

¿Por qué nos urge mejorar las condiciones de vivir de los niños latinoamericanos?

Es sumamente importante que mejoremos las condiciones de vivir de los niños latino-americanos, ya que ellos son esenciales para el bienestar del futuro. Hoy en día, se puede decir que la falta de acceso a servicios básicos es uno de los problemas más grandes que confronta a los niños a través del mundo latinoamericano. Como resultado, los niños son atrapados en una problemática sin salida: la pobreza, la cual trae consigo un menor acceso a la educación, la medicina y la vivienda. El trabajo reemplaza la educación como la primera prioridad. Según la fuente #3, algunos niños latinoamericanos carecen de buena nutrición, vacunas y alfabetismo básico. Esto concuerda con otra triste realidad: el hecho preocupante que la inversión financiera en educación, según la fuente número 3, es mucho menor en América Latina, lo cual es claramente paradójico, ya que es donde más se necesita esta clase de inversión (Fuente 2).

Pienso que si las necesidades básicas de la gente se satisficieran, entonces podrían preocuparse de los lujos como la educación. Como nos explica la fuente #1, la gente hambrienta no puede funcionar en el mundo laboral. Vivir, comer y estar libre de enfermedades son necesidades básicas del ser humano. Si esta gente no recibe los servicios básicos, ello puede causar epidemias tal como se presencia en México actualmente. Además, la educación, la planificación familiar, la nutrición y la vivienda adecuadas ayudan a la gente a que contribuyan más a sus países. Y hasta es posible que puedan aportar al futuro de su país al convertirse en políticos o doctores. Se dice que con el apoyo y el deseo todo es posible. El mundo está conectado social, económica y políticamente, entonces es nuestra responsabilidad ayudar a estas personas que, según la fuente 2, "se les priva de voz" en su futuro.

Hemos visto que nuestras acciones sí hacen una diferencia en las vidas de los niños latinoamericanos y, obviamente, se sabe que no hay soluciones rápidas y fáciles. Sin embargo, la señora Giammarino se empeñó en ayudar a una comunidad pequeña guatemalteca, demostrando que los esfuerzos pequeños pueden lograr milagros. Esperamos que otras personas reconozcan la urgencia de ayudar a estas personas necesitadas.

Translation of the Sample Student Response

Why is it urgent for us to help improve the living conditions of children in Latin America?

It is extremely important for us to improve the living conditions of Latin America's children, as they are essential to the wellbeing of the future. Nowadays, it can be said that the lack of access to basic services is one of the formidable problems that confront children throughout the Latin American world. As a result, children are trapped in a problem without solution: poverty that brings with it reduced access to education, medicine, and shelter. Work replaces education as the first priority. According to source #3, some Latin American children lack good nutrition, vaccinations, and basic literacy. This goes hand in hand with another sad reality: the frightening fact that financial investment in education in Latin America is much less (source #3), which is clearly paradoxical as it is precisely where this type of investment is needed (source #2).

I believe that if the basic needs of the people were satisfied, then they would be able to concern themselves with luxuries such as education. As source #1 explains to us, hungry people cannot function in the workplace. Living, eating, and illness prevention are basic necessities of human beings. If these people don't receive basic services, it could cause epidemics as we have witnessed recently in Mexico. Also, adequate education, family planning, nutrition, and adequate housing help people to contribute more to their respective countries. It's even possible they might contribute to the future of their countries by becoming politicians or doctors. It is said that with support and desire anything is possible. The world is connected socially, economically, and politically, and thus it is our responsibility to help those people, who, according to source #2, "are denied a voice" in their future.

We have seen that our actions do indeed make a difference in the lives of Latin American children. And obviously, we know there are no quick and easy solutions. However, Mrs. Giammarino gave of herself to help a small Guatemalan community, demonstrating that small efforts can produce miracles. We can only hope that other people recognize the urgency of helping these needy people.

Evaluation

This essay had strong vocabulary, grammar, and organization. One of the challenges with the presentational writing section is to try to refer to all the sources, because the AP often includes sources that don't have a clear correlation to each other. It is your responsibility to try to find connections between them, however minor, in order to include all of them in your analysis, your synthesis, and ultimately, your composition. Mentioning ALL the sources will help you score higher. One weakness in this essay was that it needed a greater incorporation of the sources, and possibly a deeper analysis. The writer did make some connections among the materials which, although somewhat predictable, nonetheless carried ideas from start to finish and used data to back up the conclusions. Summary was kept to a minimum and statements referred to information in the readings, which are things to remember when writing your essay. This essay would probably score in the 4 range.

PRACTICE PROMPT 1

Introducción

El siguiente correo electrónico le llegó de parte del Señor Ramón Hector Ramos de la Organización de las Naciones Unidas. Es una entrevista electrónica por una práctica profesional este verano. Tendrá 15 minutos para leer la carta y escribir su respuesta.

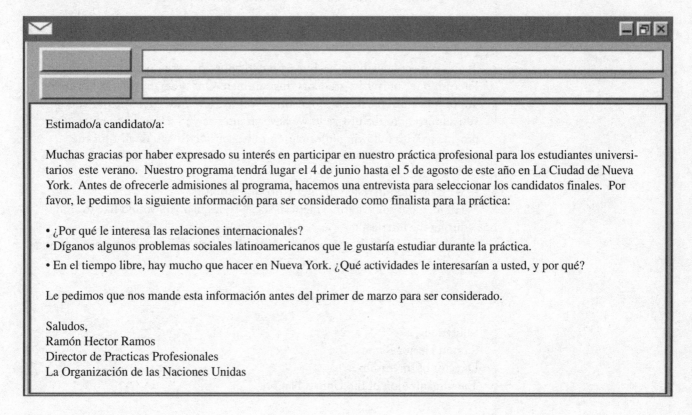

Estimado/a candidato/a:

Muchas gracias por haber expresado su interés en participar en nuestro práctica profesional para los estudiantes universitarios este verano. Nuestro programa tendrá lugar el 4 de junio hasta el 5 de agosto de este año en La Ciudad de Nueva York. Antes de ofrecerle admisiones al programa, hacemos una entrevista para seleccionar los candidatos finales. Por favor, le pedimos la siguiente información para ser considerado como finalista para la práctica:

• ¿Por qué le interesa las relaciones internacionales?
• Díganos algunos problemas sociales latinoamericanos que le gustaría estudiar durante la práctica.
• En el tiempo libre, hay mucho que hacer en Nueva York. ¿Qué actividades le interesarían a usted, y por qué?

Le pedimos que nos mande esta información antes del primer de marzo para ser considerado.

Saludos,
Ramón Hector Ramos
Director de Practicas Profesionales
La Organización de las Naciones Unidas

PRACTICE PROMPT 1 TRANSLATION

Introduction

You received the following email from Señor Ramón Hector Ramos of the United Nations. It is an electronic interview for an internship this summer. You will have 15 minutes to read the letter and write your response.

Esteemed candidate:

Thank you very much for having expressed your interest in participating in our internship for university students this summer. Our program will take place the 4th of June until the 5th of August this year in New York City. Before offering you admission to the program, we have an interview to select the finalists. Please, provide us with following information to be considered as a finalist for the internship:

- Why are you interested in international relations?
- Tell us about some Latin American social issues that you would like to study during the internship.
- In your free time, there is a lot to do in New York. What activities would interest you, and why?

We ask that you send us this information before the first of March to be considered.

Salutations,
Ramón Hector Ramos
Director of Internships
The Organization of the United Nations

PRACTICE PROMPT 2

Introducción

Este mensaje es de Señora Elena Guzman, su profesora de literatura latinoamericana. Ha recibido este mensaje porque recientemente le había pedido que le escribiera una carta de recomendación para estudiar en el programa de su universidad en Puebla, México por el primer semestre. Tendrá 15 minutos para leer la carta y escribir su respuesta.

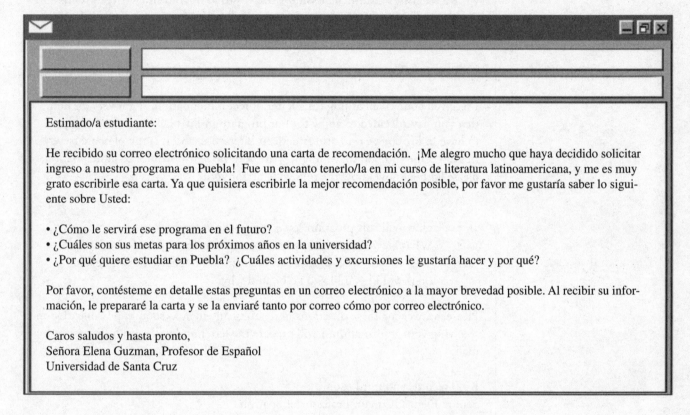

Estimado/a estudiante:

He recibido su correo electrónico solicitando una carta de recomendación. ¡Me alegro mucho que haya decidido solicitar ingreso a nuestro programa en Puebla! Fue un encanto tenerlo/la en mi curso de literatura latinoamericana, y me es muy grato escribirle esa carta. Ya que quisiera escribirle la mejor recomendación posible, por favor me gustaría saber lo siguiente sobre Usted:

• ¿Cómo le servirá ese programa en el futuro?
• ¿Cuáles son sus metas para los próximos años en la universidad?
• ¿Por qué quiere estudiar en Puebla? ¿Cuáles actividades y excursiones le gustaría hacer y por qué?

Por favor, contésteme en detalle estas preguntas en un correo electrónico a la mayor brevedad posible. Al recibir su información, le prepararé la carta y se la enviaré tanto por correo cómo por correo electrónico.

Caros saludos y hasta pronto,
Señora Elena Guzman, Profesor de Español
Universidad de Santa Cruz

PRACTICE PROMPT 2 TRANSLATION

Introduction

This message is from Señora Elena Guzman, your professor of Latin American Literature. You have received this message because recently you have asked her to write a letter of recommendation for you to study in your university's program in Puebla, Mexico for the Fall semester. You will have 15 minutes to read the letter and write your response.

Esteemed student,

I received your email asking for a letter of recommendation. I am very excited that you have decided to apply for our program in Puebla! You were a pleasure to have in my course on Latin American Literature, and it is my pleasure to write this letter for you. So that I might write you the best possible recommendation, please let me know know the following about you:

- How will this program serve you in the future?
- What are your goals for your next years at the university?
- Why do you wish to study in Puebla? Which activities and excursions would you like to go on and why?

Please, answer me these questions in detail in an email as soon as possible. Upon receiving your information, I will prepare the letter and will send it by post or by mail.

Kind regards and until soon,
Señora Elena Guzman, Professor of Spanish
University of Santa Cruz

SPEAKING

The directions for the speaking part will be given to you by the master recording. You will be told when to open the booklet containing the material. You will be asked to respond to different prompts and to record your voice. Most directions will be spoken in English, but you will be asked different types of questions in Spanish in the Directed Response part of the exam. There are two sections in the speaking part: a role-play conversation in which the student listens to a speaker and responds to prompts, and an oral presentation of two minutes based on reading and listening passages. Together, these sections comprise approximately 25 percent of your overall score.

Interpersonal Speaking: Conversation

This section integrates both listening and speaking skills in a role-play conversation. Students will be asked to interact with the recorded conversation. You will be required to answer either five or six times to various prompts. Each response will be 20 seconds long and will be timed by a beep on the recording. Before beginning, you will have the opportunity to read the outline of the simulated conversation and instructions.

Basic Approach:

1. Listen to the Scenario Carefully to Determine Context
2. Take Notes if Needed
3. Stay Relaxed and Have Some Phrases Ready

For the upcoming sample question, you may want to have a device on hand with which to record your spoken answers. This will allow you to compare your responses with the sample student responses that follow.

Ready to begin? Let's give it a try!

Sample Question

You will participate in a conversation. First, you will have 1 minute to read a preview of the conversation, including an outline of each turn in the conversation. Afterward, the conversation will begin, following the outline. Each time it is your turn to speak, you will have 20 seconds to record your response; a tone will indicate when you should begin and end speaking.	Vas a participar en una conversación. Primero, vas a tener un minuto para leer la introducción y el esquema de la conversación. Después, comenzará la conversación, siguiendo el esquema. Cada vez que te corresponda participar en la conversación, vas a tener 20 segundos para grabar tu respuesta; una señal te indicará cuando debes empezar y terminar de hablar.
You should participate in the conversation as fully and appropriately as possible.	Debes participar de la manera más completa y apropiada posible.

Introducción

Imagina que recibes un mensaje telefónico de parte del director del Departamento de Estudios para Extranjeros de una universidad latinoamericana. El director te llama para invitarte a acudir a su oficina para una entrevista sobre tu solicitud de beca. [You will hear the message on the recording.]

> **PLAY AUDIO: Track 6**

[The shaded lines reflect what you will hear on the recording.]

Entrevistador	Te saluda
Tú	Salúdalo y preséntate
Entrevistador	Te explica por qué te hace la entrevista y te hace una pregunta
Tú	Responde a la pregunta
Entrevistador	Continúa la conversación
Tú	Responde a la pregunta
Entrevistador	Continúa la conversación
Tú	Responde a la pregunta
Entrevistador	Continúa la conversación
Tú	Responde a la pregunta
Entrevistador	Continúa la conversación
Tú	Haz una pregunta

Here's How to Crack It

Use the introduction by the narrator to gain some context, jotting down a quick note or two of key vocabulary terms. Also use this to understand the context. This section is testing your ability to initiate, sustain, and conclude a conversation in a given situation as well as use language that is culturally, semantically, grammatically, and socially correct. In other words, are you using the correct *Usted* and *tú* forms? Are you being culturally appropriate in a social setting by using correct markers in your conversation, such as the subjunctive and formal commands, when necessary? Many of these situations involve traveling or studying overseas, or applying for jobs, internships, and scholarships. It would be smart to study up on some of the vocabulary involved in job applications, college courses, scholarships, internships, and so on.

Remember that you have only 20 seconds to respond to each prompt. Do not restate the question in your answer, as it wastes valuable time. Speak clearly and slowly. Don't worry if you get cut off in mid-sentence by the tone. Make it your goal to provide interesting and high-level answers that address the question or situation with correct grammar and pronunciation. Try to incorporate certain phrases that can help you introduce your answers: *Lo que es importante, Quisiera, Si fuera posible*, for example. The higher-level structure and vocabulary you use, the higher your score will be. Also, try not to use the simple way to say things; use the higher-order vocabulary. For example use *dirigirse* or *acudir* instead of *ir*. Try to use all 20 seconds as it will enable you to give two solid, high-level sentences. Remember that if you are using the *Usted* form, which is probably more often than not, you need to have all of the verbs, possessive pronouns, and especially the object pronouns in the corresponding forms. Pay attention to the Student Answers on the sample script with Student Response as these are the kinds of answers that will get you high scores.

Have these conversational phrases and relevant vocabulary ready! It will help with the entire exam, really.

> Try to fill the 20 seconds! If you have any pauses, try to convert your "uh's" into "em's", which is more common in Spanish speakers' speech patterns.

Script with Sample Student Response and Translation

Narrador:	Imagina que recibes un mensaje telefónico de parte del director del Departamento de Estudios para Extranjeros de una universidad latinoamericana. El director te llama para invitarte a acudir a su oficina para una entrevista sobre tu solicitud de beca.
	Imagine that you receive a phone message from the director of the Department of Foreign Student Studies at a Latin American university. The director calls you to invite you to his office for an interview about your scholarship application.
MA:	[Answering machine] [Beep] Buenos días, le habla el señor Guillermo Butrón, director del programa de Estudios para Extranjeros. Quisiera que pasara por mi oficina mañana para una entrevista sobre la solicitud que usted nos envió. Tengo algunas preguntas que quisiera hacerle.
	Good morning, this is Mr. Guillermo Butrón, director of the Foreign Student Studies program. I would like you to come by my office tomorrow for an interview concerning the application you submitted. I have a few questions I would like to ask you.
Narrador:	Ahora tienes un minuto para leer el esquema de la conversación.
	Now you have one minute to read the conversation outline.
	Ahora imagina que te encuentres en la oficina del señor Butrón para realizar una entrevista.
	Now imagine that you are in Mr. Butrón's office for an interview.

Entre: Buenos días. Me es muy grato conocerle en persona. Soy Guillermo Butrón, director del programa de Estudios para Extranjeros y de becas en la región latinoamericana. Por favor, pase y siéntese.

Good morning. It is a pleasure to meet you in person. I am Guillermo Butrón, director of the Foreign Student Studies program and scholarships in Latin America. Please, come in and sit down.

Tú: Es un verdadero gusto conocerle también, Señor Butrón. Soy Michael Randello de Nueva York.

It is real pleasure to meet you also, Mr. Butrón. I am Michael Randello, from New York.

Entre: Tengo su solicitud para una beca de estudios y necesito hacerle algunas preguntas para saber un poco más sobre usted. ¿Por qué le interesa estudiar en Latinoamérica?

I have your scholarship study application and I need to ask you some questions to find out a little more about you. Why are you interested in studying in Latin America?

Tú: Siempre me han llamado la atención la cultura y el idioma de esa región. Como quisiera trabajar en un empleo relacionado con América Latina, necesito hablar mejor el español y entender más a fondo su cultura y costumbres.

I have always been interested in both the culture and language of that region. Since I would like to work in a position that relates to Latin America, I need to speak Spanish better and understand in depth its culture and customs.

Entre: Ah, muy interesante. Se nota que tiene un verdadero interés en estudiar en el extranjero. ¿Dónde en Latinoamérica le gustaría estudiar y vivir, y por qué?

Ah, very interesting. I see that you have a real interest in studying abroad. Where in Latin America would you like to study and live, and why?

Tú: Definitivamente me interesaría estar en Argentina. Encuentro tanto la historia como la cultura fascinante. Además, ahí podría perfeccionar el español.

I would definitely like to be in Argentina. I find both the history and culture fascinating. In addition, there I would be able to perfect my Spanish.

Entre: Si fuera a recibir la beca, ¿qué le gustaría estudiar y por qué?

If you were to receive the scholarship, what would you like to study and why?

| Tú: | Bueno, obviamente necesitaría estudiar el español, pero como quisiera trabajar en negocios internacionales, sería buena idea que estudiara comercio, relaciones internacionales, e historia. |

Well, obviously I would need to study Spanish, but as I would like to work in international business, it would be a good idea to study commerce, international relations, and history.

| Entre: | Además de sus responsabilidades académicas, los estudiantes que reciben becas deben participar en actividades culturales. ¿Qué aspectos de la cultura del país que visitará le interesan? |

In addition to their academic responsibilities, the students who receive scholarships must participate in cultural activities. What aspects of the culture interest you in your country of choice?

| Tú: | Siempre me ha fascinado el tango. La historia y el significado del tango me son muy interesantes. Siempre soñé con aprender a bailar el tango, así que tomaré clases. |

The tango has always fascinated me. The history and meaning of the tango are very interesting. I always dreamed about learning to dance the tango, so I will take classes.

| Entre: | ¡Qué bien! Y para terminar, ¿qué preguntas tiene sobre la beca o sobre nuestro programa en general? |

How nice! And to conclude, what questions do you have about the scholarship or about our program in general?

| Tú | Por favor, dígame: ¿Cuándo empezará el programa? ¿Viviré con una familia o en una residencia estudiantil? ¿Cuándo me informarán sobre la beca? |

Please tell me: When does the program begin? Will I live with a family or in a student residence? When will I be informed about the scholarship?

Evaluation

Reflect
- Review idioms and phrases like *Dígame* to prepare for this section.
- Use all the time available to continue talking. Don't worry if you get cut off!
- Have a friend help you study by reading prompts from AP Students.

The responses by the student were rich, varied, and complete; he used excellent grammatical and vocabulary structures: conditional, subjunctive, and future tenses. The student also fulfilled the requirement of being socially appropriate by using the *Usted* command *Dígame* in the last response. Be sure to get one example of that in your response. The responses enriched and advanced the conversation; notice how the topics were addressed and developed with creative and interesting answers: the student showed an understanding of university courses, culture, and studying overseas. You should be sure to have an understanding of several Spanish-speaking countries, as you may need to discuss their culture in one of these types of questions. This response would certainly score in the 4 or 5 level.

Presentational Speaking: Cultural Comparison

This section requires you to make a presentation on a specific topic. You are given 4 minutes to read the question and plan your answer, and then 2 minutes to actually deliver your presentation. Although you are not given any material on which to base your answer, you need to reflect on the cultural knowledge you have acquired about the Spanish-speaking world, as well as the knowledge you have acquired about the community in which you live.

Try this sample question. As with the last section, you may want to have a device on hand with which to time yourself and record your presentation so that you can evaluate it later.

Brainstorm on paper and then decide how to order and structure your argument.

Basic Approach:

1. Brainstorm Key Vocab and Order your Points
2. Have Specific Regions and Examples Ready to Pull From
3. Have Transitional Phrases Ready

Sample Question

You will make an oral presentation on a specific topic to your class. You will have 4 minutes to read the presentation topic and prepare your presentation. Then you will have 2 minutes to record your presentation. In your presentation, compare your own community to an area of the Spanish-speaking world with which you are familiar. You should demonstrate your understanding of cultural features of the Spanish-speaking world. You should also organize your presentation clearly.	Vas a dar una presentación oral a tu clase sobre un tema cultural. Vas a tener 4 minutos para leer el tema de la presentación y prepararla. Después vas a tener 2 minutos para grabar tu presentación. En tu presentación, compara tu propia comunidad con una región del mundo hispanohablante que te sea familiar. Debes demostrar tu comprensión de aspectos culturales en el mundo hispanohablante y organizar tu presentación de una manera clara.

Tienes cuatro minutos para leer el tema de la presentación y prepararla.

(4 minutes)

Tema de la presentación:

¿Cómo ha afectado la tecnología la vida de las personas en su comunidad?

Compara tus observaciones acerca de las comunidades en las que has vivido con tus observaciones de una región del mundo hispanohablante que te sea familiar. En tu presentación, puedes referirte a lo que has estudiado, vivido, observado, etc.

Tienes dos minutos para grabar tu presentación.

Here's How to Crack It

This section is challenging since there are no prompts to use as a basis for your answer. It is testing your ability to produce an oral report for an extended period of time, to expound on familiar topics that require some sort of research, and to demonstrate and understand aspects of the target culture (geography, art, music, and social, economic, and political elements). There also should be some sort of comparing and contrasting going on in your response; this is an example of higher-order thinking, and the graders like to see that. The best way to prepare for this section is to become completely familiar with several countries in the Spanish-speaking world. Pick one from each major region: the Caribbean, Mexico and Central America, the Andean and Southern Cone regions of South America, and Spain. This way, you have knowledge of the different ethnic groups, history, and customs. Often, you will be asked to compare and contrast cultures, so practice doing that on your own by looking for similarities and differences when reading and comparing articles or other media. Use specific vocabulary to voice similarities and differences: *por otra parte, se parecen, se diferencian, vale mencionar que mientras una _____, la otra _____,* and so on.

Check out these phrases! Learn them. Love them.

Translation of the Question

Presentation Topic:

How has technology affected the lives of the people in your community?

Compare your observations about the communities you have lived in to your observations of a Spanish-speaking region of the world with which you are familiar. In your presentation you can refer to what you have studied, lived, observed, etc.

Sample Student Response

Les voy a hablar sobre cómo la tecnología ha empeñado un papel sumamente importante en las vidas de las personas tanto en mi comunidad como en la comunidad hispanohablante.

Yo diría que en mi comunidad la tecnología ha enriquecido la educación en las escuelas. Gracias al Internet, tenemos acceso a recursos para el estudio de idiomas —periódicos de cualquier país de Latinoamérica o España. Inclusive podemos escuchar noticieros y ver programas televisivos a cualquier hora. Hasta hemos abandonado los diccionarios, ya que podemos usar páginas de Web desde los teléfonos para descifrar palabras y entender su uso correcto en la gramática. Como resultado, mi rendimiento como estudiante ha mejorado.

En mi comunidad, veo que hay padres que pueden vigilar sus casas, empleados, niños —todo desde su teléfono celular. Los policías pueden usar tecnología especial para rastrear a niños perdidos o secuestrados a través de las torres de teléfonos celulares.

La tecnología también ha tenido efectos positivos en los países de América Latina. En Argentina, por ejemplo, la tecnología ha ayudado a conservar al medioambiente. Durante un viaje allá, presencié el uso de hidrógeno en los carros en vez de gasolina. Este uso especializado ha ayudado a que la gente use menos combustible y es económicamente beneficioso ya que combate el alto costo del petróleo. Argentina es uno de los pocos países de Sudamérica que no cuenta con vastos campos petrolíferos. También vi el uso de la tecnología en el campo médico. En Argentina hay muchas zonas retiradas y aisladas cuya población no puede acudir al servicio médico. Ahora hay trenes que viajan a través del paisaje y llevan equipo médico portátil y hasta usan el Internet para consultar con expertos en Buenos Aires, para diagnosticar al paciente por la Red. Ese programa se llama "El tren de la Esperanza" y fue creado por jóvenes médicos argentinos que se preocupaban por el bienestar de los niños. Hace 10 años nada de eso fue posible.

Hay centenares de ejemplos más; pero si tuviera que elegir un cambio tecnológico que ha revolucionado al mundo, diría que es el teléfono celular. Los teléfonos de hoy ahora nos hablan, nos guían, nos traducen, y nos conectan al Red. Gracias a la tecnología, los sueños de hace sólo un par de años de verdad pueden convertirse en realidad.

Translation of the Sample Student Response

I'm going to speak to you about how technology has played an extremely important role in the lives of people both in my community and in the Spanish-speaking community.

I would say that in my community, technology has enriched the education in schools. Thanks to the Internet, we have access to resources for the study of language—newspapers from any Latin American country or Spain. We can even listen to news broadcasts or watch television at any time. We've stopped using dictionaries since we can use web pages from our phones to decipher words and understand their correct grammatical usage. As a result, my performance as a student has improved.

In my community, I see that parents can watch their homes, employees, children—all from a cell phone. The police can use special technology to track lost or kidnapped children through cell phone towers.

Technology has also had positive effects in Latin America. In Argentina, for example, technology has helped save the environment. During a trip there, I witnessed the use of hydrogen in cars instead of gasoline. This specialized use has helped people use less gasoline, and it is economically beneficial because it combats the high price of oil. Argentina is one of the few countries in South America that does not possess vast oil fields. I also saw the use of technology in the medical field. In Argentina there are many isolated areas where the population doesn't have access to medical services. There are now trains that travel through the countryside and bring portable medical equipment and even use the Internet to consult with experts in Buenos Aires to diagnose the patient over the Internet. This program is called the "Train of Hope" and was created by young Argentinean doctors who were concerned about the wellbeing of children. Ten years ago, none of this was possible.

There are hundreds more examples, but if I had to choose one technological change that has revolutionized the world, I would say it would have to be the cell phone. The phones of today speak to us, guide us, translate for us, and connect us to the Internet. Thanks to technology, dreams from just a few years ago can now become reality.

Evaluation

This was a tough question, as it was so open ended. Although it seemed that the student was grasping at straws at first, it turned out to be a pretty good response. Overall, there was a lack of contrasting, and the two applications of technology didn't really have a common thread. However, the student clearly demonstrated knowledge of the target culture and did apply the variable of technology to both societies in a very creative way. The answer also flowed well and even gave a surprise at the end with a personal evaluation of technology's greatest contribution. It would probably score a 4, possibly a 5, given the strong grammar and organization it demonstrated.

Make notes for yourself to talk from and organize yourself. Decide which point you will talk about first, second, and so on.

Essay Practice Prompt 1

Tienes cuatro minutos para leer el tema de la presentación y prepararla.

(4 minutes)

Tema de la presentación:

¿Cuáles son las aventajas y las desventajas del teléfono celular?

Compara tus observaciones acerca de las comunidades en las que has vivido con tus observaciones de una región del mundo hispanohablante que te sea familiar. En tu presentación, puedes referirte a lo que has estudiado, vivido, observado, etc.

Tienes dos minutos para grabar tu presentación.

Essay Practice Prompt 2

Tienes cuatro minutos para leer el tema de la presentación y prepararla.

(4 minutes)

Tema de la presentación:

¿Cómo le ha afectado a usted la educación? La educación puede ocurrir por varias maneras, de maneras formales y informales. Compara tus experiencias acerca de las comunidades en las que has vivido con tus observaciones de una región del mundo hispanohablante que te sea familiar. En tu presentación, puedes referirte a lo que has estudiado, vivido, observado, etc.

Tienes dos minutos para grabar tu presentación.

Essay Practice Prompt 3

Tienes cuatro minutos para leer el tema de la presentación y prepararla.

(4 minutes)

Tema de la presentación:

¿Cómo ha afectado los medios sociales las vidas de las personas en su comunidad?

Compara tus observaciones acerca de las comunidades en las que has vivido con tus observaciones de una región del mundo hispanohablante que te sea familiar. En tu presentación, puedes referirte a lo que has estudiado, vivido, observado, etc.

Tienes dos minutos para grabar tu presentación.

REFLECT

Think about what you've learned in Part III, and respond to the following questions:

- What is your pace for an average passage of 6–8 questions? Your average pace per question?

- How will you change your approach to multiple-choice questions?

- What is your multiple-choice guessing penalty? Should you guess?

- How should you use the multiple-choice questions to help you through the listening portions?

- How should you listen to the audio recordings? What should you do as you listen?

- How will you change your approach to the interpersonal response? The persuasive essay? The conversation? The spoken presentation?

- What kinds of salutatory phrases might be useful to keep in mind for the conversation?

- What kinds of transitional phrases might come in handy for the interpersonal response, the essay, and the spoken presentation?

- What kinds of tenses should you be using for the spoken and written portions?

- Which parts of this section are you going to re-review?

- Will you seek further help, outside this book (such as from a teacher, tutor, or AP Students), on how to approach multiple-choice questions, the essay, or a pacing strategy?

Be sure to download our special supplement, "Using Time Effectively to Maximize Points," when your register your book online!

Study Break!
Before you dive into Part IV, be sure to give yourself some downtime to let your brain absorb the information you've been studying.

Part IV
Grammar Review for the AP Spanish Language and Culture Exam

HOW TO USE THIS REVIEW

In the following chapter, we'll highlight the grammar topics you should master by test day. Bear in mind that this is NOT a comprehensive review; we strongly urge you to study your textbook and class notes as well. If there is a topic that you don't fully understand or is not covered here, be sure to go through your textbook and ask your teacher about it well before test day.

Remember, a careful review of verb and grammar forms now can translate into higher-quality responses on the exam. At the end of the chapter, you'll have an opportunity to reflect on what you've absorbed and what you may need to re-review.

Chapter 3
Review of
Spanish Verb and
Grammar Forms

BASIC TERMS

Although you won't see the following terms on the test, they are important because they will come up later in the chapter. Knowing these terms will allow you to understand the rules of grammar that you're about to review.

Noun:	a person, place, thing, or idea
EXAMPLES:	Abraham Lincoln, New Jersey, a taco, a thought
Pronoun:	a word that replaces a noun
EXAMPLES:	Abraham Lincoln would be replaced by *he*, New Jersey by *it*, and a taco or thought by *it*. You'll see more about pronouns later.
Adjective:	a word that describes a noun
EXAMPLES:	cold, soft, colorful
Verb:	an action—a word that describes what is being done in a sentence
EXAMPLE:	Ron *ate* the huge breakfast.
Infinitive:	the original, unconjugated form of a verb
EXAMPLES:	to eat, to run, to laugh
Auxiliary Verb:	the verb that precedes the past participle in the perfect tense
EXAMPLE:	He *had* eaten his lunch.
Past Participle:	the appropriate form of a verb when it is used with the auxiliary verb
EXAMPLE:	They have *gone* to work.
Adverb:	a word that describes a verb, adjective, or another adverb, just as an adjective describes a noun
EXAMPLES:	slowly, quickly, happily (In English, adverbs often, but don't always, end in *-ly*.)
Subject:	the person or thing (noun) in a sentence that is performing the action

EXAMPLE:	*John* wrote the song.
Compound Subject:	a subject that's made up of two or more subjects or nouns
EXAMPLES:	*John and Paul* wrote the song together.
Object:	the person or thing (noun or pronoun) in the sentence that the action is happening to, either directly or indirectly
EXAMPLES:	Mary bought *the shirt*. Joe hit *him*. Mary gave a gift to *Tim*.
Direct Object:	the thing that receives the action of the verb
EXAMPLE:	I see *the wall*. (The wall "receives" the action of seeing.)
Indirect Object:	the person who receives the direct object
EXAMPLE:	I wrote *her* a letter. (She receives a letter.)
Preposition:	a word that marks the relationship (in space or time) between two other words
EXAMPLES:	He received the letter *from* her. The book is *below* the chair.
Article:	a word (usually a very small word) that precedes a noun
EXAMPLES:	*a* watch, *the* room

That wasn't so bad, was it? Now let's put all those terms together in a few examples.

Dominic	spent	the	entire	night	here.
subject	verb	article	adjective	dir. obj.	adverb

Margaret	often	gives	me	money.
subject	adverb	verb	indir. obj. pronoun	dir. obj.

Alison and Rob	have	a	gorgeous	child.
compound subject	verb	article	adjective	dir. obj.

PRONOUNS

You already learned that a pronoun is a word that takes the place of a noun. Now you'll review what pronouns look like in Spanish. There are three basic types.

Subject Pronouns

These are the most basic pronouns and probably the first ones you learned. Just take a moment to look them over to make sure you haven't forgotten them. Then spend some time looking over the examples that follow until you are comfortable using them.

yo	me	**nosotros/as**	us
tú	you (singular)	**vosotros/as**	you (plural)
él, ella, Ud.	him, her, you (singular)	**ellos, ellas, Uds.**	them, you (plural)

When to Use Subject Pronouns

A subject pronoun replaces a noun (like any other pronoun). In the case of the subject pronoun, the noun replaced is the subject of the sentence.

Marco no pudo comprar el helado.

Marco couldn't buy the ice cream.

Who performs the action of this sentence? Marco—so he is the subject. If we wanted to use a subject pronoun in this case, we'd replace **Marco** with **él.**

Él no pudo comprar el helado.

He couldn't buy the ice cream.

Direct Object Pronouns
A direct object pronoun replaces (you guessed it) the direct object in a sentence.

me	me	**nos**	us
te	you (*tú* form)	**os**	you (*vosotros* form)
lo/la	him, it (masc.)/ you (*Ud.* form)/ her, it (fem.)	**los/las**	them (masc./fem.)/ you (*Uds.* form)

When to Use Direct Object Pronouns
Now let's see what it looks like when we replace the direct object with a pronoun in a sentence.

Marco no pudo comprar el helado.

What couldn't Marco buy? Ice cream. Since ice cream is what's receiving the action, it's the direct object. To use the direct object pronoun, you'd replace **helado** with **lo:**

*Marco no pudo comprar**lo**.*   or   *Marco no **lo** pudo comprar.*

When the direct object pronoun is used with the infinitive of a verb, it can either be tacked on to the end of the verb (the first example), or it can come before the conjugated verb in the sentence (the second example). Here is another example.

*Voy a ver**lo**.*   I'm going to see it.

***Lo** voy a ver.*   (Both sentences mean the same thing.)

The direct object pronoun also follows the verb in an affirmative command, for example.

¡Cómelo!	Eat it!
¡Escúchame!	Listen to me!

Indirect Object Pronouns

These pronouns replace the indirect objects in sentences. Keep in mind that in Spanish, when the object is indirect, the preposition is often implied, not explicitly stated. So how can you tell the difference? In general, the indirect object is the person who receives the direct object.

me	me	**nos**	us
te	you (*tú* form)	**os**	you
le	him, her, you (*Ud.* form)	**les**	them, you (*Ud.* form)

When to Use Indirect Object Pronouns

This may seem a bit strange, but in Spanish the indirect object pronoun is often present in a sentence that contains the indirect object noun.

*Juan **le** da el abrigo al viejo.*

Juan gives the old man the coat.

Notice that the sentence contains the indirect object noun (**viejo**) and the indirect object pronoun (**le**). This is often necessary to clarify the identity of the indirect object pronoun, or to emphasize that identity. Typically, an expression of clarification is used with the pronouns **le** and **les** and **se** (see below), but is not used with other pronouns.

*María **nos** ayudó.*	María helped us.
*Juan **me** trae el suéter.*	Juan brings me the sweater.

The identity of the indirect object is obvious with the choice of pronoun in these examples and so is not necessary for clarification. It may be used, however, to emphasize the identity of the indirect object.

> *No **me** lo trajeron a mí; **te** lo trajeron a ti.*
>
> They didn't bring it to **me**; they brought it to **you.**

We would change our intonation to emphasize these words in English. This doesn't happen in Spanish; the expressions **a mí** and **a ti** serve the same function.

Se is used in place of **le** and **les** whenever the pronoun that follows begins with **l.**

¿Le cuentas la noticia a María?	Are you telling Maria the news?
*Sí, **se** la cuento **a María.***	Yes, I'm telling it to her.
¿Les prestas los guantes a los estudiantes?	Do you lend gloves to the students?
*No, no **se** los presto **a ellos.***	No, I don't lend them to them.

Notice that **le** changes to **se** in the first example and **les** to **se** in the second because the direct object pronouns that follow begin with **l.** Notice also the inclusion of **a María** and **a ellos** to clarify the identity of **se** in each example.

Prepositional Pronouns

As we mentioned earlier, there are some pronouns that take explicitly stated prepositions, and they're different from the indirect object pronouns. The prepositional pronouns are as follows.

mí	me	**nosotros/nosotras**	us
ti	you (*tú* form)	**vosotros/vosotras**	you (plural)
él/ella/Ud.	him/her/you (*Ud.* form)	**ellos/ellas/Uds.**	them/you (plural)

When to Use Prepositional Pronouns

Consider the following examples:

1. *Cómprale un regalo de cumpleaños.*   Buy him a birthday present.

2. *Vamos al teatro sin él.*   We're going to the theater **without** him.

Notice that in the first example, "him" is translated as **le,** whereas in the second, "him" is translated as **él.** What exactly is the deal with that?! Why isn't it the same word in Spanish as in English? In Spanish, the different pronouns distinguish the different functions of the word within the sentence.

In the first example, *him* is the indirect object of the verb *to buy* (Buy the gift for whom? For him—*him* receives the direct object), so we use the indirect object pronoun **le.** In the second example, however, *him* is the object of the preposition *without,* so we use the prepositional pronoun **él.** Here are some more examples that involve the prepositional pronouns. Notice that they all have explicitly stated prepositions.

*Las flores son **para** ti.*   The flowers are **for** you.

*Estamos enojados **con** él.*   We are angry **with** him.

*Quieren ir de vacaciones **sin** Uds.*   They want to go on vacation **without** you.

In two special cases, when the preposition is **con** and the object of the preposition is **mí** or **ti,** the preposition and the pronoun are combined to form **conmigo** (with me) and **contigo** (with you).

*¿Quieres ir al concierto **conmigo**?*   Do you want to go to the concert **with me**?

*No, no puedo ir **contigo**.*   No, I can't go **with you.**

When the subject is **él, ella, ellos, ellas, Ud.,** or **Uds.,** and the object of the preposition is the **same** as the subject, the prepositional pronoun is **sí,** and is usually accompanied by **mismo/a** or **mismos/as:**

*Alejandro es muy egoísta. Siempre habla de **sí mismo.***

Alejandro is very egotistical. He always talks about **himself.**

*Ellos compran ropa para **sí mismos** cuando van de compras.*

They buy clothes for **themselves** when they go shopping.

POSSESSIVE ADJECTIVES AND PRONOUNS

Possessive adjectives and pronouns are used to indicate ownership. When you want to let someone know what's whose, use the following pronouns or adjectives:

Stressed Possessive Adjectives

mío/mía	mine	**nuestro/nuestra**	ours
tuyo/tuya	yours (fam.)	**vuestro/vuestra**	yours
suyo/suya	his, hers, yours (for *Ud.*)	**suyo/suya**	theirs, yours (for *Uds.*)

Unstressed Possessive Adjectives

mi	my	**nuestro/nuestra**	our
tu	your (fam.)	**vuestro/vuestra**	your
su	his/her/your (for *Ud.*)	**su**	their, your (for *Uds.*)

When to Use Possessive Adjectives

The first question is, "When do you use an unstressed adjective, and when do you use a stressed adjective?" Check out these examples, and then we'll see what the rule is.

> *Ésta es **mi** casa.*
> This is **my** house.
>
> *Aquí está **tu** cartera.*
> Here is **your** wallet.

> *Esta casa es **mía**.*
> This house is **mine**.
>
> *Esta cartera es **tuya**.*
> This wallet is **yours**.

The difference between stressed and unstressed possessive adjectives is emphasis, as opposed to meaning. Saying "This is my house" puts emphasis on the house, while saying "This house is mine" takes the focus off of the house and stresses the identity of its owner—me. To avoid getting confused, just remember that unstressed is the Spanish equivalent of *my* and stressed is the Spanish equivalent of *mine*.

In terms of structure, there is an important difference between the two types of adjectives, but one you should be able to remember: Stressed adjectives come after the verb, but unstressed adjectives come before the noun. Notice that neither type agrees with the possessor; they agree with the thing possessed.

If it's not clear to you why these are adjectives when they look so much like pronouns, consider their function. When you say *my house*, the noun *house* is being described by *my*. Any word that describes a noun is an adjective, even if that word looks a lot like a pronoun. The key is how it's being used in the sentence.

Possessive Pronouns

Possessive pronouns look like stressed possessive adjectives, but they mean something different. Possessive pronouns *replace* nouns; they don't *describe* them.

When to Use Possessive Pronouns

This type of pronoun is formed by combining the article of the noun that's being replaced with the appropriate stressed possessive adjective. Just like stressed possessive adjectives must agree with the nouns they describe, possessive pronouns must agree in gender and number with the nouns they replace.

> *Mi bicicleta es azul.*   *La mía es azul.*
>
> **My** bicycle is blue.   **Mine** is blue.

Notice how the pronoun not only shows possession, but also replaces the noun. Here are some more examples.

> *Mis zapatos son caros.*   *Los míos son caros.*
>
> **My** shoes are expensive.   **Mine** are expensive.
>
> *Tu automóvil es rápido.*   *El tuyo es rápido.*
>
> **Your** car is fast.   **Yours** is fast.
>
> *No me gustaban los discos que ellos trajeron.*   *No me gustaban los suyos.*
>
> I didn't like the records they brought.   I didn't like **theirs.**

Reflexive Pronouns

Remember those reflexive verbs you learned about in class (**ponerse, hacerse,** and so on)? Those all have a common characteristic, which is that they indicate the action is being done to or for oneself. When those verbs are conjugated, the reflexive pronoun (which is always **se** in the infinitive) changes according to the subject.

me	myself	**nos**	ourselves
te	yourself (fam.)	**os**	yourselves (fam.)
se	him/herself/yourself (for *Ud.*)	**se**	themselves/ yourselves (for *Uds.*)

A reflexive pronoun is used when the subject and indirect object of the sentence are the same. This may sound kind of strange, but after you see some examples it ought to make more sense.

> *Alicia se pone el **maquillaje.***
>
> **Alicia** puts on makeup.
>
> What does she put on? **Makeup**—direct object.
>
> Who receives the makeup? **Alicia**—she's also the subject.

The action is thus *reflected* back upon itself: Alicia does the action and then receives it. No outside influences are involved.

Another meaning for reflexive verbs is literally that the person does something directly to or for him/herself.

> *Rosa **se cortó** con el cuchillo.*
>
> Rosa **cut herself** with the knife.
>
> *Roberto tiene que **comprarse** una libreta nueva.*
>
> Roberto has to **buy himself** a new notebook.

The Relative Pronouns (Que, Quien, and Quienes)

A relative pronoun connects a noun or pronoun to a clause that describes the noun or pronoun. Relative pronouns may represent people, things, or ideas, and they may function as subjects, direct or indirect objects, or as objects of prepositions. Unlike in English, the relative pronouns cannot be omitted in Spanish.

Let's look at some examples with relative pronouns in their various functions.

Remember that **que** is used to refer to people and things. **Quien(es)** is used to refer only to people.

1. As a subject:

Busco el libro que estaba en mi mochila.

I am looking for the book that was in my bookbag.

2. As a direct object:

Hicimos la tarea que la profesora nos asignó.

We did the assignment that the professor gave us.

3. As an indirect object:

No conozco a la prima a quien le mandé la invitación.

I don't know the cousin to whom I sent the invitation.

4. As an object of a preposition:

Ud. no conoce a los alumnos de quienes hablo.

You don't know the students whom I am talking about.

The relative pronoun **cuyo** acts as an adjective and agrees with the noun it introduces, not the possessor.

El alumno, cuyas notas son excelentes, es un chico muy simpático.

The student, whose grades are excellent, is a very nice boy.

Interrogative Words

You probably know most of your interrogative words in Spanish by this time, but it wouldn't hurt for you to review them. Remember that they all have accents when used as parts of questions. Let's look briefly at one interrogative that students commonly misuse: **Cuál** (meaning *which* or *what*) is used when a choice is involved. It's used in place of **que** before the verb **ser**, and it has only two forms: singular (**cuál**) and plural (**cuáles**). Both **cuál** and the verb **ser** must agree in number with the thing(s) being asked about.

*¿**Cuál** es tu ciudad favorita?*	**What** is your favorite city?
*¿**Cuáles** son nuestros regalos?*	**Which** presents are ours?

Demonstratives

First, learn the construction and meaning.

este/esta	this (one)	**estos/estas**	these
ese/esa	that (one)	**esos/esas**	those
aquel/aquella	that (one over there)	**aquellos/aquellas**	those (over there)

Adjective or Pronoun—Which Is It?

If the demonstrative word comes before a noun, then it is an adjective.

***Este** plato de arroz con pollo es mío.*	**This** plate of chicken and rice is mine.
***Ese** edificio es de mi hermano.*	**That** building is my brother's.

If the demonstrative word takes the place of a noun, then it's a pronoun.

*Dije que **este** es mío.*	I said that **this one** is mine.
*Sabemos que **ese** es de mi hermano.*	We know **that one** is my brother's.

When used as adjectives, these words mean *this*, *that*, and so on. When used as pronouns, they mean *this one*, *that one*, and so on.

Pronoun Summary

You should know the following types of pronouns: subject, object (direct and indirect), possessive, prepositional, reflexive, and demonstrative.

- Don't just memorize what the different pronouns look like! Recognizing them is important, but it's just as important that you understand how and when to use them.

- When selecting your final answer choices, don't forget about POE. Something simple (like the gender of a pronoun) can be easily overlooked if you're not on your toes. Before you start thinking about grammar, eliminate answers that are wrong based on flagrant stuff like gender, singular versus plural, and so on.

- If all else fails, your ear can sometimes be your guide. In learning Spanish, you probably spoke and heard the language on a pretty regular basis, and so you have a clue as to what correct Spanish sounds like. You don't want to use your ear if you can eliminate answers based on the rules of grammar, but if you've exhausted the rules and you're down to two answers, one of which sounds a lot better than the other, choose the correct-sounding one. The fact is many grammatical rules were born out of a desire to make the language sound good.

Use the grammar rules to eliminate answers you know to be wrong, and use your ear when necessary.

Drill 1: How Well Do You Know Your Pronouns?

1. El libro es _____.

   (A) mi
   (B) mío
   (C) mía
   (D) me

2. A mí _____ gusta ir al cine.

   (A) te
   (B) mío
   (C) me
   (D) tu

3. Laura _____ ayudaba a los estudiantes con la tarea.

   (A) les
   (B) se
   (C) lo
   (D) tu

4. Ana _____ dio un premio al perro por hacer un truco.

   (A) la
   (B) lo
   (C) se
   (D) le

5. A Yamil _____ gustaban todas sus clases el año pasado.

   (A) le
   (B) les
   (C) las
   (D) la

6. José _____ dio el regalo a su novia.

   (A) le la
   (B) se le
   (C) se la
   (D) se lo

7. ¿_____ aquí es la persona famosa?

   (A) Qué
   (B) Cuál
   (C) Quién
   (D) Quienes

8. ¿Para pintar el cuarto, _____ color prefieres?

   (A) qué
   (B) cuyo
   (C) quién
   (D) por qué

Drill 2: How Well Do You Know Your Pronouns?

1. ¿Maya, quieres ir de compras _____?

   (A) conmigo
   (B) contigo
   (C) con yo
   (D) con mí

2. El automóvil es _____.

   (A) su
   (B) suya
   (C) suyo
   (D) suyos

3. ¡Tu bicicleta es nuevo, pero _____ es muy vieja!

   (A) la mia
   (B) la mía
   (C) el mío
   (D) el mio

4. ¿_____ prefieres? ¿Tacos o enchiladas?

   (A) Cuál
   (B) Por qué
   (C) Quién
   (D) Cual

5. _____ casa es nuestra.

   (A) Esta
   (B) Esto
   (C) Este
   (D) Está

6. Este barco no es mío. El mío es _____.

   (A) aquella
   (B) aquellas
   (C) aquel
   (D) aquellos

7. El doctor, _____ paciente está enfermo, le recetó antibióticos.

   (A) cuya
   (B) cuyas
   (C) cuyos
   (D) cuyo

8. Alessandra _____ ponió el maquillaje.

   (A) le
   (B) lo
   (C) la
   (D) se

Drill 3: How Well Do You Know Your Pronouns?

1. ¿_____ es tu comida favorita?

   (A) Cual
   (B) Cuáles
   (C) Cuál
   (D) Quién

2. ¿Son _____ aquellos guantes que están sobre la butaca?

   (A) mío
   (B) mía
   (C) míos
   (D) mías

3. Teresa compró almuerzo por _____ porque estaba sola.

   (A) si mismo
   (B) sí misma
   (C) sí mismo
   (D) si misma

4. Mis libros están aquí, pero _____ están allí.

   (A) vuestra
   (B) vuestro
   (C) vuestros
   (D) vuestras

5. Caminé desde mi casa al trabajo simplemente porque _____ dio la gana.

   (A) se mi
   (B) se me
   (C) se le
   (D) se lo

6. ¿_____ dieron los lápices correctos a los estudiantes para el exámen?

   (A) Los
   (B) Les
   (C) Las
   (D) Se

7. Me gustaría hacer_____ abogado.

   (A) sí
   (B) mi
   (C) se
   (D) me

8. Carolina _____ cortó el pelo.

   (A) le
   (B) se
   (C) la
   (D) lo

VERBS

You probably learned what felt like a zillion different verbs and tenses in Spanish class. For the purposes of the AP Spanish Language and Culture Exam, you should focus on recognizing clues in the sentences that suggest certain tenses, and then finding the answer in the appropriate tense. Even if you don't know which answer is in the tense that corresponds to the sentence, you can still eliminate answers that definitely aren't correct. Use POE! A brief review of the tenses that show up on the test is probably a good place to begin, so let's get right to it.

The Present Tense (aka the Present Indicative)

The present tense is the easiest, and probably the first, tense that you ever learned. It is used when the action is happening in the present, as in the following example:

> *Yo **hablo** con mis amigos cada día.*
>
> I **speak** with my friends each day.

You should know the present tense inside and out if you are enrolled in an AP Spanish class, but take a quick glance at the following verb conjugations just to refresh your memory:

	trabajar	vender	escribir
yo	trabaj**o**	vend**o**	escrib**o**
tú (fam.)	trabaj**as**	vend**es**	escrib**es**
él/ella/Ud.	trabaj**a**	vend**e**	escrib**e**
nosotros/nosotras	trabaj**amos**	vend**emos**	escrib**imos**
vosotros/vosotras (fam.)	trabaj**áis**	vend**éis**	escrib**ís**
ellos/ellas/Uds.	trabaj**an**	vend**en**	escrib**en**

The Future Tense

The future tense is used to describe things that will *definitely* happen in the future. The reason we stress definitely is that there is a different verbal mode (the dreaded subjunctive) used to describe things that *may* happen. In Spanish, just as in English, there is a difference between being certain *(I will go)* and being uncertain *(I may go)*, and different forms are used for the different degrees of certainty. You'll see the fancier stuff later. First take a look at the regular future tense.

> *Mañana yo **hablaré** con mis amigos.*
>
> Tomorrow I **will speak** with my friends.

Notice that what takes two words to say in English (*will speak*) takes only one word to say in Spanish (**hablaré**). The future is a nice, simple tense (no auxiliary verb, only one word), which should be easy to spot thanks to the accents and the structure. The future is formed by tacking on the appropriate ending to the infinitive of the verb *without dropping the -ar, -er, or -ir.*

	trabajar	**vender**	**escribir**
yo	trabajar**é**	vender**é**	escribir**é**
tú (fam.)	trabajar**ás**	vender**ás**	escribir**ás**
él/ella/Ud.	trabajar**á**	vender**á**	escribir**á**
nosotros/nosotras	trabajar**emos**	vender**emos**	escribir**emos**
vosotros/vosotras (fam.)	trabajar**éis**	vender**éis**	escribir**éis**
ellos/ellas/Uds.	trabajar**án**	vender**án**	escribir**án**

Back to the Future: the Conditional

Remember the future tense? (It's the one that is used to describe actions that are *definitely* going to happen in the future.) Well, now you will learn a tense that is used to describe things that *may* happen in the future, *if* certain other conditions are met.

The conditional describes what could, would, or might happen in the future.

> Me **gustaría** hablar con mis amigos cada día.
>
> I **would like** to talk to my friends each day.
>
> Con más tiempo, **podría** hablar con ellos el día entero.
>
> With more time, I **could** speak with them all day long.
>
> Si gastara cinco pesos, solamente me **quedarían** tres.
>
> If I spent (were to spend) five dollars, I **would have** only three left.

It can also be used to make a request in a more polite way.

> ¿**Puedes** prestar atención?   ¿**Podrías** prestar atención?
>
> **Can you** pay attention?   **Could you** pay attention?

The conditional is formed by taking the future stem of the verb (which is the infinitive) and adding the conditional ending.

	trabajar	**vender**	**escribir**
yo	trabajar**ía**	vender**ía**	escribir**ía**
tú (fam.)	trabajar**ías**	vender**ías**	escribir**ías**
él/ella/Ud.	trabajar**ía**	vender**ía**	escribir**ía**
nosotros/nosotras	trabajar**íamos**	vender**íamos**	escribir**íamos**
vosotros/vosotras (fam.)	trabajar**íais**	vender**íais**	escribir**íais**
ellos/ellas/Uds.	trabajar**ían**	vender**ían**	escribir**ían**

The accented í is in the
conditional, but not in the
future.

To avoid confusing the conditional with the future, concentrate on the conditional endings. The big difference is the accented **í**, which is in the conditional, but not in the future.

FUTURE	CONDITIONAL
trabajaré	trabajaría
venderán	venderían
escribiremos	escribiríamos

The Past Tense (aka the Preterite)

The past tense is used to describe an action that had a *definite beginning and ending in the past* (as opposed to an action that may be ongoing), as in the following example:

*Ayer yo **hablé** con mis amigos.*

Yesterday I **spoke** with my friends. (The action began and ended.)

There are many different tenses that are considered past tenses—all of which describe actions that took place at various points in the past. There are, for example, different tenses for saying *I spoke, I was speaking, I have spoken,* and so on. Let's start by reviewing the most basic of these: the simple past tense.

	trabajar	**vender**	**escribir**
yo	trabaj**é**	vend**í**	escrib**í**
tú (fam.)	trabaj**aste**	vend**iste**	escrib**iste**
él/ella/Ud.	trabaj**ó**	vend**ió**	escrib**ió**
nosotros/nosotras	trabaj**amos**	vend**imos**	escrib**imos**
vosotros/vosotras (fam.)	trabaj**asteis**	vend**isteis**	escrib**isteis**
ellos/ellas/Uds.	trabaj**aron**	vend**ieron**	escrib**ieron**

The easiest forms to spot are the first and third person singular (**yo** and **él/ella/Ud.** forms) because of the accents.

The Imperfect

The imperfect is another past tense. It is used to describe actions that occurred continuously in the past and exhibited no definitive end at that time. This is different from the preterite, which describes "one-time" actions that began and ended at the moment in the past being described. Look at the two together, and the difference between them will become clearer.

To decide preterite vs. imperfect, ask yourself whether you have a "one-time" event or an ongoing one.

> *Ayer **yo hablé** con mis amigos y luego **me fui.***
>
> Yesterday **I spoke** with my friends and then **left.**
>
> (The act of speaking obviously ended, because I left afterward.)
>
> *Yo **hablaba** con mis amigos mientras **caminábamos.***
>
> **I spoke** with my friends while **we walked.**
>
> (The act of speaking was **in progress** at that moment, along with walking.)

The imperfect is also used to describe conditions or circumstances in the past, since these are obviously ongoing occurrences.

> ***Era** una noche oscura y tormentosa.*
>
> **It was** a dark and stormy night.
>
> *Cuando **tenía** diez años…*
>
> When **I was** ten years old…

In the first example, it didn't just start or just stop being a stormy night, did it? Was the dark and stormy night already a past event at that point? No. The dark and stormy night was **in progress** at that moment, so the imperfect is used, not the preterite.

In the second example, did I start or stop being ten years old at that point? Neither. Was being ten already a past event at the moment I am describing? No. I was simply in the process of being ten years old at that moment in the past, so the imperfect is the more precise tense to use.

Make sense? Good; now check out the conjugation.

	trabajar	vender	escribir
yo	trabaj**aba**	vend**ía**	escrib**ía**
tú (fam.)	trabaj**abas**	vend**ías**	escrib**ías**
él/ella/Ud.	trabaj**aba**	vend**ía**	escrib**ía**
nosotros/nosotras	trabaj**ábamos**	vend**íamos**	escrib**íamos**
vosotros/vosotras (fam.)	trabaj**abais**	vend**íais**	escrib**íais**
ellos/ellas/Uds.	trabaj**aban**	vend**ían**	escrib**ían**

Although the imperfect is similar to the other past tenses you've seen (e.g., the preterite and the present perfect) because it speaks of past actions, it looks quite different. That's the key, since half of your job is just to know what the different tenses look like. The toughest part will be distinguishing the preterite from the imperfect.

The Present Perfect

The present perfect is used to refer to an action that began in the past and is continuing into the present (and possibly beyond). It is also used to describe actions that were completed very close to the present. Compare these sentences.

<table>
<tr><td>1.</td><td>

*Ayer **hablé** con mis amigos.*
Yesterday **I spoke** with my friends.
***Decidiste** no ir al cine.*
You decided not to go to the movies.
</td></tr>
<tr><td>2.</td><td>

***He hablado** mucho con mis amigos recientemente.*
I have spoken a lot with my friends lately.
***Has decidido** hacerte abogado.*
You have decided (recently) to become a lawyer.
</td></tr>
</table>

The first examples are just the plain past tense: I started and finished talking with my friends yesterday, and you completed the process of deciding not to go to the movies. In the second examples, the use of the present perfect tense moves the action to the very recent past, instead of leaving it in the more distant past. The present perfect, then, is essentially a more precise verb form of the past, used when the speaker wants to indicate that an action happened very recently in the past.

Look for words like **ayer** or **recientemente** to help decide which tense to use.

Spotting the perfect tenses can be rather easy. This is a compound tense, meaning that it is formed by combining two verbs: a tense of the auxiliary (or helping) verb **haber** (present, imperfect, future, conditional) and the past participle of the main verb.

	trabajar	vender	escribir
yo	**he** trabaj**ado**	**he** vend**ido**	**he** escrito
tú (fam.)	**has** trabaj**ado**	**has** vend**ido**	**has** escrito
él/ella/Ud.	**ha** trabaj**ado**	**ha** vend**ido**	**ha** escrito
nosotros/nosotras	**hemos** trabaj**ado**	**hemos** vend**ido**	**hemos** escrito
vosotros/vosotras (fam.)	**habéis** trabaj**ado**	**habéis** vend**ido**	**habéis** escrito
ellos/ellas/Uds.	**han** trabaj**ado**	**han** vend**ido**	**han** escrito

Any time there is a helping verb, no matter the tense, the participle will be the same.

Most past participles are formed by dropping the last two letters from the infinitive and adding **-ido** (for **-er** and **-ir** verbs) or **-ado** (for **-ar** verbs). **Escribir** has an irregular past participle, as do some other verbs, but don't worry about it. This is no problem, since the irregulars still look and sound like the regulars, and, with respect to this tense, you still know it's the present perfect because of **haber.**

The Subjunctive

Don't give up now! Just two more verb modes (not tenses—the subjunctive is a different *manner* of speaking) and you'll be done with all this verb business (give or take a couple of special topics).

The Present Subjunctive

The present subjunctive is used in sentences that have *two distinct subjects* in *two different clauses*, generally (on this test, at least) in four situations.

For the subjunctive, look for expression of desire or emotion.

1. When a *desire* or *wish* is involved.
    *Quiero que **comas** los vegetales.*
    I want you **to eat** the vegetables.
    *Ordenamos que Uds. nos **sigan**.*
    We order you (pl.) **to follow** us.
2. When *emotion* is involved.
    *Me alegro que **haga** buen tiempo hoy.*
    I am happy that the weather **is** nice today.
    *Te enoja que tu novio nunca te **escuche**.*
    It makes you angry that your boyfriend never **listens** to you.

3. When *doubt* is involved.
   *Ellos no creen que **digamos** la verdad.*
   They don't believe that **we are telling** the truth.
   *Jorge duda que su equipo **vaya** a ganar el campeonato.*
   Jorge doubts that his team **is going** to win the championship.

4. When an *impersonal expression* or *subjective commentary* is made.
   *Es ridículo que no **pueda** encontrar mis llaves.*
   It's ridiculous that I **can't** find my keys.
   *Es importante que los estudiantes **estudien** mucho.*
   It's important that students **study** a lot.

The subjunctive is formed by taking the **yo** form of the present tense, dropping the -**o**, and adding the appropriate ending.

	trabajar	vender	escribir
yo	trabaj**e**	vend**a**	escrib**a**
tú (fam.)	trabaj**es**	vend**as**	escrib**as**
él/ella/Ud.	trabaj**e**	vend**a**	escrib**a**
nosotros/nosotras	trabaj**emos**	vend**amos**	escrib**amos**
vosotros/vosotras (fam.)	trabaj**éis**	vend**áis**	escrib**áis**
ellos/ellas/Uds.	trabaj**en**	vend**an**	escrib**an**

The Present Perfect Subjunctive

The important thing to remember about Spanish grammar is that grammar builds upon itself. To understand this next concept, you should have a strong knowledge of the previous one. Do you remember the present perfect from the previous section? Hope so! As you know, it is a compound tense made up of the auxiliary verb **haber** and the past participle of the main verb. You can apply this in the present subjunctive and it becomes the *present perfect subjunctive*. Just be sure you know all the forms of **haber** in present subjunctive: **haya, hayas, haya, hayamos, hayáis, hayan.** The past participles are the same in all the perfect tenses: **dicho, hecho, hablado, roto,** and so on. So memorize them! On the AP exam, graders want to see diversity in the tenses you use, and utilizing an advanced form of a perfect tense will look impressive.

Here are a few examples of the present perfect subjunctive using some examples you saw previously.

Still the same participle!

---

1. **Present subjunctive**
   *Te enoja que tu novio nunca te **escuche**.*
   It makes you angry that your boyfriend never **listens** to you.
   Present perfect subjunctive
   *Te enoja que tu novio nunca te **haya escuchado**.*
   It makes you angry that your boyfriend **has** never **listened** to you.

2. **Present subjunctive**
   *Ellos no creen que **digamos** la verdad.*
   They don't believe that **we are telling** the truth.
   Present perfect subjunctive
   *Ellos no creen que **hayamos dicho** la verdad.*
   They don't believe that **we have told** the truth.

Commands

Commands are very similar to the present subjunctive form, perhaps because they are an obvious attempt to tell someone what to do. Let's look briefly at the formation of the regular commands.

	hablar	**comer**	**subir**
tú (fam.)	habla, no hables	come, no comas	sube, no subas
él/ella/Ud.	hable	coma	suba
nosotros/nosotras	hablemos	comamos	subamos
vosotros/vosotras (fam.)	hablad, no habléis	comed, no comáis	subid, no subáis
ellos/ellas/Uds.	hablen	coman	suban

Remember: The affirmative **tú** form derives from the third person present singular tense, except for the verbs that are irregular in the **tú** form. The affirmative **vosotros** form comes from the infinitive: the 'r' is dropped and the 'd' is added. All other command forms come from the subjunctive. *¡Muy fácil!*

¡Trabaja con tu padre!   **¡Vende** el coche!   **¡Escribe** la carta!

Work with your father!   **Sell** the car!   **Write** the letter!

The Imperfect Subjunctive

This version of the subjunctive is used with the same expressions as the present subjunctive (wish or desire, emotion, doubt, impersonal commentaries), but it's used in the past tense.

*Quería que **comieras** los vegetales.*
I wanted you **to eat** the vegetables.
*Me alegré que **hiciera** buen tiempo ayer.*
I was happy that the weather **was** nice yesterday.
*No creían que **dijéramos** la verdad.*
They didn't believe that **we told** the truth.
*Era ridículo que no **pudiera** encontrar mis llaves.*
It was ridiculous that **I couldn't** find my keys.

One very important thing to notice in the examples above is that because the *expression* is in the past, you use the imperfect subjunctive. If you're looking at a sentence that you know takes the subjunctive, but you're not sure whether it's present or imperfect, focus on the expression. If the expression is in the present, use the present subjunctive. If the expression is in the past, use the imperfect subjunctive.

The imperfect subjunctive is also always used after the expression **como si,** which means "as if." This expression is used to describe hypothetical situations.

*Él habla como si **supiera** todo.*

He speaks as if **he knew** it all.

*Gastamos dinero como si **fuéramos** millonarios.*

We spend money as if **we were** millionaires.

The imperfect subjunctive is formed by taking the **ellos/ellas/Uds.** form of the preterite (which you already know, right?), removing the **-on,** and adding the correct ending.

	trabajar	vender	escribir
yo	trabaj**ara**	vend**iera**	escrib**iera**
tú (fam.)	trabaj**aras**	vend**ieras**	escrib**ieras**
él/ella/Ud.	trabaj**ara**	vend**iera**	escrib**iera**
nosotros/nosotras	trabaj**áramos**	vend**iéramos**	escrib**iéramos**
vosotros/vosotras (fam.)	trabaj**arais**	vend**ierais**	escrib**ierais**
ellos/ellas/Uds.	trabaj**aran**	vend**ieran**	escrib**ieran**

Verbs that are in the imperfect subjunctive shouldn't be too tough to spot when they show up in the answer choices. The imperfect subjunctive has completely different endings from the preterite. It's not a compound tense, so you won't confuse it with the present perfect. The stems are different from the present subjunctive, so distinguishing between those two shouldn't be a problem.

The Past Perfect Subjunctive

As with the present perfect subjunctive, you can extend your knowledge of the imperfect subjunctive to apply to a more advanced grammar point that graders like to see from time to time on the exam. Just one correct use of the past perfect subjunctive can elevate your score and can demonstrate mastery. Just be sure you know all the forms of **haber** in the imperfect subjunctive: **hubiera, hubieras, hubiera, hubiéramos, hubierais, hubieran.** Again, the past participles are the same in all the perfect tenses: **dicho, hecho, hablado, roto,** and on and on. So be sure to memorize them!

Here are a few examples of the past perfect subjunctive from previous examples.

> This is a tricky one: Ask yourself whether there was a question in the past about whether or not it would happen. If there was ever question, use the past perfect subjunctive.

1. **Imperfect subjunctive**
   *No creían que **dijéramos** la verdad.*
   They didn't believe that **we told** the truth.
   Past perfect subjunctive
   *No creían que **hubiéramos dicho** la verdad.*
   They didn't believe that **we had told** the truth.
2. **Imperfect subjunctive**
   *Era ridículo que no **pudiera** encontrar mis llaves.*
   It was ridiculous that **I couldn't** find my keys.
   Past perfect subjunctive
   *Era ridículo que no **hubiera podido** encontrar mis llaves.*
   It was ridiculous **that I hadn't been able** to find my keys.

Special Topics

Remember, is it a one-time event or an ongoing one?

Preterite versus Imperfect

This may be the bout of the century, amigos! By now you probably have spent a long time in class (and in your head) debating which to use. When we study grammar, we learn how to form the verb and when to use the tense. One reason this concept confuses students is because the preterite, with all of its irregulars and exceptions, can be difficult to form—whereas the imperfect can seem a little easier to form, with **-aba** and **-ía** as a base and only 3 irregulars. However, when we think about when to use them, the preterite wins the round with its simplicity.

Generally speaking, you use the preterite to express an action that happened once in the past. More specifically,

- For actions that can be viewed as single events
  Ellos vinieron a las ocho.
  They came at eight o'clock.
- For actions that were repeated a specific number of times
  Ayer escribí cinco cartas.
  Yesterday I wrote five letters.
- For actions that occurred during a specific period of time
  Vivimos allí por tres años.
  We lived there for three years.
- For actions that were part of a chain of events
  Ella se levantó, se bañó y salió de la casa.
  She got up, bathed, and left the house.
- To state the beginning or the end of an action
  Empezó a llover a las siete de la mañana.
  It began to rain at seven in the morning.

The imperfect is a bit more diverse in its application.

- For actions that were repeated habitually
  Cenábamos juntos todos los días.
  We would eat dinner together every day.
- For actions that "set the stage" for another past action
  Yo jugaba cuando entró mi papá.
  I was playing when my papa entered. (Note that *entered* is preterite.)
- For telling time
  Eran las seis de la noche.
  It was six o'clock at night.
- For stating one's age
  La niña tenía siete años.
  The little girl was seven years old.
- For mental states (usually)
  José tenía miedo de estar en público.
  José was afraid to be in public.

- For physical sensations (usually)
  Me gustaba el libro.
  I liked the book. (The book was pleasing to me.)
- To describe the characteristics of people, things, or conditions
  (usually more permanent features of the objects described)
  Era una señorita muy alta.
  She was a tall young lady.

Ser versus *Estar*

The verbs **ser** and **estar** both mean *to be* when translated into English. You may wonder, "Why is it necessary to have two verbs that mean exactly the same thing?" Good question. The answer is that in Spanish, unlike in English, there is a distinction between temporary states of being (e.g., *I am hungry*) and fixed, or permanent states of being (e.g., *I am Cuban*). Although this difference seems pretty simple and easy to follow, there are some cases when it isn't so clear. Consider the following examples:

> *El señor González _____ mi doctor.*
>
> *Cynthia _____ mi novia.*

> **Ser** = permanent states of being
>
> **Estar** = temporary states of being

Would you use **ser** or **estar** in these two sentences? After all, Cynthia may or may not be your girlfriend forever, and the same goes for Mr. González's status as your doctor. You may get rid of both of them tomorrow (or one of them may get rid of you)! So which verb do you use?

In both cases, the answer is **ser,** because in both cases there is no *foreseeable* end to the relationships described. In other words, even though they may change, nothing in either sentence gives any reason to think they will. So whether you and Cynthia go on to marry or she dumps you tomorrow, you would be correct if you used **ser.** When in doubt, ask yourself, "does this action/condition have a definite end in the near or immediate future?" If so, use **estar.** Otherwise, use **ser.** Try the following drill.

Drill 1: Ser vs. Estar

Fill in each blank with the correct form of **ser** or **estar.**

1. El regalo _____ para ti.

2. _____ enojados con el profesor. (nosotros)

3. _____ un tipo muy simpático.

4. Él ____ muy alto y _____ encima del techo.

5. La computadora _____ funcionando.

6. _____ listos para el examen. (ellos)

7. Las manzanas _____ deliciosas.

8. Los estudiantes _____ jóvenes.

Answers: 1) es 2) Estamos 3) Es 4) es.....está 5) está 6) Están 7) son 8) son

Don't assume that certain adjectives (like **enfermo,** for example) necessarily take **estar.** If you're saying someone is sick as in *ill,* then **estar** is appropriate. If you're saying that someone is sick, as in, *a sickly person,* then **ser** is correct.

Unfortunately, usage is not the only tough thing about **ser** and **estar.** They are both irregular verbs. Spend a little time reviewing the conjugations of **ser** and **estar** before you move on.

---

estar

present: estoy, estás, está, estamos, estáis, están

preterite: estuve, estuviste, estuvo, estuvimos, estuvistéis, estuvieron

pres. subj.: esté, estés, esté, estemos, estéis, estén

imp. subj.: estuviera, estuvieras, estuviera, estuviéramos, estuvierais, estuvieran

---

The other tenses of **estar** follow the regular patterns for **-ar** verbs.

```
        ser

   present:   soy, eres, es, somos, sois, son

 imperfect:   era, eras, era, éramos, erais, eran

 preterite:   fui, fuiste, fue, fuimos, fuistéis, fueron

pres. subj.:  sea, seas, sea, seamos, seáis, sean

 imp. subj.:  fuera, fueras, fuera, fuéramos, fuerais, fueran
```

The other tenses of **ser** follow the regular patterns for **-er** verbs.

Drill 2: Ser vs. Estar

1. Mi película favorita _____ dirigido por Guillermo del Toro.

    (A) estuve
    (B) es
    (C) era
    (D) fue

2. Los enchiladas _____ muy ricos, pero ahora mi estómago _____ contento.

    (A) fueron….está
    (B) fueron….es
    (C) eran…está
    (D) eran…es

3. Yo _____ de los Estados Unidos pero ahora _____ en México.

    (A) estoy…fui
    (B) soy…estoy
    (C) sería…estoy
    (D) soy…estaba

4. La falda de ella _____ muy bonita.

    (A) son
    (B) esté
    (C) está
    (D) es

5. Camilla _____ triste cuando su gato se murió.

    (A) está
    (B) era
    (C) estaba
    (D) es

6. Ella _____ rubia y _____ contenta.

   (A) está…es
   (B) es…sea
   (C) es…está
   (D) era…está

7. _____ una noche gloriosa y tranquila.

   (A) Estaba
   (B) Eran
   (C) Está
   (D) Era

8. Fernando _____ mi esposo.

   (A) es
   (B) son
   (C) está
   (D) estuve

Answers: 1) fue 2) fueron…está 3) soy…estoy 4) es 5) estaba 6) es…está 7) Era 8) es

Drill 3: Ser vs. Estar

1. ¿Dónde _____ ellos?

   (A) están
   (B) son
   (C) eran
   (D) estaba

2. ¿_____ él aburrido o cansado?

   (A) Era
   (B) Es
   (C) Está
   (D) Esté

3. Puerto Rico _____ una isla en el Mar Caribe.

   (A) era
   (B) es
   (C) fue
   (D) está

4. Fútbol _____ el deporte nacional de México.

   (A) era
   (B) fue
   (C) está
   (D) es

5. Mis padres _____ muy sabios.

   (A) es
   (B) son
   (C) están
   (D) está

6. Este momento puede _____ lo más importante del juego.

   (A) ser
   (B) estar
   (C) es
   (D) está

7. He _____ enferma por tres días.

   (A) soy
   (B) estoy
   (C) sido
   (D) estado

8. Los zapatos _____ míos.

   (A) son
   (B) están
   (C) es
   (D) soy

Answers: 1) están 2) Está 3) es 4) es 5) son 6) ser 7) estado 8) son

Conocer versus Saber

As you probably remember from Spanish I, there is another pair of verbs that have the same English translation but are used differently in Spanish. However, don't worry; knowing when to use them is really very straightforward.

> **Conocer** is for knowing people.
>
> **Saber** is for knowing facts.

The words **conocer** and **saber** both mean *to know*. In Spanish, knowing a person or a thing (basically, a noun) is different from knowing a piece of information. Compare the uses of **conocer** and **saber** in these sentences.

> ¿*Sabes* cuánto cuesta la camisa?
>
> **Do you know** how much the shirt costs?
>
> ¿*Conoces* a mi primo?
>
> **Do you know** my cousin?
>
> *Sabemos* que Pelé era un gran futbolista.
>
> **We know** that Pelé was a great soccer player.
>
> *Conocemos* a Pelé.
>
> **We know** Pelé.

When what's known is a person, place, or thing, use **conocer**. It's like the English *to be acquainted with*. When what's known is a fact, use **saber**. The same basic rule holds for questions.

> ¿*Sabe* a qué hora llega el presidente?
>
> **Do you know** at what time the president arrives?
>
> ¿*Conoce* al presidente?
>
> **Do you know** the president?

Now that you know how they're used, take a look at their conjugations.

> **conocer**
>
> **present:** conozco, conoces, conoce, conocemos, conocéis, conocen
>
> **pres. subj.:** conozca, conozcas, conozca, conozcamos, conozcáis, conozcan

The other tenses of **conocer** follow the regular **-er** pattern.

> **saber**
>
> **present:** sé, sabes, sabe, sabemos, sabéis, saben
>
> **preterite:** supe, supiste, supo, supimos, supistéis, supieron
>
> **future:** sabré, sabrás, sabrá, sabremos, sabréis, sabrán
>
> **conditional:** sabría, sabrías, sabría, sabríamos, sabríais, sabrían
>
> **pres. subj.:** sepa, sepas, sepa, sepamos, sepáis, sepan
>
> **imp. subj.:** supiera, supieras, supiera, supiéramos, supieráis, supieran

Drill 1: Saber vs. Conocer

In the following drill, fill in each blank with the correct form of **conocer** or **saber**:

1. Yo _____ a un músico ayer durante el ensayo.

2. Ellos _____ que necesitan trabajar más para obtener mejores notas.

3. Ellos no les _____.

4. Me gustaría _____ a Marc Anthony.

5. Yo _____ ayer que vivimos en la misma ciudad.

6. Ella _____ que debe estudiar mucho para la clase de química.

7. Tú no _____ a los jugadores de quienes hablo.

8. Yo no _____ la respuesta correcta.

Answers: 1) conocí 2) saben 3) conocí 4) conocer 5) supe 6) sabe 7) conoces 8) sé

Drill 2: Saber vs. Conocer

1. No _____ al director del departamento. (yo)

2. No _____ si voy a ir a la playa este fin de semana.

3. Nosotros no _____ si el profesor está enfermo o de vacaciones.

4. Vosotros _____ bien a los profesores de filosofía.

5. ¿_____ usted dónde está el restaurante nuevo?

6. Espero que yo _____ el presidente de Argentina.

7. ¡Él _____ cocinar muy bien!

8. Sí, ella y yo nos _____ bien.

Answers: 1) conozco 2) sé 3) sabemos 4) conocéis 5) Sabe 6) conozca 7) sabe 8) conocemos

Verb Summary

The tenses you need to know are the present, past, future, and perfect tenses; you also need to know the subjunctive mode (both present and imperfect) as well as the commands. In terms of memorizing and reviewing them, we think the best approach is to lump them together in the following way:

Present Tense	Past Tenses	Future Tenses	Subjunctive	Commands
Present	Preterite	Future	Present	
	Imperfect	Conditional	Imperfect	
	Present perfect			

By thinking in terms of these groupings, you'll find that eliminating answers is a snap once you've determined the tense of the sentence. That is your first step on a question that tests your knowledge of verb tenses: Determine the tense of the sentence (or at least whether it's a past, present, or future tense), and eliminate.

When memorizing the uses of the different tenses, focus on clues that point to one tense or another.

- There are certain expressions (wish or desire, emotion, doubt, and impersonal commentaries) that tell you to use the subjunctive, and whether the expression is in the present or the past will tell you which subjunctive form to use.

- To distinguish between future and conditional, focus on the certainty of the event's occurrence.

- The three past tenses are differentiated by the end (or lack thereof) of the action and when that end occurred. If the action had a clear beginning and ending in the past, use the regular past. If the action was a continuous action in the past, use the imperfect. If the action began in the past and is continuing into the present, or ended very close to the present, use the present perfect.

- Recognizing the different tenses shouldn't be too tough if you focus on superficial characteristics.

- Certain tenses have accents, while others do not.

- Review all the verb forms by studying your textbook.

Drill 1: How Well Do You Know Your Verbs?

1. Ojalá que _____ mañana.

    (A) lloverá
    (B) llueve
    (C) llueva
    (D) llovió

2. _____ un barco nuevo ayer.

    (A) Compraste
    (B) Compres
    (C) Comprarías
    (D) Comprares

3. ¡_____ la tarea!

    (A) Haces
    (B) Haz
    (C) Hiciste
    (D) Harías

4. Eduardo _____ mucho tiempo jugando el fútbol.

    (A) pasado
    (B) he pasado
    (C) ha pasado
    (D) pasaron

5. Esperaba que nosotros _____ un paseo por el parque, pero llueve ahora.

    (A) dábamos
    (B) dimos
    (C) damos
    (D) diéramos

6. Mañana _____ el partido de fútbol.

    (A) asistí
    (B) asisto
    (C) asistiré
    (D) asistía

7. No creo que _____ odiarte nunca.

    (A) pueda
    (B) puedo
    (C) pudiera
    (D) podré

8. El fin de semana pasado, nosotros _____ a Cancún.

    (A) iremos
    (B) iríamos
    (C) fuiste
    (D) fuimos

Drill 2: How Well Do You Know Your Verbs?

1. _____ una noche oscura y nublado cuando él llegó a casa.

   (A) Fue
   (B) Era
   (C) Es
   (D) Estaba

2. Me gustaría que me _____ al concierto de Tito Puentes.

   (A) acompañaste
   (B) acompañaras
   (C) acompañas
   (D) acompañes

3. Es importante lavar los dientes. _____ los dientes, por favor. (tú)

   (A) Lavas
   (B) Lávese
   (C) Lávate
   (D) Lavarse

4. Era triste que Javier no _____ el premio.

   (A) gana
   (B) gane
   (C) ganó
   (D) ganara

5. ¡Estoy alegre de que usted _____ venir!

   (A) puede
   (B) podrá
   (C) pueda
   (D) podría

6. Es cierto que ella _____ pelo rojo.

   (A) tiene
   (B) tenga
   (C) tuve
   (D) tuviera

7. Es la mejor película que _____ en mi vida.

   (A) he visto
   (B) ha visto
   (C) haya visto
   (D) hubiera visto

8. Por supuesto que _____ a la escuela mañana.

   (A) irías
   (B) irás
   (C) fuiste
   (D) fuera

Drill 3: How Well Do You Know Your Verbs?

1. Por favor, _____ la cama. (tú)

   (A) haz
   (B) haga
   (C) hiciste
   (D) hará

2. Paso mucho tiempo _____ por el parque.

   (A) corro
   (B) correr
   (C) corriendo
   (D) corre

3. Me _____ conocerse mejor.

   (A) gusto
   (B) gustaría
   (C) gusta
   (D) gustaba

4. Sus padres dijeron que _____ mejor comer la cena antes del postre.

   (A) ha sido
   (B) haya sido
   (C) he sido
   (D) hubiera sido

5. Gabriela _____ a la sala mientras sus hermanos _____ televisión.

   (A) entró…miraban
   (B) entraba…miraban
   (C) entraba…miraron
   (D) entró…miraron

6. Julio no quiere que ella _____ la verdad.

   (A) dice
   (B) diga
   (C) dirá
   (D) diría

7. Es importante _____ eficazmente.

   (A) sabe escribir
   (B) saber a escribir
   (C) saber escribiendo
   (D) saber escribir

8. No sé si Rodrigo _____ cocinar.

   (A) sabe
   (B) sepa
   (C) supiera
   (D) sabía

PREPOSITIONS

A preposition is a little word that shows the relationship between two other words. In English, prepositions are words such as *to, from, at, for, about,* and so on. In Spanish, they're words like **a, de, sobre,** and so on.

Part of what you need to know about prepositions is what the different ones mean. The other thing you need to know is how and when to use them. You need to know which verbs and expressions take prepositions and which prepositions they take. This shouldn't be too difficult to learn, but it can be tricky.

Common Prepositions and Their Uses

- **a:** to; at

  ¿Vamos a la obra de teatro esta noche?   *Llegamos a las cinco.*

  Are we going to the play tonight?   We arrived at 5:00.

- **de:** of; from

  Son las gafas de mi hermano.   *Soy de la Argentina.*

  Those are my brother's glasses.   I am from Argentina.
  (Literally, the glasses of my brother.)

- **con:** with

  Me gusta mucho el arroz con pollo.

  I like chicken with rice a lot.

- **sobre:** on; about; over

  La chaqueta está sobre la mesa.

  The jacket is on the table.

  La conferencia es sobre la prevención del SIDA.

  The conference is about AIDS prevention.

  Los Yankees triunfaron sobre los Braves en la serie mundial.

  The Yankees triumphed over the Braves in the World Series.

- **antes de:** before

  Antes de salir quiero ponerme un sombrero.

  Before leaving I want to put on a hat.

- **después de:** after

  Después de la cena me gusta caminar un poco.

  After dinner I like to walk a little.

- **en:** in

  Regresan en una hora.

  They'll be back in an hour.

  Alguien está en el baño.

  Someone is in the bathroom.

- **entre:** between

  La carnicería está entre la pescadería y el cine.

  The butcher shop is between the fish store and the cinema.

  La conferencia duró entre dos y tres horas.

  The conference lasted between two and three hours.

- **durante:** during; for

  Durante el verano me gusta nadar cada día.

  During the summer I like to swim each day.

  Trabajé con mi amigo durante quince años.

  I worked with my friend for fifteen years.

- **desde:** since; from

  He tomado vitaminas desde mi juventud.

  I've been taking vitamins since childhood.

  Se pueden ver las montañas desde aquí.

  The mountains can be seen from here.

Para versus *Por*

The prepositions **para** and **por** both mean *for* (as well as other things, depending on context), but they are used for different situations, and so they tend to cause a bit of confusion. Luckily, there are some pretty clear-cut rules as to when you use **para** and when you use **por,** because they both tend to sound fine even when they're being used incorrectly. Try to avoid using your ear when choosing between these two.

When to Use *Para*

The following are examples of the most common situations in which **para** is used. Instead of memorizing some stuffy rule, we suggest that you get a feel for what types of situations imply the use of **para,** so that when you see those situations come up on your AP Spanish Language and Culture Exam, you'll recognize them.

The preposition **para,** in very general terms, expresses the idea of *destination,* but in a very broad sense.

- **Destination in time**
  *El helado es **para** mañana.*
  The ice cream is for tomorrow. (Tomorrow is the ice cream's destination.)
- **Destination in space**
  *Me voy **para** el mercado.*
  I'm leaving for the market. (The market is my destination.)
- **Destination of purpose**
  *Compraste un regalo **para** Luis.*
  You bought a gift for Luis. (Luis is the destination of your purchase.)
  *Estudiamos **para** sacar buenas notas.*
  We study to get good grades. (Good grades are the destination of our studies.)
- **Destination of work**
  *Trabajo **para** IBM.*
  I work for IBM. (IBM is the destination of my work.)

Two uses of **para** do not indicate a sense of destination.

- **To express opinion**
  ***Para** mí, el lunes es el día más largo de la semana.*
  For me, Monday is the longest day of the week.
- **To qualify or offer a point of reference**
  ***Para** un muchacho joven, tiene muchísimo talento.*
  For a young boy, he has a lot of talent.

When to Use *Por*

Chances are, if you're not discussing destination in any way, shape, or form, and you're not engaging in the other two uses of **para,** then you'll need to use **por.** If this general rule isn't enough for you, however, study the following possibilities and you should have all the bases covered.

- **To express how you got somewhere (by)**
  *Fuimos a Italia **por** barco.*
  We went to Italy by boat.
  *Pasamos **por** esa tienda ayer cuando salimos del pueblo.*
  We passed by that store yesterday when we left the town.

- **To describe a trade (in exchange for)**
  *Te cambiaré mi automóvil **por** el tuyo este fin de semana.*
  I'll trade you my car for yours this weekend.

- **To lay blame or identify cause (by)**
  *Todos los barcos fueron destruidos **por** la tormenta.*
  All the boats were destroyed by the storm.

- **To identify gain or motive (for; as a substitute for)**
  *Ella hace todo lo posible **por** su hermana.*
  She does everything possible for her sister.
  *Cuando Arsenio está enfermo, su madre trabaja **por** él.*
  When Arsenio is ill, his mother works (as a substitute) for him.

Drill 1: Por vs. Para

1. Caminaba _____ el parque con mi esposo.

2. _____ obtener notas buenas, necesitas estudiar más.

3. ¿_____ cuánto tiempo dura la película?

4. _____ mí, prefiero pasar tiempo con mis amigos.

5. Tenéis que comprar verduras frescas _____ la fiesta.

6. _____ el Día de los Muertos, vamos a celebrar con nuestra familia.

7. Los automóviles fueron construidos _____ los alemanes.

8. Cambiaré mi pieza de chocolate _____ tu galleta.

Answers: 1) por 2) Para 3) Por 4) Para 5) para 6) Para 7) por 8) por.

Drill 2: Por vs. Para

1. La canción fue escrito _____ ella.

2. Tengo que comprar un regalo _____ el cumpleaños de mi prima.

3. Necesito un motor nuevo _____ reparar el coche.

4. Él fue a la oficina de correos _____ mandar una tarjeta de cumpleaños.

5. El grupo de estudiantes caminaban _____ los pasillos de la escuela.

6. Prefiero ir a Nueva York _____ tren.

7. _____ comenzar, gracias _____ asistir la reunión.

8. Debemos gastar dinero _____ comprar una casa.

Answers: 1) por 2) para 3) para 4) para 5) por 6) por 7) Para...por 8) para

Ir a and *Acabar de*

Ir a is used to describe what the future will bring, or, in other words, what is going to happen. The expression is formed by combining the appropriate form of **ir** in the present tense (subject and verb must agree) with the preposition **a.**

> *Mañana **vamos a** comprar el árbol de Navidad.*
>
> Tomorrow we are going to buy the Christmas tree.
>
> *¿**Vas a** ir a la escuela aun si te sientes mal?*
>
> You're going to go to school even if you feel ill?

Acabar de is the Spanish equivalent of *to have just,* and is used to talk about what has just happened. It is formed just like **ir a,** with the appropriate form of **acabar** in the present tense followed by **de.**

> ***Acabo de** terminar de cocinar el pavo.*
>
> I have just finished cooking the turkey.
>
> *Ellos **acaban de** regresar del mercado.*
>
> They have just returned from the supermarket.

Other Prepositions to Remember

Other prepositions and prepositional phrases you should know follow. Notice that many of these are merely adverbs with **a** or **de** tacked on to the end to make them prepositions.

hacia	toward
enfrente de	in front of
frente a	in front of
dentro de	inside of
fuera de	outside of

a la derecha de	to the right of
a la izquierda de	to the left of
debajo de	underneath
encima de	above, on top of
alrededor de	around, surrounding
en medio de	in the middle of
hasta	until
tras	behind
cerca de	near
lejos de	far from
detrás de	behind
(a)delante de	in front of
al lado de	next to

Preposition Summary

- Much of your work with prepositions boils down to memorization: which expressions and verbs go with which prepositions, and so on.

- You should concentrate on the boldfaced examples at the beginning of the preposition section since those are the most common. Once you're comfortable with them, the subsequent list should be a snap because many of those expressions are merely adverbs with **a** or **de** after them.

- Some verbs take prepositions all the time, some never do, and others sometimes do. This isn't as confusing as it may sound, however, because prepositions (or lack thereof) change the meanings of verbs. Consider the following:

Voy a tratar _____ despertarme más temprano.

(A) a
(B) de
(C) con
(D) sin

Which one of these goes with **tratar**? Actually, each of them does, depending on what you are trying to say. In this case you want to say *try to*, so **de** is the appropriate preposition. **Tratar con** means *to deal with*, and **tratar sin** means *to try/ treat without*, while **tratar a** doesn't mean anything unless a person is mentioned afterward; in which case it means *to treat*. None of them makes sense in this sentence. The moral of the story is don't try to memorize which verbs go with which prepositions; concentrate on meaning.

Drill 1: How Well Do You Know Your Prepositions?

1. Tenemos una reservación de restaurante _____ las ocho.

    (A) en
    (B) por
    (C) a
    (D) de

2. Ana va a casarse _____ Raul.

    (A) con
    (B) de
    (C) a
    (D) por

3. Estoy enamorado _____ ti.

    (A) de
    (B) con
    (C) a
    (D) por

4. Ellos _____ regresar a casa.

    (A) fueron de
    (B) acaban a
    (C) acaban de
    (D) hacia

5. El techo está _____ la casa.

    (A) dentro de
    (B) encima de
    (C) al lado de
    (D) frente a

6. Sigue derecho _____ al norte hasta que llegues a la ciu-
    dad.

    (A) hasta
    (B) frente
    (C) tras
    (D) hacia

7. El jardín está _____ la casa.

    (A) para
    (B) debajo de
    (C) fuera de
    (D) acabar de

8. Maya y Alejandro fueron de compras _____ obtener
    nueva ropa.

    (A) de
    (B) a
    (C) por
    (D) para

Drill 2: How Well Do You Know Your Prepositions?

1. El perro se escondió _____ la aspiradora.

   (A) al lado de
   (B) dentro de
   (C) lejos de
   (D) encima de

2. Olivia toca el piano muy bien _____ una chica joven.

   (A) por
   (B) para
   (C) a
   (D) que

3. Es un juego _____ niños, pero a mí me encanta el escondite en el parque.

   (A) para
   (B) por
   (C) con
   (D) de

4. Argentina es _____ Rusia.

   (A) al lado
   (B) en frente de
   (C) cerca de
   (D) lejos de

5. _____ ahora, he estudiado mucho.

   (A) Acabo de
   (B) Hacia
   (C) Hasta
   (D) Tras de

6. La película _____ la vida de un hombre buscando su destino.

   (A) sobre de
   (B) durante
   (C) en vez de
   (D) trata de

7. _____ nosotros, tenemos un compromiso.

   (A) Entre
   (B) Encima de
   (C) Con
   (D) Sin

8. _____ mí, hay demasiado drama entre las chicas adolescentes.

   (A) Adelante de
   (B) Hacia
   (C) Para
   (D) Por

Drill 3: How Well Do You Know Your Prepositions?

1. La cena está _____ la mesa.

   (A) debajo de
   (B) encima de
   (C) dentro de
   (D) enfrente de

2. Busco _____ unos platos para la cena.

   (A) a
   (B) por
   (C) para
   (D) no se necesita una preposición

3. Me gusta relajar un poco cuando estoy _____ casa.

   (A) dentro de
   (B) en
   (C) a
   (D) en frente de

4. Escuchaba a una lectura _____ tomaba apuntes.

   (A) sobre
   (B) para
   (C) durante
   (D) mientras

5. Fui al parque _____ completar el día de trabajo.

   (A) después de
   (B) al lado de
   (C) en frente de
   (D) acababo de

6. Caterina le gusta andar _____ las montañas.

   (A) por
   (B) para
   (C) a
   (D) encima de

7. El cuarto de baño está _____ dormitorio.

   (A) dentro del
   (B) encima del
   (C) al lado del
   (D) acaba del

8. _____ salir, Eva se puso el maquillaje.

   (A) Antes de
   (B) Después de
   (C) Durante de
   (D) En medio de

ANSWERS AND EXPLANATIONS FOR QUIZZES

Drill 1: How Well Do You Know Your Pronouns? (Page 144)

1.   The book is _____.

   (A) my
   (B) mine (m.)
   (C) mine (f.)
   (D) me

The correct word should be *mine* and should agree with **el libro**, which is masculine. Therefore, the correct answer is (B).

2.   I enjoy going to the movies.

   (A) you
   (B) mine
   (C) me
   (D) you

The verb **gustar** is used in a reflexive form to show that something is pleasing to the person. Since the sentence says **A mí,** the answer should be in the **yo** form. Eliminate (A) and (D). The answer should be an indirect object pronoun, so the correct answer is (C).

3.   Laura _____ helped the students with their homework.

   (A) les
   (B) se
   (C) lo
   (D) tu

The pronoun here refers to the students, who are the indirect object in the sentence. Eliminate (C) (direct object) and (D) (**tú** form). Remember that **se** is only used when it is followed by a direct object pronoun beginning with **l.** Since that's not the case here, eliminate (B). The correct answer is (A).

4.   Ana _____ gave a treat to the dog for doing a trick.

   (A) la
   (B) lo
   (C) se
   (D) le

The pronoun refers to the dog, which is the indirect object in the sentence. Eliminate (A) and (B) because they are direct object pronouns. Remember that **se** is only used when it is followed by a direct object pronoun beginning with **l.** Since that's not the case here, eliminate (C). The correct answer is (D).

5. Yamil _____ enjoyed all his classes last year.

   (A) **le**
   (B) les
   (C) las
   (D) la

The verb **gustar** has a backwards construction: its subject is that which pleases, and its object is the person who is pleased. So the subject of **gustar** here is **todas sus clases,** and the indirect object (with which this pronoun must agree) is Yamil. Since he is singular, choose **le.** The correct answer is (A).

6. José _____ gave the present to his girlfriend.

   (A) le la
   (B) se le
   (C) se la
   (D) **se lo**

In this sentence, there are both an indirect and a direct object pronoun. When both are present and the direct object pronoun begins with **l,** use **se** for the indirect, so eliminate (A). The indirect object pronoun will come first and then the second will be a direct object pronoun, so eliminate (B) because **le** is indirect. José's girlfriend is the indirect object (a great way to tell which object is the indirect is that it's the object after a preposition such as *to, from, for, with,* etc.) and **el regalo** is the masculine direct object. Since the direct object is masculine, the correct response is (D).

7. _____ here is the famous person?

   (A) Qué
   (B) Cuál
   (C) **Quién**
   (D) Quienes

Since the question refers to a person, eliminate (A) and (B), which both refer to things. The famous person is singular, so the correct answer is (C).

8. To paint the room, _____ color do you prefer?

   (A) **qué**
   (B) cuyo
   (C) quién
   (D) por qué

In English, *what* or *which* would be acceptable. Eliminate (B), *whose,* (C), *who,* and (D), *why.* The correct answer is (A).

Drill 2: How Well Do You Know Your Pronouns? (Page 145)

1. Maya, would you like to go shopping _____?

    (A) conmigo
    (B) contigo
    (C) con yo
    (D) con mí

The correct pronoun for *with me* in Spanish is **conmigo:** one word, rather than two. The correct answer is (A).

2. The car is _____.

    (A) su
    (B) suya
    (C) suyo
    (D) suyos

The car is singular and masculine, so the correct answer is (C).

3. Your bicycle is new, but _____ is ancient!

    (A) la mia
    (B) la mía
    (C) el mío
    (D) el mio

La bicicleta is singular and feminine, so eliminate (C) and (D). The pronoun needs an accent, so (B) is correct.

4. _____ do you prefer? Tacos or enchiladas?

    (A) Cuál
    (B) Por qué
    (C) Quién
    (D) Cual

The question is asking *which* the person prefers, so eliminate (B) and (C) because they ask *Why* and *Who* respectively. When asking a question, there needs to be an accent on **cuál,** so (A) is correct.

5. _____ house is ours.

    (A) Esta
    (B) Esto
    (C) Este
    (D) Está

Casa is feminine, so the answer must also be feminine. Eliminate (B) and (C). Choice (D) is a verb form of **estar,** not a pronoun, so eliminate this choice as well. The correct answer is (A).

6. This boat is not mine. Mine is _____.

   (A) aquella
   (B) aquellas
   (C) aquel
   (D) aquellos

The boat is singular and masculine. Therefore, (C) is the correct answer.

7. The doctor, _____ patient is sick, gave him/her antibiotics.

   (A) cuya
   (B) cuyas
   (C) cuyos
   (D) cuyo

El paciente is singular and masculine (even though the noun can be feminine): you can tell because the adjective **enfermo** is used later in the sentence. Therefore (D) is the correct response.

8. Alessandra ____ put on makeup.

   (A) le
   (B) lo
   (C) la
   (D) se

Ponerse is a reflexive verb and here it is used in the third person, so **se** is the correct form of the pronoun. Choice (D) is the correct answer.

Drill 3: How Well Do You Know Your Pronouns? (Page 146)

1. _____ is your favorite food?

   (A) Cual
   (B) Cuáles
   (C) Cuál
   (D) Quién

When asking a question, there should be an accent on the question word, so eliminate (A). The subject is singular and a thing (not a person), so eliminate (B) and (D). The correct answer is (C).

2. Are those _____ gloves that are on the armchair?

   (A) mío
   (B) mía
   (C) míos
   (D) mías

Guantes is masculine and plural (which you can also tell by looking at **aquellos**), so (C) is correct.

3. Teresa bought lunch for _____ because she was alone.

   (A) si mismo
   (B) sí misma
   (C) sí mismo
   (D) si misma

The correct idiom to express *him-* or *herself* is **sí mismo/misma.** Teresa is a feminine name and the adjective **sola** is used, so eliminate (A) and (C). There should be an accent on **sí,** so the correct answer is (B).

4. My books are here, but _____ are there.

   (A) vuestra
   (B) vuestro
   (C) vuestros
   (D) vuestras

The pronoun needs to match **libros,** which is plural and masculine. Therefore, the correct answer is (C).

5. I walked from my house to work simply because it pleased
_____ to.

(A) se mi
(B) se me
(C) se le
(D) se lo

Darse la gana is a reflexive verb phrase. Since this sentence is in first person, there should be a first person pronoun in the sentence. Eliminate (C) and (D). **Mi** is a possessive pronoun and **me** is reflexive, so (B) is the correct answer.

6. Did they give the correct pencils to the students for the
exam?

(A) Los
(B) Les
(C) Las
(D) Se

This sentence contains both a direct object **(los lápices)** and an indirect object **(los estudiantes)**. The one that must be accompanied by a pronoun is the indirect object, so eliminate (A) and (C), the direct object pronouns. Since **se** is only used when both the indirect and direct object pronouns are present (and the direct object pronoun begins with **l**), the correct answer is (B).

7. I would like to become a lawyer.

(A) sí
(B) mi
(C) se
(D) me

The verb **hacerse** is reflexive and is used in the context of becoming a member of a profession. Since the subject is *I*, a first-person pronoun is needed, so eliminate (A) and (C). **Me** is the reflexive pronoun, so the correct answer is (D).

8. Carolina _____ cut her hair.

(A) le
(B) se
(C) la
(D) lo

Cortarse is a reflexive verb, and Carolina is a third-person subject. Since this is the case, **se** is the correct pronoun. The correct answer is (B).

Drill 1: How Well Do You Know Your Verbs? (Page 168)

1. May it _____ tomorrow.

   (A) lloverá
   (B) llueve
   (C) llueva
   (D) llovió

The expression **ojalá** indicates subjunctive, so the correct answer must be (C).

2. _____ a new boat yesterday.

   (A) Compraste
   (B) Compres
   (C) Comprarías
   (D) Comprares

The clue for time in this sentence is **ayer,** meaning *yesterday,* so the verb must be in past tense. Choice (A) is the simple preterite, so keep this choice. Choice (B) is simple present, so eliminate it. **Comprarías** is conditional and **comprares** is future, so eliminate these choices as well. The correct answer is (A).

3. _____ the homework!

   (A) Haces
   (B) Haz
   (C) Hiciste
   (D) Harías

This is a command, so the verb must be in the command form, whether formal or informal. Therefore, the correct verb must be **Haz** or **Hace.** Only one of these is present, so (B) is the correct response.

4. Eduardo _____ a lot of time playing soccer.

   (A) pasado
   (B) he pasado
   (C) ha pasado
   (D) pasaron

The sentence is not very clear about the tense, but the subject is singular and third person. Eliminate (A) because this is only the participle without a helping verb that is conjugated. In (B), **he** is first person, so eliminate this choice too. Choice (C) is in the third person, so keep it, and eliminate (D) because it is a plural form. The correct answer is (C).

5. I hoped that we _____ a walk through the park, but
    now it's raining.

    (A) dábamos
    (B) dimos
    (C) damos
    (D) diéramos

The clue here is **Esperaba que,** which indicates desire and therefore must be followed by the subjunctive. Since **Esperaba** is imperfect, the imperfect subjunctive is necessary. Therefore, (D) is the correct answer.

6. Tomorrow _____ the soccer game.

    (A) asistí
    (B) asisto
    (C) asistiré
    (D) asistía

There is a time trigger here: **Mañana.** Therefore, the verb must be in the future tense. Choice (A) is first person preterite, so eliminate this choice. Choice (B) is in the present tense, which is incorrect as well. Choice (C) is in the future, so keep this choice. Choice (D) is the imperfect, so eliminate this one as well. The correct answer is (C).

7. I don't believe _____ ever hate you.

    (A) pueda
    (B) puedo
    (C) pudiera
    (D) podré

The phrase **No creo que** needs subjunctive because it expresses doubt. Eliminate (B) and (D) since they are indicative. **Creo** is present tense, so the subjunctive should also be present. Therefore, (A) is correct.

8. Last weekend, we _____ to Cancún.

    (A) iremos
    (B) iríamos
    (C) fuiste
    (D) fuimos

The time trigger here is **El fin de semana pasado,** which indicates past tense. Eliminate (A) and (B). Choice (C) is in the tú form, but the sentence contains **nosotros.** Only (D) agrees.

Drill 2: How Well Do You Know Your Verbs? (Page 169)

1. _____ a dark and cloudy night when he returned home.

   (A) Fue
   (B) Era
   (C) Es
   (D) Estaba

There is a preterite verb at the end of the sentence, so there must also be a past-tense verb at the beginning of the sentence. Eliminate (C). When setting the stage, as in this sentence, use the imperfect tense. Eliminate (A), which is preterite. Between **ser** and **estar, ser** is the correct verb to use here. Therefore, (B) is the correct answer.

2. I would like that _____ me to the Tito Puentes concert.

   (A) acompañaste
   (B) acompañaras
   (C) acompañas
   (D) acompañes

The beginning of the sentence expresses desire, so use the subjunctive. Eliminate (A) and (C). The sentence uses the conditional, indicating that the concert is in the future, so use the present subjunctive. Therefore, (D) is the correct answer.

3. It is important to brush your teeth. _____ your teeth, please. (tú)

   (A) Lavas
   (B) Lávese
   (C) Lávate
   (D) Lavarse

This sentence needs the informal form, so eliminate (B) and (D). The sentence is a command, so eliminate (A), which is the simple present tense. The correct answer is (C).

4. It was sad that Javier did not _____ the prize.

   (A) gana
   (B) gane
   (C) ganó
   (D) ganara

Since this sentence expresses emotion, use the subjunctive. The only choice here is **ganara,** so the correct answer is (D).

5.   I am happy that you _____ come!

(A) puede
(B) podrá
(C) pueda
(D) podría

This sentence shows emotion, so use the subjunctive here. The only option for subjunctive is (C).

6.   It is certain that she _____ red hair.

(A) tiene
(B) tenga
(C) tuve
(D) tuviera

Since the sentence shows certainty, do not use the subjunctive, but rather use the indicative. The sentence is in the present, so use the simple present tense. The correct answer is (A).

7.   It is the best movie that _____ in my life.

(A) he visto
(B) ha visto
(C) haya visto
(D) hubiera visto

The clue here is **mi vida,** so the verb needs to be first person. Eliminate (B). Since it is clear that the person saw the movie, the indicative is needed. Eliminate (C) and (D), and the correct answer is (A).

8.   Of course _____ to school tomorrow.

(A) irías
(B) irás
(C) fuiste
(D) fuera

The sentence has a trigger word **mañana,** so eliminate the past tense choices (C) and (D). Choice (A) contains the conditional and (B) contains the future tense. Since there is not a **si** clause in the sentence, there is no need for the conditional. Choice (B) is correct.

Drill 3: How Well Do You Know Your Verbs? (Page 170)

1. Please, _____ the bed. (tú)

    (A) haz
    (B) haga
    (C) hiciste
    (D) hará

This is a command, and it must be in the informal form. Therefore, (A) is correct.

2. I spend a lot of time _____ through the park.

    (A) corro
    (B) correr
    (C) corriendo
    (D) corre

There is already a conjugated verb in the sentence without a **que:** usually this means the sentence will use an infinitive or a progressive tense. Eliminate (A) and (D). It does not make sense to use the infinitive; the meaning would be *I spend a lot of time to run*, so the progressive is the correct choice. Choice (C) is correct.

3. I would like to know you better. (formal)

    (A) gusto
    (B) gustaría
    (C) gusta
    (D) gustaba

The conditional is used as a formality with the verb **gustar** to express want or desire. Therefore, (B) is correct.

4. Their parents said to them _____ better to eat dinner before dessert.

    (A) ha sido
    (B) haya sido
    (C) he sido
    (D) hubiera sido

The parents expressed preference in the past, though it is not certain that the children did what the parents suggested they do. Therefore, use the subjunctive; eliminate (A) and (C). Since the first part of the sentence is in past tense, use a past subjunctive. Choice (D) is correct.

5. Gabriela _____ the room while her brothers _____ television.

    (A) entró…miraban
    (B) entraba…miraban
    (C) entraba…miraron
    (D) entró…miraron

Gabriela did a singular action while her brothers did a continual action, both in the past. The singular action should be expressed with the preterite, while the continual action should be expressed with the imperfect. Therefore, (A) is correct.

6. Julio does not want for her _____ the truth.

    (A) dice
    (B) diga
    (C) dirá
    (D) diría

Julio expresses desire in the first part of the sentence, so use the subjunctive. The only option here is (B).

7. It is important _____ effectively.

    (A) sabe escribir
    (B) saber a escribir
    (C) saber escribiendo
    (D) saber escribir

There is already a conjugated verb in the sentence: this usually indicates the need for an infinitive or a progressive tense. Eliminate (A) since **sabe** is conjugated. In English, the sentence is trying to say *It is important to know how to write effectively,* so there are two infinitives needed. Eliminate (C) because it contains a progressive tense instead. Since the infinitive already includes the *to* in it, the **a** in Spanish is not necessary. Choice (D) is correct.

8. I don't know whether Rodrigo _____ to cook.

    (A) sabe
    (B) sepa
    (C) supiera
    (D) sabía

Since the sentence is expressing doubt, use the subjunctive. Eliminate (A) and (D). Since the first part of the sentence is in the present tense, (B) is correct.

Drill 1: How Well Do You Know Your Prepositions? (Page 177)

1. We have a restaurant reservation _____ eight o'clock.

   (A) en
   (B) por
   (C) a
   (D) de

When talking about a meeting time, use **a** to replace the English *at*. Choice (C) is correct.

2. Ana is going to marry _____ Raul.

   (A) con
   (B) de
   (C) a
   (D) por

The correct idiom is **casarse con,** which is a bit counterintuitive to English speakers. Therefore, (A) is correct.

3. I am in love _____ you.

   (A) de
   (B) con
   (C) a
   (D) por

The correct idiom for *in love with* is **enamorada/o de.** The correct answer is (A).

4. They _____ returned home.

   (A) fueron de
   (B) acaban a
   (C) acaban de
   (D) hacia

This sentence is a bit tricky. The infinitive **regresar** comes right after the blank, so there must be a conjugated verb in the blank. Eliminate (D), since there is not a verb there. **Fueron** means *they went,* which does not make sense in the sentence, so eliminate (A) as well. The correct idiom between (B) and (C) is **de,** meaning *to have just* done something. The correct answer is (C).

5.   The roof is _____ the house.

(A) dentro de
(B) encima de
(C) al lado de
(D) frente a

The roof of a house should be above the house. Choice (A) means *inside,* so eliminate this choice. Choice (B) works, so keep it. Choice (C) means *next to,* and (D) means *in front of,* so eliminate these too. Choice (B) is correct.

6.   Continue straight _____ the north until you arrive at the city.

(A) hasta
(B) frente
(C) tras
(D) hacia

The meaning of the word should be along the lines of *toward* the north. **Hasta** means *until,* so eliminate (A). Choice (B) is close: *facing,* but it is not idiomatically correct, so eliminate this choice as well. **Tras** means *through,* which does not make sense in context: eliminate (C). The only word that means *toward* is **hacia.** The correct answer is (D).

7.   The garden is _____ the house.

(A) para
(B) debajo de
(C) fuera de
(D) acabar de

The garden is most likely *outside* the house, though there may be some exceptions. **Para** does not work here because with it, the sentence means *The garden is in order to the house,* so eliminate (A). The garden would not be *underneath* the house, so eliminate (B) as well. Keep (C), since it matches the prediction of *outside* the house. Choice (D) does not make sense grammatically, roughly translating to *to have just the house.* Choice (C) is correct.

8.   Maya and Alejandro went shopping _____ get new clothes.

(A) de
(B) a
(C) por
(D) para

Maya and Alejandro went shopping *in order to* get new clothes. Whenever it works to use *in order to* in the sentence, use **para.** The correct answer is (D).

Drill 2: How Well Do You Know Your Prepositions? (Page 179)

1. The dog hid itself _____ the vacuum.

    (A) al lado de
    (B) dentro de
    (C) lejos de
    (D) encima de

If the dog is hiding from the vacuum, it wants to get *away* from the vacuum. Only **lejos de** puts space between the dog and the vacuum, so the correct answer is (C).

2. Olivia plays the piano very well _____ a young child.

    (A) por
    (B) para
    (C) a
    (D) que

The English translation would be *for a young child*. Therefore, this is a **por** vs. **para** question. The correct idiom for this type of sentence is **para,** so (B) is correct.

3. It is a game _____ children, but I love hide-and-seek in the park.

    (A) para
    (B) por
    (C) con
    (D) de

It is a game for children; the word *for* here tells you that this is a **por** vs. **para** question. The correct idiom here is **para** because it is *intended for* children. The correct answer is (A).

4. Argentina is _____ Russia.

    (A) al lado
    (B) en frente de
    (C) cerca de
    (D) lejos de

Argentina is not *next to* Russia, so eliminate (A), which is also missing a word **(de).** It is not *in front of* Russia either, so eliminate (B). Since it is not *near* or *around* Russia, eliminate (C) as well. The correct answer is (D), meaning *far from* Russia.

5. _____ now, I have studied a lot.

    (A) Acabo de
    (B) Hacia
    (C) Hasta
    (D) Tras de

The sentence intends to say *until now,* so the correct idiom to express this in Spanish is **Hasta ahora.** Choice (A) does not make sense in context (*to have just now*), and neither does (B), *towards now.* Choice (D) means *behind,* so this is incorrect as well. The correct answer is (C).

6. The movie _____ the life of a man in search of his destiny.

    (A) sobre de
    (B) durante
    (C) en vez de
    (D) trata de

To express that a movie, book, play, etc. is *about* something, use the idiom **tratar de.** The correct answer is (D).

7. _____ us, we have an agreement.

    (A) Entre
    (B) Encima de
    (C) Con
    (D) Sin

We have an agreement *between* us. Therefore, the proper preposition is **entre.** The correct answer is (A).

8. _____ me, there is too much drama amongst adolescent girls.

    (A) Adelante de
    (B) Hacia
    (C) Para
    (D) Por

The phrase *For/to me* to express *in my opinion* in Spanish is **para mí.** Therefore, (C) is correct.

Drill 3: How Well Do You Know Your Prepositions? (Page 180)

1. The dinner is _____ the table.

   (A) debajo de
   (B) encima de
   (C) dentro de
   (D) enfrente de

Hopefully dinner is not *under, inside,* or *in front of* the table, eliminating (A), (C), and (D) respectively. Choice (B) is correct.

2. I am in search of _____ some plates for dinner.

   (A) a
   (B) por
   (C) para
   (D) no se necesita una preposición

The verb **buscar** means *to look for*, so there is no preposition needed. The preposition is already part of the verb itself. Choice (D) is correct.

3. I enjoy relaxing a bit when I am _____ home.

   (A) dentro de
   (B) en
   (C) a
   (D) en frente de

To express *at home,* the correct idiom is **en casa,** making (B) correct. The idiom is not *inside the house,* so eliminate (A). Choice (C) is used when a person is going home, not when a person is already at home. Choice (D) does not make much sense in context *(in front of the house).* Choice (B) is correct.

4. I was listening to a lecture _____ I was taking notes.

   (A) sobre
   (B) para
   (C) durante
   (D) mientras

Sobre means *over,* which does not make sense in this context, since one thing is happening while another thing is also happening in this sentence. **Para** does not work either, since one does not listen to a lecture *in order to* take notes, eliminating (B). **Durante** is tempting, but the correct idiom is **mientras.** The correct answer is (D).

5. I went to the park _____ to complete the workday.

    (A) después de
    (B) al lado de
    (C) en frente de
    (D) acababo de

There are not many clues here, though there is most likely a time trigger since the work day is complete. **Después de** works because one could go to the park *after* the workday. Keep (A). Choice (B) does not make sense because one could not go to the park *next to* complete the workday. Eliminate (B). Choice (C) makes the same error as (B), showing spatial orientation, so eliminate this one as well. Choice (D) carries the right intention, but it is idiomatically and grammatically incorrect, conjugating a second verb without a **que** in the sentence. Choice (A) is correct.

6. Caterina enjoys walking _____ the mountains.

    (A) por
    (B) para
    (C) a
    (D) encima de

This is a **por** vs. **para** question. Here, the idiom is to *walk through* the mountains, so use **por** to express this. The correct answer is (A).

7. The bathroom is _____ bedroom.

    (A) dentro del
    (B) encima del
    (C) al lado del
    (D) acaba del

The bathroom hopefully is not *inside* or *on top of the* bedroom, so eliminate (A) and (B) respectively. Choice (C) makes sense: *next to the* bedroom. Choice (D) does not make sense in the sentence: *to have just the* bedroom. The correct answer is (C).

8. _____ leaving, Eva put on makeup.

    (A) Antes de
    (B) Después de
    (C) Durante de
    (D) En medio de

One would assume that Eva put on makeup *before* leaving, so the correct answer is (A).

REFLECT

Respond to the following questions:

- Of which topics discussed in this chapter do you feel you have achieved sufficient mastery to use effectively in an essay?

- On which topics discussed in this chapter do you feel you need more work before you can use them effectively in an essay?

- Of which topics discussed in this chapter do you feel you have achieved sufficient mastery to use effectively in a spoken response?

- On which topics discussed in this chapter do you feel you need more work before you can use them effectively in a spoken response?

- What parts of this chapter are you going to re-review?

- Will you seek further help, outside this book (such as from a teacher, tutor, or AP Students), on any of the content in this chapter—and if so, on what content?

Part V
Practice Tests

Practice Test 1

Following are the audio track numbers for **Practice Test 1.**

- Track 7: Selección 1 (Fuente 2)

- Track 8: Selección 2 (Fuente 2)

- Track 9: Selección 3

- Track 10: Selección 4

- Track 11: Selección 5

- Track 12: Presentational Writing (Fuente 3)

- Track 13: Interpersonal Speaking: Conversation

It's a good idea to have a device handy with which to record and time yourself for the speaking sections.

Good luck!

AP® Spanish Language and Culture

SECTION I: Multiple-Choice Questions

DO NOT OPEN THIS BOOKLET UNTIL YOU ARE TOLD TO DO SO.

Instructions

Section I of this examination contains 65 multiple-choice questions. Fill in only the ovals for numbers 1 through 65 on your answer sheet.

Indicate all of your answers to the multiple-choice questions on the answer sheet. No credit will be given for anything written in this exam booklet, but you may use the booklet for notes or scratch work. After you have decided which of the suggested answers is best, completely fill in the corresponding oval on the answer sheet. Give only one answer to each question. If you change an answer, be sure that the previous mark is erased completely. Here is a sample question and answer.

<table>
<tr><td>Sample Question</td><td>Sample Answer</td></tr>
</table>

Chicago is a   Ⓐ ● Ⓒ Ⓓ
(A) state
(B) city
(C) country
(D) continent

Use your time effectively, working as quickly as you can without losing accuracy. Do not spend too much time on any one question. Go on to other questions and come back to the ones you have not answered if you have time. It is not expected that everyone will know the answers to all the multiple-choice questions.

About Guessing

Many candidates wonder whether or not to guess the answers to questions about which they are not certain. Multiple choice scores are based on the number of questions answered correctly. Points are not deducted for incorrect answers, and no points are awarded for unanswered questions. Because points are not deducted for incorrect answers, you are encouraged to answer all multiple-choice questions. On any questions you do not know the answer to, you should eliminate as many choices as you can, and then select the best answer among the remaining choices.

At a Glance

Total Time
1 hour and 35 minutes
Number of Questions
65
Percent of Total Grade
50%
Writing Instrument
Pencil required

Part A

Interpretive Communication: Print Texts

You will read several selections. Each selection is accompanied by a number of questions. For each question, choose the response that is best according to the selection and mark your answer on your answer sheet.	Vas a leer varios textos. Cada texto va acompañado de varias preguntas. Para cada pregunta, elige la mejor respuesta según el texto e indícala en la hoja de respuestas.

Selección número 1

Introducción

La siguiente entrevista apareció en una revista latinoamericana en junio 2014.

Este profesor de Educación Física, de 35 años y oriundo de Santiago de Chile, hizo realidad un sueño que muchos bailarines caribeños anhelan: ser bicampeón mundial de rumba. ¡Y en Europa! Hace ya casi diez años, Cristian Vera dejó su país y se trasladó a España para ejercer su profesión y también su gran pasión: la danza. En dicho continente ha viajado por múltiples países enseñando este baile tropical y participando también en diferentes competencias. Anécdotas y experiencias tiene muchas. Aquí podemos conocer algunas.

¿Cómo llega un chileno a convertirse en bicampeón mundial de rumba?

En Barcelona se realiza cada año el festival cubano más importante de Europa; y en ese evento se lleva a cabo una competencia de carácter mundial denominada "Buscando al rumbero". Es un concurso individual donde cada competidor, proveniente de distintos lugares del mundo, muestra su talento en el baile. En mi primera participación, en 2011, salí segundo y luego logré dos años seguidos el primer lugar. Después de eso, me convertí en el primer profesor no cubano en enseñar folclore en ese festival.

¿Cómo llegaste a la rumba? ¿Qué fue lo que te motivó a practicar esta disciplina?

Lo que me inspiró fue una película: "Dance With Me"; ahí vi a los protagonistas bailando salsa en Cuba. La verdad es que siempre tuve el baile en la sangre porque toda mi familia se dedica a esto. Cada día, cuando me levanto tengo deseos de bailar; y sigo teniendo las mismas ganas y energía que al inicio. Por eso, además, me he ido perfeccionando en la danza. Cada día voy aprendiendo algo nuevo de distintos tipos de bailes.

¿Por qué has desarrollado tu carrera en Europa?

En el año 2007 me fui becado a la Universidad ITK de Leipzig para realizar un postgrado en Ciencias Aplicadas al fútbol. Luego de eso, estuve tres meses en España realizando una pasantía en el club Villareal, que era dirigido en ese momento por Manuel Pellegrini. Ahí el preparador físico del equipo me habló de un máster que él había hecho en Barcelona. Por eso luego de volver a Chile y trabajar un tiempo, junté dinero y emprendí rumbo nuevamente a la Madre Patria para inscribirme en ese curso de especialización.

¿Crees tú que este tipo de baile es hoy más popular en Europa que en Latinoamérica?

En el Viejo Continente tienen una ventaja: los países están cerca y los vuelos no son costosos. De esta forma, los bailarines y aficionados a danzas como la salsa pueden viajar a diferentes competencias y festivales. Los concursos tienen gran éxito porque a la gente no solo le apasiona el baile sino que además tienen la posibilidad de acudir en masa. Hay mucha demanda.

Los bailes latinos son alegres y sensuales. ¿Es eso lo que le gusta al europeo de estos ritmos?

Los europeos, en general, son disciplinados y en el caso de la danza se enfocan bastante en tratar de conocer a fondo la cultura del baile. Muchos, incluso, aprenden español para entender las canciones; no solo quieren bailar y hacer una mímica. Yo creo que todos los europeos que aprenden a bailar danzas cubanas quieren ir a conocer Cuba.

¿Y qué impresión se lleva la gente cuando ve a un bailarín chileno enseñando salsa cubana?

Yo nunca he estado en Cuba. Pero mucha gente me pregunta cómo es posible que baile con ritmo y estilo tan marcadamente tropical. Me confunden con cubano, y no precisamente por mi acento, sino por mi forma de bailar. Te puede jugar en contra, por supuesto, porque hay un tema de tradición y referencia con los cubanos, pero creo que aquel que se la juega por esto y lo siente en la piel, va a tener éxito.

GO ON TO THE NEXT PAGE.

¿Te ves o te sientes como un embajador en Europa de la salsa?

El cubano es muy celoso de su cultura. Cuando saben que yo bailo salsa, pueden tener una especie de prejuicio al principio. Pero una vez que me ven en la pista de baile, todo cambia. Yo espero que me juzguen siempre por lo que hago. Y en ese sentido, he logrado ganar el respeto de los grandes maestros cubanos de la salsa. Me parece que más que un embajador propiamente tal, me gusta verme como una persona que ha podido dar el ejemplo de que si se puede bailar salsa o rumba sin ser cubano. Me gusta poder representar a toda esa gente.

---

1. ¿Quién es Christian Vera?

   (A) Un maestro cubano de la salsa

   (B) Un profesor chileno de rumba y salsa que vive en España

   (C) Un profesor español de rumba y salsa que vive en Cuba

   (D) Un maestro chileno de la salsa

2. ¿Por qué les gustan a los europeos los ritmos latinos?

   (A) Porque son alegres y sensuales

   (B) Porque es más fácil conquistar las mujeres con el baile

   (C) Porque pueden conocer la cultura de Cuba

   (D) Porque ofrecen contrasto a la disciplina que existe en Europa

3. ¿Cómo llegó Vera a la rumba?

   (A) Era una parte fundamental de su cultura.

   (B) Era una parte integral de su familia, y entonces su padre le enseñó.

   (C) Pasó un rato en Cuba para aprender la rumba.

   (D) Vio una película de baile latino y fue inspirado por ella.

4. ¿Por qué ha desarrollado su carrera en España?

   (A) Había estudiado en Europa con una beca cuando conoció a un maestro en Barcelona.

   (B) Pasó parte de su infancia en Europa y quería regresar.

   (C) Aprendió el baile en Latinoamérica primero y decidió a moverse a España.

   (D) Es el primer enseñador no cubano en enseñar el folclore cubano.

5. ¿Cómo aceptan los otros bailarines al chileno cuando baila la salsa?

   (A) Los europeos lo aceptan como cubano.

   (B) Al principio hay un poco de prejuicio, pero todo cambia cuando Vera está bailando.

   (C) Nunca puede bailar tan bien como los cubanos.

   (D) Siempre le aceptan como un cubano sin preguntas.

6. ¿Qué responde Vera al entrevistador a la última pregunta?

   (A) Responde que sí, es el embajador oficial a Cuba.

   (B) Responde que no, es demasiado presión para él.

   (C) Responde que sí, desea ser el embajador de baile para todos.

   (D) Responde que no, los cubanos no lo aceptan cuando está en la pista de baile.

GO ON TO THE NEXT PAGE.

Selección número 2

Introducción

El siguiente artículo apareció en 2009 en una revista del cine Español.

Política, Películas y Poder en España

El cine español es el pulso político de España. Aparte de ser uno de los países más grandes del cine experimental, es uno que había expresado los triunfos y los fracasos del gobierno.

En 1929, Luis Buñuel y Salvador Dalí hicieron la cinta *Un Chien Andalou* para expresar sus sentimientos radicales hacia el estado de España y la modernización del mundo. Ellos, en su cinta surrealista, trataron de ilustrar el impacto de la modernización de la mujer, la religión y el estado. Cuando comenzó la Segunda República, los ciudadanos socialistas rechazaron tradiciones españolas como la iglesia católica y la monarquía, a favor del mismo industrialismo e innovación con que trata esta película de Buñuel y Dalí. Durante la Segunda República se dio el comienzo de la libertad política en España, y la película refleja la nueva manumisión de expresión religiosa y política. Desafortunadamente, después de la Guerra Civil en España, la dictadura de Franco censuró la mayoría de los cineastas.

Durante el régimen de Francisco Franco, que empezó en el 1939, el gobierno controlaba las redes de comunicación y la mayoría del cine, pero algunos directores pudieron evitar la censura por medio de la sátira. Maestros del cine, como Luis García Berlanga y Juan Antonio Bardem crearon obras que por fuera parecían estar lejos de los temas políticos, pero en realidad ridiculizaban la sociedad alta y los conservadores. *Muerte de un ciclista*, de Bardem, es el paradigma de esta dicotomía porque cuenta una historia de muerte y romanticismo trágico, pero también incluye una sutil ironía para ilustrar las diferencias entre clases sociales durante la dictadura.

Después de la muerte de Franco, directores descubrieron una libertad de expresión nueva en España sin la amenaza de censura. *¿Qué he hecho para merecer esto?*, de Pedro Almodóvar en 1984, fue un gran ejemplo de la nueva emancipación sexual y política en el cine, lo cual era una analogía del nuevo gobierno después de Franco. Todos los personajes de la película (una prostituta, un traficante, una abuela, una madre, y más), tienen características con las cuales el público se identifican en seres agradables, mostrando un gran aumento de aprobación social en España.

Hoy en día, los directores pueden expresarse de cualquier manera que deseen. Cineastas como Almodóvar, Alejandro Amenábar y Woody Allen tienen éxito con las audiencias contemporáneas examinando temas controversiales, aún escandalosos, que muestran el cambio profundo en el sentimiento público y gubernamental.

GO ON TO THE NEXT PAGE.

7. ¿Cuál es el propósito del artículo?

   (A) Describe cómo el cine ha cambiado con el ambiente político en España, pero a veces ofrece una crítica del gobierno.

   (B) Relata unos cineastas importantes y sus obras.

   (C) Aconseja sobre los peligros de la censura.

   (D) Muestra cómo los cineastas durante el régimen de Franco usaron la sátira e ironía para evitar la censura del gobierno.

8. Se menciona *Un chien andalou* para

   (A) celebrar el genio de Dalí y Buñuel

   (B) dar un ejemplo de innovación en el cine español para mostrar la modernización política

   (C) mostrar el gran éxito del cine durante los años veinte y treinta

   (D) ilustrar el impacto del surrealismo durante la Segunda República

9. La influencia de Franco en el cine era una de

   (A) celebración

   (B) censura

   (C) horror

   (D) sátira

10. Podemos inferir que

    (A) *Muerte de un ciclista* es la mejor película de la época de Franco

    (B) después de la Segunda Republica, no había ninguna libertad en el país

    (C) hoy en día, solo los temas polémicos tienen éxito en el cine español

    (D) Almodóvar, Buñuel y Bardem tuvieron éxito con sus películas

11. ¿Qué pasó en el cine española después de Franco?

    (A) Hubo un período de ideales conservadores que restringió a muchos directores.

    (B) Pedro Almodóvar creó un escándalo con su película *¿Qué he hecho para merecer esto?*

    (C) Hubo una nueva libertad para los cineastas de hacer lo que quisieran.

    (D) El legado de Franco permeaba el país.

12. Se menciona a Pedro Almodóvar, Alejandro Amenábar y Woody Allen para

    (A) sugerir que los directores son amigos que se tienen alta estima

    (B) dar ejemplos de directores exitosos del cine contemporáneo en España

    (C) mostrar que ellos revolucionaron el cine tanto como Dalí y Buñuel

    (D) demostrar que temas controversiales y escándalos son los únicos que les gustan a las audiencias contemporáneas

GO ON TO THE NEXT PAGE.

Selección número 3

Introducción

El siguiente artículo apareció en un periódico hispánico en diciembre 2016.

Cuba es hoy el país de moda. Personalidades como El Papa Francisco, Beyoncé, Rihanna y Pelé han llegado en avalancha hasta esta hermosa isla del Caribe. Sin embargo, fue la visita del presidente norteamericano Barack Obama una de las más trascendentes, quizás porque hacía 88 años un mandatario estadounidense no venía al país caribeño. Pero no es solo la estadía en sí, sino también su significado: Obama en Cuba representó el posible fin de la "Guerra Fría".

Para David Soler, Subdirector de la Oficina de Patrimonio Cultural de Cienfuegos, una ciudad con amplias ofertas de turismo cultural, el país ha aumentado los números de turistas extranjeros paulatinamente, y "con la reanudación de las relaciones diplomáticas y comerciales con EE.UU., se espera que aumente drásticamente la presencia de empresarios y turistas norteamericanos. Somos la nación más cercana que tienen después de México y Canadá", explica.

Como argumenta este investigador de la cultura cubana, todos los estadounidenses que vendrán a Cuba a invertir o a hacer turismo, traen su cultura y sus formas de comerciar, de proyectarse y hasta de comer, y los cubanos poco a poco tratarán de adecuar los servicios y negocios a este nuevo tipo de turista/empresario.

"Fíjate cómo puede verse influenciada la cultura cubana, podría pasar nuevamente lo ocurrido con la llegada del primer crucero norteamericano a La Habana a inicios de mayo de este año; los visitantes fueron recibidos por mulatas voluptuosas vestidas con los símbolos patrios cubanos. Así contribuyeron a asentar los estereotipos sobre nuestro pueblo: que esta es solo una tierra de mulatas bailarinas, de ron y de tabaco, cuando la realidad es mucho más rica que eso", se queja Soler.

Según afirma el subdirector, todos estos cambios conducen a un intercambio cultural muy peligroso, donde el que viene de fuera trata de implantar sus formas y su cultura. "El cubano, interesado en que los norteamericanos inviertan aquí, puede cometer el error de responder solamente a los intereses del norteño y olvidarse de su identidad y cultura", señala.

Aunque todavía no ha llegado la oleada grande, el investigador asegura que se espera pronto. "La gente aquí se está preparando para ello, estudiando más inglés, alistando sus negocios para el turista estadounidense y estudiando las costumbres norteñas, a veces menospreciando las propias", nos confiesa con pesar este amante del patrimonio cultural cubano.

Todos los cambios ocurridos desde el 17 de diciembre de 2014, cuando ambos presidentes anunciaron el restablecimiento de relaciones diplomáticas, apuntan a un futuro inmediato muy relacionado con el turismo y los servicios, obviamente enfocados en el mercado norteamericano. Los cubanos, lógicamente, ven la "reconciliación" como una fuente de ingresos directa.

El cambio puede traer transformaciones más allá de lo político e influir grandemente en los negocios entre ciudadanos de ambas naciones. Jenny Lleonart Cruz, joven emprendedora cubana y dueña de un lujoso hostal privado en Cienfuegos, asegura que "una cosa tan sencilla como tener una cuenta de PayPal o aceptar pagos con tarjetas de crédito es algo que se avecina. Eso beneficiaría mucho el cobrar o pagar bienes y servicios. También posibilitaría el comercio electrónico en Cuba. Hasta cosas tan sencillas como ir a Miami a comprar suministros para mi hostal sería factible".

Pedro Gómez, residente de La Habana, es más cauteloso y señala que los cubanos no pueden dar el brazo a torcer y caer de nuevo en el sistema capitalista. "Es lo que quieren los americanos. Para ahí no podemos volver porque en esa época se sufría mucho por la economía tan desigual que había. Por eso hay que tener mucho cuidado con lo que se avecina, los cambios pueden ser peligrosos también".

Definitivamente los vientos de cambios que soplan en Cuba con el restablecimiento de las relaciones con EE.UU. modificarán la vida de los cubanos, pero también de algunos países de América Latina. Algunos de estos se beneficiarán o perjudicarán, como los polos turísticos de Punta Cana y la Riviera Maya, que ven una gran competencia en una Cuba abierta al mercado norteamericano.

En tanto, los cubanos caminan en su día a día por las calles de este país y sueñan con cambios milagrosos. Tienen la esperanza de que de una forma u otra, este puente político que se tendió entre las dos naciones no se rompa de nuevo, y funja como vía al desarrollo económico de los habitantes de esta hermosa isla, que emerge del centro del Caribe.

GO ON TO THE NEXT PAGE.

13. ¿Cuál es el propósito del artículo?

    (A) El puente político entre Cuba y los Estados Unidos todavía está débil.

    (B) Los cambios económicos pueden ser difíciles para Cuba en este punto de transición.

    (C) El restablecimiento de las relaciones con EE.UU. modificarán la vida de los cubanos.

    (D) El fin del embargo y mandatorio significa unos cambios económicos para la isla.

14. Por qué se mencionan a El Papa Francisco, Beyoncé, Rihanna y Pelé en el primer párrafo?

    (A) Son embajadores a Cuba para sus países respectivas.

    (B) Quieren viajar a Cuba, pero no es posible hasta el fin de la "Guerra Fría".

    (C) Fueron unas de las primeras personas que viajaron a Cuba despúes del fin del mandatorio estadounidense.

    (D) Son algunos artistas que han dado conciertos en Cuba.

15. En el segundo párrafo, David Soler espera que

    (A) la economía cubana sufra a causa de recursos desiguales

    (B) el cambio sea el fin de la "Guerra Fría"

    (C) el cambio aumente la presencia del comercio y turismo

    (D) la influencia cubana cambie el mundo

16. ¿Por qué se menciona Paypal y tarjetas de crédito en el párrafo 8?

    (A) Son elementos de la economía norteño que pueda cambiar los negocios cubanos.

    (B) Son indicadores del comercio electrónico en Cuba.

    (C) Son métodos de pagar en los negocios cubanos.

    (D) Son peligros para los negocios de Cuba porque tienen intereses norteños.

17. ¿Qué piensa Pedro Gómez del cambio económico en Cuba?

    (A) Piensa que el capitalismo va a destruir el país.

    (B) Piensa que hay que tener cuidado porque hay una desigualdad de recursos.

    (C) Piensa que es invaluable para que los cubanos aprendan inglés.

    (D) Piensa que el futuro de la economía cubana es el turismo.

18. Según el último párrafo, ¿qué esperan los cubanos?

    (A) Esperan que la economía cubana desarrolle a ser próspera en el Caribe.

    (B) Esperan que los presidentes de los dos países sean amigos.

    (C) Esperan que el puente político que se tendió entre las dos naciones se rompa de nuevo.

    (D) Esperan que Cuba adapte a la cultura norteña.

GO ON TO THE NEXT PAGE.

Selección número 4

Introducción

El siguiente panfleto apareció en 2015 por el Acción Global de Salud.

Reduciendo las Inequidades de Salud en el Mundo

La crisis contemporánea de la salud mundial es un reflejo de las crecientes inequidades que existen entre los países y dentro de ellos. Los avances científicos y tecnológicos han aportado a un mejoramiento de la salud de algunos. Sin embargo, cada vez más gente vive en la pobreza y 30.000 niños mueren cada día.

El Observatorio Global de Salud 2005–2006 presenta las disparidades en salud y llama la atención hacia los mecanismos mediante los cuales los gobiernos, instituciones internacionales y la sociedad civil pueden aplicar para combatirlas.

Los trabajadores de la salud en particular pueden jugar un papel vital en transformar la retórica sobre derechos universales de la salud y ciudadanía global en una realidad. Aquellos que viven en las zonas más ricas del mundo tienen la particular responsabilidad de presionar hacia un cambio.

La interdependencia generada bajo la globalización incrementa estas responsabilidades éticas.

Los temas cubiertos por el *Observatorio* son diversos, pero todos ellos destacan las inequidades económicas, sociales y políticas que destruyen la salud.

Este documento de campaña enfoca áreas claves donde las presiones colectivas deben ejercerse.

■ Construyendo un mundo justo

La conquista de un mundo justo donde se elimine la pobreza y desarrolle la salud implica cambiar la manera en que la economía global es manejada, e incrementar sustancialmente la transferencia de recursos de los países centrales hacia los países periféricos.

■ Defendiendo y extendiendo el sector público

La reparación y desarrollo de los sistemas de atención en salud pública son cruciales para detener las amenazas de la mercantilización y reducir los crecientes abismos sociales y de salud. Este reporte propone una agenda de diez puntos para la acción.

■ Migración, farmacéuticas y grandes corporaciones

La migración de trabajadores de la salud, las normas globales de propiedad intelectual que incrementan los precios de las medicinas y el impacto de las multinacionales en salud destacan como tres ejemplos de la manera en que la globalización y la subordinación de los derechos de la salud a objetivos comerciales afectan directamente la salud y los sistemas de salud a través del mundo.

■ Tomando acciones frente a los cambios climáticos y al militarismo

El cambio climático global y el militarismo son dos de las más importantes causas presentes y futuras de deterioro de la salud a través del mundo. La incapacidad actual de enfrentar dicha problemática de modo significativo señala la urgente necesidad de mayor movilización de la sociedad civil, de las organizaciones populares y de los trabajadores de la salud para arrancar soluciones más efectivas y justas.

■ Afirmando el liderazgo por la salud global en la Organización Mundial de la Salud

El mundo necesita una agencia de salud multilateral que sea capaz de proteger y promover la salud, reducir las desigualdades y asegurar la vigencia plena de los derechos universales frente a las necesidades básicas y de salud. Para que esto suceda, la OMS requiere más recursos y ser más sensible a las necesidades de los pueblos, alcanzando estándares de administración mejores.

Acción Global de la Salud ("Global Health Action") demanda al *Observatorio* en recomendar una agenda que oriente la lucha de los trabajadores de la salud y los gestores de la campaña.

GO ON TO THE NEXT PAGE.

19. ¿Cuál es el propósito del panfleto?

    (A) El panfleto quiere diseminar información sobre la salud global y unas razones para los cambios mundiales.

    (B) El panfleto quiere mostrar los problemas que no se pueden resolver.

    (C) Acción Global de la Salud es la organización más equipado a solucionar los conflictos mencionados.

    (D) El mundo necesita una agencia de salud multilateral que sea capaz de proteger y promover la salud.

20. Según el autor en el primer párrafo, ¿por qué hay una crisis contemporánea de salud mundial?

    (A) Las agencias hoy en día son incapaces de ayudar y promover la salud con sus pocos recursos.

    (B) El militarismo ha destruido la salud pública.

    (C) Los avances científicos y tecnológicos destruyeron el orden del mundo.

    (D) Hay un crecimiento de inequidades que existen entre los países y dentro de ellos.

21. En el primer párrafo, ¿por qué se incluyó "Sin embargo, cada vez más gente vive en la pobreza y 30.000 niños mueren cada día"?

    (A) Es increíble que tantos niños mueren cada día.

    (B) Hay una yuxtaposición entre la gente con buena salud pública y la gente que no la tiene.

    (C) Se necesita más recursos y ser más sensible a las necesidades de los pueblos para salvar a los niños.

    (D) Los niños sufren a causa de la globalización y la subordinación de los derechos de la salud.

22. ¿Como se refiere a un "mundo justo" en el panfleto?

    (A) Un mundo justo puede cambiar la manera en que la economía global es manejada.

    (B) Un mundo justo salva vidas porque puede proteger la gente y promover la salud.

    (C) Es un mundo en que todos pueden vivir en armonía.

    (D) Es un mundo que tiene precios bajos para las medicinas para los ricos.

23. ¿Qué tiene que ver el sector público con la salud pública?

    (A) Puede obtener recursos importantes para los niños.

    (B) Es una de las causas presentes y futuras del deterioro de la salud a través del mundo.

    (C) Mantiene y crece el militarismo.

    (D) Puede detener las amenazas de la mercantilización.

24. ¿Por qué se menciona el militarismo en el panfleto?

    (A) Se menciona para reducir las desigualdades entre países.

    (B) Es una de las más importantes causas de deterioro de la salud global.

    (C) Se menciona los militares como las organizaciones populares de salud.

    (D) El militarismo proporciona empleo a muchos trabajadores.

25. Todas son metas de la Acción Global de la Salud SALVO:

    (A) reparar y desarrollar los sistemas de salud pública

    (B) reducir desigualdades económicas

    (C) asegurar la vigencia plena de los derechos universales

    (D) aumentar los precios de las medicinas

GO ON TO THE NEXT PAGE.

Selección número 5

Introducción

El siguiente artículo es sobre el horario de la noche en España.

España: un lugar para los noctámbulos

El siguiente artículo apareció en una revista estadounidense en 2008.

El español duerme una hora menos al día que sus vecinos europeos; no puede conciliar su vida profesional con la familiar y su productividad laboral es una de las más bajas de Europa. Y todo por culpa de sus peculiares horarios: se come y se cena tarde, la jornada de trabajo se alarga considerablemente y la gente se acuesta pasada la medianoche. Estos horarios existen desde los años 40, pero ahora son cuestionados. La alternativa es adoptar los europeos, pero ¿será el español capaz de ello?

Según recomienda la Organización Mundial de la Salud, una persona debe dormir ocho horas diarias. Cansancio, sueño, estrés invaden los hogares españoles y las consultas de los médicos. La doctora Rosa García López-Tello afirma que "el déficit crónico de sueño se está convirtiendo en el mayor factor de riesgo cardiovascular". Insiste en que lo más saludable es tener un sueño reparador y dormir unas ocho horas en el caso de los adultos y entre diez y doce en el de los niños.

Todo esto merma la productividad. Estudios demuestran que las empresas que han adoptado medidas para que sus empleados tengan horarios más razonables aumentan el rendimiento, optimizan los recursos y, lo principal, tienen trabajadores más felices. Este directivo de una multinacional europea apunta a otra consecuencia: "No se está para nada en armonía con los horarios de tus colegas europeos. Pasas alrededor de cuatro horas en las que no puedes comunicarte con ellos, ya que cuando terminan de comer empiezas tú, finalizando la comida cuando ellos están concluyendo su jornada laboral. Esto provoca muchas dificultades a la hora de trabajar en un entorno multinacional".

Jaime Albuerne es un ejecutivo comercial que por motivos profesionales viaja con frecuencia a Alemania. "Es verdad que allí todo es más ordenado, pero cuando tengo que cenar a las 18:00 siempre pienso: '¡Pero si en España todavía están con la merienda!'" Jaime cree que ese "orden" no va con el español. "Aquí tenemos muchas horas de sol, nos gusta la vida en la calle, trasnochar aunque sea en casa. No veo al español cenando tan pronto".

En España nadie está a salvo de estos horarios tardíos. Al salir tarde del trabajo, los comercios han de ampliar sus horas de apertura hasta bien entrada la noche para facilitar las compras a sus clientes. Lo mismo ocurre con cines, teatro y televisión.

Por su parte, la hostelería ubicada en zonas turísticas ha de hacer jornadas muy extensas, ya que se intenta complacer al español pero también al extranjero. La idea es que este último no se sienta muy desarraigado y pueda comer o cenar a las mismas horas que en su país de origen.

Otro sector de la población muy perjudicado es el infantil. Los niños acaban la escuela mucho antes de que sus padres terminen de trabajar, lo cual les obliga a numerosas actividades extraescolares que les mantienen ocupados y cuidados.

Teresa Pozas, maestra en educación infantil, señala que "hay muchos niños que echan muchas horas en el cole, ya que existe el servicio de madrugadores, donde los monitores se ocupan de ellos una o dos horas hasta que empiecen las clases. Después de la jornada escolar se pueden quedar a participar en actividades extraescolares. Al final, pasan muchísimas horas en la escuela".

Sara Berbel, doctora en Psicología Social y experta en este tema, explica que "durante la época de la industrialización los europeos habían adoptado jornadas laborales larguísimas y muy rígidas. Tras la guerra, las naciones más avanzadas vieron que no eran buenas para la productividad y se modernizaron. Pero España entró en una dictadura y todo ese proceso modernizador se paralizó".

En gran parte de América Latina los horarios son muy similares a los españoles. Berbel explica que ello se debe fundamentalmente a dos factores: el gran impacto que tuvo allí la cultura española y el hecho de que estos países tampoco se hayan modernizado tras la industrialización. En América del Norte, los horarios coinciden con los europeos.

Para la argentina Betty Mendoza todo es mucho más simple: "Somos latinos y nos gusta vivir así, aprovechando a tope el día, de forma un poco más desordenada". Llegó a España hace 15 años y comprobó que los horarios eran los mismos que en su país. "Ahora todo el mundo habla de cambiarlos, pero no veo por qué. Somos millones de personas que vivimos así desde hace años y creo que funcionamos muy bien", concluye.

GO ON TO THE NEXT PAGE.

26. ¿Cuál es el propósito del artículo?

    (A) El artículo busca explicaciones para las diferencias entre el horario español y los de otros países europeos.

    (B) Los españoles tienen un déficit crónico de sueño y están de riesgo cardiovascular.

    (C) La industrialización todavía no se ha sucedido en España.

    (D) Las empresas españoles que han adoptado medidas para que sus empleados tengan horarios más razonables tienen trabajadores más felices.

27. ¿Por qué dice Jaime Albuerne "¡Pero si en España todavía están con la merienda!"?

    (A) La mayoría de los alemanes no saben a que hora es.

    (B) Según su horario normal, es demasiado temprano para cenarse.

    (C) El horario español es mejor que el de Alemania.

    (D) No sabe por qué los negocios alemanes tienen sus horarios trabajadores así.

28. Según el quinto párrafo, ¿qué ocurre con los cines, el teatro y la televisión?

    (A) Tienen que servir los turistas y necesitan horarios diferentes que los demás trabajadores.

    (B) Los muchachos pasan mucho tiempo en la escuela, y entonces necesitan el divertimento después.

    (C) Tienen horarios de apertura para servir a toda la gente.

    (D) Es difícil para la gente ir al cine y al teatro después de trabajar.

29. En el noveno párrafo, ¿cómo explica Sara Berbel el horario de España?

    (A) La guerra civil fue un desastre que paralizó el país.

    (B) La dictadura limitó el proceso de modernización en España.

    (C) La industrialización no le gustaba a los españoles.

    (D) La cultura de España tuvo un gran efecto sobre los países latinoamericanos.

30. En el último párrafo, ¿qué nota Betty Mendoza?

    (A) Hay que reparar el horario español porque no coincide con los de los otros países europeos.

    (B) Las avanzas de industrialización deben ser implementadas en España y Argentina.

    (C) Le gusta la cultura española porque funciona para ella.

    (D) Hay elementos similares entre los horarios latinos y españoles, y le gustan así.

GO ON TO THE NEXT PAGE.

Part B

Interpretive Communication: Print and Audio Texts (combined)

You will listen to several audio selections. The first two audio selections are accompanied by reading selections. When there is a reading selection, you will have a designated amount of time to read it.

For each audio selection, first you will have a designated amount of time to read a preview of the selection as well as to skim the questions that you will be asked. Each selection will be played twice. As you listen to each selection, you may take notes. Your notes will not be scored.

After listening to each selection the first time, you will have 1 minute to begin answering the questions; after listening to each selection the second time, you will have 15 seconds per question to finish answering the questions. For each question, choose the response that is best according to the audio and/or reading selection and mark your answer on your answer sheet.

Vas a escuchar varias grabaciones. Las dos primeras grabaciones van acompañadas de lecturas. Cuando haya una lectura, vas a tener un tiempo determinado para leerla.

Para cada grabación, primero vas a tener un tiempo determinado para leer la introducción y prever las preguntas. Vas a escuchar cada grabación dos veces. Mientras escuchas, puedes tomar apuntes. Tus apuntes no van a ser calificados.

Después de escuchar cada selección por primera vez, vas a tener un minuto para empezar a contestar las preguntas; después de escuchar por segunda vez, vas a tener 15 segundos por pregunta para terminarlas. Para cada pregunta, elige la mejor respuesta según la grabación o el texto e indícala en la hoja de respuestas.

GO ON TO THE NEXT PAGE.

Selección número 1

Fuente número 1

Primero tienes 4 minutos para leer la fuente número 1.

Introducción

En Panamá, y muchos países de América Latina, muchas personas llevan uniformes al trabajo o a la escuela. Pero hoy en día, con la globalización de la economía, diferentes generaciones se preguntan si los uniformes son necesarios. Este artículo apareció en la prensa panameña en febrero de 2012.

Uso De Uniformes: Un Hábito Muy Latino

Aquí en Panamá, los uniformes son muy comunes. Lo utilizan desde las microempresas hasta el propio gabinete presidencial de la República. ¿Pero de dónde viene este éxito de los uniformes en Panamá? Dos hechos importantes de la historia del siglo XX contribuyeron a cambiar la percepción de los uniformes. El primero de ellos fue la integración masiva de mujeres en la fuerza laboral. El segundo hecho, y el más decisivo, fue el comienzo de la Era Espacial.

Unas personas creen que estas nuevas tendencias inspiradas en la tecnología y en la ciencia-ficción influenciaron el espíritu de la gente y su forma de vestir. En todos lados las personas querían uniformarse y ser parte de esta gran "revolución futurista".

Las aerolíneas fueron las primeras en usar este nuevo estilo. Cambiaron las sencillas vestimentas de tipo naval por uniformes de diseñador. Pronto fueron adaptados por compañías alrededor del mundo para sus empleados. En muchas partes fue una moda pasajera, pero no en Panamá. El negocio de los uniformes se convirtió en un trabajo muy rentable.

Pero el hecho de entregar uniformes no significa que los empleados sean personas mal vestidas o de mal gusto. En Panamá, si la gente no tiene un "código de vestuario", automáticamente escogerá prendas frescas y ligeras, ideales para soportar el calor tropical. Pero no son adecuadas para un ambiente serio y profesional. Muchas personas que utilizan uniformes piensan que es práctico y realmente les simplifica el proceso de prepararse para ir a trabajar. Pero a otras no les gusta la idea de tener que usar uniformes.

En la actualidad, camisetas sencillas con logos son la forma más popular de uniformes en Panamá. Representan el estado más simple y casual del uniforme. Muchas empresas, especialmente bancos e instituciones estatales, utilizan aún uniformes formales de varias piezas. Sin embargo, es una tendencia que va en disminución, ya que el negocio de la costura, que en su tiempo fue un próspero sector, también va decayendo.

Adapted from "Uso De Uniformes: Un Hábito Muy Latino," by María Carolina Crespo. Used by permission of VeinteMundos.com.

GO ON TO THE NEXT PAGE.

Fuente número 2

Tienes dos minutos para leer la introducción y prever las preguntas.

Introducción

Esta grabación trata de los uniformes en el trabajo o la escuela. Los siguientes entrevistados comparten sus opiniones sobre los uniformes. La grabación dura aproximadamente tres minutos.

Ahora escucha la fuente número dos.

PLAY AUDIO: Track 7

Ahora tienes un minuto para empezar a responder a las preguntas para esta selección. Después de un minuto, vas a escuchar la grabación de nuevo.

(1 minute)

Ahora escucha de nuevo.

PLAY AUDIO: Track 7

Ahora termina de responder a las preguntas para esta selección.

31. ¿Qué evento contribuyó a cambiar la percepción de los uniformes del siglo XX?

(A) Los ambientes serios y profesionales demandaron los uniformes.

(B) A la gente le gustaba la ciencia-ficción y fue inspirada por las historias del género.

(C) La integración de las mujeres en la fuerza laboral.

(D) Muchas empresas, especialmente bancos e instituciones estatales, utilizaban uniformes de varias piezas.

32. ¿Generalmente, quiénes usan los uniformes en los EE. UU.?

(A) Los productores de televisión

(B) Los profesores en la universidad

(C) Los bomberos y militares

(D) Los asistentes jurídicos

33. Se menciona la frase, la "revolución futurista", para

(A) referirse a la revolución social inspirada por la ciencia-ficción

(B) hablar del "código de vestuario" que existe en todos los modos de trabajo

(C) ilustrar la creencia de que unas personas que llevaban uniformes al trabajo querían uniformarse

(D) describir la integración de mujeres en la fuerza laboral

34. ¿Por qué se menciona el clima en la discusión de los uniformes?

(A) Muestra que el clima tropical se presta para usar prendas ligeras, pero no son suficientemente profesionales para los ambientes serios.

(B) Las prendas frescas son ideales para el ambiente profesional.

(C) El código de vestuario depende del clima.

(D) En Panamá, toda la gente quiere vestirse de ropa ligera para soportar el calor.

35. ¿Cuál es el tono de Eduardo?

(A) Perplejo

(B) Negativo

(C) Odioso

(D) Estático

36. Según la fuente auditiva, ¿cuál es la opinión de los entrevistados jóvenes?

(A) Ellos odian la idea de los uniformes.

(B) Depende de la profesión del individuo.

(C) Sólo a las personas más conservadoras les gusta.

(D) Ellos son indiferentes porque es parte de la cultura.

GO ON TO THE NEXT PAGE.

37. Todas son razones que dan los entrevistados para llevar los uniformes SALVO:

    (A) Crean un sentido de pertenencia.

    (B) Cubren cosas como tatuajes.

    (C) El salario se puede invertir en cosas más importantes que ropa de trabajo.

    (D) No permiten expresar la individualidad.

38. ¿A cuáles de los entrevistados les gustan los uniformes?

    (A) Eduardo y Roberto Sánchez

    (B) Liz y Eduardo

    (C) Liz y Roberto Sánchez

    (D) Roberto Sánchez y María Carolina

39. ¿Cuál de las afirmaciones mejor resume este artículo?

    (A) Muchos de los uniformes para el trabajo son de mal gusto.

    (B) El futuro de los uniformes está condenado porque los negocios de costura están decayendo.

    (C) Muchas personas tienen distintas opiniones sobre el uso de los uniformes en el trabajo.

    (D) Hubo muchos cambios en la economía del siglo XX que contribuyeron al uso de los uniformes.

GO ON TO THE NEXT PAGE.

Selección número 2

Fuente número 1

Primero tienes tres minutos para leer la fuente número 1.

Introducción

Esta información apareció en el sitio de Web globalchange.org, sobre la deserción escolar de los jóvenes en América Latina. Las estadísticas son de agosto de 2013.

¿Por qué abandonan la escuela secundaria los jóvenes latinoamericanos?

Con uno de cada dos estudiantes que no termina secundaria, la deserción escolar afecta a jóvenes de todos los sectores de la sociedad. Sin embargo, los siguientes grupos registran tasas elevadas de abandono escolar de forma desproporcionada.

Son muchos los factores que influyen en la deserción escolar. Históricamente, problemas de acceso han propiciado altas tasas de deserción escolar en América Latina. En las últimas décadas, los países latinoamericanos han logrado avances notables en el acceso a la educación secundaria.

Si bien los problemas económicos y de acceso siguen suponiendo obstáculos para la educación en ciertas zonas, no ilustran la historia completa de la situación actual. Varios factores influyen en el abandono escolar y las razones por las que los jóvenes dejan los estudios pueden sorprender. Según datos de encuestas de hogares de 8 países, la mayoría de los estudiantes entre 13 y 15 años que no van a la escuela identifican la falta de interés —por encima de los problemas económicos, de acceso o familiares— como la razón principal de abandono escolar.

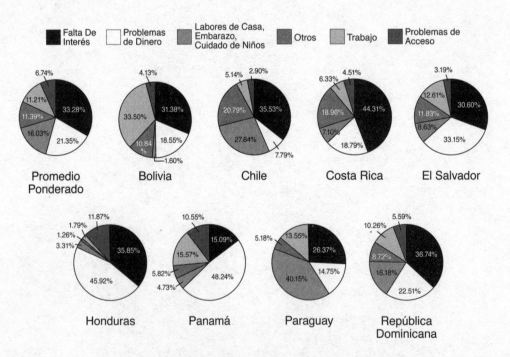

GO ON TO THE NEXT PAGE.

Fuente número 2

Tienes dos minutos para leer la introducción y prever las preguntas.

Introducción

Esta grabación trata de la deserción escolar. La grabación es una conversación entre dos amigos, Miguel y Loren, que viven en Zacapa, Guatemala. La grabación dura aproximadamente tres minutos.

Ahora escucha la fuente número dos.

> **PLAY AUDIO: Track 8**

Ahora tienes un minuto para empezar a responder a las preguntas para esta selección. Después de un minuto, vas a escuchar la grabación de nuevo.

(1 minute)

Ahora escucha de nuevo.

> **PLAY AUDIO: Track 8**

Ahora termina de responder a las preguntas para esta selección.

40. ¿Cuál es el propósito del artículo y de las estadísticas?

    (A) Los estudiantes entre 13 y 15 años necesitan trabajar y ayudar a sus familias.

    (B) Hay muchas razones por la deserción escolar y la razón más grande identificada es la falta de interés.

    (C) No se sabe por qué hay una falta de interés en los estudiantes entre 13 y 15 años de edad.

    (D) Todavía los problemas económicos y de acceso siguen suponiendo obstáculos para los jóvenes.

41. ¿Según los datos, cuál es la razón más indicada de la deserción escolar por jóvenes entre 13 y 15 años?

    (A) Falta de interés

    (B) Trabajo

    (C) Problemas de acceso

    (D) Problemas de dinero

42. Todas las siguientes son razones de abandonar la escuela secundaria SALVO

    (A) problemas de acceso

    (B) falta de interés

    (C) embarazo y cuidado de niños

    (D) presión de los padres

43. Las razones mayores para la falta de asistencia en Bolivia son

    (A) falta de interés y labores de casa

    (B) falta de interés y problemas de dinero

    (C) falta de interés y trabajo

    (D) falta de interés y problemas de acceso

44. Se puede inferir que

    (A) todos los jóvenes en Latinoamérica tienen una falta de interés en los estudios escolares

    (B) las razones de la deserción escolar varían dependiendo del país

    (C) los problemas de acceso son del pasado

    (D) los problemas económicos y de acceso siguen suponiendo obstáculos grandes en todas partes

45. ¿Cuál es el problema principal de Miguel?

    (A) A Miguel le falta interés en sus estudios secundarios.

    (B) Necesita ayudar a sus padres.

    (C) Necesita solicitar una beca para asistir a la universidad.

    (D) Necesita encontrar empleo.

46. ¿Quiénes son María, Joaquín, y Carolina?

    (A) Son los amigos de Miguel y Loren.

    (B) Son los hermanos menores de Loren.

    (C) Son los hermanos mayores de Miguel.

    (D) Son los hermanos menores de Miguel.

47. ¿Qué va a hacer Miguel durante su año sabático?

    (A) Va a cuidar a sus niños y trabajar para su padre.

    (B) Va a asistir a la Universidad de Guatemala y después la Facultad de Medicina.

    (C) Va a trabajar con su padre mientras cuida de sus hermanos con su madre.

    (D) Va pasar un rato trabajando y viajando con su padre.

GO ON TO THE NEXT PAGE.

Interpretive Communication: Audio Texts

Selección número 3

Introducción

Primero tienes un minuto para leer la introducción y prever las preguntas.

La siguiente grabación fue parte de un BROADCAST del "Mundo de deportes," un programa de radio dedicado a los deportes de todas partes.

Ahora escucha la selección.

PLAY AUDIO: Track 9

Ahora tienes un minuto para empezar a responder a las preguntas para esta selección. Después de un minuto, vas a escuchar la grabación de nuevo.

(1 minute)

Ahora escucha de nuevo.

PLAY AUDIO: Track 9

Ahora termina de responder a las preguntas para esta selección.

48. ¿Cómo es el campo de golf de Saint Andrew's en Escocia?

 (A) Nuevo y moderno

 (B) Pintoresco

 (C) Histórico y prestigioso

 (D) Innovador

49. ¿Qué tiempo hacía durante el torneo?

 (A) Hacía un tiempo agradable.

 (B) Hacía calor.

 (C) Nevaba.

 (D) Hacía un tiempo tempestuoso.

50. ¿Cómo reaccionó Alfonso García frente al tiempo variable en Escocia?

 (A) Se sintió frustrado.

 (B) Se sintió muy a gusto.

 (C) Se sintió nostálgico.

 (D) Se sintió triste.

51. ¿Cómo se interesó Alfonso García en el golf?

 (A) Jugaba golf con su padre.

 (B) Acompañaba a su abuelo en el campo de golf.

 (C) Jugaba golf con su hermana.

 (D) Jugaba golf con su abuela.

52. ¿Cómo pasa Alfonso la mayoría de su tiempo?

 (A) Descansando con sus padres en Buenos Aires

 (B) Viajando en el Tour de la PGA

 (C) Jugando tenis con su hermana menor, Patricia

 (D) Pasando tiempo con su abuelo maternal

GO ON TO THE NEXT PAGE.

Selección número 4

Introducción

Primero tienes un minuto para leer la introducción y prever las preguntas.

Esta grabación trata del feminismo en España. La grabación es parte de una conferencia sobre el feminismo en España.

Ahora escucha la selección.

PLAY AUDIO: Track 10

Ahora tienes un minuto para empezar a responder a las preguntas para esta selección. Después de un minuto, vas a escuchar la grabación de nuevo.

(1 minute)

Ahora escucha de nuevo.

PLAY AUDIO: Track 10

Ahora termina de responder a las preguntas para esta selección.

53. ¿Cómo interpretan algunos el movimiento feminista en España?

   (A) Una lucha política

   (B) Una cuestión artística

   (C) Una competencia entre iguales

   (D) Un concurso de belleza

54. ¿Cuál característica de la cultura española se puede considerar como el opuesto del movimiento feminista?

   (A) El marianismo

   (B) La honra

   (C) La dignidad

   (D) El machismo

55. Según la conferencia, ¿cuál es el objetivo ideológico del movimiento feminista?

   (A) El triunfo de la mujer sobre el hombre

   (B) La aceptación del marianismo en todo el mundo

   (C) Una identidad individual para la mujer

   (D) La apreciación de la cultura tradicional

56. Según la conferencia, ¿qué pensamiento surgió en la época de Franco?

   (A) Un pensamiento radical

   (B) Un pensamiento tradicional

   (C) Un pensamiento progresivo

   (D) Un pensamiento feminista

57. Según la conferencia, ¿qué debemos guardar de la sociedad tradicional machista?

   (A) El papel de la mujer como madre

   (B) El marianismo

   (C) El papel de la mujer subordinada al hombre

   (D) El machismo

GO ON TO THE NEXT PAGE.

Selección número 5

Introducción

Primero tienes un minuto para leer la introducción y prever las preguntas.

La siguiente grabación trata de los juegos olímpicos especiales convocado el pasado agosto. La grabación es una entrevista con Alejandro Martínez, entrenador triunfante del torneo de los juegos olímpicos especiales.

Ahora escucha la selección.

> **PLAY AUDIO: Track 11**

Ahora tienes un minuto para empezar a responder a las preguntas para esta selección. Después de un minuto, vas a escuchar la grabación de nuevo.

(1 minute)

Ahora escucha de nuevo.

> **PLAY AUDIO: Track 11**

Ahora termina de responder a las preguntas para esta selección.

58. ¿Cómo se interesó Alejandro Martínez en los juegos olímpicos especiales?

    (A) Siempre había participado en los juegos especiales.

    (B) Su hermano participaba en los juegos especiales.

    (C) Su hijo respondió favorablemente a los deportes.

    (D) Su esposa está muy metida en los juegos especiales.

59. ¿Cuándo se dedica Alejandro completamente a los juegos especiales?

    (A) Los fines de semana

    (B) Durante las vacaciones escolares

    (C) En invierno

    (D) En verano

60. Según la entrevista, ¿por qué no trabaja exclusivamente con los juegos especiales?

    (A) Porque no gana suficiente dinero

    (B) Porque es maestro de matemáticas

    (C) Porque su hija le ocupa mucho tiempo

    (D) Porque no podría soportarlo

61. ¿Por qué le gusta a Alejandro trabajar con los niños?

    (A) Porque son jóvenes

    (B) Porque son honestos

    (C) Porque tienen mucho interés

    (D) Porque tienen más habilidad

GO ON TO THE NEXT PAGE.

62. Según la entrevista, ¿por qué es terapéutico el ejercicio físico?

    (A) Porque practican ejercicios especiales

    (B) Porque los entrenadores tienen educación en terapia física

    (C) Porque es divertido

    (D) Porque les hace sentir mejor a los niños mentalmente y físicamente

63. ¿Cómo se caracteriza el espíritu colectivo de los niños?

    (A) No saben colaborar con el grupo.

    (B) Entienden instintivamente cómo colaborar.

    (C) No saben funcionar físicamente.

    (D) Hay mucha competencia entre los grupos.

64. Según la entrevista, ¿cuál característica describe mejor a los niños que participan en los juegos olímpicos especiales?

    (A) Son muy delgados.

    (B) Son muy delicados.

    (C) Son muy dedicados.

    (D) Son delegados a los juegos especiales.

65. ¿Qué recomienda Alejandro a las familias que no quieren participar en los juegos?

    (A) Que se enteren de los eventos planeados

    (B) Que sigan su corazón

    (C) Que organicen sus propios juegos con los juegos especiales

    (D) Que no participen

END OF SECTION I

IF YOU FINISH BEFORE TIME IS CALLED, YOU MAY CHECK YOUR WORK ON THIS SECTION

SPANISH LANGUAGE AND CULTURE

SECTION II

Approximate Time—85 minutes

50% of total grade

Interpersonal Writing: Email Reply

| You will write a reply to an email message. You will have 15 minutes to read the message and write your reply.

Your reply should include a greeting and a closing, and should respond to all the questions and requests in the message. In your reply, you should also ask for more details about something mentioned in the message. Also, you should use a formal form of address. | Vas a escribir una respuesta a un mensaje electrónico. Vas a tener 15 minutos para leer el mensaje y escribir tu respuesta.

Tu respuesta debe incluir un saludo y una despedida, y debe responder a todas las preguntas y peticiones del mensaje. En tu respuesta, debes pedir más información sobre algo mencionado en el mensaje. También debes responder de una manera formal. |

Introducción

Este mensaje es de su profesor del colegio. Ha recibido este mensaje porque recientemente le había pedido que le escribiera una carta de recomendación para su solicitud de ingreso a la universidad. Tendrá 15 minutos para leer la carta y escribir su respuesta.

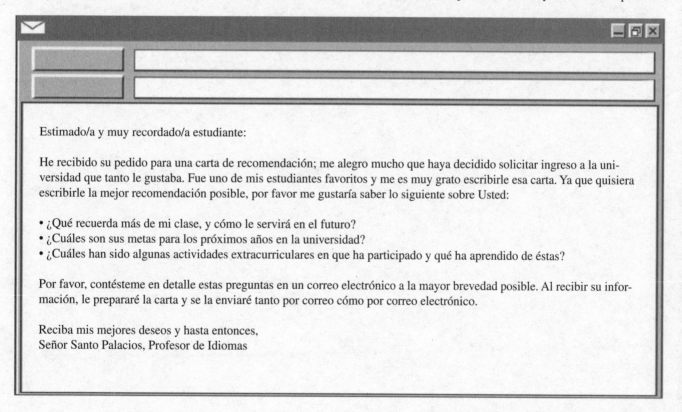

Estimado/a y muy recordado/a estudiante:

He recibido su pedido para una carta de recomendación; me alegro mucho que haya decidido solicitar ingreso a la universidad que tanto le gustaba. Fue uno de mis estudiantes favoritos y me es muy grato escribirle esa carta. Ya que quisiera escribirle la mejor recomendación posible, por favor me gustaría saber lo siguiente sobre Usted:

• ¿Qué recuerda más de mi clase, y cómo le servirá en el futuro?
• ¿Cuáles son sus metas para los próximos años en la universidad?
• ¿Cuáles han sido algunas actividades extracurriculares en que ha participado y qué ha aprendido de éstas?

Por favor, contésteme en detalle estas preguntas en un correo electrónico a la mayor brevedad posible. Al recibir su información, le preparé la carta y se la enviaré tanto por correo cómo por correo electrónico.

Reciba mis mejores deseos y hasta entonces,
Señor Santo Palacios, Profesor de Idiomas

GO ON TO THE NEXT PAGE.

Presentational Writing: Persuasive Essay

You will write a persuasive essay to submit to a Spanish writing contest. The essay topic is based on three accompanying sources, which present different viewpoints on the topic and include both print and audio material. First, you will have 6 minutes to read the essay topic and the printed material. Afterward, you will hear the audio material twice; you should take notes while you listen. Then, you will have 40 minutes to prepare and write your essay.	Vas a escribir un ensayo persuasivo para un concurso de redacción en español. El tema del ensayo se basa en las tres fuentes adjuntas, que presentan diferentes puntos de vista sobre el tema e incluyen material escrito y grabado. Primero, vas a tener 6 minutos para leer el tema del ensayo y los textos. Después, vas a escuchar la grabación dos veces; debes tomar apuntes mientras escuchas. Luego vas a tener 40 minutos para preparar y escribir tu ensayo.
In a persuasive essay, you should present the sources' different viewpoints on the topic, and also clearly indicate your own viewpoint and defend it thoroughly. Use information from all of the sources to support your essay. As you refer to the sources, identify them appropriately. Also, organize your essay into clear paragraphs.	En un ensayo persuasivo, debes presentar los diferentes puntos de vista de las fuentes sobre el tema, expresar tu propio punto de vista y apoyarlo. Usa información de todas las fuentes para apoyar tu punto de vista. Al referirte a las fuentes, identifícalas apropiadamente. Organiza también el ensayo en distintos párrafos bien desarrollados.

Tema del ensayo:

¿Cómo nos afecta la vida el calentamiento global?

GO ON TO THE NEXT PAGE.

Fuente número 1

Introducción

Este artículo apareció en un sitio de Internet de España en mayo de 2008.

Las consecuencias del calentamiento global asociadas con un aumento en el nivel de mar

Con la destrucción de la capa de ozono, observamos una mayor penetración de rayos solares al planeta. Estos, a su vez, contribuyen a una expansión térmica de los océanos y el derretimiento de grandes números de montañas glaciares y de los casquetes de hielo ubicados en las partes orientales de las Tierras Antárticas y Groenlandia. Ya con estos niveles elevados del mar, se pronosticarán graves cambios para el porvenir del planeta.

El nivel del mar ya aumentó en entre 4 y 8 pulgadas en el siglo pasado. Se predice que los niveles del mar podrían aumentar en desde 10 hasta 23 pulgadas para el año 2100. Lamentablemente los niveles vienen creciendo más de lo previsto —la capa de hielo de Groenlandia ha disminuido en la última década. Este declive contribuye aproximadamente una centésima de pulgada anualmente al aumento del nivel del mar. La cifra parece ser mínima a primera vista, pero hay que tener en cuenta que Groenlandia cuenta con alrededor de 10% de la masa total del hielo mundial. Si el hielo de Groenlandia fuera a derretirse, los niveles de los mares mundiales podrían aumentar en hasta 21 pies. Este año, por primera vez, los barcos pudieron pasar por las aguas árticas sin la ayuda de un barco rompehielos. O sea, que las predicciones de los científicos que el hielo empezaría a derretirse han acontecido 25 años por adelantado. Esto también significará graves consecuencias para el planeta. Ya se pronostica que el oso polar, los lobos marinos y ciertas especies de pingüinos estarán al borde de la extinción en pocos años.

Con la destrucción de los glaciares y casquetes del hielo, más agua dulce entra al mar, y así aumentando los niveles actuales. Estos derretimientos provocarán inundaciones severas en áreas costeñas. Si el nivel de mar subiera apenas 6 metros, arrasaría con lugares como Miami, Florida y San Francisco, California en los Estados Unidos; en China dejaría hundidas a ciudades como Shangai y Beijing, y en India, la ciudad de Calcuta estaría bajo agua. Estos últimos tres centros urbanos figuran entre las ciudades más pobladas del mundo.

GO ON TO THE NEXT PAGE.

Fuente número 2

Introducción

Este artículo apareció en la prensa argentina en julio de 2008.

Advertencia: El calentamiento global traerá consigo graves consecuencias sobre la vida y la salud humana

"No es ninguna especulación —es una realidad. Los días del planeta están contados. Ya es la hora de actuar y poner en marcha programas de planificación y contingencia", comentó Francisco García, director general de la Organización de Preservación Mundial, en rueda de prensa durante la undécima convocatoria general de La Semana del Planeta celebrada en Buenos Aires, Argentina. Representantes de más de 35 países se reunieron en la capital argentina para discutir, analizar data y formular planes de acción para que las organizaciones internacionales y nacionales entendieran con mayor profundidad las consecuencias del calentamiento global. Es su esperanza, que una vez armados con esta información los países adopten programas para evitar un desastre que, según García, "está al acecho".

Una de las charlas más alarmantes dio a conocer las cifras actuales sobre enfermedades y desastres por el mundo. El doctor alemán Martin Teuscher, profesor de la Universidad de Tübingen, explicó que el ser humano ya ha sido expuesto a varias enfermedades causadas por cambios o exageraciones del clima. "Es una realidad que hemos estado viviendo durante este siglo. Pero fíjense que con el cambio climático, las bajas serán aún mayores. Intensificarán el balance delicado entre el desastre y la prosperidad, entre tener hogar y ser desamparado, y finalmente, entre la vida y la muerte". Señaló, en concreto, que mundialmente mueren más de 4 millones de personas por la malnutrición, más de 2 millones por enfermedades diarreicas, y 1,2 millones por enfermedades como la malaria. Indudablemente, estas cifras aumentarán con el cambio del clima mundial. Dijo Teuscher que no estaría fuera de lo posible que esas cifras triplicaran en apenas 5 o 10 años.

Los descensos no pararán ahí. Con las temperaturas más cálidas, los insectos y otros organismos maléficos tendrán más oportunidad de desarrollarse y contagiar a los seres humanos como resultado. Se espera que ocurrirán más brotes de dengue y epidemias de malaria. Ambas enfermedades se trasmiten por la picadura de mosquitos. El calentamiento global favorece a estos insectos portadores de enfermedades. Otro resultado del calentamiento global son las inundaciones, las cuales proveen el ambiente ideal para la cría de mosquitos y las temidas pandémicas de cólera. Los recientes estudios realizados por los científicos ilustran la gravedad del problema del calentamiento global. En apenas 15 años, el número de personas en el continente de África expuesta a la malaria podrá llegar a las 100 millones. Globalmente, el dengue podrá amenazar a casi unos 2.000 millones de personas.

El calentamiento global ha traído trastornos en los climas mundiales, y cada año se manifiestan cambios y matices climáticos jamás vistos anteriormente. Por ejemplo, las olas de calor en Europa y los Estados Unidos significan miles de muertos cada año y los huracanes cada vez se vuelvan más devastadores y potentes. "El huracán Katrina de 2005 y el Huracán Mitch de 1998 destrozaron grandes partes del territorio americano", puntualizó Felipe Fonseca, meteorólogo mexicano que habló sobre los cambios sufridos en el Golfo de México por el calentamiento global. "Estos efectos sociales, económicos y políticos, aún se sienten. En 50 años podríamos encontrar partes del América del Norte bajo agua".

Las emisiones ocasionadas por los automóviles, camiones y aviones envenenan el aire que respiramos. Esa contaminación del aire causa casi un millón de muertes al año. Según los estimados citados por los expertos, por cada grado centígrado que aumente la temperatura global, habrá casi 30.000 muertos anuales adicionales por enfermedades cardiorrespiratorias. Con los recientes aumentos de precio de los combustibles, la demanda no ha disminuido lo suficiente para reducir la contaminación del aire. Muchos temen que con el crecimiento de las economías emergentes de Asia, más el gran número de chóferes que tendrán acceso a automóviles, el daño ambiental continúe perjudicando cualquier intento de conservar el medioambiente.

"El individuo sí tiene el poder para hacer una diferencia", explica Rachel Johnson, estudiante alemana y miembro de GreenWatch, un movimiento estudiantil que educa a jóvenes sobre la conservación y el reciclaje. "Esa bolsa plástica que arrojas a la basura sin pensarlo tardará un centenar en descomponerse. La gasolina y el petróleo influencian casi todos los aspectos de nuestra vida, y al mismo tiempo perjudican al nuestro bienestar y el del planeta. Tenemos que cambiar nuestra manera de pensar y actuar ahora. En mi país hay un dicho que dice: *Macht es jetzt! Warte nicht auf bessere Zeiten.* (¡Hazlo ahora! No esperes mejores momentos.) Si no hacemos el esfuerzo ahora, nuestras futuras generaciones se condenarán a una vida sin vida".

GO ON TO THE NEXT PAGE.

Fuente número 3

Introducción

Este informe, que se titula "Los expertos señalan mayores riesgos de salud por el calentamiento global" se emitió por la emisora hispanoamericana Enteramérica en julio de 2005.

Ahora escucha la fuente número tres.

> **PLAY AUDIO: Track 12**

Ahora escucha de nuevo.

> **PLAY AUDIO: Track 12**

Ahora tienes cuarenta minutos para preparar y escribir un ensayo persuasivo.

(40 minutes)

GO ON TO THE NEXT PAGE.

Interpersonal Speaking: Conversation

You will participate in a conversation. First, you will have 1 minute to read a preview of the conversation, including an outline of each turn in the conversation. Afterward, the conversation will begin, following the outline. Each time it is your turn to speak, you will have 20 seconds to record your response. You should participate in the conversation as fully and appropriately as possible.	Vas a participar en una conversación. Primero, vas a tener un minuto para leer la introducción y el esquema de la conversación. Después, comenzará la conversación, siguiendo el esquema. Cada vez que te corresponda participar en la conversación, vas a tener 20 segundos para grabar tu respuesta. Debes participar de la manera más completa y apropiada posible.

Tienes un minuto para leer la introducción.

Introducción

Has solicitado una posición de aprendiz en una empresa multinacional latinoamericana. Imagina que recibes una llamada telefónica del director del Departamento de Recursos Humanos para hablar sobre la posición que has solicitado.

> **PLAY AUDIO: Track 13**

Entrevistador	Te saluda
Tú	Contesta la pregunta
Entrevistador	Te hace una pregunta
Tú	Responde a la pregunta
Entrevistador	Continúa la conversación
Tú	Responde a la pregunta
Entrevistador	Continúa la conversación
Tú	Responde a la pregunta
Entrevistador	Continúa la conversación
Tú	Contesta que no es posible y ofrece una alternativa
Entrevistador	Continúa la conversación
Tú	Despídete

GO ON TO THE NEXT PAGE.

Presentational Speaking: Cultural Comparison

You will make an oral presentation on a specific topic to your class. You will have 4 minutes to read the presentation topic and prepare your presentation. Then you will have 2 minutes to record your presentation.	Vas a dar una presentación oral a tu clase sobre un tema cultural. Vas a tener 4 minutos para leer el tema de la presentación y prepararla. Después vas a tener 2 minutos para grabar tu presentación.
In your presentation, compare your own community to an area of the Spanish-speaking world with which you are familiar. You should demonstrate your understanding of cultural features of the Spanish-speaking world. You should also organize your presentation clearly.	En tu presentación, compara tu propia comunidad con una región del mundo hispanohablante que te sea familiar. Debes demostrar tu comprensión de aspectos culturales en el mundo hispanohablante y organizar tu presentación de una manera clara.

Tienes cuatro minutos para leer el tema de la presentación y prepararla.

(4 minutes)

Tema de la presentación:

Se sabe que los idiomas enriquecen la vida de uno. Explica de qué manera los idiomas han influenciado la sociedad en que tú vives y en otra ciudad hispanohablante que tú hayas observado, estudiado o visitado.

Compara tus observaciones acerca de las comunidades en las que has vivido con tus observaciones de una región del mundo hispanohablante que te sea familiar. En tu presentación, puedes referirte a lo que has estudiado, vivido, observado, etc.

Tienes dos minutos para grabar tu presentación.

STOP

END OF EXAM

Practice Test 1:
Answers and
Explanations

ANSWER KEY

Section I

1.	B	23.	D	45.	B
2.	C	24.	B	46.	D
3.	D	25.	D	47.	C
4.	A	26.	A	48.	C
5.	B	27.	B	49.	D
6.	C	28.	C	50.	A
7.	A	29.	B	51.	B
8.	B	30.	D	52.	B
9.	B	31.	C	53.	A
10.	D	32.	C	54.	D
11.	C	33.	C	55.	C
12.	B	34.	A	56.	B
13.	D	35.	B	57.	A
14.	C	36.	B	58.	C
15.	C	37.	D	59.	D
16.	A	38.	C	60.	B
17.	B	39.	C	61.	B
18.	A	40.	B	62.	D
19.	A	41.	A	63.	B
20.	D	42.	D	64.	C
21.	B	43.	C	65.	A
22.	A	44.	B		

Section II

See explanations beginning on page 265.

SECTION I

Interpretive Communication: Print Texts (Page 206)

Selection 1: Translated Text and Questions, with Explanations

Introduction

The following interview appeared in a Latin-American magazine in June 2014.

This Physical Education teacher, 35 years old and a native of Santiago, Chile, realized a dream that many Caribbean dancers yearn for: to be two-time world champion of rumba. And in Europe! Almost 10 years ago, Christian Vera left his country and moved to Spain to practice his profession and great passion: dance. In said continent, he has traveled many countries teaching this tropical dance and also participating in different competitions. He has many anecdotes and experiences. Here we will come to know a few.

How has it come to be that a Chilean became the two-time world champion of rumba?

The most important Cuban festival in Europe is held in Barcelona every year; and during that event there is a world competition called "Searching for the Rumba Dancer." It is an individual competition in which every competitor, coming from different parts of the world, shows his or her dance talent. In my first participation, in 2011, I came second and then I managed first place two years in a row. After that, I became the first non-Cuban teacher to teach folklore at that festival.

How did you arrive at rumba? What was it that motivated you to practice this discipline?

What inspired me was a movie: *Dance With Me;* there I saw the protagonists dancing salsa in Cuba. The truth is that I always had dance in my blood because all my family is dedicated to it. Every day when I wake, I want to dance; and I still have the same enthusiasm and energy as in the beginning. That is also why I have been perfecting my dance. Every day I am learning something new from different types of dance.

Why has your career developed in Europe?

In the year 2007, I had a scholarship to the ITK University in Leipzig to obtain a postgrad in Applied Sciences toward soccer. After that, I was in Spain for three months doing an internship with Villareal club, which was directed at the time by Manuel Pellegrini. There, the team's physical trainer told me about a masters that he had done in Barcelona. That's why after returning to Chile and working for a time, I gathered money and again headed to the Mother Country to enroll myself in that course of specialization.

Do you believe that this type of dance is today more popular in Europe than in Latin America?

In the old continent there is an advantage: The countries are very close and flights are not expensive. Thus, the dancers and aficionados of dances like salsa can travel to different competitions and festivals. The competitions have lots of success because the people are not only impassioned about dance, but also have the possibility of attending en masse. There is a lot of demand.

Latin dances are lively and sensual. Is that what Europeans like about these rhythms?

Europeans, in general, are disciplined and in the case of dance they focus a lot on trying to get to know in depth the culture of the dance. Many even learn Spanish in order to understand the songs; they don't just want to dance and mimic. I believe that all the Europeans who learn to dance the Cuban dances want to get to know Cuba.

And what impression do people get when they see a Chilean dancer teaching Cuban salsa?

I never have been to Cuba. But many people ask me how it is possible that I dance with rhythm and style so markedly tropical. They mistake me for a Cuban, and not precisely because of my accent, but rather because of the way I dance. It can work against you, of course, because there is a theme of tradition and reference among Cubans, but I believe that whoever goes with that and feels it in his or her skin will have success.

Do you see yourself as or feel like an ambassador of salsa in Europe?

Cubans are very protective over their culture. When they find out that I dance salsa, they can have a type of prejudice at first. But once they see me on the dance floor, everything changes. I hope that they judge me always for what I do. And in that sense, I have come to earn the respect of the great Cuban salsa masters. It seems to me that more than an ambassador proper, I like to see myself as a person who has the power to be an example that yes, one can dance salsa or rumba without being Cuban. I enjoy being able to represent all of those people.

1. Who is Christian Vera?
   (A) A Cuban salsa master
   (B) A Chilean rumba and salsa teacher who lives in Spain
   (C) A Spanish rumba and salsa teacher who lives in Cuba
   (D) A Chilean salsa master

Christian Vera is Chilean, so eliminate (A) and (C). He teaches rumba and salsa in Spain, so (B) is the correct answer.

2. Why do Europeans enjoy Latin rhythms?
   (A) Because they are lively and sensual
   (B) Because it is easier to seduce women with dance
   (C) Because they can get to know Cuban culture
   (D) Because they offer contrast to the discipline that exists in Europe

Vera talks about how Europeans want to get to know the culture better by learning Spanish, among other things, so (C) is the correct choice. The interviewer asks about the lively and sensual nature of the dances, as in (A), but that is not the answer that Christian gives. The correct answer is (C).

3. How did Vera arrive at rumba?
   (A) It was a fundamental part of his culture.
   (B) It was an integral part of his family, and therefore his father taught him.
   (C) He spent some time in Cuba to learn rumba.
   (D) He saw a movie about Latin dance and was inspired by it.

Christian tells the interviewer about the time he watched *Dance With Me* and was inspired, so (D) is correct. He does say that dance is in his blood, but does not say that rumba was part of his culture or that his father taught him to dance, eliminating (A) and (B). He has never been to Cuba, eliminating (C). The correct answer is (D).

4. Why has his career developed in Spain?

   (A) He had studied in Europe with a scholarship when he met a teacher in Barcelona.

   (B) He spent part of his childhood in Europe and wanted to return.

   (C) He learned to dance in Latin America first and decided to move to Spain.

   (D) He is the first non-Cuban to teach Cuban folklore.

He talks about his scholarship to study Applied Sciences in Leipzig and then his internship in Spain. That is when he learned of his future teacher in Barcelona. The correct answer is (A).

5. How do other dancers accept the Chilean when he dances salsa?

   (A) The Europeans accept him as a Cuban.

   (B) At first there is a bit of prejudice, but everything changes when Vera is dancing.

   (C) He can never dance as well as the Cubans.

   (D) They always accept him as Cuban without question.

Choice (A) is only partially correct, while (B) more fully explains how others view him and accept him. Choice (C) is too harsh, and (D) is not true because they do question him.

6. How does Vera respond to the interviewer's last question?

   (A) He responds that yes, he is the official ambassador to Cuba.

   (B) He responds that no, that is too much pressure for him.

   (C) He responds that yes, he wants to be the dance ambassador for everyone.

   (D) He responds that no, the Cubans do not accept him on the dance floor.

Christian says that he wants to be an example for anyone who wants to dance, even if that dance is not part of their culture. Therefore, he wants to be an ambassador for everyone. The correct answer is (C).

Selection 2: Translated Text and Questions, with Explanations

Introduction

The following article appeared in 2009 in a Spanish film magazine.

Politics, Films, and Power in Spain

Spanish cinema is the political pulse of Spain. Aside from being one of the most important countries in experimental film, it is one that has expressed the triumphs and failures of the government.

In 1929, Luis Buñuel and Salvador Dali made the film *Un Chien Andalou* to express their radical sentiments on the state of Spain and the modernization of the world. They, in their surrealist film, address the impact of the modernization of women, religion, and Spain. At the start of the Second Republic, socialist citizens rejected Spanish traditions such as the Catholic Church and the monarchy in favor of industrialism and innovation, the subjects of Buñuel and Dali's film. The Second Republic was one of the first glimpses of political liberty in Spain, and the film reflects the new freedom of religious and political expression. Unfortunately, Franco's dictatorship after the Spanish Civil War censored the majority of filmmakers.

During the regime of Francisco Franco, which began in 1939, the government controlled the communication networks and the majority of films, though some directors were able to avoid censorship through satire. Masters of the cinema, such as Luis García Berlanga and Juan Antonio Bardem, created works that, on the surface, appeared far removed from political subjects, but in reality made fun of the conservative upper class. *Death of a Cyclist* by Bardem is the paradigm of this dichotomy because it tells the story of death and tragic romance, but also includes a subtle irony to illustrate the differences between social classes during the dictatorship.

After Franco's death, directors discovered new freedom of expression that flourished in Spain without the threat of censorship. *What Have I Done to Deserve This?!*, by Pedro Almódovar in 1984, was a great example of the new sexual and political freedom in film, which was an analogy for the new government after Franco. All the characters of the film (a prostitute, a drug dealer, a grandmother, a mother, and more), possess endearing traits with which the public identifies and which make them likable, showing the large increase in social acceptance in Spain.

Today, directors can express themselves by whatever means they choose. Directors such as Almódovar, Alejandro Amenábar, and Woody Allen are successful with contemporary audiences, examining controversial, even scandalous, topics, which shows the profound change in public and government sentiment.

7. What is the purpose of the article?

(A) **It describes how film has changed with the political climate in Spain, though at times it offers criticism of the government.**

(B) It mentions some important filmmakers and their works.

(C) It warns against the dangers of censorship.

(D) It shows how filmmakers during Franco's rule used satire and irony to resist government censorship.

Choice (A) is the correct answer. The purpose of the article is to show how Spanish cinema has paralleled the liberal and conservative swings of the government. In addition, some filmmakers have used their work to criticize the government. While it does talk about some important filmmakers and their works, those are not the main focus of the article (B). While the author is against censorship (C), and some filmmakers did use satire and irony during Franco's regime (D), neither were the primary point of the article.

8. *Un Chien Andalou* is mentioned in order to

(A) praise the genius of Dali and Buñuel

(B) **give an example of innovation in Spanish film to show political modernization**

(C) show the great success of the cinema during the 1920s and 30s

(D) address the impact of surrealism during the Second Republic

Un Chien Andalou is an example of the overall innovation and modernization happening in Spain and around the world during that time. Though Dali and Buñuel are considered geniuses by most, that is beyond the scope of the passage and not the reason for the film's mention in the second paragraph (A). Choice (C) is not the focus of the paragraph, and (D) is never mentioned in the passage, so (B) is correct.

9. Franco's influence on cinema was one of

(A) celebration

(B) **censorship**

(C) horror

(D) satire

Choice (B) is correct. Franco's influence was one of oppression, in which filmmakers had to censor themselves so as to not anger the government. Horror, (C), is too extreme. Celebration, (A), is too positive, while satire, (D), describes some of the films themselves rather than Franco's regime.

10. It can be inferred that
    (A) *Death of a Cyclist* is the best film from the time of Franco
    (B) after the Second Republic, there was absolutely no freedom in the country
    (C) today, only controversial topics have success in Spanish film
    (D) Almodóvar, Buñuel, and Bardem had success with their films

Choice (D) is correct. The only sentence we can infer from the passage is that the filmmakers mentioned were successful because we have proof in the last paragraph. Choices (A), (B), and (C) are extreme answers, containing superlatives and exaggerated language.

11. What happened in Spanish cinema after Franco?
    (A) There was a period of conservative ideals that restricted many directors.
    (B) Pedro Almodóvar created a scandal with his film *What Have I Done to Deserve This?!*
    (C) There was new freedom for directors to make what they wanted.
    (D) The legacy of Franco permeated the country.

Choice (C) is correct. After Franco, directors had new freedom to do as they pleased in their work without the threat of censorship (fourth paragraph). Choice (A) is the opposite of what happened after Franco, while (B) and (D) go beyond the information offered in the passage.

12. Pedro Almódovar, Alejandro Amenabar, and Woody Allen are mentioned in order to
    (A) suggest that the directors are friends and hold each other in high esteem
    (B) give examples of successful directors of contemporary Spanish film
    (C) show that they revolutionized film as much as did Dali and Buñuel
    (D) show that controversial and scandalous themes are the only ones that contemporary audiences enjoy

Choice (B) is correct. The directors mentioned in the last paragraph are examples of those who have recently had success in contemporary Spanish film. Though we might hope it is true, we do not know from the passage that they are all friends (A). The comparison to Dali and Buñuel is not supported by the text (C), and (D) is extreme.

Selection 3: Translated Text and Questions, with Explanations

Introduction

The following article appeared in a Hispanic newspaper in December 2016.

Cuba is a hot spot today. Personalities such as Pope Francis, Beyoncé, Rihanna, and Pelé have flocked to the lovely Caribbean island. Nevertheless, the visit of the U.S. president Barack Obama was one of the most momentous, perhaps because it had been 88 years since a United States head of state traveled to the Caribbean country. But it is not just the visit itself, but also its significance: Obama in Cuba represented the possible end of the "Cold War."

For David Soler, deputy director of the Office of Cultural Heritage of Cienfuegos, a city with ample cultural tourism on offer, the country has increased the numbers of foreign tourists gradually, and "with the resumed diplomatic relations and commerce with the United States, we hope this will dramatically increase the presence of North American businesses and tourists. We are the closest nation they have after Mexico and Canada," he explains.

As this investigator of Cuban culture argues, all the United States citizens who will come to Cuba to invest or be tourists bring their culture and their forms of trade, of portraying themselves, and even of eating; little by little the Cubans will try to adapt their services and businesses to this type of tourist/businessperson.

"Notice how Cuban culture can be influenced, how what happened with the arrival of the first North American cruise to Havana in early May this year might repeat: The visitors were received by voluptuous mixed-race women dressed in patriotic Cuban symbols. In this way they contributed to reinforcing stereotypes of our people: that this is just a land of mixed-race dancers, of rum and tobacco, when in reality it is much richer than that," grumbles Soler.

According to the deputy director, all these changes lead to a very dangerous cultural interchange, where those who arrive from abroad try to put in place their own forms and culture. "Cubans, interested in North American investment here, may make the mistake of responding only to northern interests and forgetting their own identity and culture," he notes.

Even though the larger wave has not yet arrived, the investigator assures that it is expected soon. "The people here are preparing for it, studying more English, preparing their businesses for U.S. tourists, and studying northern customs, at times looking down on their own," this lover of Cuban culture confesses to us with a heavy heart.

All the changes that have occurred since December 17, 2014, when both presidents announced the reestablishment of diplomatic relations, point to an immediate future closely linked with tourism and services, obviously focused on the North American market. The Cubans, logically, see the "reconciliation" as a source of direct revenue.

The change can bring transformations beyond the political and greatly influence business between citizens in both nations. Jenny Lleonart Cruz, a young Cuban businesswoman and owner of a luxurious private inn in Cienfuegos, says that "something as simple as having PayPal or accepting credit card payments is something that is just around the corner. This would help a lot with receipt of and payment for goods and services. It would also make electronic commerce in Cuba possible. Even something as simple as going to Miami to buy supplies for my inn would be feasible."

Pedro Gómez, Havana resident, is more cautious and notes that Cubans cannot allow themselves to give in and fall again into a capitalist system. "That is what the Americans want. We cannot return to that because in that time there was much suffering because of economic inequality. So Cuba must be very careful with what approaches; the changes can be dangerous as well."

Definitely, the winds of change that blow in Cuba with the reestablishment of relations with the United States will change the lives of Cubans, but also of some other Latin American countries. Some of these will benefit or be harmed, such as the tourist attractions of Punta Cana and the Mayan Riviera, which see great competition with Cuba open to the North American market.

Meanwhile, Cubans go on with their day-to-day through the streets of the country and dream about miraculous changes. They have hope that in one form or another, this political bridge extending between both nations will not break again, and will function as a pathway to economic development for the inhabitants of this beautiful island, which rises from the center of the Caribbean.

13. What is the point of the article?

    (A) The political bridge between Cuba and the United States is still fragile.

    (B) The economic changes may be difficult for Cuba during this transition.

    (C) The reestablishment of relations with the United States will change the lives of Cubans.

    (D) The end of the embargo and mandate signifies some economic changes for the island.

Choices (A) and (B) are mentioned in the passage, but they are not the main focus of the passage. Choice (C) predicts the future, which is impossible to do, so eliminate (C) as well. The wording of (D) indicates that changes are likely to occur, making this the correct choice.

14. Why are Pope Francis, Beyoncé, Rihanna, and Pelé mentioned in the first paragraph?

    (A) They are ambassadors to Cuba for their respective countries.

    (B) They want to travel to Cuba, but it is not possible until the end of the "Cold War."

    (C) They were some of the first people to visit Cuba after the end of the United States mandate.

    (D) They are some of the artists who have given concerts in Cuba.

The only true statement in this question is (C). They are not literally ambassadors, eliminating (A), and it is possible for them to visit since they did so already, eliminating (B). It is not stated in the article that they have given concerts in Cuba (Pope Francis most likely hasn't given any concerts in Cuba), eliminating (D). The correct answer is (C).

15. In the second paragraph, David Soler hopes that

    (A) the Cuban economy suffers because of unequal resources

    (B) the change will be the end of the "Cold War"

    (C) the change will increase the presence of commerce and tourism

    (D) Cuban influence will change the world

David Soler mentioned many things about the previous economy and what he hopes will happen, but does not state that there are unequal resources at present, eliminating (A). He does not mention anything about the Cold War, eliminating (B), nor does he mention (D). The correct answer is (C).

16. Why are PayPal and credit cards mentioned in paragraph 8?

    (A) They are elements of the northern economy that could change Cuban businesses.

    (B) They are indicators of electronic commerce in Cuba.

    (C) They are methods of payment in Cuban businesses.

    (D) They are dangers for Cuban businesses because they contain northern interests.

PayPal and credit cards are simple things that the northern economy takes for granted, but are not existent in Cuba. These elements introduced into Cuba's economy could create change. They are not indicators of electronic commerce since they do not yet exist in Cuba, nor are they current methods of payment, eliminating (B) and (C). They are never mentioned as dangerous, eliminating (D). The correct answer is (A).

17. What does Pedro Gómez think of the economic change in Cuba?

    (A) He thinks that capitalism will destroy the country.

    (B) He thinks that Cuba should be cautious because there is an inequality of resources.

    (C) He thinks it is invaluable that Cubans learn English.

    (D) He thinks the future of the Cuban economy is tourism.

Gómez is cautious about the reestablishment and what it will mean for the country's the economy, but (A) is too extreme. He never mentions (C) or (D), so the answer must be (B). He says that they should be cautious.

18. According the last paragraph, what do Cubans hope?

   (A) They hope that the Cuban economy develops to be prosperous in the Caribbean.

   (B) They hope that the presidents of the two countries can be friends.

   (C) They hope that the political bridge that was made between the two nations breaks again.

   (D) They hope that Cuba adapts to northern culture.

The Cubans are optimistic, but there is no information about (B) or (D) in the last paragraph. It says the opposite of (C), so the correct answer is (A).

Selection 4: Translated Text and Questions, with Explanations

Introduction

The following pamphlet appeared in 2005 from Global Health Action.

Reducing the Inequalities of World Health

The contemporary world health crisis is a reflection of the growing inequalities that exist between countries and within them. Scientific and technological advances have contributed to an improvement in the health of some people. Nevertheless, there are ever more people living in poverty, and 30,000 children dying every day.

The Observatory of World Health 2005–2006 presents disparities in health and calls attention to the mechanisms that governments, international institutions, and civil society can apply to combat them.

Health workers in particular can play a vital role in transforming the rhetoric about universal health rights and global citizenship into a reality. Those who live in more prosperous areas of the world have a particular responsibility to push toward change.

The interdependence generated under globalization increases these ethical responsibilities.

The topics covered by the *Observatory* are diverse, but all of them highlight the economic, social, and political inequalities that destroy health.

This campaign document focuses on key areas where collective pressure should be exercised.

■ **Constructing a just world**
   The achievement of a just world in which poverty is eliminated and health is developed entails changing the way the global economy is run, and substantially increasing the transfer of resources from central countries to peripheral ones.

■ **Defending and extending the public sector**
   The repair and development of public health care systems are crucial to stop the threats of commercialization and to reduce widening social and health chasms. This report proposes a ten-point agenda of action.

■ **Migration, pharmaceuticals, and large corporations**
   The migration of health workers, the global norms of intellectual property that increase the prices of medicine, and the impact of multinational corporations on health stand out as three examples of the manner in which globalization and subordination of health rights to commercial objectives directly affect health and systems of health throughout the world.

■ **Taking action in the face of climate change and militarization**
   The change in global climate and militarism are two of the most important causes, present and future, of the deterioration of health throughout the world. The current inability to confront said predicament in any significant way

indicates an urgent need for better mobilization of civil society, popular organizations, and health workers to pull off more effective and just solutions.

■ **Affirming leadership for global health in the World Health Organization**
The world needs a multilateral health agency that is capable of protecting and promoting health, reducing inequalities, and securing full protection of universal rights with regard to basic needs and health. In order for this to succeed, the WHO requires more resources and to be more sensitive to the needs of the people, achieving higher administration standards.

Global Health Action demands that the *Observatory* recommend an agenda that is oriented towards the fight of health workers and campaign administrators.

19. What is the purpose of the pamphlet?

    (A) The pamphlet seeks to disseminate information about global health and some reasons for world changes.

    (B) The pamphlet seeks to show the problems that cannot be solved.

    (C) Global Health Action is the best-equipped organization to solve the mentioned conflicts.

    (D) The world needs a multilateral health agency capable of protecting and promoting health.

The pamphlet does not say that the problems cannot be solved, nor that the Global Health Action is the best organization, so eliminate (B) and (C). The pamphlet does state that the world needs an agency like the one described in (D), but that is not the primary purpose. Choice (A) is the best description of the passage as a whole.

20. According to the author in the first paragraph, why is there a contemporary world health crisis?

    (A) Agencies today are incapable of helping and promoting health with the few resources they have.

    (B) Militarism has destroyed public health.

    (C) Scientific and technological advances destroyed the order of the world.

    (D) There has been a growth of inequalities that exist between countries and within them.

Choice (A) is offensive to the agencies in place today and (B) is extreme, so those may be eliminated. Choice (C) is both extreme and untrue in its use of recycled words, so eliminate (C) as well. The correct answer is (D).

21. In the first paragraph, why does the author include "Nevertheless, there are ever more people living in poverty, and 30,000 children dying every day"?

    (A) It is unbelievable how many children die every day.

    (B) There is juxtaposition between those who have good public health and those who do not.

    (C) It is necessary to have more resources and to be more sensitive to the needs of the people to save the children.

    (D) The children suffer due to globalization and subordination of global health rights.

While it might be awful how many children die every day, the purpose for the author's inclusion of this phrase is to create a juxtaposition between those who benefit from the scientific advances and those who remain in poverty. Choices (C) and (D) are not mentioned in the passage, but recycle words from the passage. Therefore, the correct answer is (B).

22. How does the pamphlet refer to a "just world"?

    (A) A just world can change the manner in which the global economy is run.

    (B) A just world saves lives because it can protect people and promote health.

    (C) It is a world in which everyone can live in harmony.

    (D) It is a world that has low medicine prices for the rich.

In the first bullet point of the passage, it is stated that a just world will be achieved through managing the global economy. While (B) and (C) might be true, they are not explicitly stated in the passage. Choice (D) is a reversal of what the passage states later on. The correct answer is (A).

23. What does the public sector have to do with public health?

    (A) It can obtain important resources for children.

    (B) It is one of the present and future causes of the deterioration of health throughout the world.

    (C) It maintains and grows militarism.

    (D) It can stop the threats of commercialization.

The public sector paragraph talks about stopping or hindering the spread of commercialization, so the correct answer is (D). It does not talk about children, militarism, or that it is a cause of health deterioration in the world. Therefore, the answer is (D).

24. Why does the pamphlet mention militarism?

    (A) It is mentioned to reduce inequalities between countries.

    (B) It is one of the most important causes of global health deterioration.

    (C) Militaries are mentioned as popular health organizations.

    (D) Militarism provides employment to many workers.

Militarism is one of the largest problems, according to the passage. It does not reduce inequalities between the countries (in fact, it may do the opposite), eliminating (A). It is certainly not one of the health organizations, eliminating (C), and (D) is irrelevant. Choice (B) is correct.

25. All of the following are goals of Global Health Action EXCEPT:

    (A) repairing and developing systems of public health

    (B) reducing economic inequalities

    (C) securing full protection of universal rights

    (D) raising the prices of medicines

Global Health Action does not raise the price of medicines, but rather tries to do the opposite to make health-care affordable. The correct answer is (D).

Selection 5: Translated Text and Questions, with Explanations

Introduction

The following article is about Spain's late-night schedule.

Spain: A Place for Night Owls

The following article appeared in a United States magazine in 2008.

Spaniards sleep one hour less each day than their European neighbors; they cannot reconcile professional life with familial and labor productivity is much lower than that of other Europeans. And all because of their peculiar schedules: they eat and dine late, the workday is lengthened considerably, and people go to bed past midnight. These schedules have existed since the 1940s, but now are questioned. The alternative is to adopt European schedules, but will Spaniards be capable of this?

According to recommendations of the World Health Organization, a person should sleep 8 hours daily. Exhaustion, sleep, stress invade Spanish homes as well as doctor visits. Doctor Rosa García López-Tello states, "Chronic sleep deficit is turning into the biggest cardiovascular risk factor." She insists that the healthiest thing to do is to get restorative sleep and to sleep eight hours for adults and between 10 and 12 for children.

All this decreases productivity. Studies show that businesses that have adopted measures for their employees to have more reasonable schedules increase efficiency, optimize resources, and, most importantly, have happier workers. This directive of a European multinational points to another consequence: "These schedules are not at all in harmony with those of your European colleagues. You go through about four hours in which you cannot communicate with them, and when they finish eating you start, and when you finish eating they're done with their workday. This creates many difficulties when working in a multinational setting."

Jaime Albuerne is a business executive who for professional reasons travels frequently to Germany. "It is true that there, everything is more organized, but when I have to eat at 18:00 I always think 'But in Spain it's still snack time!'" Jaime believes that this "order" doesn't work for the Spaniard. "Here we have many hours of sun, we like life in the street, stay up all night even at home. I don't see the Spaniard eating dinner so early."

In Spain, no one is spared these late schedules. Because everyone leaves work late, businesses have to lengthen the hours they are open well into the night to facilitate shopping for their clients. The same occurs in movie theaters, theater, and television.

For their part, the hotel industry located in tourist zones have to do very long days, since the intent is to please b Spaniards and foreigners. The idea is that the latter does not feel uprooted and can eat or dine at the same hours countries of origin.

The other sector of the population that is harmed is children. Children finish school much earlier th work, which obligates them to do numerous extracurricular activities so they remain occupied and

Teresa Pozas, a teacher in early childhood education, states, "There are many children wh school, since there exists early morning care, where monitors keep them for an hour or tw the school day, they can stay to participate in extracurricular activities. All in all, they sp

Sara Berbel, doctor of Social Psychology and expert in this topic, explains: "Durin Europeans had adopted very long and rigid work days. After the war, the most advan good for productivity and they modernized. But Spain entered into a dictatorship a paralyzed."

In large part, Latin American schedules are similar to those of Spaniards. Be two factors: The great impact that Spanish culture had there and the fact that 147 industrialization either. In North America, the schedules coincide with the E

For Argentinian Betty Mendoza everything is much simpler: "We are Latinos and we like to live this way, taking full advantage of the day, in a more disorganized way." She arrived to Spain 15 years ago and confirmed that the schedules were the same as in her country. "Today all the world talks of changing them, but I don't see why. We are millions of people and we have lived that way for years and I believe we function very well," she concludes.

26. What is the point of the article?

   (A) The article searches for explanations for the differences between the Spanish schedule and those of other European countries.

   (B) The Spaniards have a chronic sleep deficit and are at cardiovascular risk.

   (C) Industrialization still has not happened in Spain.

   (D) Spanish businesses that have adopted measures so that their employees have more reasonable hours and happier workers.

The article mentions (B) and (D), but they are not the main point of the passage. Choice (C) is too extreme to be the correct answer; rather the article states that it did not develop in Spain the way it did in other countries. The correct answer is (A).

27. Why does Jaime Albuerne say "But in Spain it is still snack time!"?

   (A) The majority of Germans do not know what time it is.

   (B) According to his normal schedule, it is too early to eat dinner.

   (C) The Spanish schedule is better than the German.

   (D) He doesn't understand why German businesses have their work hours this way.

Jaime is saying it is still snack time for him because in Spain they eat dinner much later than 18:00. That is not to say that one schedule is better than the other, eliminating (C), nor that he does not understand the German schedule, eliminating (D). Choice (A), that the majority of Germans do not know what time it is, is ridiculous. The correct answer is (B).

28. According to the fifth paragraph, what happens with movie theaters, theaters, and television?

   (A) They have to serve tourists and therefore need different hours than those of the workers.

   (B) Children spend a lot of time in school, and therefore need entertainment afterwards.

   (C) They have business hours that serve the Spanish people.

   (D) It is difficult for people to go to the movies or to the theater after working.

fifth paragraph states that business hours are extra-long for Spanish retailers, and for movie theaters, the-
and televison as well, so that people can go to the cinemas and theaters after work since they work later.
ccommodate the odd hours rather than making it difficult, eliminating (A) and (D). While children
d entertainment after school, that is not stated in the passage, eliminating (B). The correct answer

th paragraph, how does Sara Berbel explain the Spanish schedule?

ivil war was a disaster that paralyzed the country.

tatorship limited the process of modernization in Spain.

did not like industrialization.

culture had a large effect on Latin American countries.

While (A) might be true according to some opinions, it is too extreme according to this passage, and it recycles words from the passage. Choice (B) says the same while making it less extreme and includes the modernization process Berbel mentions. Choice (C) is untrue, and (D) is irrelevant to the question. The correct answer is (B).

30. In the last paragraph, what does Betty Mendoza point out?
    (A) It is necessary to fix the Spanish schedule because it doesn't coincide with those of other European countries.
    (B) The advances of industrialization should be implemented in Spain and Argentina.
    (C) She likes Spanish culture because it works for her.
    (D) There are similar elements between Latin American and Spanish schedules, and she likes them that way.

Mendoza seems to like the schedules and she felt at home in Spain because its schedule was very similar to that of Argentina, where she is from. She does not believe it is necessary to fix the schedule, nor that industrialization should be implemented in Spain and Argentina, eliminating (A) and (B). Choice (C) may be true, but it is not what she points out. The fact that they are similar is her point, so (D) is correct.

Interpretive Communication: Print and Audio Texts (Combined) (Page 216)

Selection 1: Translated Texts and Questions, with Explanations

Source 1
Introduction: In Panama, and in many Latin American countries, many people wear uniforms to work or to school. Today, however, with economic globalization, there is a dialogue among generations about whether uniforms are necessary. This article appeared in the Panamanian press in February 2012.

The Use of Uniforms: A Very Latino Habit

Here in Panama, uniforms are common. They are used from the smallest businesses to the presidential cabinet of the Republic. But where did this success of uniforms in Panama come from? Two important movements in 20th-century history contributed to the change in perception of uniforms. The first of these was the massive integration of women in the workforce. The second cause, and the more crucial, was the start of the Space Age.

Some people may believe that these new tendencies were inspired by technology and science fiction, and thus influenced people's spirits and way of dressing. On all sides, people wanted to make themselves uniform and part of this "futuristic revolution."

The airlines were the first to use this new style. They changed from the simple, naval-type vestments to designer uniforms. Soon, they were adapted by companies around the world for their employees. In many places, this was a passing style, but not in Panama. The business of uniforms became a very lucrative trade.

Giving up uniforms does not mean that employees will be badly dressed or in poor taste. In Panama, if the people do not have a "dress code," they will automatically choose fresh and light garments, ideal for bearing the tropical heat. However, these are not adequate for serious or professional environments. Many people who use uniforms think it is practical and it actually simplifies their process of preparing for work. However, others do not like the idea of having to use uniforms.

Nowadays, simple shirts with logos are the most popular form of uniforms in Panama. They represent the most simple and casual state of the uniform. Many businesses, especially banks and state institutions, still use multi-piece formal uniforms. Nevertheless, it is a tendency that is decreasing now that the sewing business, which in its time was a prosperous sector, is also declining.

Source 2

Introduction: This recording is about uniforms in the workplace or at school. The following interviewees share their opinions about uniforms. The recording lasts approximately three minutes.

(NARRATOR)   Source: the opinions of people of various ages on the subject of uniforms for work or school.

María Carolina, Panamanian, upon arrival in the United States to pursue higher education.

(PERSON 1)   Here, the entire world can wear what they want to work! Almost no one, with the exception of police, firefighters, and military officials, has to wear uniforms to go to work or school. I love their freedom of expression!

(NARRATOR)   Roberto Sánchez, 62 years old, owner and designer of a uniform factory in Panama.

(PERSON 2)   For me it was the most natural thing, the world of suits, ties, fabrics, buttons, zippers, threads, and insignias. Uniforms create a sense of belonging. They better work conditions, given that there is no time lost in choosing what to wear. Furthermore, people can invest their salaries in more important things than buying clothes for work.

(NARRATOR)   Eduardo is 35 years old, and a producer for a TV channel.

(PERSON 3)   I have never understood the reason for a person with a creative job to have to wear a uniform. It pigeonholes you in a style and doesn't permit you to express your true individuality.

(NARRATOR)   Rebecca de Suiza, from the United States, is an English professor at the National University of Panama.

(PERSON 4)   In my country, uniforms are situation-specific to some professions, such as doctors, nurses, or military members. They also have some ceremonial uses. It is interesting to see that, here in Panama, they are for everyone. To me it seems professional.

(NARRATOR)   Liz, a legal assistant, who works in a legal firm.

(PERSON 5)   For many people, the use of uniforms is difficult. For those with specific physical conditions such as being overweight, it is difficult to wear uniforms. However, even with a normal physique, there are other reasons for wearing uniforms: tattoos.

Many people do not feel comfortable addressing people with tattoos or have prejudices, especially in Latin America. The sleeves of my work blouses are a bit short, so I try to adjust their fit a bit so that my tattoos are not seen.

31. What event contributed to the change in the perception of uniforms in the 20th century?
    (A) The more serious and professional atmospheres demanded uniforms.
    (B) People liked science fiction and were inspired by the genre's stories.
    (C) There was an integration of women into the workforce.
    (D) Many businesses, especially banks and state institutions, used multi-piece uniforms.

Choice (C) is correct. The integration of women into the workplace and the start of the Space Age were two reasons for uniforms mentioned in the first paragraph. It does not say that people were inspired by science fiction or its stories (B), though it was offered as a possible explanation for the popularity of uniforms. Choice (A) is extreme, as professional atmospheres do not "demand" uniforms, and, while (D) is true, it is not a reason for a change in the perception of uniforms.

32. Generally, who uses uniforms in the United States?
    (A) TV producers
    (B) University professors
    (C) Firefighters and members of the military
    (D) Legal assistants

Choice (C) is correct. Though all these professions are mentioned in the audio, only the firefighters and military members are said to have uniforms in the United States.

33. The phrase "futurist revolution," is used to
    (A) refer to the social revolution inspired by science fiction
    (B) talk about the "dress code" that exists in all modes of work
    (C) illustrate that some people wore uniforms to conform
    (D) describe the integration of women into the workforce

Choice (C) is correct. The "futurist revolution" is a figure of speech that refered to the rise of uniforms and the urge of individuals to feel unified. It is in reference to science fiction novels that contain uniformed cultures, but it is not a social revolution inspired by the genre (A). Choice (B) is extreme, and (D) is not quite true. While it coincides with the integration of women into the workplace, the quote relates to science fiction novels.

34. Why is the climate mentioned in the discussion of uniforms?
    (A) It shows that the tropical climate lends itself to light fabrics, but these are not sufficiently professional for serious environments.
    (B) Light fabrics are ideal for the professional environment.
    (C) The dress code depends on the environment.
    (D) In Panama, everyone wants to dress in light fabrics to tolerate the heat.

Choice (A) is correct. The light fabrics lend themselves well to the tropical climate of Panama, according to the fourth paragraph. However, they are not suitable for more serious workplaces. This is the opposite of (B). While (D) is more or less in line with what individuals want to wear in the hot climate, it is both too extreme and not the reason for its mention in the passage. Choice (C) both is incorrect and goes beyond the text.

35. What is Eduardo's tone?
    (A) Perplexed
    (B) Negative
    (C) Hateful
    (D) Ecstatic

Choice (B) is correct. Eduardo is not in favor of uniforms for his work as a television director, as he believes it stifles creativity. Choice (C) is too strong, and (D), while the opposite of (C), is also an extreme answer. Choice (A) does not work either because he is not confused about his feelings.

36. According to the audio source, what is the opinion of the younger interviewees?
    (A) They hate the idea of uniforms.
    (B) It depends on the individual's profession.
    (C) Only the most conservative people like it.
    (D) They are indifferent because it is part of the culture.

Choice (B) is correct. There are varying opinions among the interviewees, according to profession, age, and other related elements. Choice (A) is too extreme, and only one or two interviewees dislike the idea of uniforms. There is nothing that states whether they are conservative or not (C), and the interviewees are certainly not indifferent to uniforms, as all of them have opinions.

37. All are reasons that the interviewees give for wearing uniforms EXCEPT:
    (A) They create a sense of belonging.
    (B) They cover things such as tattoos.
    (C) One's salary can be used on more important things than on work clothes.
    (D) They do not allow one to express one's individuality.

Choice (D) is correct. Eduardo is not in favor of uniforms as a TV producer because he says they do not allow him to express his creativity. Therefore, this is not a reason for wearing uniforms. Roberto states that uniforms can create a sense of belonging (A), and that one can use one's salary on more important things than work clothes (C). Liz mentions that she appreciates covering up tattoos at her workplace with her uniform (B).

38. Which of the people interviewed are in favor of uniforms?
    (A) Eduardo and Roberto Sánchez
    (B) Liz and Eduardo
    (C) Liz and Roberto Sánchez
    (D) Roberto Sánchez and María Carolina

Choice (C) is correct. Eduardo is not in favor of uniforms, which eliminates (A) and (B). María Carolina is not necessarily opposed to uniforms, but she does not support them, and she seems rather excited to see that people in America wear whatever they want, which eliminates (D) as well. Liz and Roberto are both in favor of uniforms, despite Liz pointing out some difficulties with them initially.

39. Which of the following statements best summarizes the article?
    (A) Many work uniforms are in bad taste.
    (B) The future of uniforms is doomed because sewing businesses are dwindling.
    (C) Many people have differing opinions about the use of uniforms at work.
    (D) There were many changes in the economy during the 20th century that contributed to the use of uniforms.

Choice (C) is correct. Clearly, from both the text and audio sources, there are many varying opinions and issues surrounding uniforms for work or school. Choice (B) predicts the future, and it is too harsh to say that the future of uniforms is "doomed." Choice (A), when taken out of context, is neither true nor the main point of the passage. Choice (D) is true, though it is not the main point of the passage or audio.

Selection 2: Translated Texts and Questions, with Explanations

Source 1

Introduction

This information appeared on the website GlobalChange.org, about school dropout amongst youths in Latin America. The statistics are from August 2013.

Why do young Latin Americans abandon secondary school?

With one out of every two students not finishing secondary school, school dropout affects young people in all sectors of society. Nevertheless, the following groups demonstrate disproportionately elevated dropout rates.

There are many factors that influence dropping out of school. Historically, access problems have contributed to high dropout rates in Latin America. In the last decades, however, Latin American countries have achieved notable advances in access to secondary education.

Although problems related to the economy and access continue to pose obstacles for education in certain places, they do not illustrate the complete story of the present situation. Various factors influence school dropout rates, and the reasons for which young people leave their studies can be surprising. According to the data from home surveys in 8 countries, the majority of students between 13 and 15 years old who do not go to school identify a lack of interest—above economic, access, or familial problems—as the principal reason for dropping out of school.

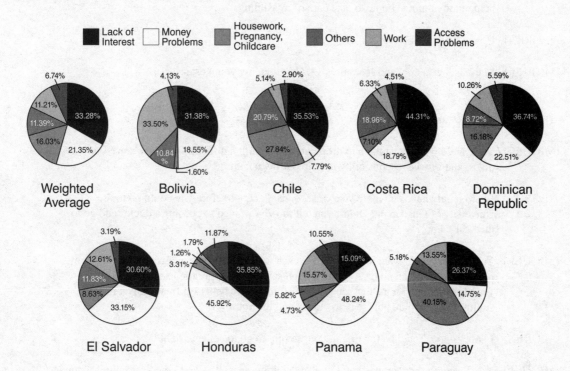

Source 2

Introduction: This recording is about dropping out of school. It is a conversation between two friends, Miguel and Loren, who live in Zacapa, Guatemala. The recording lasts approximately three minutes.

(MIGUEL) Hi Loren!

(LOREN) Hi Miguel! How are you?

(MIGUEL) Well, I've been all right, though a bit preoccupied. And you?

(LOREN) I'm well, thanks. What's wrong?

(MIGUEL) I'm thinking about dropping out of school, at least for a bit. I'm not sure what to do.

(LOREN) Oh, no! But you're such a good student!

(MIGUEL) Thank you. I don't really want to.

(LOREN) Why are you thinking of abandoning your studies, Miguel?

(MIGUEL) Well, my mother needs help caring for my little brother and two sisters, and my father needs help in his grocery store. I'm thinking about taking a year off to work for him and help out my mom at home to take care of my siblings.

(LOREN) How old are your siblings?

(MIGUEL) María is 8 years old and Joaquin is 12. Carolina, my youngest sister, is 6 years old.

(LOREN) And they are still in school?

(MIGUEL) Yes…and I don't want them to drop out of school. It's difficult for me because I am the oldest and I feel a responsibility to help out my parents.

(LOREN) But you only have one more year of secondary school before you could go to the University of Guatemala! Didn't you tell me you wanted to become a doctor and go to medical school?

(MIGUEL) Yes, I know! I still want to go to medical school. If I only take one year off to help my parents, I hope I can go back to finish high school and apply for a scholarship next year. In that time, I hope that the grocery store will be better off financially, and that my siblings will be more able to help out around the house.

(LOREN) I hope so too. You'd be the first in your family to go to college, right?

(MIGUEL) Yes. I want to set a good example for my siblings as well as go to medical school. I am determined to go back and finish secondary school.

(LOREN) I'm so glad to hear that! Please let me know if I can help.

(MIGUEL) Thank you very much, Loren. I am going to study chemistry during my free time, and perhaps you could help me.

(LOREN) Of course. I will share my notes with you, and we could study together.

(MIGUEL) That sounds great.

(LOREN) Sounds good to me too. You are going to complete your studies!

(MIGUEL) Well, we should go to class. See you later!

(LOREN) Goodbye!

40. What is the purpose of the article and statistics?
    (A) Students between 13 and 15 years of age need to work and help out their families at home.
    (B) **There are many reasons for dropping out of school, and the greatest reason reported is lack of interest.**
    (C) It is not known why there is a lack of interest in students between 13 and 15 years of age.
    (D) There are still economic and access problems that continue to pose obstacles for young people.

Choice (B) is the correct answer. The primary purpose of the article and statistics is to give various reasons for young people dropping out of secondary school, the biggest of which the study found to be lack of interest. Choice (C) is not mentioned in either of the sources, though the lack of interest is indeed a surprising finding. Both (A) and (D) are true, as some students need to work and others have access or money problems, but neither is the main point of the passage.

41. According to the data, what is the most commonly reported reason for dropping out of school in youth ages 13 to 15?
    (A) **Lack of interest**
    (B) Work
    (C) Access problems
    (D) Money problems

Choice (A) is the correct answer. Both the text and statistics suggest that lack of interest is the most reported reason for dropping out of school among students ages 13 to 15. All other choices are reported in the statistics, though not to the same degree.

42. All the following are reasons for abandoning secondary school EXCEPT
    (A) access problems
    (B) lack of interest
    (C) pregnancy and caring for children
    (D) **pressure from parents**

Choice (D) is the correct answer. All the reasons in (A), (B), and (C) are categories in the statistics. Pressure from parents is never mentioned in the audio or text sources.

43. The greatest reasons for lack of attendance in Bolivia are
    (A) lack of interest and household chores
    (B) lack of interest and money problems
    (C) **lack of interest and work**
    (D) lack of interest and access problems

Choice (C) is the correct answer. The greatest reasons for leaving school in Bolivia are lack of interest and the need to find work. The trap answer, (B), reports the weighted average across all countries, not specifically for Bolivia. Choice (A) would be correct for Chile, to the right of Bolivia, and (D) pairs lack of interest with access problems, a less common reported reason for leaving school in that country.

44. It can be inferred that
    (A) all young people in Latin America lack interest in their studies
    (B) the reasons for leaving school vary by country
    (C) access problems belong to the past
    (D) economic and access problems continue to be major obstacles in all places

Choice (B) is the correct answer. The reasons for dropping out of school vary by country. Problems of access have improved greatly, but are still factors in the present day (C). Though these access and money problems continue to be obstacles in all places, they are no longer the greatest problems (D). Choice (A) is extreme and offensive because not all young Latin Americans lack an interest in school.

45. What is Miguel's main dilemma?
    (A) Miguel lacks interest in his secondary school studies.
    (B) He needs to help his parents.
    (C) He needs to apply for a scholarship to attend the university.
    (D) He needs to find work.

Choice (B) is the correct answer. Miguel needs to help his parents by working in his father's grocery store and helping out at home. He is going to help his mother take care of his younger sisters and brother. He does say that he will apply for a scholarship to attend the university, but it is not Miguel's main concern, nor will he do so during his year off (C). He does not lack interest in his studies because he wants to become a doctor (A), and he does not need to find work because he will be working for his father at the grocery store (D).

46. Who are Maria, Joaquin, and Carolina?
    (A) They are friends of Miguel and Loren.
    (B) They are Loren's younger siblings.
    (C) They are Miguel's older siblings.
    (D) They are Miguel's younger siblings.

Choice (D) is the correct answer. Maria, Joaquin, and Carolina are Miguel's younger siblings, not Loren's.

47. What is Miguel going to do during his year off?
    (A) He is going to take care of his children and work for his father.
    (B) He is going to attend the University of Guatemala and medical school after that.
    (C) He is going to work with his father while caring for his siblings with his mother.
    (D) He is going to spend some time working and traveling with his father.

Choice (C) is the correct answer. Miguel is going to help his father in the grocery store and care for his younger siblings with his mother. His younger siblings are not his children (A), and he needs to finish secondary school before he can attend the University of Guatemala (B). Choice (D) is half-right because he is going to work for his father, but there is no mention of him traveling with his father.

Interpretive Communication: Audio Texts (Page 223)

Selection 3: Translated Text and Questions, with Explanations

Introduction

The following recording was part of a broadcast of "World of Sports," a radio program dedicated to sports from all parts of the world.

(NARRATOR) The Argentine Alfonso García wins the golf championship in Scotland.

(WOMAN) The tumultuous and cold weather here in St. Andrew's, Scotland, yesterday was the catalyst for some extraordinarily high scores in the international golf championship, which was won by the young Argentinian Alfonso García. García, who is only twenty-two years old, is the first Argentinian to win this championship at St. Andrew's, the most historic and perhaps the most prestigious golf course in the world. The efforts of the golfers were complicated throughout the three-day tournament by an implacable wind and intermittent rain squalls.

"I have never experienced such a violent and tempestuous wind," the excited golfer said yesterday. And when he was asked how the weather affected his game, the young Argentinian replied, "At the beginning, I didn't know how to adapt well to the wind and calculate it into each shot. Later, the rain squalls bothered me quite a bit. The first day when I scored a 75, I was feeling very frustrated. But during the second day, when I realized that the other players were also struggling, it was much easier for me to concentrate. I began to think I might actually be able to win this tournament."

García, who comes from a family of athletes, is the first of his family to play golf at the professional level. His father was a tennis champion in the seventies, and his younger sister, Patricia, is also a tennis player. Alfonso spends the majority of his time traveling on the PGA tour, but when he is not traveling, he lives with his parents in Buenos Aires. They say that he acquired his passion for golf from his maternal grandfather, who used to take him out on the golf course regularly.

Certainly, Alfonso García is a new star in the sport of golf.

48. What is the golf course like in St. Andrews, Scotland?
    (A) New and modern
    (B) Picturesque
    (C) **Historic and prestigious**
    (D) Innovative

The correct answer is (C). The golf course is said to be historic and prestigious. Something historic is certainly not new and modern, so that eliminates (A). The golf course may be picturesque (B) but it is not described that way in the narrative. Choice (D), innovative, is never mentioned.

49. What was the weather like during the tournament?

    (A) The weather was nice.

    (B) The weather was hot.

    (C) It was snowing.

    (D) The weather was tempestuous.

The correct answer is (D). There are various references to the tempestuous weather, primarily the wind and the rain squalls.

50. How did Alfonso García react to the variable weather in Scotland?

    (A) He felt frustrated.

    (B) He felt at ease.

    (C) He felt nostalgic.

    (D) He felt sad.

The correct answer is (A); he felt very frustrated initially. Later, he realized that the other players were experiencing the same challenges, and he was able to regain his focus.

51. How did Alfonso García become interested in golf?

    (A) He played golf with his father.

    (B) He accompanied his grandfather to the golf course.

    (C) He played golf with his sister.

    (D) He played golf with his grandmother.

The correct answer is (B). It is stated in the narrative that he accompanied his maternal grandfather to the golf course frequently. Reference is made to his father and his sister, but not in reference to golf, so (A) and (C) are eliminated. His grandmother is never mentioned, which easily eliminates (D).

52. How does Alfonso spend the majority of his time?

    (A) Relaxing with his parents in Buenos Aires

    (B) Traveling on the PGA Tour

    (C) Playing tennis with his little sister, Patricia

    (D) Spending time with his maternal grandfather

Choice (B) is the correct answer. Alfonso spends the majority of his time touring with the PGA. He spends his downtime with his parents in Buenos Aires, but the recording specifically says that the majority of his time goes to touring. We might assume so, but there is no proof that Alfonso plays tennis with his sister Patricia, and it certainly is not how he spends the majority of his time (C). The article mentions Alfonso's grandfather, who taught him the love of golf, but his grandfather took him to the golf courses mostly when he was young (D).

Selection 4: Translated Text and Questions, with Explanations

Introduction

This recording is about feminism in Spain. The recording is part of a conference about feminism in Spain.

Feminism in Spain is a strong force. For some it is a political battle. For others it is an economic matter. Yet others search for a theoretical liberation, including a sexual liberation. One thing is certain: It is a movement that continues growing with increasing force. What interests us here is the situation in Spain today. We will examine how the peninsular movement sprang out of Spanish culture and what directions it is likely to take. It is very important that we look at this brand of feminism as a product of Spanish culture. Of course, there is a universal movement going on outside of Spain. However, there are some specific characteristics of the movement in Spain that play a key role in its development there. It will help us to examine a few facets of Spanish culture and later turn our attention to the current state of feminism in Spain today.

One characteristic well-rooted in the Spanish culture, and perhaps the most opposed to feminism, is "machismo." Historically, in Spanish society, it is the man who makes decisions. It seems that the informal social laws are written by men to favor men. The concepts of honor and dignity are also very important. What comes out of all of this, then, is the idea of the strong and dignified man, who protects and assures the future of the woman. Similarly, the concept of "marianismo" establishes the desired qualities in the ideal Spanish woman. Also influenced by the ideas of honor and dignity, "marianismo" defines the domain of the woman in the home. Subordinated by the man, the woman personifies the qualities of obedience and self-sacrifice. Almost as if she were to exist through her association with the man, the woman is seen as fulfilled by her union in marriage to the man. After leaving the home of her father, the woman moves on to the home of her husband. Historically, in this culture there was no room for feminist independence.

The reverberations of these basic concepts from Spanish culture provide the foundation for the feminist movement today. According to its own ideology, the feminist movement looks for an individual identity for the woman. Feminists want to reject the traditional concepts of "machismo" and "marianismo." The difficult part, however, is penetrating deeply into a culture that has a long history with these cultural values. The more rooted a culture is in "machismo," the more difficult the struggle for feminism will be.

Now, let us turn our attention to the contemporary situation in Spain today. The reign of Franco marks a period of rigid censorship. This oppressive regime reinforced the traditional values of Spanish culture. It was almost as if it had resuscitated the concepts of "machismo" and "marianismo" in the society of the forties. Or perhaps they never died. In any case, there is most decidedly an important cultural foundation. What comes out of the Franco period are the reverberations of thought that have carried over from the Middle Ages. For that reason, the feminist movement was faced with a monumental obstacle. The feminists in Spain were looking for a way to express and communicate their protest. There are, among the feminist movement in Spain, those who want greater social or political freedom while others seek the complete elimination of traditional roles for women. There are militant groups and intellectual groups. Thus, the feminist movement in Spain is diverse and growing.

How can we evaluate such a movement? Surely, the extremes and excesses of a "machista" society should be eliminated. It is also essential that the independent identity of the woman be recognized. But with a radical approach, are we also prepared to lose all of the characteristics of femininity? It would seem that there are some traditional feminine roles worth maintaining, such as the nurturing mother figure, the sensible figure, etc. A search for complete equality, without limits or distinctions, surely would be the beginning of a great loss: the loss of the distinct feminine. The role of women in the family, for example, shouldn't be compromised. Furthermore, the characteristics typically considered feminine, such as sensitivity and capacity for emotion, have value in and of themselves. It is important, of course, that in this search for feminine recognition, we don't lose the meaning of femininity. What we need now is to bring about knowledge of feminine reality in a society previously steeped in masculine reality.

53. How do some interpret the feminist movement in Spain?

    (A) As a political battle

    (B) As an artistic issue

    (C) As a competition between equals

    (D) As a beauty pageant

The correct answer is (A), a political battle. There is no reference made to artistic issues, which eliminates (B). It is clearly not a competition between equals, which eliminates (C). Choice (D) goes against all of the ideals described in the selection regarding a feminine identity.

54. Which characteristic of Spanish culture can be considered opposite to the ideals of the feminist movement?

    (A) *Marianismo*

    (B) Honor

    (C) Dignity

    (D) *Machismo*

The correct answer is (D). It should be pretty clear that honor and dignity would not go against feminist ideals, so (B) and (C) should be eliminated immediately. That leaves *marianismo* and *machismo*. If you understood what was said about *marianismo*, you know that *marianismo* defines the role of women in the home and idealizes the qualities of obedience and sacrifice. While these ideals do not seem to support the feminist movement, they are minor in comparison with the ideals that go along with *machismo*. In reality, both terms refer to cultural attitudes that clash with the modern feminist movement. However, the more obvious choice is *machismo*, which the selection, in fact, describes as "perhaps the most opposed to feminism."

55. According to the selection, what is the ideological objective of the feminist movement?

    (A) The victory of woman over man

    (B) The acceptance of *marianismo* in all parts of the world

    (C) An individual identity for woman

    (D) The appreciation of the traditional culture

The correct answer is (C), an individual identity for woman. Choice (A) is extreme, and the selection did not advocate extremist measures. Choice (B) may be tempting because it uses the term *marianismo*, but *marianismo* is really a cultural view of women that grew out of the veneration of the Virgin Mary, and should not be confused with the feminist movement. Choice (D) is actually the opposite of what the selection is describing. The baggage of the traditional culture must be shed to find an individual identity for woman.

56. According to the selection, what type of thinking surfaced during the Franco era?

(A) Radical thinking

(B) Traditional thinking

(C) Progressive thinking

(D) Feminist thinking

The correct answer is (B), traditional thinking. Franco was very traditional and very conservative. That eliminates (A) and (C). Feminist thinking, (D), came about much later in Spain.

57. According to the selection, what should we keep from the traditional *machista* society?

(A) The role of the woman as mother

(B) *Marianismo*

(C) The role of the woman as subordinated to the man

(D) *Machismo*

The correct answer is (A), the role of the woman as mother. Both *marianismo* and *machismo* need to be overcome to move on to a greater state of gender equality, which eliminates both (B) and (D). Choice (C) is clearly one of the reasons to create a feminist movement and would most certainly not be desirable in a culture free of gender bias.

Selection 5: Translated Text and Questions, with Explanations

Introduction

The following recording is about the Special Olympic Games, which convened last August. The recording is an interview with Alejandro Martinez, a trainer who was triumphant at the recent tournament of the Special Olympic Games.

(NARRATOR)   Now you are going to hear an interview with Alejandro Martínez, victorious coach from the recent competition of the Special Olympic Games held in Vermont last August. Alejandro is a coach of many sports, including soccer, tennis, swimming, and field hockey.

(NARRATOR)   Alejandro, first of all, how did you get involved with the world of the Special Olympic Games?

(MARTÍNEZ)   Well, I have always been interested in sports. When I was in college, I played four sports during all four years, so sports have been a fundamental part of my life. The other fundamental part of my life, in chronological order, not order of importance, is my son, Carlos. Carlos was born eight years ago with a mild form of cerebral palsy. I noticed that with increased movement and physical activity, he felt better. For that reason, I have devoted myself to the Special Olympics. We have met other children like Carlos and other families like ourselves. It has been a very positive experience.

(NARRATOR)   Do you work with the Special Olympics all year long?

(MARTÍNEZ)   I wish I could devote myself to the Special Olympics 100 percent, but I also have a job. I am a high school mathematics teacher. So I work with the Special Olympics during the summers, which is the busiest time.

(NARRATOR)   It seems that you are drawn to professions that deal with children. Do you have any other children?

(MARTÍNEZ)   Yes, I have a daughter who just turned four last month. It is true that I enjoy working with children. They are more innocent and honest than adults.

(NARRATOR)   What would you say is the most difficult part of your work with the Special Olympics?

(MARTÍNEZ)   Well, we are faced with new obstacles every day. Perhaps the most difficult part for me is recognizing my own limitations. Frequently, I try to do much more than is reasonable in a day. And the worst thing is that the kids are the same way. Once they have become enthused by an idea or a training exercise, for example, they want to practice for hours without resting. They are very dedicated.

(NARRATOR)   It seems that you too are very dedicated. How do you explain the phenomenal success of your teams?

(MARTÍNEZ)   Well, I think there are two important factors. The first factor is that physical exercise has a very positive effect on the mind and body. It is incredibly therapeutic. It makes the kids feel better physically. And mentally, they are more alert. Of course, they also enjoy the benefits that we all gain when we participate in a physical sport. Our kids feel the pride and dignity that medicine or medical treatment cannot give them. The second factor that contributes to our success is the dedication of our kids. The kids are completely dedicated to their team. They understand instinctively the importance of the group and of working together. Each one of them is completely dedicated to the program. Without them, it would never work. Without our kids, the Special Olympics would not exist.

(NARRATOR)   What is Carlos's favorite sport?

(MARTÍNEZ)   Without a doubt, his favorite sport is American football, perhaps because he knows that I played in college.

(NARRATOR)   What would you recommend to other families with children who at the moment do not participate in the Special Olympic games? Maybe they think these games are silly or too juvenile.

(MARTÍNEZ)   I recommend that they call as soon as possible to find out about the upcoming events that are planned. One only has to go to one competition to see the advantages of this program. It's a great organization. The volunteers are very generous and dedicated. It's a very important experience for the children and for the families.

(NARRATOR)   Well, Alejandro Martínez, many thanks for being here with us.

58. How did Alejandro Martínez become interested in the Special Olympic Games?
   (A) He had always participated in the Special Games.
   (B) His brother participated in the Special Games.
   (C) His son responded favorably to sports.
   (D) His wife is very involved in the Special Games.

The correct answer is (C), his son responded favorably to sports. There is no mention of his wife or brother, which eliminates both (B) and (D) easily. Choice (A) is really a restatement of the question and not an answer to the question.

59. When does Alejandro devote himself entirely to the Special Olympics?

    (A) On weekends

    (B) During school vacations

    (C) In the winter

    (D) In the summer

Because Alejandro is a high school teacher, he has his summers off and devotes himself to the Special Olympics. There is no mention made of the school vacations (B), except the summer vacation, which is best described by (D). It is also not stated in the dialogue whether or not Alejandro spends time working for the Special Olympics on weekends (A). However, it's pretty clear that he is *entirely* devoted to the games during the summer.

60. According to the interview, why does he not work full time for the Special Olympics?

    (A) Because he doesn't earn enough money

    (B) Because he is a math teacher

    (C) Because he spends a lot of time on his daughter

    (D) Because he couldn't take it

The correct answer is (B); he mentions that he would dedicate 100% of his time, but he also has a full time job as a math teacher. There is no mention made of money, so that eliminates (A). At first glance, (C) would seem possible as children generally occupy a person's time, but this is not stated in the selection. Choice (D) is an excuse that many people make, but Alejandro does not.

61. Why does Alejandro enjoy working with children?

    (A) Because they are young

    (B) Because they are honest

    (C) Because they are very interested

    (D) Because they are gifted

The correct answer is (B), as he mentions that he prefers working with children because they are more "honest and innocent." There are no specific mentions of age, interest level, or talent, so the other choices are not correct in this situation.

62. According to the interview, why is physical exercise therapeutic?

    (A) Because they practice therapeutic exercises

    (B) Because the coaches have studied physical therapy

    (C) Because it's fun

    (D) Because it makes the kids feel better mentally and physically

The correct answer is (D), because it makes the kids feel better mentally and physically. Choices (B) and (C) may be true, but they are not mentioned in the interview. Choice (A) simply does not answer the question.

63. How is the collective spirit of the kids characterized?

    (A) They don't know how to collaborate in a group.

    (B) They understand instinctively how to collaborate.

    (C) They don't know how to function physically.

    (D) There is a lot of competition among the groups.

The correct answer is (B), they understand instinctively how to collaborate. Choice (A) is the exact opposite of the correct answer. Choices (C) and (D) are either completely false, or simply not mentioned in the interview.

64. According to the interview, which characteristic best describes the children who participate in the Special Olympic Games?

    (A) They are very thin.

    (B) They are very delicate.

    (C) They are very dedicated.

    (D) They are delegates.

The correct answer is (C), they are very dedicated. The other choices are designed to sound and look alike in an effort to confuse you. You, of course, will know your vocabulary and will not be fooled!

65. What does Alejandro recommend to the families who don't participate in the Special Olympic Games?

    (A) That they find out about the planned events

    (B) That they follow their hearts

    (C) That they organize their own games

    (D) That they don't participate

The correct answer is (A), that they find out about the planned events. None of the other choices were mentioned in the interview, although they may be true. Be sure to answer the questions according to the interview.

SECTION II

Interpersonal Writing: Email Reply (Page 227)

Translation of the Question

Introduction: This message is from your high school teacher. You have received this message because recently you had asked him to write a letter of recommendation for your college application.

Dear and most remembered student:

I have received your request for a letter of recommendation; I am happy you have decided to apply to the university that you liked so much. You were one of my favorite students, and it is a pleasure for me to write that letter. Since I would like to write the best recommendation letter possible for you, I would like to know the following about you:

- What do you remember most from my class and how will it serve you in the future?
- What are some of your goals for the upcoming years in the university?
- What are some of the extracurricular activities in which you have participated and what have you learned from them?

Please answer these questions in detail as soon as possible in an email reply. Upon receiving your information, I will prepare the letter and I will send it you both by mail and by email.

My best wishes and until soon,
Señor Santo Palacios, Language Teacher

Sample Student Response

Estimado Profesor Palacios:

Es un verdadero placer saludarlo nuevamente. Aunque han pasado un par de años desde que estuve en su clase, recuerdo con mucha nostalgia los buenos momentos que pasamos en el curso. Sobre todo recordaré las lecciones no sólo académicas, sino también las aplicaciones que tuvieron a la vida real. Aprendí a siempre dar mi mejor esfuerzo en todo lo que lleva mi nombre, y que nunca debo darme por vencido ante las situaciones difíciles en la vida.

Me dirijo a usted ya que pienso que usted es el profesor que mejor me conoce y mejor me describirá a la universidad. Puesto que el español será mi concentración en la universidad, mi meta es ser traductor o interprete y trabajar con una empresa multinacional en América Latina. Durante mis años universitarios, me gustaría retarme con cursos en otros idiomas. Otra meta que tengo, y ojalá se haga realidad, es estudiar por un año en una universidad extranjera.

Las actividades extracurriculares que más me impresionaron en el colegio fueron el equipo de tenis, el club de español y el club de servicio comunitario. En el Club de tenis aprendí la importancia de trabajar en equipo y la importancia de la práctica para mejorar las destrezas de uno. En el club de español, tuve la oportunidad de viajar a España y experimentar la cultura directamente. Viajé solo por primera vez en la vida y creo que representé bien a mi escuela y a mi país. Aprendí también que los estereotipos que mucha gente tiene son falsas, y una meta mía en el futuro es ayudar a combatirlos. Y en el club de servicio comunitario, vi que ayudar a los demás es ayudar a uno mismo.

Le doy las gracias por ser un ejemplo positivo en mi vida académica, y por haberme brindado su conocimiento y sabiduría tras los años.

Un saludo cordial,
Josh Messinger

Translation of the Sample Student Response

Dear Professor Palacios:

It is indeed a pleasure to greet you once again. Although a few years have passed since I was last in your class, I remember with great nostalgia the good times we students had in the course. Above all I will remember the lessons: not only academic, but also the applications that they had to real life. I learned to always give my best effort in everything that reflects upon me, and to never give up when facing difficult situations in life.

I am contacting you because I believe you are the teacher who knows me best and can best describe me to the university. Given that Spanish will be my college major, my goal is to be a translator or interpreter and work with a multinational company in Latin America. During my university studies, I would like to challenge myself with classes in other languages. Another goal I have, which I hope is realized, is to study for a year in an overseas university.

The extracurricular activities that most impacted me in high school were the tennis team, the Spanish Club, and the Community Service Club. On the tennis team I learned the importance of working with others and the importance of refining one's skills. In the Spanish Club, I had the opportunity to travel to Spain and experience the culture directly. I traveled alone for the first time in my life, and I think I represented both my school and my country well. I also learned that stereotypes that many people have are untrue, and my future goal is to help combat them. And finally, in the Community Service club, I saw that helping others really is helping oneself.

I thank you for being a positive role model in my academic career and for having bestowed your knowledge and wisdom throughout the years.

Cordial greetings,

Josh Messinger

Evaluation

Sometimes the AP exam picks topics from "out of left field" which can sometimes catch a student off guard. This essay really forced the writer to reflect on his goals and plans. Perhaps you don't have those defined yet. That doesn't matter. It is okay to make up things to fulfill the answers. The readers are not concerned whether you played tennis in high school or not; they are more concerned with how you answered the question. The exam in some way will ask you to talk about yourself or your academic experience, so make sure you have those details clear in your head so you can access them quickly.

Overall, this essay fulfilled all requirements, and maintained good grammar throughout. It also was logically organized and had a clear beginning and showed cultural appropriateness in the opening and closing and in the register used. There was a lack of transition between some of the sentences and a few awkward translations (*retarme con cursos, mi concentración*), but it would most likely receive a 4.

Presentational Writing: Persuasive Essay (Page 228)

Essay topic:

How does global warming affect our lives?

Translation for Source 1

Introduction

This article appeared on an Internet site in Spain in May of 2008.

The Consequences of Global Warming Associated with a Rise in Sea Level

With the destruction of the ozone layer we are observing more solar radiation penetrating to the planet's surface. This in turn contributes to thermal expansion of the oceans and the melting of great numbers of glacial mountains and of the icecaps found in the eastern parts of Antarctica and Greenland. With these elevated sea levels, serious changes for the future of the planet are already being forecasted.

Sea level already rose by between 4 and 8 inches during the last century. It's predicted that sea levels could rise by 10 to 23 inches by the year 2100. Unfortunately levels are rising more than predicted—the Greenland icecap has shrunk in the last decade. This shrinking contributes approximately a hundredth of an inch annually to the sea level rise. This figure might seem minimal at first glance, but one has to keep in mind that Greenland makes up around 10% of the world's total ice mass. If all Greenland's ice were to melt, world sea levels could rise up to 21 feet. This year for the first time ships were able to pass through Arctic waters without the help of icebreaker boats. That is to say, the predictions of scientists that the ice would begin to melt have come true 25 years ahead of schedule. This also will mean grave consequences for the planet. Already it is predicted that polar bears, sea lions, and certain species of penguins are facing extinction in only a few years.

With the destruction of glaciers and icecaps, more fresh water enters the ocean, adding to current levels. These melts cause severe flooding in costal areas. If the sea level were to rise even 6 meters, places such as Miami, Florida and San Francisco, California in the United States would be devastated; in China cities such as Shanghai and Beijing would be left sunken; and in India the city of Calcutta would be underwater. These last three urban centers figure among the most populous cities in the world.

Translation for Source 2

Introduction

This article appeared in the Argentinian press in July of 2008.

Warning: Global Warming Will Bring Grave Consequences for Human Life and Health

"It's not speculation at all—it's a reality. The planet's days are numbered. Now is the time to act and put in place planning and contingency programs," commented Francisco García, general director of the World Preservation Organization, at a press conference during the eleventh general convocation of the Week of the Planet celebrated in Buenos Aires, Argentina. Representatives of more than 35 countries met in the Argentinian capital to discuss, analyze data, and formulate action plans so that international and national organizations might understand the consequences of global warming at a deeper level. It is their hope that once armed with this information, countries may introduce programs to avoid a disaster that, according to García, "is lying in wait."

One of the most alarming talks gave information about the current figures on illnesses and disasters around the world. German doctor Martin Teuscher, professor at the University of Tübingen, explained that human beings have already been exposed to various illnesses caused by changes or exaggerations of the climate. "The reality is that we've been living during this century. But notice that with the change in climate, the lows will be even lower. It will intensify the delicate balance between disaster and prosperity, between having a home and being helpless, and finally between life and death." He specifically stressed that more than 4 million people die, worldwide, of malnutrition; more than 2 million of diarrheal sicknesses; and 1.2 million of diseases such as malaria. Undoubtedly, these figures will grow with the global change in climate. Teuscher said it would not be impossible for these figures to triple within a mere 5 or 10 years.

The forewarnings do not stop there. With warmer temperatures, insects and other pests will have the opportunity to spread and infect more humans as a result. It is expected that more outbreaks of dengue fever and malaria epidemics will occur. Both sicknesses are transmitted by mosquito bites. Global warming favors these disease-transmitting insects. Another result of global warming is flooding, which produces the ideal environment for mosquitoes to breed and for the feared cholera pandemics. Recent studies carried out by scientists illustrate the gravity of the global warming problem: In barely 15 years, the number of people exposed to malaria on the African continent could reach the hundred millions. Globally, dengue fever could threaten almost 2 billion people.

Global warming has brought upheavals in worldwide climates, and each year previously unknown changes and nuances of climate become evident. For example, heat waves in Europe and the United States mean thousands of deaths each year, and hurricanes are becoming more and more devastating and powerful. "Hurricane Katrina in 2005 and Hurricane Mitch in 1998 destroyed large swaths of American territory," pointed out Felipe Fonseca, a Mexican meteorologist who spoke about the changes the Gulf of Mexico has suffered due to global warming. "Their social, economic, and political effects are still being felt. In 50 years we'll find parts of North America underwater."

Automobile, truck, and plane emissions poison the air we breathe. That air pollution causes almost a million deaths per year. According to the estimates cited by the experts, for each degree Celsius the global temperature increases, there will be almost 30,000 additional deaths per year due to heart and lung diseases. With the recent rise in gas prices demand has not diminished enough to reduce air pollution. Many also fear that with the growth of the emerging Asian economies, plus the huge number of drivers that will have access to automobiles, the environmental damage will continue to stymie any attempt at environmental conservation.

"Individuals do have the power to make a difference," explains Rachel Johnson, German student and member of GreenWatch, a student movement that educates youth about conservation and recycling. "That plastic bag you throw in the trash without thinking about it will take a century to break down. Gasoline and petroleum influence almost every aspect of our lives, and at the same time put our wellbeing, and that of the planet, in danger. We must change our way of thinking, and act now. In my country we have a saying: *Macht es jetzt! Warte nicht auf bessere Zeiten.* (Do it now! Don't wait for a better moment.) If we don't make the effort now, our future generations will be condemned to a life without life."

Translation for Source 3 (Audio Track 12)

Introduction

This report, titled "Experts Point to Greater Health Risks Because of Global Warming," was broadcast on the Latin American radio station Enteramérica in July of 2005.

LH: Good afternoon, listening friends. This is Laura Heredia speaking, and I have the pleasure of presenting to you the very esteemed scientist Dr. Michelet Zamor, of the University of Miami. Besides being a university professor, Dr. Zamor is a contributing author of the report on the health risks caused by global warming presented by the Environmental Protection Agency at the recent meeting of experts during the commemoration of International Health Day celebrated at the United Nations in New York. Doctor, thank you for being with us. Please, tell us: Which of the discoveries in your report stood out the most?

MZ: Well, upon analyzing data submitted by many sources worldwide, scientists around the world detailed an elevated rate of deaths due to heat waves, will-o'-the-wisps, and the sicknesses and smog caused by global warming. It's the first time in the history of the world that scientists have recognized the grave risks presented by global warming, not just to human beings, but also to foods, energy, and water, upon which human survival depends.

LH: I hadn't thought about it that way. Many people think that global warming is just a question of hotter summers and less snow in the winter.

MZ: If only it were so simple. The risks to human health, to society in general, and to the environment increase as much with the rate as with the magnitude of climate changes. The fault for global warming undoubtedly belongs with human beings. The documents put out by the EPA suggest that climate extremes and illnesses transmitted by fleas and other organisms can kill more people as temperatures rise. Likewise, allergies may worsen because the climatic changes will produce more pollen. Smog, a principal cause of respiratory and pulmonary ailments, also counts among the threats to the world's population. At the same time, however, global warming may mean fewer sicknesses and deaths due to the cold.

LH: What has been the biggest obstacle to adopting legislation to prevent the dangers of global warming?

MZ: While scientists point to the connection between health and climate change, the government, for its part, has not done so—has not even recognized it. This recognition, many believe, would obligate the government to regulate greenhouse gases. This certainly would open a Pandora's box in the search for the governmental effort and support necessary to lend weight and importance to the necessity of embarking on the task of understanding and preventing the devastating consequences of global warming.

Sample Student Response

El calentamiento global trae consigo graves riesgos al bienestar del planeta. El ritmo al cual han crecido tanto la población mundial como la expansión industrial han puesto en peligro las defensas naturales del planeta. Como resultado, en la Tierra hay una mayor tendencia a ocurrir acontecimientos perjudiciales como desastres naturales, escasez de comida, brotes de enfermedades, y una disminución de recursos vitales para sobrevivir. Por consiguiente, nuestras vidas han cambiado también.

Yo diría que los cambios más drásticos se han presenciado en nuestra vida diaria. Los precios de gasolina, comida, y transportación han aumentado muchísimo recientemente. Por ello, nuestra vida económica cotidiana es más difícil. Muchas personas han sufrido ya que sus sueldos no rinden como antes y les es difícil que su presupuesto les alcance para todo lo necesario. Y como recientemente ha surgido conciencia para preservar el planeta, estamos viendo programas de reciclar, ahorrar energía, compartir viajes, explotar recursos locales, descubrir fuentes de energía, y hasta salvar los animales que están en peligro de extinción, particularmente en las zonas antárticas. La calidad de nuestras vidas ha bajado también por el calentamiento global. Por ejemplo, en muchos países subdesarrollados, las cifras de muertes causadas por el calentamiento global han crecido. Las enfermedades como la malaria tendrán más víctimas como nunca ya que el calentamiento global permite que los insectos proliferen y sobrevivan con más facilidad. El derretimiento del hielo de Antártica traerá más inundaciones y consigo más casos de cólera y otras enfermedades. Yo mismo he observado el crecimiento de alergias y problemas cardiorrespiratorios entre la gente de mi familia. Y tal como predijeron los expertos, estos problemas están manifestándose ahora. Si hubiéramos hecho caso a las advertencias de los expertos hace años, tal vez no nos habríamos encontrado en esta situación tan desconsolada.

Finalmente, el calentamiento global ha cambiado nuestra forma de pensar. Se han despertado nuevas maneras de planificar el futuro. Los expertos están educando al público para que varíe su forma de pensar y su percepción en el mundo. El individuo se ha dado cuenta de que sí se puede hacer una diferencia al preservar el planeta y consumir más prudentemente. La gente está tratando de hacer lo posible para preservar el medio ambiente. Cada día se ve más programas para ayudar a preservar los recursos naturales, minerales y humanos del planeta. Solo esperamos que no sea demasiado tarde.

En resumen, se reconoce que el planeta en si es la base de nuestra existencia y supervivencia. El calentamiento global, fenómeno creado por el ser humano, ha llegado a tal punto que por fin el mundo ha reconocido su importancia, y como resultado, ha tratado de modificar su forma de pensar y actuar. Sin embargo, el daño es extenso, y requiere que también los gobiernos apoyen toda opción necesaria para salvar al mundo. Solo el tiempo dirá si este esfuerzo es suficiente.

Translation of the Sample Student Response

Global warming brings with it severe risks to the wellbeing of the planet. The rhythm at which both the world population as well as industrial expansion has grown have endangered the natural defenses of the planet. As a result, on Earth there is an increased tendency toward detrimental events such as natural disasters, food shortages, sickness outbreaks, and a decrease in the vital resources necessary for survival. As a result, our lives have changed as well.

I would say that the most drastic changes have been evident in our daily lives. The prices of gas, food, and transportation have gone up tremendously recently. For that reason, our daily economic life is even more difficult. Many people have suffered since their salaries don't go as far as before and it is difficult for their budgets to cover all of their needs. And given that recently there has been an increase in consciousness towards preserving the planet, we are seeing programs for recycling, saving energy, ride sharing, using local resources, discovering alternative energy sources, and even saving endangered animals, particularly in the Antarctic zones. Our quality of life has also gone down as a result of global warming. For example, in many underdeveloped countries, the number of deaths caused by global warming has grown. Sicknesses like malaria will have more victims than ever because global warming allows insects to thrive and to survive more easily. The melting of Antarctic ice will bring more floods and with that more cases of cholera and other sicknesses. I myself have observed an increase in allergies and cardio-respiratory problems among my own family members. And just as the experts predicted, these problems are becoming evident now. If we had paid attention to the experts' warnings years ago, perhaps we wouldn't have found ourselves in this sad situation.

Finally, global warming has changed our way of thinking. New ways of planning the future have been formed. Experts are educating the public to change its way of thinking and its perception of the world. The individual has realized that one can indeed make a difference by preserving the planet and consuming more wisely. People are taking the necessary steps to save the environment. Each day we see more programs to help preserve the planet's natural, mineral, and human resources. We only hope that it is not too late.

In summary, it is known that the planet itself is the key to our existence and survival. Global warming, a phenomenon created by human beings, has come to the point where the world has finally recognized its importance, and as a result, has modified its way of thinking and acting. However, the damage is extensive and requires that governments also support all the necessary options in order to save the planet. Only time will tell whether this effort is enough.

Evaluation

This essay expresses ideas clearly and in an organized manner. It has a good flow and transitions, and it displays excellent grammatical control and breadth of vocabulary. At the end of the introduction, there should be some reference to the topics of the following paragraphs to ease transitions. Another improvement would be to tie the articles in a little bit more, as it referenced them in mostly general terms. Some specifics from the articles could have strengthened the essay. The writer didn't specifically identify the sources mentioned. Perhaps a few lines where he could have said "According to Source #1...." However, given the strong style, grammar, and organization, this essay would have still scored extremely well.

This essay has some very good grammatical points that you should try to use in your essay: Use of good transitions: *Por ello, en resumen, Finalmente, Tal como*. Advanced vocabulary: *ya que, consigo, se reconoce que*. Good use of subjunctive: *Esperamos que, Requiere que, para que*. Good use of verbs: *surgir, rendir, predecir, manifestarse, proliferar, sobrevivir, modificar*. Advanced/Native structures: *tanto… como; les es difícil*.

A good way to make a winning essay is to find vocabulary and expressions that you can use or modify to fit most essays. Choose a few expressions in each of the above categories from essays and readings and try to start inserting them in your essays each time you write in class. For example, "Por ello" is a more sophisticated way to say "por eso," and this is exactly the type of thing the readers are looking for in the essays. Keep a checklist and always try to incorporate some of them into your essay. It will definitely make a good impression with the readers. In addition, try to use a variety of tenses: The above essay used present tense, present progressive, present subjunctive, future, preterite, and conditional. Readers especially like to see the advanced tenses and past subjunctive as well. Don't be afraid to go over the minimum word requirement either; generally you do better by writing more as opposed to less.

Interpersonal Speaking: Conversation (Page 232)

Script with Sample Student Response and Translation

Narrador: Has solicitado una posición de aprendiz en una empresa multinacional latinoamericana. Imagina que recibes una llamada telefónica del director del Departamento de Recursos Humanos para hablar sobre la posición que has solicitado.

You have applied for an internship in a Latin American multinational company. Imagine that you receive a phone message from the director of Human Resources to speak about the position that you have applied for.

Ahora tienes un minuto para leer el esquema de la conversación.

Now you have one minute to read the conversation outline.

Ahora imagina que recibas una llamada del señor Rivero para realizar una entrevista.

Now imagine that you receive a phone call from Mr. Rivero to speak about the position.

MA: Buenos días, le habla el señor Luis Rivero, director de Recursos Humanos de la Empresa Mundiales. Me gustaría hacerle algunas preguntas por teléfono sobre su solicitud. Primero, cuénteme por favor. ¿Qué le motivó a solicitar una posición de aprendiz en nuestra compañía?

Good morning, this is Mr. Luis Rivero from the Human Resources Department of the Mundiales Company. I would like to ask you a few questions by phone about your application. First, please tell me, what prompted you to apply for a position in our company?

Tú: Pues, como su compañía cuenta entre los líderes de su industria, me pareció buena idea solicitar una posición con ustedes para poder aprender más sobre la industria.

Well, since your company is among the leaders of its industry, it seemed like a good idea for me to apply for a position to learn more about the industry.

MA: Muy bien. ¿Qué destrezas y habilidades podrá aportar a nuestro lugar de trabajo?

Very good. What skills and abilities could you contribute to our workplace?

Tú: Hablo tres idiomas: el español, el inglés y el francés. Además, domino varios programas de computadora y soy muy bueno resolviendo problemas.

I speak three languages: Spanish, English, and French. In addition, I am proficient in many computer programs and I am very good at resolving problems.

MA: ¿Qué dirían sus patrones o jefes anteriores sobre personalidad y calidad de trabajo?

What might your previous employers say about your personality and the quality of your work?

Tú: Dirían que soy puntual, leal y que trabajo bien en grupos. En cuanto a mi calidad de trabajo, dirían que soy trabajador, organizado y diligente.

They would say I am punctual, loyal, and that I work well in group situations. In terms of my work quality, they would say I am hard-working, organized, and diligent.

MA: Quisiera saber, ¿cuándo está disponible para trabajar y cuándo podrá empezar?

I would like to know: when are you available to work and when could you start?

Tú: Como las clases terminan a finales de junio, puedo trabajar los meses de julio y agosto. Puedo comenzar el 5 de julio.

As school finishes at the end of June, I can work in July and August. I can start July 5.

MA: Me gustaría que pasara por nuestra oficina para que conociera a algunos de mis compañeros de trabajo. ¿Podrá pasar por la oficina mañana a las 10 de la mañana?

I would like for you to come by our office in order to meet some of my work colleagues. Could you stop by tomorrow at 10 in the morning?

Tú: Desafortunadamente, asisto a la escuela hasta las tres de la tarde. ¿Sería posible que le visitara a las 4?

Unfortunately, I have school until 3 P.M. Would it be possible for me to visit at 4 P.M.?

MA: No hay ningún inconveniente. Nos vemos entonces en esa fecha y hora.

No problem. We'll see you then at that date and time.

Tú: Espero con ganas poderle conocer mañana. Que pase buen día. Adiós.

I look forward to seeing you tomorrow. Have a nice day. Goodbye.

Evaluation

The answers were clear, appropriate, and had some complex structures like conditional and past subjunctive *(sería posible que le visitara)*, and subjunctive *(que pase buen día)*. The rest of the responses advanced the conversation and more than fulfilled the requirements. It would receive at least a 4 due to the quality of its grammar and topic development.

Presentational Speaking: Cultural Comparison (Page 233)

Translation of the Question

It is known that languages enrich us. Explain in what way languages have influenced the society in which you live and in another Spanish-speaking city that you have observed, studied, or visited.

Compare your observations about the communities in which you have been with those of a region of the Spanish-speaking world that you have studied. You can refer to what you have studied, experienced, observed, etc.

Sample Student Response

Los idiomas no sólo facilitan la comunicación entre otros, sino que también aportan la oportunidad de que las culturas se asimilen. En los Estados Unidos vemos cada día más que estamos desarrollando una sociedad bilingüe. Hay más de 40 millones de hispanos viviendo en los Estados Unidos. Este grupo reserva poder económico, social y político, e influencian los acontecimientos en muchas de las comunidades donde viven. Pero al nivel humano, como cualquier inmigrante, el hispano-hablante trae consigo una larga y rica cultura también. Como resultado de este tremendo oleaje de inmigrantes, la música, comida, vocabulario y lenguaje de la sociedad reflejan una mayor influencia hispana. En mi comunidad, hay letreros bilingües, servicios bilingües y mayores oportunidades de empleo para los bilingües. Casi cada solicitud de empleo hoy en día busca candidatos bilingües.

Paraguay es un país que disfruta una rica cultura gracias a los idiomas. Cuando los españoles asentaron el país, no erradicaron la cultura indígena. Es más, los pioneros españoles aprendieron el idioma de los indígenas—el guaraní. A la vez, los guaranís aprendieron el español. Ambos idiomas son lenguas oficiales de Paraguay, y casi todos los paraguayos dominan los dos. El guaraní es el idioma del amor, de la música, de la poesía y de la vida cotidiana, mientras que el español se usa en los periódicos, la televisión y los negocios. Cada uno ocupa un lugar en la sociedad, y el país como resultado, ha beneficiado.

Hoy en día en muchos lugares del mundo hay movimientos que están a favor de adoptar un solo idioma oficial. Pero realmente vemos que la sociedad beneficia y hasta se vuelve más tolerante al tener varios idiomas presentes en la sociedad.

Translation of the Sample Student Response

Languages not only facilitate our communication with others, but they also allow cultures to assimilate with each other. In the United States we see each day more and more that were are developing a bilingual society. There are more than 40 million Hispanics living in the United States. This group holds economic, political, and social power, and influences the events in many of the communities in which they live. But at the same time, like any immigrant, the Hispanics bring with them a rich and long cultural tradition. As a result of this tremendous wave of immigration, the music, food, vocabulary, and language of society reflect a growing Hispanic influence. In my community there are bilingual signs, services, and greater work opportunities for bilinguals. Almost every job application today seeks bilingual candidates.

Paraguay is a country that enjoys a rich culture thanks to its languages. When the Spanish settled in the country, they did not eradicate the native culture. They actually learned the language of the natives—Guarani. The Guarani in turn learned Spanish. Both languages are official languages of Paraguay, and almost all Paraguayans speak both fluently. Guaraní is the language of love, music, poetry, and daily life, while Spanish is used in newspapers, television, and business. Each one occupies a place in society, and the country, as a result, has benefitted.

Nowadays, in many parts of the world, there are movements to adopt one official language. However, we truly see that society benefits from multiple languages and even becomes more tolerant when different languages are present in daily life.

Evaluation

The response got better as it went along. The question really wanted to hear more about the personal experience of the writer, which to some extent was absent in the first paragraph. The second paragraph was much stronger because it demonstrated a familiarity with another culture, and most importantly, specific facts. This is what you will need to make the grade on this section. You could have chosen other options: Puerto Rico, Andean languages, Panamá. Notice how you will need to know information on the various regions of the Spanish-speaking world. This response fulfilled the requirements, was well composed, and showed knowledge of the culture. It would have scored 4 on the AP exam.

Practice Test 2

Following are the audio track numbers for Practice Test 2.

- Track 14: Selección 1 (Fuente 2)

- Track 15: Selección 2 (Fuente 2)

- Track 16: Selección 3

- Track 17: Selección 4

- Track 18: Selección 5

- Track 19: Presentational Writing (Fuente 3)

- Track 20: Interpersonal Speaking: Conversation

Again, make sure you have a device handy with which to record and time yourself for the speaking sections.

Good luck!

AP® Spanish Language and Culture

DO NOT OPEN THIS BOOKLET UNTIL YOU ARE TOLD TO DO SO.

Instructions

Section I of this examination contains 65 multiple-choice questions. Fill in only the ovals for numbers 1 through 65 on your answer sheet.

Indicate all of your answers to the multiple-choice questions on the answer sheet. No credit will be given for anything written in this exam booklet, but you may use the booklet for notes or scratch work. After you have decided which of the suggested answers is best, completely fill in the corresponding oval on the answer sheet. Give one answer to each question. If you change an answer, be sure that the previous mark is erased completely. Here is a sample question and answer.

At a Glance
Total Time 1 hour and 35 minutes **Number of Questions** 65 **Percent of Total Grade** 50% **Writing Instrument** Pencil required

Sample Question   Sample Answer

Chicago is a   Ⓐ ● Ⓒ Ⓓ
(A) state
(B) city
(C) country
(D) continent

Use your time effectively, working as quickly as you can without losing accuracy. Do not spend too much time on any one question. Go on to other questions and come back to the ones you have not answered if you have time. It is not expected that everyone will know the answers to all the multiple-choice questions.

About Guessing

Many candidates wonder whether or not to guess the answers to questions about which they are not certain. Multiple choice scores are based on the number of questions answered correctly. Points are not deducted for incorrect answers, and no points are awarded for unanswered questions. Because points are not deducted for incorrect answers, you are encouraged to answer all multiple-choice questions. On any questions you do not know the answer to, you should eliminate as many choices as you can, and then select the best answer among the remaining choices.

Part A

Interpretive Communication: Print Texts

You will read several selections. Each selection is accompanied by a number of questions. For each question, choose the response that is best according to the selection and mark your answer on your answer sheet.	Vas a leer varios textos. Cada texto va acompañado de varias preguntas. Para cada pregunta, elige la mejor respuesta según el texto e indícala en la hoja de respuestas.

Selección número 1

Introducción

La siguiente selección es un fragmento de un cuento corto.

Mamá, Ana y la chiquitina fueron a visitar al abuelo, pero el pobre papá no pudo ir porque tuvo que quedarse en casa para trabajar.

—¿Qué haré yo sin ti? —dijo él.

Línea —Te escribiré cartas, tres cartas, —contestó Ana—. Te diré lo que estemos haciendo aquí sin ti.

5 —¿Sabes escribir una carta? —pregunto papá.

—¡Oh sí, la puedo escribir! —dijo Ana—. Ya tengo siete años. Verás que puedo escribir una carta.

Ana se divirtió mucho. Un día dijo:

—Abuelita, ¿puedo tomar una pluma? Quiero escribir a Papá.

—Sí —dijo su abuela—, en el escritorio hay plumas.

10 Ana corrió al escritorio de su abuelo.

—¡Oh, Abuelita! Aquí hay una pluma muy rara.

—Ésta es una pluma de ave —dijo la abuela—. Tu abuelo la cortó para mí. Es una pluma de ganso; en tiempos pasados todo el mundo escribía con plumas de ave.

—Me parece muy bonita —dijo Ana—. No creo que pueda escribir con ella.

15 Tomó otra pluma y se fue. Al poco tiempo, volvió al escritorio. Y allí vio que la chiquitina había tomado la pluma de ave y había escrito con ella a su papá. ¡Y qué carta había escrito! Ana se dio cuenta de que había derramado la tinta sobre el escritorio.

—¡Oh, chiquitina, chiquitina! ¿por qué has hecho esto?

Mamá envió la carta de la chiquitina a su papá y él dijo que se alegraba de recibir las dos cartas.

Aracataca, 12 de Julio de 1917.

20 Mi querido Papá:

Nos estamos divirtiendo mucho. Mi abuelito tiene un gran caballo oscuro. Algunas veces me monta en el caballo. ¡Es tan divertido! Juego mucho en el prado. Mi abuelito me deja pasear sobre los montones de hierba y recojo moras para mi abuelita. Nos dan queso con el café.

Quisiera que estuvieses aquí con nosotros. La chiquitina te ha escrito una carta. Tomó la pluma de ave de nuestra abuela, y 25 derramó la tinta. ¿Puedes leer su carta? Dice que ha escrito: "¿Cómo estás, papá? Te quiero mucho".

Tu hijita,
Ana

GO ON TO THE NEXT PAGE.

1. ¿Cómo se puede entender de qué se trata la carta de la chiquitina?

   (A) Según la carta misma

   (B) Según la carta de Ana

   (C) Según lo que dice la abuela al padre

   (D) Según el narrador

2. ¿Quién duda que Ana pueda escribir la carta?

   (A) La abuela

   (B) El padre

   (C) El abuelo

   (D) La chiquitina

3. Según la selección ¿por qué escribe Ana "¿Puedes leer su carta?" a su padre?

   (A) Porque sabe que su padre tiene la vista débil

   (B) Porque sabe que la carta ha llegado

   (C) Porque cree que no puede leer la carta de la chiquitina

   (D) Porque sabe que en tiempos pasados todo el mundo escribía con plumas de ave

4. La siguiente oración se puede añadir al texto: "Captada por la novedad, la manoseaba por un rato, luego la retornó a su recinto". ¿Dónde serviría mejor la oración?

   (A) Línea 10

   (B) Línea 14

   (C) Línea 18

   (D) Línea 25

5. ¿Quién es la "ella" (línea 16) con que la chiquitina escribió la carta?

   (A) La abuela

   (B) La pluma

   (C) Ana

   (D) La madre

6. ¿Por qué busca una pluma Ana?

   (A) Porque quiere escribir tres cartas

   (B) Porque quiere escribir un libro

   (C) Porque quiere derramar la tinta

   (D) Porque necesita a su padre

7. ¿Quién manda la carta a Papá?

   (A) La abuela

   (B) Ana

   (C) La chiquitina

   (D) La madre

GO ON TO THE NEXT PAGE.

Selección número 2

Introducción

El siguiente artículo apareció en la prensa boliviana en junio de 2001.

¡Cuidado! Cebras Trabajando En La Calle

No son personajes de Disney o mascotas que promocionan una marca o producto. Las "cebras" que circulan por las calles de La Paz tienen un trabajo muy especial: son educadores urbanos que enseñan a la gente a caminar con seguridad por toda la ciudad. Día a día, cubren su cuerpo con un disfraz y una máscara: se mueven, saltan, gritan y agitan banderines para llamar la atención de los peatones. Según datos de la organización municipal "Cultura Ciudadana" alrededor de 240 jóvenes trabajan en dos turnos, cuatro horas por día y veinte horas a la semana.

El tráfico vehicular y peatonal es cada vez mayor en la ciudad sede del gobierno boliviano. Los automóviles no respetan los semáforos y la gente cruza las calles por cualquier lugar. El caos es total. La vida de la gente, especialmente de los niños, está en permanente peligro. Por eso, la autoridad municipal decidió tomar medidas concretas. Así nacieron las "cebras".

En el año 2001, la alcaldía creó un proyecto a través de la entidad "Cultura Ciudadana" con el fin de descongestionar el tráfico vehicular. "Las cebras emergieron con el objetivo de indicar el paso peatonal a los ciudadanos de a pie", aclara Kathia Salazar, coordinadora del "Proyecto Cebras". Este movimiento de "Cultura Ciudadana" se inició en Colombia. Ahí se trabajaba con mimos educadores. En las calles, grupos de niños y estudiantes hacían juegos para demostrar cómo debía cruzarse un paso peatonal.

La representante municipal afirma que este proyecto posee dos pilares fundamentales: educativo y social. La mayoría de los muchachos que trabaja como cebras tiene entre 16 y 22 años y está autorizada por la municipalidad para descongestionar el tráfico vehicular y facilitar el tránsito de los peatones.

"Los requisitos para trabajar como cebra son la voluntad, el emprendimiento, la creatividad y los deseos de salir adelante. Desde la alcaldía nos comprometemos a acompañar un proyecto de vida", revela Salazar.

Todos los días, las cebras se cubren el cuerpo con trajes de algodón y tela blanca adornada con líneas de color negro. Mientras los peatones desesperados avanzan a la orden del semáforo, ellas bailan, juegan, bromean y gesticulan sin cesar. Cuando se van, los niños y ancianos las extrañan y el caos retorna a las calles. El sueldo mensual que perciben asciende a 450 bolivianos (unos U.S. $65). Las líderes o guías pueden llegar a ganar hasta Bs.1000 (cerca de U.S. $144) por su exclusividad al Proyecto Cebras.

Cultura ciudadana

Julia Andrea Marca (21 años) trabaja como cebra desde hace un año y nueve meses. Para ejercer el cargo de educadora urbana tuvo que asistir a varios talleres de enseñanza y aprendizaje impartidos por Kathia Salazar. "Los niños me abrazan y agarran con mucho cariño. Con esto, buscamos educar y enseñar a los infantes", señala. Julia estudia además todas las mañanas en la Universidad Mayor de San Andrés y cursa el primer año de Bioquímica. "La única experiencia negativa que tuve durante este tiempo fue que un auto me atropelló, pero no fue un accidente muy grave. En un principio, la gente no conocía el paso peatonal. Pero ahora, gracias a nosotros, los ciudadanos respetan las señales de tránsito", agrega.

Amanda Pinos (29 años), lleva ocho años en esta iniciativa municipal. Brinca por las calles en cuanto la luz del semáforo cambia a roja. Día a día, se ubica muy cerca de la Plaza del Estudiante y de esta forma, evita que los conductores se pasen por alto el semáforo y provoquen incidentes y más congestionamiento vial. Su función principal radica en transmitir valores de Cultura Ciudadana a toda la gente. "He visto accidentes muy terribles, es algo realmente muy triste", indica. "La tarea principal de los educadores urbanos es generar reflexión en cada uno de los ciudadanos de La Paz y generar concienciación de la forma más cariñosa y respetuosa". Pinos, quien se desempeña como guía del proyecto, relata que las "cebras son jóvenes interesados en participar de esta familia y los educadores urbanos van aconsejando con la prevención". Añade que algunas frases que dicen a los peatones son: "Señor cuídese mucho"; "tenga cuidado, por favor"; "no cruce las calles"; ¡alto por favor!".

Para nuestras entrevistadas trabajar como cebra es más un oficio que una profesión. Para varias de ellas, el trabajo de educadora urbana significa una forma de apoyar, querer, amar y cambiar la ciudad. Así de sencillo.

¿La Paz?

El Censo Nacional de 2001 reportó una población de 1.552.156 habitantes en toda el área metropolitana de La Paz, incluyendo la ciudad de El Alto. La población estimada al año 2010 es de cerca de 2 millones de habitantes, sin incluir a El Alto, de casi 1,2 millones de personas. En su conjunto forman la aglomeración urbana más grande del país. Según Datos del Instituto Nacional de Estadística de Bolivia, el parque automotor en La Paz llegó a cerca de 220.000 vehículos en

GO ON TO THE NEXT PAGE.

2009. Si bien existen leyes y multas que regulan el tráfico en La Paz, la mayoría de los choferes no respetan la luz roja del semáforo. Mucho menos el derecho de los peatones, ni las líneas de cruce. Es por ese motivo que las cebras se encuentran en casi todas las esquinas de la ciudad, ayudando a la gente a cruzar la calle, y disciplinando a los conductores, desde las primeras horas de la mañana hasta caer la noche.

Used by permission of VeinteMundos.com

8. ¿Cuál es el propósito de este artículo?

   (A) Presentar una forma graciosa de lidiar con un problema urbano

   (B) Narrar las experiencias de jóvenes que se unen a una causa

   (C) Demostrar que los empleos pueden ser tanto satisfactorios como educativos

   (D) Ilustrar cómo una ciudad respondió a una necesidad urgente con creatividad

9. ¿Cuál de las siguientes afirmaciones mejor resume el artículo?

   (A) Es casi imposible cambiar la forma de pensar de la gente.

   (B) En América del Sur, por no contar con fondos para obras públicas como los países del Primer Mundo, hay que buscar alternativas para resolver problemas.

   (C) Una ciudanía educada y respetuosa puede mejorar la vida y bienestar de todos.

   (D) Tantos los choferes como los peatones juegan un papel en la seguridad de todos.

10. ¿Qué podemos inferir de las cifras sobre el Censo Nacional en 2001 y 2009?

   (A) Por la crisis económica, más personas están convirtiéndose en peatones.

   (B) Por la explosión demográfica, la autoridad municipal simplemente no puede acomodar tantos peatones en las calles.

   (C) Los números de automóviles no han aumentado al ritmo del crecimiento de la población.

   (D) Con el aumento del número de residentes en La Paz y las afueras en años recientes, ahora hay mayores riesgos para el peatón.

11. Si fueras a realizar una investigación más profundizada sobre el mismo tema del artículo, ¿a cuál de la siguientes fuentes te acudirías?

   (A) El censo boliviano de 2013

   (B) Planificación Urbana de La Paz

   (C) El ministerio de Transporte y Carreteras

   (D) El Registro Civil

12. ¿Cuál es un punto negativo del programa?

   (A) Los choferes no necesariamente respetarían a un joven vestido de cebra de la misma manera que respetarían a un policía o miembro del ejército.

   (B) Las cebras siempre tendrán el riesgo de ser arrollados por vehículos.

   (C) El pago y las horas que reciben los trabajadores apenas alcanza para mantenerse uno.

   (D) Los fondos atados al programa podrían ser revocados en cualquier momento.

13. ¿Cuál es el problema que trata este proyecto?

   (A) La mayor incidencia de accidentes

   (B) Los peatones no saben dónde cruzar las calles por falta de indicaciones

   (C) Los choferes básicamente ignoran las leyes de transito

   (D) Los conflictos entre peatón y chofer son cada día más comunes

GO ON TO THE NEXT PAGE.

Selección número 3

Introducción

El siguiente artículo apareció en un sitio de Internet en 2013.

República del Paraguay
Sudamérica
Población: 6,800,284 (2013)
Lengua: Español y Guaraní
Moneda: Guaraní

El Guaraní en Paraguay

Fue perseguido y prohibido por varias décadas en Paraguay. Nunca pudo ser enseñado formalmente. Pero sirvió como mecanismo de defensa en las guerras y hoy es hablado por casi nueve millones de personas en diferentes países de Sudamérica. A partir de 1992 es idioma oficial junto con el español en todo Paraguay. El guaraní ha sorteado grandes desafíos a lo largo de los años y aún pretende hacerlo, en pleno siglo XXI.

Según el censo poblacional de 2002, la población indígena de Paraguay llega casi a los 100.000 habitantes y reúne a más de 17 etnias. Pese a que la cifra no es significativa dentro del total nacional (el país cuenta con casi 7 millones de habitantes), el 87% de los paraguayos habla guaraní. Por lo tanto, esta nación latinoamericana es bilingüe.

¿Y por qué tanta gente habla esta lengua originaria? Según María Antonia Rojas, del instituto cultural "Ateneo Guaraní", el dialecto pertenece a los primeros habitantes de esta zona de Sudamérica y ha sido defendido como idioma por los propios paraguayos. "Es así como hoy en día, constituye un elemento transcendental en la cultura cotidiana", afirma la licenciada.

Comenzando por el nombre Paraguay, que significa "río que sale al mar", este idioma ha formado parte de la cultura del país. Es más, una gran cantidad de nombres de plantas, animales, canciones, comidas y actitudes puede ser señalada únicamente en esta lengua.

Pese a la fuerte defensa hecha por los paraguayos, durante mucho tiempo el idioma guaraní fue prohibido, incluso a través de persecución política, incluyendo castigos a todos los niños y jóvenes que lo hablasen en las escuelas y colegios. Esa realidad cambió cuando la dictadura de Alfredo Stroessner (1954–1989) cayó y se creó una nueva constitución. De esta forma, le otorgó el rango de oficial junto al español en 1992. A partir de ese momento y con el nuevo sistema educativo, el guaraní fue enseñado obligatoriamente en todas las escuelas del país. Además, recientemente fue aprobada una ley que protege a 20 idiomas de todo el territorio y que crea las condiciones para proteger la cultura que hay detrás de estas lenguas. La nueva normativa permitirá que la ortografía y gramática guaraní sean oficiales; además, se contará con un diccionario unificado de esta lengua.

GO ON TO THE NEXT PAGE.

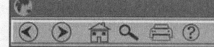

Lengua moderna

Este idioma, además de ser oficial en Paraguay, lo es también en Bolivia (junto al quechua y aymara), en la provincia argentina de Corrientes y en el municipio brasileño de Takuru. A partir de 2005 es el tercer idioma del Mercado Común del Sur (MERCOSUR), luego del castellano y el portugués. En los centros de compras paraguayos como mercados, restaurantes y galerías se usa el guaraní; los comerciantes atraen a sus clientes con esta lengua. Algunos programas de TV lo utilizan y los locutores de radio emplean el idioma para comunicarse. En diferentes tipos de celebraciones festivas, tanto la música como los discursos son en guaraní. "El guaraní no es una lengua primitiva, sino que es un idioma moderno, vivo e interesante como cualquier otro utilizado hoy" señala David Galeano Olivera, director del "Ateneo de Lengua y Cultura Guaraní". El catedrático agrega que "a pesar de los problemas que tuvo durante toda su historia, es una lengua del tercer milenio, que es hablada por casi 9 millones de personas en toda Sudamérica".

Su importancia no solo radica en el uso cotidiano, sino también en la investigación y estudio que hay al respecto. Es enseñado no solamente en universidades paraguayas, argentinas y brasileñas, sino también en prestigiosos centros de estudios de EE.UU. y Europa. Universidades como La Sorbona (Francia), Mainz (Alemania), Autónoma de Madrid (España), Zurich (Suiza) y Bari (Italia) tienen cátedras de esta lengua y cursos de postgrado. Las clases son dictadas tanto por académicos paraguayos como por investigadores europeos, muchos de ellos con una importante permanencia en Paraguay. Algunos eran diplomáticos, mientras que otros simplemente fueron seducidos por esta lengua.

Es así como también en Internet, el guaraní ha tenido gran auge, y hoy se encuentra presente en miles de sitios. Es más, en la Web se le conoce a esta lengua nativa como ta'anga veve, que significa "imágenes que vuelan". "Las lenguas que tienen poca o ninguna presencia en Internet son aquéllas que están condenadas a la muerte o la desaparición", reflexiona Olivera. Y es así como tanto Google como Wikipedia tienen su versión del avañe'e ("idioma del hombre"). En la red podemos encontrar desde traductores en línea hasta poemas en este idioma. Sin embargo, el mercado digital aún resulta complicado para el guaraní. Como idioma casi oral, poca gente lee o escribe en esta lengua. Por eso, la demanda es aún reducida por parte de la gente común, no así por curiosos y académicos. Esto constituye un nuevo desafío para el guaraní, y probablemente no sea el único que le queda a esta lengua que ha sabido sobrevivir a lo largo de los años.

Used by permission of VeinteMundos.com

GO ON TO THE NEXT PAGE.

14. El guaraní sufrió subyugación en Paraguay por motivos

    (A) lingüísticos

    (B) nacionalistas

    (C) políticos

    (D) económicos

15. ¿Qué podemos inferir del gobierno de Alfredo Stroessner?

    (A) Fue un gran defensor del idioma.

    (B) Creía que un solo idioma debe ser el idioma oficial.

    (C) Alentó el uso de guaraní en guerras como defensa.

    (D) Le otorgó el rango de idioma oficial al guaraní.

16. El idioma ha podido superar los varios intentos de eliminarlo ya que

    (A) hay presencia en los países vecinos

    (B) los paraguayos lo perciben como parte integral de su cultura y nación

    (C) es diferente de otros idiomas indígenas ya que tiene una parte escrita

    (D) la constitución garantizó su sobrevivencia

17. Un reto para la sobrevivencia de guaraní en la época tecnológica es que

    (A) hay poca demanda para su traducción

    (B) hasta ahora la demanda para aprender el guaraní solo existe en los centros académicos

    (C) la mayoría de los hablantes no dominan ni la lectura ni la escritura en la lengua

    (D) tiene poca presencia en Internet

18. La situación de Paraguay es única comparada con otros países sudamericanos ya que

    (A) es el único país que tiene dos idiomas oficiales

    (B) una población no indígena habla un idioma indígena

    (C) ha protegido a todas sus idiomas indígenas por legislación

    (D) el renacimiento del idioma ha traído consigo muchos retos no percibos antes

19. El interés en el exterior hacia el guaraní tiene su ímpetu a causa de

    (A) el comercio con otros países

    (B) el hecho que es el tercer idioma más utilizado en el Cono Sur

    (C) los académicos que lo estudiaron y lo enseñaron por interés en la cultura paraguaya

    (D) su nueva presencia en la Red

20. ¿Cuál de las siguientes afirmaciones mejor resume el artículo?

    (A) Sin el guaraní, Paraguay deja de ser Paraguay.

    (B) El guaraní tiene una posición delicada en el mundo de los idiomas.

    (C) La sobrevivencia del guaraní sólo lo pueden garantizar los paraguayos.

    (D) El guaraní merita el mismo respeto que recibe el español.

GO ON TO THE NEXT PAGE.

Selección número 4

Introducción

El siguiente artículo apareció en la prensa chilena el septiembre de 2000.

El Lado B de la Fiestas Patrias

Este año, los chilenos celebraron "el doble" de tiempo sus fiestas nacionales. La razón se debe a que junto a los tradicionales días libres del 18 y 19 de septiembre, se agregaron otros dos más: 17 y 20. Bueno, se trataba de las festividades del Bicentenario de la Independencia y había que celebrarlo como corresponde. Resultado: las jornadas festivas fueron viernes, sábado, domingo y lunes… ¡uf! Un fin de semana largo completo, que incluye casi unas mini vacaciones para toda la población, tiene sus consecuencias. El aumento de peso producto del alto número de calorías de las carnes asadas y bebidas alcohólicas, junto con las deudas acumuladas, terminan siendo protagonistas.

En las tradicionales fondas y ramadas chilenas, recintos especialmente construidos de ramas para las Fiestas Patrias, hasta el propio Presidente de la República debe bailar la cueca. Más aún, sobre todo cuando los medios de comunicación siempre están presentes en esta celebración nacional.

Los precios de comidas y bebidas típicas son altos en estos lugares: una empanada de pino cuesta alrededor de 800 pesos (U.S. $1,5), un choripán mil pesos (U.S. $2) y una cerveza de 350 cc dos mil pesos (U.S. $4). Si se tiene en cuenta que un asado promedio para cuatro personas (más la correspondiente cantidad de bebida, vino y pisco) tiene un costo de 27 mil pesos (U.S. $55), no es un misterio que se necesita tener "sólidos ingresos".

Dado que muchos chilenos no cuentan con los suficientes recursos para ello, es común que en esta época pidan créditos de consumo que los distintos bancos ofrecen para aumentar su presupuesto. Laura Soto, jefa División Créditos de Consumo del Banco CrediChile sucursal Viña del Mar, afirma que "septiembre es un mes en el que generalmente hay más demanda de créditos. Si bien a fin de año se entregan más préstamos de dinero, por las fiestas de Navidad y Año Nuevo, además de las vacaciones, este mes de septiembre ha sido comparativamente mejor que en el pasado. Tal vez por las celebraciones del Bicentenario".

Soto señala que los créditos van de los 150 mil (U.S. $300) hasta los ¡11 millones de pesos! (U.S. $24.000). "Es exagerado, pues para financiar viajes o la compra de un auto se justificaría, pero no en esta fecha". Sin embargo, aclara, el porcentaje de deudores es bajo, ya que en general la gente logra pagar los préstamos. Según sostienen expertos, las principales causas para no pagar la deuda son la pérdida del trabajo o compromisos con otro organismo financiero.

Más dinero para celebrar

En Chile un 60% de las empresas privadas entrega aguinaldos, una cantidad de dinero extra, a sus trabajadores en Fiestas Patrias. El rango varía entre los 22 y los 325 mil pesos (U.S. $45 y U.S. $750), y junto a Perú son los únicos países de Latinoamérica que incluyen estas gratificaciones en su estructura del sueldo. No sólo las compañías privadas dan aguinaldos; los organismos públicos también lo hacen. Los montos se dan de acuerdo a cuánto reciba el empleado: a quienes reciben alrededor de 500 mil pesos (U.S. $1.000) mensuales o una cantidad menor les corresponde aproximadamente 50 mil pesos (U.S. $100).

Para Ricardo Iglesias, Licenciado en Historia y Máster en América Latina Contemporánea, "lo más probable es que el entusiasmo se deba a que el 18 y 19 de septiembre son las únicas fiestas nacionales. En el resto del continente están los carnavales, los cuales tienen un significado religioso: celebran la cuaresma, los 40 días restantes para Semana Santa, como ocurre en Brasil y Uruguay". A juicio de Iglesias, otro aspecto positivo de los carnavales es que "la gente se disfraza y no es posible determinar su condición social. Además, la fiesta se desarrolla en un solo lugar. En el caso chileno, ocurre que hay bastantes ramadas y fondas, teniendo como resultado que cada persona escoge de acuerdo a su gusto y conveniencia, situación que trae consigo falta de unión entre los compatriotas". El profesor está convencido que en Chile falta una "cultura de festejos", por lo que los excesos con el alcohol podrían encontrar ahí su causa. "En Chile a la gente le gusta beber alcohol, porque simplemente le gusta. Creo que no se relaciona con las crisis económicas que nos han afectado o con penas puntuales. Cualquier excusa sirve para comprar abundante cantidad de alcohol, siendo el 18 de septiembre una fecha ideal".

Riesgo de sobrepeso

Otro tema que suele complicar en las Fiestas Patrias es el exceso de calorías consumidas. "Una persona puede subir entre uno y cinco kilogramos, según las calorías que acumule, pensando que son cuatro días feriados", afirma Janet Cossio, directora de la carrera de Nutrición y Dietética de la Universidad Andrés Bello. En el caso que la persona termine pagando altas sumas de dinero mensuales y si además engordó los tradicionales kilogramos extra, en Chile se usa una frase muy conocida como consuelo: A final de cuentas, lo comido y lo bailado no me lo quita nadie.

Used by permission of VeinteMundos.com

GO ON TO THE NEXT PAGE.

21. ¿Qué papel desarrolla el alcohol en Chile durante estas celebraciones?

    (A) El consumo del alcohol aumenta durante la crisis económica.

    (B) El consumo de alcohol es parte de cualquier costumbre cultural en Chile.

    (C) Las penalidades de la borrachería son severas y limitan el consumo.

    (D) El alto consumo del alcohol influencia la mayor tasa de obesidad en Chile.

22. ¿Cómo se diferencia el ambiente social durante las celebraciones en Chile y sus países vecinos?

    (A) Durante estas celebraciones las clases sociales en Chile se mezclan más de lo normal.

    (B) En los otros países, tal vez por la anonimidad, hay más probabilidad de que las clases sociales se mezclen.

    (C) Las celebraciones chilenas tienden a ser más cortas.

    (D) El gobierno hace que los patrones de los empleados les provean un dinero extra durante la época de las fiestas patrias.

23. ¿Qué opina Soto en cuanto a los préstamos realizados durante la época de las Fiestas Patrias?

    (A) Que muchos chilenos no cumplen con su deuda

    (B) Que no tiene sentido asumir un préstamo gigantesco para una sencilla celebración

    (C) Que los préstamos otorgados durante septiembre sobrepasan los de las épocas navideñas

    (D) Que la proporción de préstamos se vincula directamente al estado de la economía

24. ¿Qué son ramadas?

    (A) Viviendas temporales

    (B) Quioscos

    (C) Un cobertizo hecho de árboles

    (D) Un escenario

25. ¿Por qué se prolongó la celebración este año?

    (A) Cayó en un fin de semana.

    (B) Para poder estimular la economía chilena.

    (C) Coincidieron con la celebración de 200 años de independencia del país.

    (D) Lo mandó el presidente chileno para honrar la cueca.

26. Al final del artículo, ¿a qué se refiere la frase, "Al final de cuentas, lo comido y lo bailado no me lo quita nadie"?

    (A) La diversión que experimenta uno valió la pena.

    (B) Durante una celebración uno no cuida la dieta.

    (C) La comida y el baile son selecciones individuales y dependen del gusto del uno.

    (D) No hay remedio para una decisión que ya se tomó.

GO ON TO THE NEXT PAGE.

Selección número 5

Introducción

Las siguientes son unos anuncios clasificados en la prensa peruana.

TELEFÓNICA DE PERÚ

LIMA, PERÚ

Selecciona:

Asistente de Recursos Humanos

Aquellos que estén interesados en esta posición, deberán tener experiencia mínima en lo siguiente:

- Diploma de universidad o poder demonstrar cuatro años de cursos académicos en empresas, administración, o recursos humanos. Por lo mínimo, 2 años de experiencia en recursos humanos, control de archivos—altas y bajas, presentaciones a los administradores, compensación, comunicación con gerentes y abogados sobre temas legales y atención de reclamos.

- La persona para esta posición tendrá entre 25 y 35 años de edad, vive en la área de Lima y Villa El Salvador, y busca una posición de 40 horas por semana.

La empresa ofrece beneficios que incluyen: salario anual, medicina prepaga, vacaciones y días de enfermo, opciones en acciones y posibilidad de desarrollo.

Por favor aplicar antes del 30 de junio por sitio de Web: www.telefonica.peru.la

---

PALMEROS AUTOMATION

CALABASAS, CALIFORNIA

USA

Selecciona:

Ingeniero/Gerente de Proyectos para Automación

Lima, Perú

Palmeros Automation, N.A. seleccionara una persona para la posición de ingeniero/a en la planta localizada en Lima, Perú. Experiencia en lo siguiente es necesario:

- Diploma de universidad (graduado/a) ingeniero o eléctrico, mínimo 5 años de experiencia como gerente de manejo integral de proyectos en automación industrial

- Funciones serán: diseño de arquitectura y ofertas, lanzamiento de proyectos, control de archivos, asignación de recursos, negociación con proveedores

- Manejo oral y escrito del idioma inglés e español. Viajará dentro y fuera del país.

Palmeros Automation es un líder en el mercado internacional de Ingeniería. Si usted está interesado en esta posición, por favor mande su CV con historia de salario antes del 30 de junio por nuestro sitio de Web: www.palmeros-automation.com

---

GO ON TO THE NEXT PAGE.

27. ¿Cuál es el propósito de los avisos?

    (A) Dos compañías que buscan llenar el mismo tipo de posición

    (B) La misma compañía buscando nuevos empleados

    (C) Dos compañías que buscan llenar dos posiciones muy diferentes

    (D) Dos compañías en Lima, Perú buscando llenar posiciones

28. ¿Cuál es la diferencia entre los dos avisos?

    (A) Una compañía está en la industria técnica y la otra en financia

    (B) Solamente las funciones de trabajo y los beneficios

    (C) Una compañía está en Perú y la otra busca llenar la posición en California

    (D) Las funciones de cada posición, el lugar donde las compañías están establecidas, y el tipo de empresas

29. ¿Cuál de las siguientes frases comunica la misma intención que "Aquellos que estén interesados en esta posición"?

    (A) Si busca una posición nueva

    (B) ¡Váyase de su trabajo!

    (C) Todas las posiciones en la compañía están disponibles

    (D) Si busca una posición por corto plazo

30. ¿Qué perspectiva cultural representa principalmente estos dos avisos?

    (A) Las opciones de trabajo en los Estados Unidos para gente latina

    (B) Las oportunidades disponibles para trabajo

    (C) La importancia de trabajar para compañías chicas

    (D) El valor del diploma universitario

GO ON TO THE NEXT PAGE.

Part B

Interpretive Communication: Print and Audio Texts (combined)

You will listen to several audio selections. The first two audio selections are accompanied by reading selections. When there is a reading selection, you will have a designated amount of time to read it.	Vas a escuchar varias grabaciones. Las dos primeras grabaciones van acompañadas de lecturas. Cuando haya una lectura, vas a tener un tiempo determinado para leerla.
For each audio selection, first you will have a designated amount of time to read a preview of the selection as well as to skim the questions that you will be asked. Each selection will be played twice. As you listen to each selection, you may take notes. Your notes will not be scored.	Para cada grabación, primero vas a tener un tiempo determinado para leer la introducción y prever las preguntas. Vas a escuchar cada grabación dos veces. Mientras escuchas, puedes tomar apuntes. Tus apuntes no van a ser calificados.
After listening to each selection the first time, you will have 1 minute to begin answering the questions; after listening to each selection the second time, you will have 15 seconds per question to finish answering the questions. For each question, choose the response that is best according to the audio and/or reading selection and mark your answer on your answer sheet.	Después de escuchar cada selección por primera vez, vas a tener un minuto para empezar a contestar las preguntas; después de escuchar por segunda vez, vas a tener 15 segundos por pregunta para terminarlas. Para cada pregunta, elige la mejor respuesta según la grabación o el texto e indícala en la hoja de respuestas.

GO ON TO THE NEXT PAGE.

Selección número 1

Fuente número 1

Primero tienes 4 minutos para leer la fuente número 1.

Introducción

En abril de 2013, la junta legislativa del estado de Florida tuvo unas mesas redondas sobre la posibilidad de aumentar la edad mínima para sacar el permiso de aprendiz de conducir de 15 a 16 años, y la edad mínima para licencia completa de 17 a 18 años. El primer artículo es una presentación de parte de Lorena Pérez, abogada y presidente de la organización, Salvando la Juventud. La segunda selección es un informe de radio que presenta las ideas de varios jóvenes estadounidenses sobre esta propuesta.

Discurso, Lorena Pérez, ante la Junta Legislativa Hispana, Tallahassee, Florida, presentado en mayo de 2013.

Los conductores adolescentes: No hay prisa

"Estimados compañeros: pueden imaginar la angustia que abarca a un padre al recibir esa llamada telefónica informándole que ha fallecido su único hijo en un accidente automovilístico. Muchas veces es más que alguien se encuentre en el lugar equivocado en el momento inoportuno. Más bien, se trata de que a nuestros adolescentes les carezcan la madurez y la experiencia como chóferes. Accidentarse hoy en día es demasiado fácil. No tienen por qué estar recorriendo las carreteras y calles a su temprana edad, y menos con otros amigos en el coche. Los riesgos a la vida sobrepasan cualquier beneficio otorgado por tener la licencia a muy temprana edad.

Según las cifras del gobierno, mueren más de 42.000 personas anualmente en accidentes automovilísticos. Esto sobrepasa las cifras de todas las guerras en las cuales ha luchado nuestra nación. Y de esas muertes, los chóferes adolescentes entre las edades de 16 y 19 comprenden más del 40% del total. Es de esperarse que mientras los chóferes vayan aumentando de edad, conseguirán más años de experiencia, más madurez, y como resultado, las cifras empezarán a bajar.

En muchos estados, la legislación reciente tiene como meta reducir esos números a través de programas de adiestramiento y estándares para licenciamiento por edad. Es mejor que repartamos los derechos de manejar gradualmente. De esa manera los chóferes jóvenes poseerían licencias restringidas, y poco a poco irían mejorando y adquiriendo entrenamiento obligatorio. Cada año recibiría mayores derechos siempre y cuando hayan cumplido con las horas de entrenamiento ya sean de cursos prácticos o de aprendizaje formal. Así aumentamos en etapas su nivel de experiencia.

No es una idea nueva; muchos estados están examinando la posibilidad de adoptar ese plan, y muchos que lo apoyan proponen que ese umbral sea de 18 años. Muchos países europeos ya tienen como edad mínima los dieciocho años para otorgar las licencias de manejar. Otros países han impuesto limitaciones en cuanto a los límites de velocidad, los horarios, el uso de las carreteras y hasta identificación expuesta en el vehículo para identificar chóferes juveniles.

Muchos adolescentes opinarán que con estas leyes pretendamos negarles su independencia o sus derechos. Al contrario, tenemos la obligación de proteger a nuestros ciudadanos más vulnerables. Algunos científicos mantienen que existen diferencias de madurez entre los 16 y los 18 años, y se sabe que en cuanto al desarrollo el ser humano no alcanza niveles de madurez en decisiones ejecutivos hasta el final de los años adolescentes o hasta que se llegue a los 20 años. Les exhorto que consideren esta importante oportunidad para salvarles la vida a nuestros jóvenes".

GO ON TO THE NEXT PAGE.

Fuente número 2

Tienes 2 minutos para leer la introducción y prever las preguntas.

Introducción

Las opiniones de estos jóvenes aparecieron en un grupo focal sobre el tema de conductores adolescentes en Miami.

Ahora escucha la fuente número dos.

PLAY AUDIO: Track 14

Ahora tienes un minuto para empezar a responder a las preguntas para esta selección. Después de un minuto, vas a escuchar la grabación de nuevo.

(1 minute)

Ahora escucha de nuevo.

PLAY AUDIO: Track 14

Ahora termina de responder a las preguntas para esta selección.

31. Los jóvenes entrevistados mayormente opinan que
    (A) económicamente es necesario que manejen
    (B) tendrán que depender más de los adultos si la edad mínima se reduce
    (C) no hay necesidad de elevar la edad mínima para manejar ya que no logra nada
    (D) socialmente es imprescindible que los jóvenes manejen

32. Lorena Pérez basa su teoría en la necesidad de elevar la edad mínima de manejar
    (A) en experiencia propia
    (B) en la inferencia que la edad trae madurez
    (C) en pruebas científicas de otros países europeos
    (D) en el hecho que los jóvenes no pueden diferenciar entre lo bien y lo mal

33. Diría Lorena Pérez que un factor que contribuye a los muertos elevados por accidentes automovilísticos es
    (A) legislación leve
    (B) la falta de suficiente horas de práctica
    (C) el número de compañeros en el carro
    (D) falta de madurez o desarrollo

34. ¿Cuál sería un ejemplo de mayor adiestramiento?
    (A) Evaluación de destrezas prácticas después de cierto tiempo
    (B) Intervención académica
    (C) Entrevistas para determinar el nivel de madurez
    (D) Experiencia práctica

35. ¿Cuál de las afirmaciones mejor resume este artículo?
    (A) Hay posibilidades de salvarles la vida a algunos jóvenes si se cambia la edad mínima para manejar a los 18 años.
    (B) Aunque hay información que indica que el requisito de una mayor edad puede traer beneficios, los jóvenes tienen necesidad de manejar.
    (C) Las muertes por accidentes automovilísticos son el ímpetu para cambiar la edad mínima para manejar.
    (D) Se requiere más prueba científica para determinar con absoluta seguridad si la edad del chofer realmente influencia la tendencia de accidentarse.

GO ON TO THE NEXT PAGE.

36. ¿Cuál es el tono de la presentación de Lorena Pérez?

    (A) Inconvincente

    (B) Emocionante

    (C) Práctica

    (D) Lógica

37. Según la fuente auditiva, ¿cuál es el tono de John Grant?

    (A) Negativo

    (B) Arrogante

    (C) Desconfiado

    (D) Preocupado

38. ¿Cuál de los jóvenes opina lo mismo que Lorena Perez sobre la madurez y edad para conducir?

    (A) John Grant

    (B) Cielo Ramirez

    (C) Barri Marlowe

    (D) Felicia Badillo

GO ON TO THE NEXT PAGE.

Selección número 2

Fuente número 1

Primero tienes 4 minutos para leer la fuente número 1.

Introducción

El siguiente es un anuncio para los estudios en línea, un nuevo programa de la Universidad Nacional de España.

¡Estudia a la Universidad Nacional de España, en cualquier parte del mundo!

La vida contemporánea se ha transformado de muchas formas, sobre todo el mundo de correo electrónico y el Internet. El Internet ha cambiado la educación de muchas maneras, incluyendo la educación superior. Ahora, no se importa dónde estés ni cuánto tiempo tienes: puedes tomar cursos universitarios de modalidad línea con la Universidad Nacional de España en nuestro nuevo departamento de educación a distancia.

Los beneficios de estudiar en línea:

- Tienes la oportunidad de organizar tus horarios propios.
- Puedes ahorrar tiempo y dinero.
- Adquieres la responsabilidad de tu propio aprendizaje.
- Puedes enfocarte en los estudios cuando tienes el tiempo.
- Puedes aprender de manera rápida y eficiente.

No importa dónde estés.

- Alumnos, profesores y tutores pueden estar en cualquier lugar para participar en sus cursos en línea, y sólo requieren una computadora con acceso al Internet.
- Con la mayor accesibilidad, se puede reducir el tiempo de aprendizaje.

Tienes un horario flexible.

- La universidad virtual es flexible y el aula está abierta 24 horas al día, 7 días a la semana.
- Además de que te permite organizarte para cumplir tus actividades en tiempo y forma.

Recursos disponibles en línea:

- Bibliotecas electrónicas, revistas y bases de datos
- Laboratorios electrónicos completos relacionados con matemáticas, química, física, biología y electrónica
- Textos electrónicos de literatura e historia

Interacción entre estudiantes y el profesor:

- Durante el curso, se formarán grupos en línea para elaborar y repasar trabajos de la clase.
- Las interacciones entre tú y el profesor serán dinámicas y podrás usar las horas de oficina.

Un ambiente activo:

- Podrás introducir puntos para discusión relacionados al tema y responder a cuestionamientos del profesor o de tus compañeros.
- Participarás en presentaciones en línea, seminarios y proyectos.

GO ON TO THE NEXT PAGE.

Fuente número 2

Tienes dos minutos para leer la introducción y prever las preguntas.

Introducción

Esta grabación trata del aprendizaje en línea. Es una conversación entre una representante de la Universidad Nacional de España y un estudiante potencial. La grabación dura aproximadamente tres minutos.

Ahora escucha la fuente número dos.

PLAY AUDIO: Track 15

Ahora tienes un minuto para empezar a responder a las preguntas para esta selección. Después de un minuto, vas a escuchar la grabación de nuevo.

(1 minute)

Ahora escucha de nuevo.

PLAY AUDIO: Track 15

Ahora termina de responder a las preguntas para esta selección.

39. ¿De qué se trata este anuncio?

    (A) El aprendizaje en línea es el mejor método de continuar los estudios universitarios.

    (B) La vida contemporánea se ha transformado de muchas formas.

    (C) Para acomodarse a la vida moderna, el e-learning es una manera de estudiar en todas partes del mundo.

    (D) Para participar en los cursos en línea, sólo se requiere una computadora con acceso al Internet.

40. ¿Cómo ha cambiado la vida contemporánea?

    (A) La gente se muda mucho, y por eso no pueden terminar sus estudios en un solo lugar.

    (B) El Internet y el correo electrónico ofrecen una manera fácil de comunicarse con otras partes del mundo.

    (C) Ahora, mucha gente necesita más flexibilidad para cumplir los estudios.

    (D) Se puede ahorrar tiempo y dinero, y reducir el nivel de estrés porque las redes de comunicación están abiertas.

41. Según el anuncio y la grabación, los profesores y profesores en prácticas

    (A) son amables con los estudiantes

    (B) publican los resultados de los exámenes en el foro estudiantil antes del día del examen

    (C) son accesibles por medio del foro estudiantil, las horas de oficina y correo electrónico

    (D) tienen que trabajar con el secretario de la universidad para asignar los créditos

42. Podemos inferir que

    (A) el estudiante en la grabación se va a graduar temprano porque está tomando cursos en línea

    (B) los cursos en línea son más fáciles y reducen el nivel de estrés en los estudiantes

    (C) el ambiente de e-learning puede cambiar dependiendo de las necesidades de los estudiantes

    (D) se puede transferir los créditos fácilmente a todas las otras universidades, sin ningún problema

GO ON TO THE NEXT PAGE.

43. Según el anuncio, todas las siguientes frases promocionan los estudios en línea SALVO:

    (A) La sala de clase está abierta 24 hora al día, 7 días a la semana.

    (B) Las horas de estudio son flexibles y pueden cambiar dependiendo de cada alumno.

    (C) Los estudiantes pueden dar respuestas a las preguntas del profesor y de sus condiscípulos.

    (D) Los estudios en línea son como tutorías para los estudios en carne y hueso.

44. Según la grabación, se menciona el cálculo, el álgebra lineal y la estadística porque

    (A) son las materias favoritas del alumno

    (B) el estudiante quiere tomar unos cursos de matemática en el departamento de educación a distancia

    (C) son los cursos más populares en el e-learning

    (D) el estudiante quiere estudiar estadística y quiere obtener más información sobre el curso

45. ¿Cuál pregunta tiene el estudiante para la representante?

    (A) Qué hacer si tiene preguntas para el profesor

    (B) Si los cursos son divertidos

    (C) Si los profesores o los profesores en prácticas corrigen los exámenes

    (D) Cuáles son los prerrequisitos para tomar los cursos de álgebra lineal

46. Los créditos de los estudios en línea

    (A) son decididos por el foro estudiantil

    (B) se transfieren fácilmente a todas las universidades

    (C) sólo se transfieren a la Universidad Nacional de España

    (D) se pueden transferir a la mayoría de otras universidades

47. ¿Qué decide hacer el estudiante?

    (A) Se matricula en el curso de álgebra lineal.

    (B) Decide pensar un poco más antes de matricularse.

    (C) Se inscribe en el primer nivel de estadística.

    (D) Quiere hablar con un profesor de e-learning.

GO ON TO THE NEXT PAGE.

Interpretive Communication: Audio Texts

Selección número 3

Introducción

Primero tienes un minuto para leer la introducción y prever las preguntas.

Esta grabación se basa en una investigación realizada por la revista Veinte Mundos y trata de los pros y las contras de la cirugía estética.

Ahora escucha la selección.

PLAY AUDIO: Track 16

Ahora tienes un minuto para empezar a responder a las preguntas para esta selección. Después de un minuto, vas a escuchar la grabación de nuevo.

(1 minute)

Ahora escucha de nuevo.

PLAY AUDIO: Track 16

Ahora termina de responder a las preguntas para esta selección.

48. ¿Cuál es el propósito del artículo?

   (A) Presentar cómo la cultura afecta la estética

   (B) Enseñar hasta dónde puede llegar una obsesión

   (C) Explicar por qué Colombia se ubica a la vanguardia de la cirugía estética

   (D) Comparar y contrastar la estética en Colombia y los EE.UU.

49. Según el artículo, ¿qué significa la frase "valor agregado"?

   (A) Recuperar algo perdido

   (B) Llegar a un acuerdo

   (C) Postularse para un acenso en el trabajo

   (D) Mejorar su posición ya sea social o económica

50. La cirugía plástica para muchos es conveniente ya que

   (A) la recuperación tiende a ser rápida

   (B) no hay que viajar al exterior

   (C) quita la necesidad de hacer régimen

   (D) mejora la autoestima inmediatamente

51. Según el artículo, el doctor Edilson Machabajoy López advierte que

   (A) la cirugía no resuelve todos los problemas de uno

   (B) la cirugía puede ser hasta dañina al paciente

   (C) la cirugía estética es una decisión personal que trae diferentes resultados para cada persona

   (D) ninguna de estas respuestas es correcta

GO ON TO THE NEXT PAGE.

52. ¿Cuál es la diferencia entre los servicios de cirugía estética en Colombia y en los Estados Unidos?

(A) La calidad no es la misma en Colombia.

(B) Los candidatos en Colombia pueden combinar servicios de salud con el turismo.

(C) No hay edad mínima en Colombia para someterse a una intervención estética.

(D) La tasa de crecimiento en Colombia es mayor que la de los EE.UU.

53. Según el artículo, ¿cuál puede ser una decepción que podrá resultar de la cirugía estética?

(A) Las personas pueden convertirse en adictas de la cirugía y perder el aspecto natural de su físico.

(B) Los problemas de autoestima no desaparecen completamente.

(C) Los resultados nunca quedan exactamente como uno piensa.

(D) Muchas veces una sola cirugía no resuelve el problema; varias sesiones son necesarias.

GO ON TO THE NEXT PAGE.

Selección número 4

Introducción

Primero tienes un minuto para leer la introducción y prever las preguntas.

Belisario Féliz Jiménez, conocido por todos como "Beli", vino al mundo un 8 de marzo de 1909. Durante estos 101 años ha tenido una cómplice sin igual: la música, que según él, le mantiene fuerte y vivo. Y es que desde los ocho años de edad este anciano dominicano se dejó seducir por la magia musical del sonido que hace el acordeón. Es sin dudas, un apasionado de este instrumento y continúa tocando, por lo que se le considera un verdadero hito del folklore dominicano.

Ahora escucha la selección.

> **PLAY AUDIO: Track 17**

Ahora tienes un minuto para empezar a responder a las preguntas para esta selección. Después de un minuto, vas a escuchar la grabación de nuevo.

(1 minute)

Ahora escucha de nuevo.

> **PLAY AUDIO: Track 17**

Ahora termina de responder a las preguntas para esta selección.

54. ¿Cuántos años tenía "Beli" (Belisario Féliz Jiménez) cuando se hizo esta entrevista?
    - (A) 93
    - (B) 103
    - (C) 101
    - (D) 100

55. ¿Por qué el papa de Beli no lo dejaba tocar el acordeón?
    - (A) Porque tenía un trauma de infancia.
    - (B) Porque quería que Beli estudiara.
    - (C) Porque no le gustaba el sonido del instrumento.
    - (D) Porque no era un instrumento tradicional dominicano.

56. Además de crear ritmos, a Beli le fascinan
    - (A) bailar al ritmo del merengue
    - (B) las mujeres que bailan al ritmo del acordeón
    - (C) cantar canciones dominicanas
    - (D) aprender a tocar nuevos instrumentos

57. ¿Qué es lo único que Beli le pide a Dios?
    - (A) Más hijos
    - (B) Morirse sin dolores
    - (C) Salud y no morirse todavía
    - (D) Reconocimiento de sus admiradores

58. ¿Qué es lo que más aprecia de la vida hoy en día?
    - (A) La admiración de su familia, la salud, la larga vida y la música
    - (B) La admiración de los presidentes, la salud, la larga vida y la música
    - (C) El amor de su mujer, la salud, la larga vida y la música
    - (D) La oportunidad de haber conocido a varios presidentes

GO ON TO THE NEXT PAGE.

59. Cuando Beli dice "Yo estaba asfixiado de mi acordeón" implica que

    (A) ya no soportaba más al instrumento

    (B) le consumía su vida por completo

    (C) el costo de mantenerlo era sumamente caro

    (D) fue la causa de mucho conflicto con su padre

60. ¿Qué nos enseña esta entrevista?

    (A) El esfuerzo de una persona puede mejorar la vida de los demás.

    (B) Con las ganas, todo es posible.

    (C) La pobreza no es un obstáculo al éxito.

    (D) La música es una lengua internacional que todos entendemos.

GO ON TO THE NEXT PAGE.

Selección número 5

Introducción

Primero tienes un minuto para leer la introducción y prever las preguntas.

La siguiente grabación trata de la rica cultura de Perú.

Ahora escucha la selección.

> **PLAY AUDIO: Track 18**

Ahora tienes un minuto para empezar a responder a las preguntas para esta selección. Después de un minuto, vas a escuchar la grabación de nuevo.

(1 minute)

Ahora escucha de nuevo.

> **PLAY AUDIO: Track 18**

Ahora termina de responder a las preguntas para esta selección.

61. El Perú es un país que
    (A) sufre aislamiento por tener tantas zonas geográficas
    (B) fue colonizado por europeos e indígenas
    (C) disfruta de una diversidad la cual no posee todos los países del continente
    (D) perdió mucho de su sabor indígena a causa de la influencia europea

62. Las tradiciones europeas abundan
    (A) tanto en la costa como en la selva
    (B) en la sierra mayormente
    (C) en las tres zonas
    (D) en la costa debido a la inmigración europea

63. ¿Quién sería el autor de este artículo?
    (A) Un político peruano
    (B) Un promovedor de turismo peruano
    (C) Un antropólogo peruano
    (D) Un sociólogo peruano

64. ¿Qué relación existe entre la geografía y la etnia en el Perú?
    (A) Mayormente los indígenas son la población predominante en 2 de las 3 regiones principales.
    (B) La decisión de las tribus de no asimilarse hace que la selva sea la parte más atrasada del Perú.
    (C) La geografía es el factor determinante en la composición étnica y cultural del país.
    (D) Por el aislamiento geográfico hay poco contacto entre los grupos étnicos en el Perú.

65. ¿Cuál es un ejemplo de la asimilación en el Perú?
    (A) La preservación del quechua
    (B) La diversidad europea en la costa
    (C) La siesta y el lonche
    (D) La enseñanza del español en la selva

END OF SECTION I

> IF YOU FINISH BEFORE TIME IS CALLED, YOU MAY CHECK YOUR WORK ON THIS SECTION.

SPANISH LANGUAGE AND CULTURE

SECTION II

Approximate Time—85 minutes

50% of total grade

Interpersonal Writing: Email Reply

You will write a reply to an email message. You have 15 minutes to read the message and write your reply.	Vas a escribir una respuesta a un mensaje electrónico. Vas a tener 15 minutos para leer el mensaje y escribir tu respuesta.
Your reply should include a greeting and a closing and should respond to all the questions and requests in the message. In your reply, you should also ask for more details about something mentioned in the message. Also, you should use a formal form of address.	Tu respuesta debe incluir un saludo y una despedida, y debe responder a todas las preguntas y peticiones del mensaje. En tu respuesta, debes pedir más información sobre algo mencionado en el mensaje. También debes responder de una manera formal.

Introducción

Este mensaje es de la fundación Manos a la Obra. Ha recibido este mensaje porque recientemente le había solicitado trabajo como voluntario/a en Honduras. Tendrá 15 minutos para leer la carta y escribir su respuesta.

GO ON TO THE NEXT PAGE.

MANOS A LA OBRA
FUNDACIÓN DE OBRAS BENEFICAS
LA CEIBA, HONDURAS
www.manosalaobra.com

Estimado Estudiante:

Gracias por su interés en trabajar como voluntario/a en Honduras. La siguiente carta es para informarle de una oportunidad para participar en un programa de reconstrucción de casas en Honduras este verano. El programa dura 4 semanas y usted vivirá con una familia hondureña en la ciudad La Ceiba que se encargara de su hospedaje, comidas y necesidades personales. El programa nuestro se encargara de su vuelo a Honduras, transportación dentro del país, seguro médico, y entrenamiento de voluntario. Esa información le llegara pronto.

Como ya sabe, el año pasado varios huracanes devastaron la costa atlántica de Honduras y en su camino quedo destrozada la pequeña industria pesquera de la cual dependían los residentes para mantener a sus familias. Honduras carece de una infraestructura nacional para ayudar a los miles de personas necesitadas que residen en estas áreas costeñas.

Nuestra agencia se responsabiliza por colocar a los voluntarios en el área que mejor emprenda su experiencia y talento. Por ello, le ofrecemos la oportunidad de trabajar en diferentes áreas:

EDUCACIÓN: En Honduras más de la mitad de la población vive en pobreza y más de 400.000 personas están desempleadas. Tiene una de las tasas de alfabetización más bajas de América Latina. Los voluntarios necesitan ser modelos para enseñar habilidades básicas, inglés y español a jóvenes en los pueblos rurales.

SERVICIO DE SALUD: Aunque no es necesario tener experiencia médica, los voluntarios también pueden ayudar a los profesionales en orfelinatos y escuelas primarias especialmente en las zonas más retiradas.

DESARROLLO DE LA COMUNIDAD: Hay muchas áreas en que un voluntario puede ayudar a una comunidad a sostenerse. Puede trabajar con organizaciones que contribuyen a la tasa de empleo y crecimiento económico: estas se concentran mayormente en formar talleres de tejer, obras de construcción, reutilizar materiales recicladas como bicicletas, y más importante aun, arar la tierra.

GO ON TO THE NEXT PAGE.

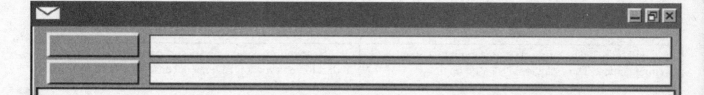

CONSTRUCCION: Las viviendas muchas veces vienen siendo covachas con techo de paja o estaño. Muchas veces no tienen ni ventanas ni pisos. No resisten la destrucción de terremotos ni huracanes. Como voluntario de construcción, trabajara con arquitectos y carpinteros a mejorar la calidad de viviendas en solo un par de horas. Es una excelente oportunidad de mejorar la calidad de vida y el nivel de esperanza entre los residentes de un pueblo. El año pasado construimos 7000 casas de cemento y ladrillo en más de 45 pueblos hondureños.

Favor de incluir una respuesta en la cual indica:

- en qué área prefiere trabajar y por que
- que otras habilidades posee que puedan ser útiles durante su estadía
- alguna situación personal que debamos tener en cuenta para hacer su estadio lo más agradable posible
- algunas preguntas que tenga sobre el programa

Esperamos con muchas ganas su respuesta. Siempre a sus órdenes,

Delfin Carrasquillo
Coordinador, Manos a la Obra, La Ceiba Honduras

GO ON TO THE NEXT PAGE.

Presentational Writing: Persuasive Essay

You will write a persuasive essay to submit to a Spanish writing contest. The essay topic is based on three accompanying sources, which present different viewpoints on the topic and include both print and audio material. First, you will have 6 minutes to read the essay topic and the printed material. Afterward, you will hear the audio material twice; you should take notes while you listen. Then, you will have 40 minutes to prepare and write your essay. In your persuasive essay, you should present the sources' different viewpoints on the topic and also clearly indicate your own viewpoint and defend it thoroughly. Use information from all of the sources to support your essay. As you refer to the sources, identify them appropriately. Also, organize your essay into clear paragraphs.	Vas a escribir un ensayo persuasivo para un concurso de redacción en español. El tema del ensayo se basa en las tres fuentes adjuntas, que presentan diferentes puntos de vista sobre el tema e incluyen material escrito y grabado. Primero, vas a tener 6 minutos para leer el tema del ensayo y los textos. Después, vas a escuchar la grabación dos veces; debes tomar apuntes mientras escuchas. Luego vas a tener 40 minutos para preparar y escribir tu ensayo. En un ensayo persuasivo, debes presentar los diferentes puntos de vista de las fuentes sobre el tema, expresar tu propio punto de vista y apoyarlo. Usa información de todas las fuentes para apoyar tu punto de vista. Al referirte a las fuentes, identifícalas apropiadamente. Organiza también el ensayo en distintos párrafos bien desarrollados.

Tema del ensayo:

¿Se debe cambiar la semana escolar de 5 a 4 días?

GO ON TO THE NEXT PAGE.

Fuente número 1

Introducción

El siguiente artículo se creó en la Junta Directiva de Educación del Distrito #242 de Los Ángeles sobre la posibilidad de ofrecerles a padres la opción de reducir la semana escolar de 5 a 4 días.

---

15 de junio de 2008

Tema: Cambiando la rutina: Reducir la semana escolar de 5 a 4 días

Estimados padres:

Entiendo cómo la inflación reciente y el aumento en el costo de la vida han afectado a ustedes y sus familias. Es un tiempo difícil para todos. Ya sufriendo del aumento en el costo de combustible para los buses, de calentar y enfriar los edificios, de alimentar a los estudiantes y de casi todos los materiales, los distritos escolares alrededor del país están considerando la idea de reducir la semana escolar de 5 a 4 días. Es una opción que debemos considerar seriamente.

Más de 150 escuelas a través del país ya han adoptado esta opción y por lo visto están contentos con los resultados. Un distrito en Topeka, Kansas ha adoptado un horario de martes a viernes y terminó ahorrando $248.000 de un presupuesto de $8,7 millones. Ese dinero se utilizó en reembolsos a los residentes del distrito. También reportaron mejoras de asistencia estudiantil y mejores resultados en los exámenes estandarizados.

Existen otros beneficios. Un fin de semana de tres días proveerá más tiempo familiar, algo que falta en la sociedad de hoy. Además, los estudiantes podrían dedicarles más tiempo a las asignaturas escolares sin la presión de una semana escolar de 5 días.

Los gastos asociados con el mantenimiento de nuestros edificios y la transportación de nuestros estudiantes son agobiantes. Como nos confronta un futuro inseguro de precios de combustible, tenemos que actuar ahora. Obviamente, la reducción de gastos es la respuesta, y agregar 1,5 horas a cada día escolar y así eliminar un día completo representa ahorros económicos significativos sin la necesidad de sacrificar trabajos, instrucción académica ni programas estudiantiles. Sin estos ahorros, los estudiantes que viven a menos de 2 millas de sus escuelas perderán el beneficio de la transportación gratuita proveída por el distrito.

Les invito a que asistan al foro público que se celebrará en la Escuela Fleetwood el 23 de julio de 2008 a las 7 de la noche. Ahí podemos dialogar más sobre este asunto.

Atentamente,
Luis Maldonado
Superintendente, Distrito 242

GO ON TO THE NEXT PAGE.

Fuente número 2

Introducción

El siguiente artículo apareció en un diario estadounidense en agosto de 2004.

---

5 – 1 = Éxito

Es un día escolar para la mayoría del país, pero no lo es para Erica Bongiardina, una estudiante del cuarto grado en la escuela Betsy Ross en Aspen, Colorado, los viernes los pasa en el pisto de esquí con su familia. "Me encanta. Tengo un fin de semana de 3 días, ¡es súper nítido!"

Su escuela estrenó la semana de cuatro días este año, principalmente para reducir costos en el presupuesto. Según los oficiales de la escuela, la escuela redujo en un 20% sus costos de transportación, servicios alimenticios, limpieza y combustible. En total estiman gozar de un ahorro de $200.000.

Varios estados han experimentado con una semana escolar de 4 días. Lo que no ha hecho la escuela Betsy Ross es reducir el currículo académico: las clases son más largas y se ha agregado un periodo adicional de estudio. La escuela empieza a las 8:30 A.M. y termina a las 4:15 P.M. para los estudiantes, "lo cual representa un día bastante largo", explica Sophie Zbeig, directora de la escuela.

"Una semana comprimida significa que los estudiantes tienen que aplicarse aún más, aprenden la importancia de tener disciplina. Los estudiantes simplemente no tienen tiempo para meterse en problemas", explica Zbeig.

Los resultados hablan

Un estudio reciente en el estado de Colorado demuestra que no hay diferencia académica en los resultados en los exámenes estatales entre los estudiantes de escuelas de cuatro o cinco días semanales. "Hay menos ausencias. Las actividades como deportes se programan los viernes, así que los estudiantes no pierden horas de estudio durante la semana. Y los padres tienden a programar citas o asuntos familiares los viernes, y entonces ya no tienden a sacarlos de la escuela de lunes a jueves", ofrece Zbeig.

"Lo bonito también es que te da un día completo para pasarlo bien con mis hijos. Y cuando tengan la edad, pueden trabajar un día más para conseguir las cosas que necesitan, que me ayuda económicamente", dice Carina Guichane, una madre de tres hijos de 6 a 14 años.

Otro beneficio potencial es con el día más largo, los estudiantes estarán llegando a casa a la misma hora que sus padres, lo cual elimina la necesidad de buscar ayuda para cuidar a los niños, otro beneficio económico. Sin embargo, los viernes presentan un problema para algunos que necesitan ahora buscar alguien que cuide a sus niños un día completo.

Los que niegan los beneficios de la semana reducida indica que los estudiantes estadounidenses, que por años han sido inferiores a los estudiantes europeos y asiáticos en las ciencias y matemáticas, estarán perdiendo la oportunidad de competir globalmente. Algunos temen que con un fin de semana más larga, los estudiantes no retendrán la misma cantidad de información.

GO ON TO THE NEXT PAGE.

Fuente número 3

Tienes 30 segundos para leer la introducción.

Introducción

Reunion de padres, Junta Directiva Educativa, 23 de julio de 2008, Fleetwood School. Los siguientes residentes de Los Ángeles expresaron sus opiniones sobre la propuesta de cambiar la semana escolar de cinco a cuatro días.

Ahora escucha la fuente número tres.

> **PLAY AUDIO: Track 19**

Ahora escucha de nuevo.

> **PLAY AUDIO: Track 19**

Ahora tienes cuarenta minutos para preparar y escribir un ensayo persuasivo.

(40 minutes)

GO ON TO THE NEXT PAGE.

Interpersonal Speaking: Conversation

You will participate in a conversation. First, you will have 1 minute to read a preview of the conversation, including an outline of each turn in the conversation. Afterward, the conversation will begin, following the outline. Each time it is your turn to speak, you will have 20 seconds to record your response.	Vas a participar en una conversación. Primero, vas a tener un minuto para leer la introducción y el esquema de la conversación. Después, comenzará la conversación, siguiendo el esquema. Cada vez que te corresponda participar en la conversación, vas a tener 20 segundos para grabar tu respuesta.
You should participate in the conversation as fully and appropriately as possible.	Debes participar de la manera más completa y apropiada posible.

Tienes un minuto para leer la introducción.

Introducción

Tu amiga Laura te llama para hablarte sobre una experiencia que tuviste el fin de semana pasado cuando fuiste a las montañas a divertirte.

> **PLAY AUDIO: Track 20**

Laura	Te saluda
Tú	Salúdala, Dile tu evaluación del viaje
Laura	Te hace una pregunta
Tú	Contesta la pregunta
Laura	Te hace una pregunta
Tú	Contesta la pregunta
Laura	Te hace una pregunta
Tú	Contesta que no es posible y ofrece una alternativa
Laura	Continua la conversación
Tú	Contesta la pregunta
Laura	Continua la conversación
Tú	Contesta la pregunta
Laura	Se despide

GO ON TO THE NEXT PAGE.

Presentational Speaking: Cultural Comparison

You will make an oral presentation on a specific topic to your class. You will have 4 minutes to read the presentation topic and prepare your presentation. Then you will have 2 minutes to record your presentation.	Vas a dar una presentación oral a tu clase sobre un tema cultural. Vas a tener 4 minutos para leer el tema de la presentación y prepararla. Después vas a tener 2 minutos para grabar tu presentación.
In your presentation, compare your own community to an area of the Spanish-speaking world with which you are familiar. You should demonstrate your understanding of cultural features of the Spanish-speaking world. You should also organize your presentation clearly.	En tu presentación, compara tu propia comunidad con una región del mundo hispanohablante que te sea familiar. Debes demostrar tu comprensión de aspectos culturales en el mundo hispanohablante y organizar tu presentación de una manera clara.

Tienes cuatro minutos para leer el tema de la presentación y prepararla.

(4 minutes)

Tema de la presentación:

En nuestra sociedad vemos que las tradiciones de la cultura defina un pueblo. Sin embargo, lo que hace la vida interesante son las diferencias entre culturas. En tu experiencia, compara y contrasta algunas tradiciones culturales que has observado en tu comunidad con las de otros países del mundo hispanohablante.

Tienes dos minutos para grabar tu presentación.

STOP

END OF EXAM

Chapter 7
Practice Test 2:
Answers and
Explanations

ANSWER KEY

Section I

1.	B	23.	B	45.	A
2.	B	24.	C	46.	D
3.	C	25.	C	47.	A
4.	B	26.	A	48.	C
5.	B	27.	C	49.	D
6.	A	28.	D	50.	C
7.	D	29.	A	51.	B
8.	D	30.	B	52.	B
9.	C	31.	A	53.	A
10.	D	32.	B	54.	C
11.	C	33.	B	55.	B
12.	B	34.	D	56.	B
13.	C	35.	A	57.	C
14.	C	36.	D	58.	A
15.	B	37.	C	59.	B
16.	B	38.	D	60.	B
17.	C	39.	C	61.	C
18.	B	40.	B	62.	D
19.	C	41.	C	63.	B
20.	A	42.	C	64.	A
21.	B	43.	D	65.	C
22.	B	44.	B		

Section II

See explanations beginning on page 340.

SECTION I

Interpretive Communication: Print Texts (Page 278)

Selection 1: Translated Texts and Questions, with Explanations

Introduction

The following selection is an excerpt from a short story.

Mom, Ana, and the baby went to visit Grandpa, but poor Dad could not go because he had to stay at home to work.

"What shall I do without you?" he asked.

"I will write you letters, three letters," Ana answered. "I will tell you what we are doing here without you."

"Do you know how to write a letter?" asked Dad.

"Oh, yes, I can write one!" said Ana. "I am seven now. You will see that I can write a letter."

Ana had a very good time. One day she said, "Grandma, may I take a pen? I want to write to Dad."

"Yes," said Grandma, "there are pens on the desk."

Ana ran to Grandpa's desk. "Oh, Grandma! This is such a strange pen!"

"That is a quill pen," said her Grandma. "Grandpa made it for me. It is a goose quill; in the old days, everybody used to write with quill pens."

"I think it is very pretty," said Ana. "I don't think I can write with it."

She took another pen and went off. In a little while she went back to the desk. And there she saw that the baby had taken the quill pen and she had been writing to Dad with it. And what a letter she had written! Ana realized that she had spilled the ink over the desk.

"Oh, baby, baby! What did you do that for?"

Mom sent baby's letter to Dad, and he said he was glad to get both letters.

ANA'S LETTER TO HER FATHER.

Aracataca, July 12, 1917.

Dear Dad:

We are having a very good time. Grandpa has a big bay horse. Sometimes he puts me on the horse's back. It is such fun! I play in the field a great deal. Grandpa lets me walk on the haycocks and I pick berries for Grandma. They give us cheese with our coffee.

I wish you were here with us. Baby has written you a letter. She took Grandma's quill pen, and she spilled the ink. Can you understand her letter? She says she wrote, "How are you, Dad? I love you a lot."

Your little girl,

Ana

1. How can one understand what the baby's letter is about?

   (A) According to the letter itself

   (B) According to Ana's letter

   (C) According to what the grandmother says to the father

   (D) According to the narrator

Because the baby's "writing" consists of spilling ink all over the desk, her letter cannot be understood by itself (A), which is why Ana facetiously asks her father whether he can read it and then offers a translation of what the baby was trying to say. She does this within her letter to her father, making (B) the correct answer. You could have eliminated (C) because the grandmother and the father do not have a conversation in this selection. The narrating voice does not offer any information about the contents of the letter, so (D) is also incorrect.

2. Who doubts that Ana can write the letter?

   (A) Her grandmother

   (B) Her father

   (C) Her grandfather

   (D) The baby

This is a straightforward comprehension question. After Ana indicates that she will write letters, Ana's father introduces doubt by asking her whether she knows how to write a letter in the first place, making (B) the correct answer.

3. According to the selection, why does Ana write, "Can you understand her letter?" to her father?

   (A) Because she knows he has poor vision

   (B) Because she knows the letter has arrived

   (C) Because she knows he cannot read the baby's letter

   (D) Because she knows that in the old days everyone used to write with quill pens

Ana asked her father whether he could read the baby's letter, knowing that he could not because it was illegible. Choice (C) is correct. Choice (D) merely rehashes some of the text and (A) and (B) are entirely unrelated.

4. The following sentence can be added to the text: **"Fascinated by the novelty, she handled it for a moment, and then she returned it to its proper place."** Where would this sentence fit best?

   (A) Line 10

   (B) Line 14

   (C) Line 18

   (D) Line 25

This passage becomes confusing because the word **pluma** here is used to refer to both a feather pen and a regular pen. The reader may have difficulty in distinguishing between the two. As the feather pen is a source of fascination to the young girl, she would naturally pick it up and examine it. In line 10, she hasn't discovered the feather pen yet. Line 14 would be the best fit, as she remarks how beautiful it is and that she doesn't think she can write with the feather pen. Immediately afterwards, she takes a regular pen and leaves, implying she had put the feather pen back. Thus, (B) is the best answer.

5. Who is the "her" ("it") with whom the baby writes the letter (line 16)?

   (A) The grandmother

   (B) The pen

   (C) Ana

   (D) The mother

Since the mother is not mentioned in this scene, you can eliminate (D) right away. If you look closely at the line, the only possible answer is (B), as the **ella** (*it* in English) refers to **la pluma,** which is a feminine noun and not a person. You know that no one wrote the letter with the baby because she was unsupervised.

6. Why does Ana look for a pen?

   (A) Because she wants to write three letters

   (B) Because she wants to write a book

   (C) Because she wants to spill the ink

   (D) Because she needs her father

This seems like an easy question, but notice how far into the question set you had to work to get here. Because the questions do not move in a clear order of difficulty, be sure not to trap yourself by spending too much time on a question you find yourself struggling with. Doing this would rob you of the points you could earn with questions like this. The entire plot of this passage is Ana writing a letter to her father: (A) is the correct answer.

7. Who sends the letter to Dad?

   (A) The grandmother

   (B) Ana

   (C) The baby

   (D) The mother

This question may seem strange, but it is actually the mother who sends the letter, not the baby (C), the grandmother (A), or Ana (B), who is the one who writes the letter. Therefore, (D) is the correct answer.

Selection 2: Translated Text and Questions, with Explanations

Introduction

The following article appeared in the Bolivian press in June 2001.

Careful! Zebras Working on the Street

They aren't Disney characters or mascots that are promoting a brand or a product. The "zebras" that circulate through the streets of La Paz have a very special job: they are urban educators who teach people to walk safely throughout the city. Each day, they cover their bodies with costumes and masks: they move, jump, yell, and wave flags to call the attention of pedestrians. According to the municipal organization "City Culture," around 240 young people work in two shifts, four hours a day and 20 hours a week.

The vehicle and pedestrian traffic is getting worse each day in this city, which is the center of the Bolivian government. The automobiles don't respect the traffic lights and people cross the streets any place they can. It's total chaos. People's lives, especially those of the children, are in constant danger. For that reason, the municipal authority decided to take concrete measures. Thus were born the "zebras."

In 2001, the mayor's office created a project through "City Culture" with the goal of lessening vehicle traffic. "The zebras emerged with the objective of showing the pedestrians how to cross the street," explained Kathia Salazar, coordinator of the "Zebra Project." This "City Culture" movement began in Colombia. There, the organization worked with mimes/educators. In the streets, groups of children and students played games to demonstrate how one should cross at crosswalks.

The municipal representative explains that this project possesses two fundamental pillars: educational and social. The majority of young people who work as "zebras" are between 16 and 22 years old and are authorized by the municipality to decongest the vehicular traffic and to facilitate pedestrian transit.

"The requirements to work as a zebra are strong will, effort, creativity, and the desire to get ahead. On the part of the mayor's office, we are committed to staying with this project," revealed Salazar.

Every day the zebras cover their bodies with cotton suits and white fabric with black stripes. When impatient pedestrians cross against the traffic lights they dance, play, joke, and gesture nonstop. When they leave, the children and elderly miss them and chaos returns to the street. The monthly salary can be up to 450 Bolivianos (about U.S. $65). The leaders or guide can earn up to Bs. 1000 (about 144 U.S. dollars) for their exclusivity to the Zebra Project.

City Culture

Julia Andrea Marca (21 years old) has been working as a zebra for 1 year and 9 months. To practice the role of urban educator, she had to attend various teaching and learning workshops taught by Kathia Salazar. "The children hug me and grab me with so much love. With this, we try to educate and teach the young ones," she indicates. Julia also studies every morning at the University of San Andres, where she is in her first year of biochemistry. "The only negative experience I've had during this time was when I got hit by a car, but it wasn't a very serious accident. Initially, people didn't know to use the crosswalks. But now, thanks to us, the citizens respect the traffic signals," she adds.

Amanda Pinos (29 years old) has been working for 8 years on this municipal initiative. She jumps through the streets as soon as the traffic light turns red. Each day she stands very close to the Student Plaza, and by doing so she prevents drivers from going through red lights, causing accidents and more road congestion. Her principal function lies in transmitting the values of City Culture to everyone. "I have seen fairly terrible accidents; it is something truly sad," she says. "The principal job of the urban educators is to generate reflection on the part of each citizen of La Paz and generate awareness in the most loving and respectful way." Pinos, who currently works as a project leader, explains that "the zebras are young people who are interested in participating in this family and being urban educators who advise about prevention." She adds that some phrases that they say to pedestrians include: "Sir, be careful," "Be careful please," "Don't cross the street," "Stop please!"

For our interviewees, working as a zebra is more of a service than just a job. For many of them, the job of urban educator means a way to support, love, and change the city. It's that simple.

La Paz?

The 2001 National Census reported a population of 1,552,156 inhabitants in all of the metropolitan areas of La Paz, including the city of El Alto. The population estimate for the year 2010 was close to 2 million inhabitants without including El Alto, with its almost 1.2 million people. Together they form the largest urban area in the country. According to the data from the Bolivian National Institute of Statistics, the number of cars in La Paz reached close to 220,000 in 2009. Although there are laws and fines that regulate the traffic in La Paz, the majority of drivers do not respect the red light—even less, the rights of the pedestrians or the crosswalk. It's for this reason that the zebras can be found on almost every corner in the city, helping people cross the street and training the drivers from early morning till nightfall.

8. What is the purpose of this article?

   (A) To present a comical way to deal with an urban problem

   (B) To tell the experiences of young people who joined an important cause

   (C) To demonstrate how jobs can be both satisfying and educational

   (D) To illustrate how a city responded creatively to an urgent need

The best answer is (D). Choices (B) and (C) are true, but are not topics that prevail throughout the article. Choice (A) is somewhat true, but the zebras were not meant to be comical: they were based on previous models in other places, and were perhaps chosen more for their easily visibility.

9. Which of the following statements best summarizes the article?

    (A) It is almost impossible to change people's way of thinking.

    (B) In South America, because of the lack of funds for public works compared to First World countries, it's necessary to look for alternative solutions to problems.

    (C) An educated and respectful populace can improve the lives and wellbeing of others.

    (D) Both drivers and pedestrians play a role in everyone's safety.

The correct answer is (C). Choice (B) is assuming information not in the article. Choice (A) is a judgment also not supported in the text. Choices (C) and (D) are both correct, but (C) is more true of the article as a whole, as the program aims to educate and teach respect among all parties on the street. The AP often goes for this type of questioning, where you must really split hairs to pick the better answer.

10. What can we infer from the 2001 and 2009 census data?

    (A) Due to the economic crisis, more people are becoming pedestrians.

    (B) Due to the demographic explosion, the municipal authority cannot accommodate so many pedestrians in the street.

    (C) The number of cars has not increased at the same rate as the population.

    (D) With the increased number of residents in La Paz and the outskirts in recent years, there are more challenges for pedestrians.

The population explosion does mean more pedestrians and probably more drivers, which means (D) is the best answer.

11. If you were to do a more in-depth investigation of the topic discussed in the article, which one of these sources might you use?

    (A) The Bolivian census of 2013

    (B) The Urban Planning Board of La Paz

    (C) The Ministry of Highways and Transportation

    (D) The Civil Registry

One would most likely want to know how the program is working, which would mean investigating the number of accidents and automotive-pedestrian incidents, making (C) the best answer.

12. What is a downside of the program?

    (A) Drivers won't necessarily respect a young person dressed a zebra in the same way that they would respect a police officer or army officer.

    (B) The zebras will always have the risk of being hit by cars.

    (C) The pay and hours that the zebras work are barely enough to live on.

    (D) The funds for the program could be revoked at any time.

Choice (A) is somewhat correct, but (B) is the better answer, as the accidents are mentioned in the article. Choices (C) and (D) are not referenced in or implied by the article.

13. What is the problem addressed by this project?

(A) The high incidence of accidents

(B) That pedestrians don't know where to cross the street due to lack of instructions

(C) That drivers basically ignore the traffic laws

(D) That conflicts between driver and pedestrian are more common each day

Choices (A) and (D) are not supported by any data. The project was more to help pedestrians stay safe and to keep drivers from going through red lights and ignoring the law, which is also mentioned in the census information. Thus (C) is the best answer.

Selection 3: Translated Text and Questions, with Explanations

Introduction

The following article appeared on an Internet site in 2013.

Republic of Paraguay
South America
Population: 6,800,284 (2013)
Language: Spanish and Guarani
Currency: Guarani

Guarani in Paraguay

It was persecuted and prohibited for many decades in Paraguay. It could never be taught formally. But it served as a defense mechanism in wars and today is spoken by almost 9 million people in different South American countries. Since 1992 it has been, along with Spanish, the official language in all of Paraguay. Guarani has overcome many great challenges throughout the years and still faces challenges, even in the 21st century.

According to the 2002 census, the indigenous population of Paraguay is almost 100,000 inhabitants and includes more than 17 ethnic groups. In spite of the fact that this number is not significant within the total population (the country has almost 7 million people), 87% of Paraguayans speak Guarani. Therefore, this Latin American nation is bilingual.

And why do so many people speak the country's original language? According to Maria Antonia Rojas of the cultural institute "Guarani Symposium," the dialect belongs to the first inhabitants of this zone of South America, and has been defended by the Paraguayans themselves. "Nowadays it is like a transcendental element in the daily culture," she says.

Beginning with the name Paraguay, which means "river that flows into the sea," this language has formed part of the country's culture. In addition, many of the names of plants, animals, songs, foods, and attitudes can be expressed only in this language.

In spite of the strong defense made by the Paraguayans, for many years the Guarani language was prohibited, including by political persecution and punishment for all the children and teenagers who spoke it at school. That changed when the dictatorship of Alfredo Stroessner (1954–1989) fell and a new constitution was created. As a result, it was given official status alongside Spanish in 1992. From this moment on, and with the new educational system, Guarani was required to be taught in all the schools in the country. Also, a law was recently approved that protects 20 languages throughout the country and creates the conditions to protect the cultures associated with those languages. The new laws will allow Guarani writing and grammar to now be considered official; in addition, there will be a unified dictionary in the language.

Modern Language

This language, aside from being an official one in Paraguay, is also one in Bolivia (along with Quechua and Aymara), in the Argentinean province of Corrientes, and in the Brazilian state of Takuru. Since 2005, it is the third language in MERCOSUR, after Spanish and Portuguese. In Paraguayan shopping centers, such as markets, restaurants, and malls, Guarani is used; the sellers attract buyers with this language. Some TV shows use it and the radio announcers use it to communicate. In different types of festive celebrations, both the music and speeches are in Guarani. "Guarani is not a primitive language, but rather a modern, alive, and interesting one, like any other language used today," explains David Galeano Olivera, director of Guarani Language and Culture Foundation. The professor adds, "In spite of the problems that it has had throughout its history, it is a language of the third millennium, that is spoken by almost 9 million people in all of South America."

Its importance lies not only in its daily use, but also in the investigation and study of the language. It is taught not only in Paraguayan, Argentinean, and Brazilian universities, but also in prestigious learning centers in the United States and Europe. Universities such as the Sorbonne (France), Mainz (Germany), Autonomous University of Madrid (Spain), Zurich (Switzerland), and Bari (Italy) have departments for this language and post-graduate courses. The classes are given by Paraguayan academics as well as European researchers, many of them with permanent residences in Paraguay. Some were diplomats, while others were just seduced by this language.

Guarani has also experienced a great resurgence on the Internet and today is found on thousands of sites. In addition, on the Web it is known as "ta'anga veve" which means "images that fly." "Languages that have little or no Internet presence are condemned to death or disappearance," reflects Olivera. And thus it is that Google as well as Wikipedia have their version of avañ'e (language of man). On the Web we can find anything from online translators to poems in this language. However, the digital market has even made things complicated for Guarani. Since it is a mostly oral language, few people read or write in it. For that reason, there is little interest on the part of the common people, unlike among those curious about the language and academics. This constitutes a new challenge for Guarani, and probably will not be the only one this language that has learned to survive throughout the years has left to face.

14. Guarani suffered subjugation in Paraguay for _____ motives.

   (A) linguistic

   (B) nationalistic

   (C) political

   (D) economic

The correct answer is (C), which is evidenced by the article's mention of political persecution.

15. What can we infer about the government of Alfredo Stoessner?

   (A) It was a great defender of the language.

   (B) It believed that only one language should be the official one.

   (C) It promoted the use of Guarani as a defense in war.

   (D) It granted Guarani the rank of official language.

The correct answer is (B). As one of the most notorious self-centered leaders of his time, Stoessner was not keen on preserving the Guarani culture. All the positive changes for the language, as the article mentions, were made after his downfall.

16. The language has been able to overcome various attempts to eliminate it, since

   (A) it is present in neighboring countries

   (B) Paraguayans perceive it as an integral part of their nation and culture

   (C) it is different from other languages since it has a written component

   (D) the constitution guaranteed its survival

The article discusses how Paraguayans defended the language and how it is now an integral part of the culture, making (B) the correct answer.

17. A challenge to the survival of Guarani in the technological age is that
    (A) there is not much demand for its translation
    (B) until now, the demand to learn Guarani has only existed in academic centers
    (C) the majority of its speakers don't read or write the language well
    (D) it has a small presence on the Internet

Guarani is a mostly spoken language. Written elements are only recently becoming commonplace, due to legislation and technology. The issue is that most Paraguayans never had a need to write or read it; thus the correct answer is (C).

18. The situation in Paraguay is unique compared with other South American countries because
    (A) it is the only South American country with two official languages
    (B) a non-indigenous population speaks an indigenous language
    (C) it has protected all of its languages with legislation
    (D) the rebirth of the language has brought many unanticipated challenges

The article mentions that only 100,000 true indigenous people live there, but 87 percent of the population speaks Guarani. Thus, the correct answer is (B).

19. The overseas interest in Guarani is due to
    (A) commerce between countries
    (B) the fact that it is the third most utilized language in the Southern Cone
    (C) the academic experts who have studied and taught it because of their interest in Paraguayan culture
    (D) the new presence it enjoys on the Web

Guarani is enjoying a thriving international resurgence due to academic study overseas and Paraguayans living abroad, so the correct answer is (C).

20. Which of the following statements best summarizes the article?
    (A) Without Guarani, Paraguay would not be Paraguay.
    (B) Guarani holds a delicate position in the world of language.
    (C) The survival of Guarani can only be guaranteed by the Paraguayans themselves.
    (D) Guarani deserves the same respect as Spanish.

The article discusses how the language is so intertwined in the culture that, without it, Paraguay would lose much of its identity and character. Thus the correct answer is (A).

Selection 4: Translated Text and Questions, with Explanations

Introduction

The following article appeared in the Chilean press in September 2000.

Side B of the National Holidays

This year, Chileans celebrated "double" time during their Independence Day celebrations. The reason is that in addition to the traditional days off, the 18th and 19th of September, two more were added, the 17th and the 20th. Well, it was due to the fact that the Bicentennial Independence festivities had to be celebrated correctly. The result: the holidays were Friday, Saturday, Sunday, and Monday…. Oof! A complete long weekend that included practically a mini-vacation for the whole population has its consequences. The increase in weight resulting from the high number of calories in barbecued meat and alcoholic beverages, along with accumulated debt, wind up being the outcome.

In the traditional Chilean outdoor huts, constructed especially for the independence celebrations, even the president of the Republic himself is supposed to dance the Cueca, especially when the media are always present at this national celebration.

The prices of typical food and drinks are high in these places: a pineapple empanada costs around 800 pesos (U.S. $1.50), a chorizo sandwich 1000 pesos (U.S. $2), and a 0.35L beer 2000 pesos (U.S. $4). When one keeps in mind that the average barbeque for four people (along with the corresponding amount of drinks, wine, and Pisco) costs twenty-seven thousand pesos (U.S. $55), it's not a mystery that one must have a "solid income."

Given that most Chileans don't have sufficient resources for this, it is common at this time to ask for loans that various banks offer in order to increase their budgets. Laura Soto, head of the credit consumption division of the bank "CrediChile," Viña del Mar branch, affirms that "September is a month in which there is generally more demand for loans. Even if at the end of the year they are handing out more loans because of Christmas and New Year's in addition to vacations, this September has been comparatively better than in the past. Maybe it's because of the bicentennial celebrations."

Soto shows that the loans granted go from 150,000 (U.S. $300) up to 11 million pesos! (U.S. $24,000). "It's too much: using loans to buy a car or pay for a trip would be justifiable, but not just for this holiday." However, she clarifies that the percentage of indebted people is low given that in general, the people are able to pay off their loans. According to experts, the principal causes for not paying the debts are loss of jobs or commitments to another financial institution.

More Money for Celebration

In Chile, 60% of private companies hand out bonuses, an extra amount of money workers receive during the patriotic celebrations. The range varies between 22 and 325 thousand pesos (U.S. $45 and $750), and along with Peru, Chile is the only Latin America country that includes these bonuses in its salary structure. Not only do companies provide bonuses, public organizations do as well. The amount varies according to what the employee receives; some receive 500,000 pesos (U.S. $1,000) monthly and others receive a lesser quantity that corresponds to 50,000 pesos (U.S. $100).

For Ricardo Iglesias, a graduate in history with a master's degree in contemporary Latin American affairs, "The enthusiasm is probably due to the fact that the 18th and 19th of September are the only national celebrations. In the rest of the continent, there are carnivals which have a religious meaning; they celebrate Lent, the 40 remaining days until Holy Week, like in Brazil and Uruguay." According to Iglesias, another positive aspect of the carnivals is that "people wear costumes and it's not possible to determine their social class. In addition, the party takes place in just one place. In the case of Chile, the result is that there are many ramadas and refreshment stands, the result being that each person chooses according to his or her tastes and convenience, a situation that brings about a lack of unity among compatriots." The professor is convinced that in Chile, there is a lack of celebratory culture because of such celebrations leading to alcohol abuse. "In Chile, people like to drink alcohol simply because they like it. I don't think it has anything to do with the economic crisis that has affected us, or with prompt penalties. Any excuse is fine in order to buy a large amount of alcohol, and the 18th of September is the perfect date."

Risk of Obesity

Another topic that tends to come up during the patriotic celebrations is excessive calorie consumption. "A person can gain between 1 and 5 kilograms according to the number of calories they accumulate, assuming there are 4 days of celebrations," explains Janet Cossio, director of the school of nutrition and diet at Andres Bello University. In the case that a person winds up paying high amounts of monthly payments and if they also gained the traditional kilograms, in Chile, a very well-known phrase is used as consolation: when all is said and done, no one can take away from me all the eating and dancing I've done.

21. What role does alcohol play during these celebrations in Chile?
    (A) Consumption increases during the economic crisis.
    (B) Consumption of alcohol is part of any cultural celebration in Chile.
    (C) The penalties for drunkenness are severe and limit the consumption.
    (D) The high consumption of alcohol influences the higher obesity rate in Chile.

The article discusses how, among Chileans, any celebration is an excuse to drink.

22. How is the social environment in Chile different during these celebrations compared to its neighboring countries?
    (A) During these celebrations the social classes in Chile mix more than usual.
    (B) In other countries, maybe because of the anonymous factor, there is more probability that the social classes may mix.
    (C) Chilean celebrations tend to be shorter.
    (D) The government makes employers provide workers extra money during the patriotic celebrations.

The article discusses that *Carnaval* is a long celebration with masks and costumes, which may be a reason why people who do not know each other may be more inclined to socialize.

23. What does Laura Soto think about the loans made during the period of Patriotic Festivals?
    (A) That many Chileans do not honor their debt
    (B) That it doesn't make sense to assume a large loan simply for a patriotic celebration
    (C) That the loans granted during September surpass those given during Christmastime
    (D) That the proportion of loans is directly tied to the economy

Laura states that it is justifiable to take out a loan for a car or a trip, but not simply for a celebration during the month of September.

24. What are ramadas?
    (A) Temporary housing
    (B) Stands
    (C) A shelter made from trees
    (D) A setting

The article discusses the word **ramas,** which means *branches.*

25. Why was the celebration longer this year?
    (A) It fell on a weekend.
    (B) To stimulate the Chilean economy.
    (C) It coincided with the celebration of 200 years of Independence.
    (D) The Chilean president ordered it as homage to the Cueca.

The article discusses the bicentennial celebration, which is a 200-year celebration.

26. At the end of the article, what does the following phrase refer to?
"Al final de cuentas, lo comido y lo bailado no me lo quita nadie".

(A) The fun that one experiences is worth it.

(B) During a celebration one doesn't stick to a diet.

(C) Food and dance are individual selections that depend on individual tastes.

(D) There's no undoing a decision you already made.

This phrase is used when one has paid a price for partying or drinking heavily.

Selection 5: Translated Texts and Questions, with Explanations

Introduction

The following are classified announcements in a Peruvian newspaper.

TELEFÓNICA OF PERU
LIMA, PERU

Hiring:
Human Resources Assistant

Those who are interested in this position should have the following experience as a minimum:

- University diploma or be able to demonstrate four years of academic courses in business, management, or human resources. At least 2 years' experience in human resources, archive management of high and low priority files, presentations to managers, compensation, communication with managers and lawyers about legal issues, and customer complaints.

- The person for this position will be between the ages of 25 and 35, live in the Lima and Villa El Salvador area, and will be looking for a position of 40 hours per week.

The company offers benefits including: annual salary, health insurance plans, vacation and sick days, stock options, and possibilities of advancement.

Please apply before June 30 through our website: www.telefonica.peru.la

PALMEROS AUTOMATION
CALABASAS, CALIFORNIA
USA

Hiring:
Engineer/Project Manager for Automation

Lima, Peru

Palmeros Automation, N.A. will select a person for the position of engineer and Project Manager at the plant located in Lima, Peru. Experience in the following is required:

- University Diploma (graduate) engineer or electrician, minimum of 5 years experience as Project Manager in industrial automation

- Functions will be: architectural design and offers, launching projects, archive management, resource allocation, negotiation with suppliers

- Command of both oral and written English and Spanish. Will travel within and outside the country.

Palmeros Automation is a leader in the international engineering market. If you are interested in this position, please send your resume with salary history before June 30 through our website: www.palmeros-automation.com

27. What is the purpose of these ads?
    (A) Two companies that are looking to fill the same type of position
    (B) The same company looking for new employees
    (C) Two companies that are looking to fill two very different positions
    (D) Two companies in Lima, Peru, looking to fill positions

The two ads are for job postings. The first is for a telephone company located in Peru, searching for a Human Resources Assistant. The second is for an automation company located in California, searching for a Project Manager/Engineer to run its plant in Peru. Choices (A) and (B) are incorrect based on this information. Choice (D) is incorrect because both companies are not located in Peru. The correct answer is (C).

28. What is the difference between these ads?
    (A) One company is in the technical industry and the other in finance
    (B) The job descriptions and benefits only
    (C) One company is in Peru and the other is looking to fill a position in California
    (D) The job descriptions, the locations where the companies are established, and the type of companies

There are many differences between these two companies. POE is the way to go here! Choice (A) is incorrect because although one could be in the technical industry, the other is not in finance. Choice (B) is incorrect because there are more differences between the two than just the job descriptions and benefits. Choice (C) is partially correct. The job descriptions, the locations where the companies are established, and the type of companies differ between the two. Choice (D) is correct.

29. Which of the following phrases communicates the same intention as "Those who are interested in this position…"?
    (A) If you are looking for a new position
    (B) Leave your job!
    (C) All of the positions within the company are available
    (D) If you are looking for a part-time position

The phrase states *those who are interested in the position:* thus we must find something that is similar and conveys the same intention/meaning. Choice (B) can be eliminated right away. Choice (C) is never stated since each of these ads is looking to fill one position. Choice (D) is incorrect because the ad describes a position requiring 40 hours per week. Choice (A) is the best answer.

30. What cultural perspective do these two ads primarily represent?
    (A) The job options in the United States for Latin American people
    (B) The opportunities available for work
    (C) The importance of working for small companies
    (D) The value of having a university diploma

The cultural perspective of these two ads represents the public sphere—careers and jobs. Choice (A) is not correct. These two ads do not represent the job options in the United States. Choice (C) can't be proven since it's not stated that each of these companies are small companies. On the contrary, the ad for Palmeros Automation states that it's a leader in international markets. Choice (D) can be disproven as well since only one ad requires a university diploma. The other ad mentions that course substitutions are possible. Choice (B) is the correct answer. Culturally, these ads represent the opportunities available for work.

Interpretive Communication: Print and Audio Texts (Combined) (Page 289)

Selection 1: Translated Texts and Questions, with Explanations

Source 1

Introduction

In April 2013, the Legislature of the State of Florida conducted some round tables about the possibility of raising the minimum age for obtaining a learner's permit from 15 to 16 years of age and the minimum age for obtaining a driver's licence from 17 to 18 years. The first article is a presentation by Lorena Perez, lawyer and president of the organization Saving the Youth. The second selection is a radio report that presents the ideas of various American youths about this proposition.

Speech, Lorena Perez, before the Hispanic Legislature, Tallahassee, Florida, presented in May 2013

Adolescent Drivers: There Is no Rush

"Esteemed colleagues: you can imagine the anguish that parents take on after receiving a telephone call informing them that their only son has passed away in an automobile accident. Many times, it is more that someone is in the wrong place at an inopportune moment. What is more, our adolescents lack maturity and experience as drivers. Accidents today are too easy. They do not need to be traversing the highways and streets at their young age, much less with their friends in the car. The risk to their lives surpasses whatever benefits are granted by having a license at an early age.

According to government figures, more than 42,000 people die annually in car accidents. This surpasses the number of deaths in all wars that have been fought by this nation. And, of these deaths, adolescent drivers between the ages of 16 and 19 comprise more than 40% of the total. It is to be expected that, as drivers age, they have more years of experience, more maturity, and, as a result, the numbers will start to fall.

In many states, recent legislation has been aiming to reduce these numbers though driving schools and standardized licensing ages. It is better that we give the privilege to drive gradually. This way, young people would have restricted licenses, and, little by little, would continue to improve and to acquire required training. Every year, they would receive more rights provided that they complete the practice hours, whether from practice courses or formal learning. Thus we increase the level of experience in stages.

It is not a new idea; many states are examining the possibility of adopting this plan, and many who support it propose that the threshold be 18 years of age. Many European countries already have eighteen as a minimum age to be awarded a driving license. Other countries have put into practice limitations with respect to speed limits, hours, highway usage, and even exposed identification on the vehicles to identify young drivers.

Many adolescents believe that these laws we hope for will deny them their independence or rights. On the contrary: we have an obligation to protect our most vulnerable citizens. Some scientists maintain that there are differences in maturity between the ages of 16 and 18, and it is known that, in terms of human development, one does not reach levels of maturity in executive decisions until the end of the adolescent years or until 20 years of age. I exhort you to consider this important opportunity to save the lives of our young people."

Source 2

Introduction

The opinions of these youths appeared in a focus group about adolescent drivers in Miami.

Radio Report

Next, you will hear the opinions of several youths about the possibility of raising the minimum driving age.

Amanda Estevez, 18

"I see the problem in another way. Yes, it is important to get more practice, and my parents are completely in favor of me continuing to get whatever experience I can. But you have to take into account that many students of 16 or 17 years of age need transportation to school activities and sports practice, and to socialize or to study in the library. If young people cannot drive until they are 18, then their parents will have to compensate."

Felicia Badillo, 16

"Perhaps it would be better to raise the minimum age because older adolescents are more mature."

John Grant, 17

"How will I get to work? I work after school, and both my parents work. I do not have the resources to take a taxi every day, and there are no reliable lines of public transportation. My income is an important part of family expenses. This is another example of a generation of adults who fear and limit the opportunities of young people. First they limit cigarettes, censor movies, and now they are interfering with the driving age. It will not stop there, I assure you."

Barri Marlowe, 16

"The economy also would be affected if young people could not drive, similarly to if it were to pass that illegal immigrants would be deported. There would not be people to occupy those vacant jobs. What's more, the young people would earn less money, and, for the most part, there would be less consumption on their part of products and services, and the country's economy would suffer a lot. We contribute a lot as consumers in the national economy."

Alex Nestle, 16

"It is said that more than a quarter of young people, age 16, work outside the home during the school year, and more than one third during the summer, when school is not in session. Businesses would suffer a lot if their workers could not get to their businesses."

Cielo Ramirez, 18

"Maybe it isn't essential that we change the minimum age. If all the states were to have required classes starting at 15 years of age, we would be more skilled at driving, and we would have that additional experience before embarking on the roads."

31. The interviewed teens for the most part believe that

   (A) it is economically necessary for them to drive

   (B)   they will have to depend on adults more if the minimum age is lowered

   (C)   there is no need to raise the age to drive since it doesn't achieve anything

   (D)   socially it is vital for teens to drive

The majority of the teens interviewed cited economic reasons for needing to drive.

32. Lorena Pérez bases her theory about the need to raise the minimum driving age on

   (A) personal experience

   (B) the inference that age brings maturity

   (C) scientific studies from other European countries

   (D) the fact that youth can't tell the difference between right and wrong

Lorena Perez classifies maturity as a key factor in assuming the responsibility to drive.

33. Lorena Pérez would say that a contributing factor to the high death toll due to automobile accidents is

   (A) weak legislation

   (B) the lack of enough practice hours

   (C) the number of companions in the car

   (D) lack of maturity or development

Lorena Pérez is a proponent of gradually providing full driving privileges after courses and training.

34. What would be an example of further training?

   (A) An evaluation of skills after a certain period of time

   (B) Academic intervention

   (C) Interviews to determine maturity level

   (D) Practical experience

All of the other options are ways of determining skill level, while (D) discusses practical experience, which is, in essence, training.

35. Which of these statements best summarizes the article?

   (A) It might be possible to save the lives of some of the youth if the minimum driving age is changed to 18 years.

   (B) Although there is data that indicates that the requirement of a higher driving age can bring benefits, young people need to drive.

   (C) Deaths from auto accidents are the impetus to change the minimum driving age.

   (D) More scientific investigation is needed to determine with absolute certainty whether the age of the driver truly influences the tendency to have accidents.

Be careful! This question refers to the article only; thus even though (B) is the best summary of both sources, the question refers to the article, which discusses saving lives by raising the age. Therefore, (A) is the best answer.

36. What is the tone of Lorena Perez's presentation?

   (A) Unconvincing

   (B) Emotional

   (C) Practical

   (D) Logical

Lorena Pérez discusses many sources, and although she makes some emotional references to losing lives, overall she uses data and reasoning to prove her point. Thus, the best answer is (D).

37. According to the auditory source, what is John Grant's tone?
   (A) Negative
   (B) Arrogant
   (C) Distrusting
   (D) Worried

John Grant thinks that this will be part of the continuing limitation of young people's rights.

38. Which of the young people has the same opinion as Lorena Perez about maturity and driving age?
   (A) John Grant
   (B) Cielo Ramirez
   (C) Barri Marlowe
   (D) Felicia Badillo

Most of the young respondents are against raising the driving age for various reasons. Felicia Badillo (D) agrees that the minimum driving age should be raised because more maturity is necessary. Cielo Ramirez (B) also partially agrees with Lorena's position: however, she argues for state requirements of additional training, since she believes the key factor is skill, not maturity.

Selection 2: Translated Texts and Questions, with Explanations

Source 1

Introduction

The following is an advertisement for online studies, a new program of the National University of Spain.

Study at the National University of Spain, from Any Part of the World!

Contemporary life has transformed in many ways, especially the world of email and the Internet. The Internet has changed the face of education in many ways, including higher education. Now, it doesn't matter where you are or how much time you have: you can take university-level courses online with the National University of Spain in our new distance-learning department.

The Benefits of Online Study:
- You have the opportunity to organize your own hours.
- You can save time and money.
- You take responsibility for your own learning.
- You can focus on your studies when you have time.
- You can learn quickly and efficiently.

It doesn't matter where you are.

- Students, professors, and tutors can be in any location to participate in their online courses, requiring only a computer with Internet access.
- With better accessibility, you can reduce your learning time.

You have a flexible schedule.

- The virtual university is flexible, and the classroom is open 24 hours per day, 7 days per week.
- In addition, you can organize your time so that you can complete all your other activities and commitments.

Available Resources Online:

- Online libraries, magazines, and databases
- Complete online laboratories for mathematics, chemistry, physics, biology, and electronics
- Online texts for literature and history

Interaction between students and the professor:

- During the course, online groups will form to elaborate on and to review assignments from class.
- Interactions between you and the professor will be dynamic, and you may use office hours.

An active environment:

- You can introduce points of discussion related to the subject and respond to questions from the professor or your classmates.
- You will participate in online presentations, seminars, and projects.

Source 2

Introduction

This recording is about online learning. It is a conversation between a representative of the National University of Spain and a prospective student. The recording lasts approximately three minutes.

(REPRESENTATIVE) Good day! How can I help you?

(STUDENT) Hello! I would like to study math in college, so I would like to take some introductory courses online to save a bit of money.

(R) Of course! What courses are you interested in?

(S) Well, I am taking calculus now in secondary school, and I think it would be good to take some courses in linear algebra or statistics. How many are there?

(R) Sure! There are three levels of statistics courses, and an introduction to linear algebra. The prerequisite for this course is calculus, so therefore you would be prepared to take it.

(S) Excellent. I only have a few questions about online learning because I have never taken an e-learning course before. What do I do if I have a question for my professors?

(R) You can use the course's forum to ask a question, or you can directly ask the professor during office hours or by email.

(S) And also, what happens with exams and course assignments?

(R) The professor and graduate assistants correct all assignments and exams, and publish the solutions on the student forum.

(S) How does the student forum work?

(R) Well, the forum is for the students. They at times are vocal, especially in Political Science courses, and they have animated conversations. The professors also participate in the debates and offer questions to the students. Other forums, like those of math or science, are calmer, but they still create academic environments for the students and professors.

(S) Wonderful! My last question is this: will the online credits transfer to my in-person studies?

(R) Yes. If you attend the National University of Spain, you can transfer credits easily. You can transfer the credits to the majority of other universities as well, but you would need to speak with the registrar of that university for more details.

(S) But, for the majority of universities, the credits will transfer?

(R) Yes. The distance-learning department offers the same credits for online courses as for in-person courses. The courses are the same, and the only difference is that you can attend classes at home.

(S) Thank you. That sounds great! May I enroll in the linear algebra course?

(R) Of course!

39. What is the advertisement about?
   (A) Online learning is the best method for continuing one's university studies.
   (B) Contemporary life has changed in many ways.
   (C) To accommodate modern life, e-learning is a way to study in all parts of the world.
   (D) To participate in online courses, one only needs a computer with Internet access.

Choice (C) is the correct answer. The advertisement is about e-learning, which offers a more flexible method of taking university courses. Choice (A) is too extreme because it says that online learning is the best method. Neither (B) nor (D) is the main point of the advertisement.

40. How has contemporary life changed?
   (A) People move a lot, and, because of this, they cannot finish their studies in only one place.
   (B) The Internet and email offer an easy way to communicate with other parts of the world.
   (C) Now, many people need more flexibility to finish their studies.
   (D) One can save time and money, and reduce stress levels because the networks of communication are open.

Choice (B) is the correct answer. The advertisement states in the first paragraph that the Internet and email have changed the lines of communication, and have thus revolutionized how we communicate. While it is true that people move a lot, it goes beyond the scope of the passage to say that they cannot finish their studies in only one place (A). Choices (C) and (D) are both off-topic, though mentioned elsewhere in the text.

41. According to the advertisement and recording, the professors and graduate assistants
    (A) are nice to the students
    (B) publish the solutions to the exams on the student forum before exam days
    (C) are accessible through the student forum, office hours, and by email
    (D) have to work with the registrar of the university to assign credits

Choice (C) is the correct answer. The professors and graduate assistants are easily accessible through the forum, during office hours, and by email. We hope they are nice to the students, but that goes beyond the scope of the text (A), and they publish solutions to the exams AFTER exams, not before (B). Lastly, we do not know whether the professors or graduate assistants have to work with the registrars or not (D).

42. We can infer that
    (A) the student in the recording will graduate early because he is taking online courses
    (B) online courses are easier and reduce stress levels in students
    (C) the environment of e-learning can change for the various needs of the students
    (D) one can transfer credits easily to all other universities without a problem

Choice (C) is the correct answer. The only choice that we can prove from the text and recording is that e-learning offers students flexibility for their various needs. We do not know whether the student in the recording will graduate early from college (A), and (D) is extreme because it says credits transfer easily to all other universities. Choice (B) is never mentioned either, and could possibly be a detractor for online learning if the courses are easier, and therefore not as worthwhile to the students.

43. According to the advertisement, all of the following phrases promote online studies EXCEPT:
    (A) The classroom is open 24 hours per day, 7 seven days per week.
    (B) The hours of study are flexible, and can change for every student.
    (C) Students can respond to questions posed by the professor and their classmates.
    (D) Online studies are like tutorials for in-person studies.

Choice (D) is the correct answer. Online studies are not described anywhere in the text or recording as tutorials for in-person studies. They are meant to be freestanding classes in which students can earn credits, the same as in any brick-and-mortar class at a university. Students are able to interact and respond to other members of the class (C), and can choose their hours of study (B). Also, the classroom is always open (A), allowing flexible hours of study (B) to be possible.

44. According to the recording, calculus, linear algebra, and statistics are mentioned because
    (A) they are the student's favorite subjects
    (B) the student would like to take some math courses in the distance-learning department
    (C) these are the most popular courses in e-learning
    (D) the student wants to study statistics, and would like more information on the course

Choice (B) is the correct answer. The student expresses that he would like to take some math courses in the distance-learning department to get a head start on some college courses for his major. As he has only taken calculus, we cannot know that these are the student's favorite subjects (A), and it goes beyond the scope of the text and recording to say that these are the most popular e-learning classes (C). Choice (D) is a trap answer, as he is interested in possibly studying statistics, though he has not decided on it. He is more interested in the different types of math courses that are available for him to choose from.

45. Which question does the student have for the representative?
    (A) What to do if he has questions for the professor
    (B) Whether the courses are fun
    (C) Whether the professors or graduate assistants correct the exams
    (D) What the prerequisites are in order to take the linear algebra course

Choice (A) is the correct answer. The student asked how he could ask questions of the professor, about credit transfer, and how exams and assignments work in online courses. He does not ask whether the courses are fun (B), or who corrects the exams (C). He also does not ask about the prerequisites for linear algebra: the representative volunteers that information instead (D).

46. The credits from online learning
    (A) are decided by the student forum
    (B) transfer easily to all universities
    (C) only transfer to the National University of Spain
    (D) can transfer to the majority of universities

Choice (D) is the correct answer. The credits from online learning, as we learned from the recording, transfer to most other universities, though the details depend on the respective schools' registrars. Choice (B) is too extreme, and (C) is too narrowly focused. Choice (A) does not make sense.

47. What does the student decide to do?
    (A) He enrolls in the linear algebra course.
    (B) He decides to think a bit more before enrolling.
    (C) He enrolls in the first level of statistics.
    (D) He would like to talk with an e-learning professor.

Choice (A) is the correct answer. The student decides to enroll in the linear algebra course at the end of the conversation. He does not enroll in any of the statistics courses at the end of the conversation (C), and he never asks to speak with an e-learning professor (D). Since he enrolls in the linear algebra course, he clearly does not spend more time thinking before enrolling (B).

Interpretive Communication: Audio Texts (Page 296)

Selection 3: Translated Text and Questions, with Explanations

Introduction

This recording is based on an investigation carried out by *Veinte Mundos* magazine, and it deals with the pros and cons of plastic surgery.

Report: The Plastic Surgery Boom

Since plastic surgery appeared, many people have had the opportunity to better their physical appearances easily and quickly. Many do not even care about the costs said operations involve. It is no longer necessary to resort to long hours at the gym or strict diets to obtain a good body. Colombia has taken this phenomenon by storm in recent years. The obsession with beauty has come to this country to position itself as one of the prime locations for plastic surgery on the world level.

The Colombian Society of Plastic Surgery (SCCP) affirms that, every year, more than ten thousand aesthetic interventions are done in this country, a figure that has grown 70% in the last decade. Moreover, the costs are less, compared with those in countries such as the United States. In North America, a nose surgery costs eight thousand dollars, while in Colombia, it can be done for half the cost.

Why has this phenomenon occurred? In the 90s, when narcotic trafficking problems invaded the country, the "narco-dollars" allowed many women easy access to plastic surgery. The high demand for this practice generated the best quality service and continually lowered prices.

This obsession with bodily perfection puts Colombia at the "top" of plastic surgery today. This nation relies on a developed industry, in which more than seven hundred specialized plastic surgeons work. The aesthetic cult extends to all types, races, and social strata in this country. Recall that Colombia has the highest concentration of beauty pageants, and their women have gone to the finals of Miss Universe on twenty-one occasions.

Doctor Edilson Machabajoy Lopez affirms that motivations for subjecting oneself to plastic surgery are related to achieving added value. "Many times, they want to rekindle romantic relationships or obtain better work. Nevertheless, these are false illusions. The results of plastic surgery can create psychological problems and less than satisfactory results for the patient."

The same Colombian culture has created a sort of familiarity and confidence necessary to subject oneself to plastic surgery. Not only for the ease of cost, but also for the cult of the ideal body. At the same time, cosmetologists have increased their sales by 55%, according to the National Department of Colombian Statistics (DANE).

Surgery and Tourism

The cost of an operation in Colombia is between 20 and 80% cheaper than in other countries. In addition, local tourism agents include extras: airplane tickets, lodging, and guided excursions through the many typical locations in the country. This is why many famous people, like Maradona, travel frequently to Colombia in order to get plastic surgery. This phenomenon has grown Colombian national tourism. Many agencies offer a unique combination of tourism, health, aesthetics, and beauty. This permits patients, on a national and international level, to access different aesthetic surgical treatments and medically specialized services, while enjoying a pleasant stay in Colombia. The majority come from Canada, the United States, Mexico, and the United Kingdom.

Pros and Cons

In Colombia, plastic surgery has also come into popularity amongst young people who turn 15 years old. They ask their parents for the present of a body enhancement with surgery, instead of a trip or large party. In spite of the fact that specialists advise against it until the body is fully formed, many parents, in the end, concede to the desires of their children.

Dagoberto Gómez (52 years), public employee of Cali, explains that he has seen the suffering of his 16-year-old daughter to lose weight. He has agreed to cooperate in arranging plastic surgery for her ("The problem will be solved quickly, and she will be happy"), even though his wife does not agree with the decision, as she has seen news of young women dying from having these types of operations performed on them.

"I have many friends who have had surgeries done to enlarge their breasts, and it appears to me that they have recovered fine," assures Marínela Fernández, 32, of Popayán. "It betters their self-esteem, and, for the most part, they seem more secure and beautiful. It seems to me that to invest money in your body is the best option."

Fabián Martínez (29 years), a lawyer in Bogotá, suggests that he agrees with the surgeries when they are really necessary. "But there are cases in which the women abuse them and end up looking very artificial. Many return to surgeries because they want to look like their favorite stars, not to correct defects in their bodies."

Even so, if you go to have a surgery of this type, it becomes very important to take the necessary precautions: for example, to investigate whether the chosen clinic is legal, and to ask whether the surgeons are certified.

The deaths from plastic surgeries have called many people's attention. Generally, the victims are young, healthy women who dream of having a better figure. Since many people search for prices that are too economical, they fall into the hands of doctors with doubtful ability.

Men in Comparison to Women
The most commonly practiced plastic surgeries in the operating rooms vary according to whether the patients are men or women. The first opt chiefly for scalp implants and liposuction. Women, on the other hand, prefer to eliminate fat from their eyelids, modify their noses, and augment or reduce their breasts.

Used by permission of VeinteMundos.com

48. What is the purpose of this article?

(A) To present how culture affects our view of aesthetics

(B) To show to what point an obsession can grow

(C) To explain why Colombia is at the vanguard of plastic surgery

(D) To compare and contrast aesthetics between Colombia and the United States

The article talks about Colombia's booming industry and the way surgery is a part of life there. The other choices are correct to a degree, but are not the overall theme of the article. Remember, you are looking for the best answer, and (C) is the most applicable to the article as a whole.

49. According to the article, what does "valor agregado" mean?

(A) Recover something lost

(B) Come to an agreement

(C) Prime oneself for a promotion at work

(D) Improve one's social or economic position

Valor agregado means *added value,* and in the article it is used to talk about a competitive edge people seek with cosmetic surgery.

50. Plastic surgery is convenient for many because

(A) recovery tends to be quick

(B) one need not travel overseas

(C) it eliminates the need for dieting and exercise

(D) it immediately improves self-esteem

The article mentions that the majority of surgeries, such as liposuction, give immediate results without the need for exercising or dieting.

51. According to the article, Doctor Edilson Machabajoy López warns that
    (A) surgery can't resolve all of your problems
    (B) surgery can even be harmful for the patient
    (C) cosmetic surgery is a personal decision that brings different results to each person
    (D) none of these responses is correct

The doctor warns in the passage about surgery people have to look like someone else or regain a lost love, but which can instead bring depression and unsatisfactory results.

52. What is the difference between cosmetic surgery in Colombia and in the United States?
    (A) The quality is not the same in Colombia.
    (B) Potential patients in Colombia can combine health services and tourism.
    (C) There is no minimum age in Colombia for having cosmetic surgery.
    (D) The growth rate in Colombia is higher than in the United States.

Colombia attempts to attract European and American tourists with "surgery and tourism" packages.

53. According to the article, what might be a problem that could result from cosmetic surgery?
    (A) People become addicted to the procedures and stop looking natural.
    (B) Self-confidence issues do not go away completely.
    (C) The results never turn out exactly as one planned.
    (D) Many times, one surgery doesn't resolve the problem and multiple sessions become necessary.

Fabian Martinez talks about women "abusing" plastic surgery and looking artificial.

Selection 4: Translated Text and Questions, with Explanations

Interview: Beli, a Life Made of Music

Introduction

Belisario Féliz Jiménez, known by all as "Beli," came into the world on the 8th of March in 1909. During those 101 years, he has had an unparalleled companion: music, which, according to him, keeps him strong and lively. From 8 years of age, this ancient Dominican was seduced by the musical magic of the sound the accordion makes. He is, without a doubt, a lover of this instrument, who continues playing, which is why some consider him a milestone of Dominican folklore.

When did your love for the accordion begin?

I was still very small and restless when I started to tease and play with the accordion. It began as a game, and, 93 years later, I continue being an enthusiast of the instrument.

Can one say, then, that between you and the accordion was "love at first tone?"

Yes, of course. I remember the first time I played an accordion, I felt an inner desire to never let it go ever again. I remember that I hid in a closet because it was my father's and I took it secretly. I spent hours making noise with it. My father had an accordion because he played it when he was young. But he did not like it, and therefore did not want me to play, according to him, because he did not want anything to distract my mind from my studies and school. You know how elderly people from before were. So, every time he came home from work and found me playing, he would hit me and punish me.

Then, how did you learn to play?

My father was very stubborn, and never taught me. Neither did I go to a music school. I learned by myself. I listened to the sounds that came from the accordion, and created melodies afterward. I continued learning little by little. When you like something, you learn it.

And thereafter you continued playing?

No. I always knew that playing the accordion was my vocation, but it was a fragile part of my life that I gave up because of pressure from my father, who wanted his son to have a stable job. When I was an adolescent, I worked with a farmer, which was what one did at the time. Also, at another time, I worked as a coal miner. But, I always continued playing because a friend would come, a neighbor, or family member would search for me to play in a wedding or at a birthday. And for me, what I really enjoyed was the accordion, and therefore, I went and left my job.

And it didn't bother you to say goodbye and leave work incomplete?

No, because in that moment I was caught by my accordion. I didn't want to leave it, and it was the most important thing to me.

And why has playing the accordion fascinated you so much?

I liked to create rhythms, but also, one of the things I most enjoyed was that I had many admirers. The women of the time would go crazy to hear me play, and I enjoyed playing for them to see how, with my rhythm, those wide and long dresses they wore back then would move.

It draws attention that, at your age, you have the physical strength and memory to play. What is your secret?

Well, to me, my memory fails me when I try to remember some names or dates, but never do I forget a musical note. The melody is not in my brain, but in my heart, and my heart never ages. It's true that I get tired at times. But what I do is play seated. I stand for a short while, and when I tire, I go back and sit down.

Do you also play other instruments?

Yes, of course. I know how to play the pandero and the güira: the mangulina, carabiné, and the merengue, which are the most danced here in the south, or at least used to be danced. You know that now the youth have other music.

And what do you think about that?

There are strange things, but there is also good music. I just leave them alone, because here we have a saying that says: "To each crazy, his own topic."

In all the south of the Dominican Republic, poverty abounds. To play the accordion was, in addition to art, a source of work?

Of course, yes. To me, they paid me to play, and playing my accordion supported and raised my 20 declared children as well as some wild ones we have there [he smiles]. That's why I say that in music, in addition to the love of art, I also encountered a way to survive.

And today you continue playing and working?

I remain "accordion in hand." I play at parties and political events around here.

You are a man of 101 years; you must have many anecdotes…

Oof, I have many, many. I will tell you one about president Trujillo, who was a dictator. Well, in one of the regime controls, I fell prisoner. I went to play at a party, and one of the officials who worked for Trujillo incarcerated me for this and no more, without me doing anything. I didn't have a lawyer or anything because that was for rich people. Then, as I was a musician, I began to play to entertain myself. You know that we Dominicans, from the moment we hear the music, we start to move our feet, and there was a moment in which the official could not resist my rhythm. He took me out of the cell, and we finished with everyone in the prison dancing. We made a tremendous party.

Well, thanks to your accordion, you hobnobbed with a Dominican president.

Not only with one. I also knew professor Juan Bosch, who was a good president. One time, he made a competition for all the musicians of the country, and I won.

Is there something you think you have not achieved?

Well, I only ask God for health and to not take me yet. I know that I am a "chin" past age, but I still want to continue living.

Today, now that you are a very old man, what do you appreciate most about life now?

My family's admiration, above all, my 82 grandchildren. My health, my long life, and music—these are the greatest things I have.

54. How old was "Beli" (Belisario Féliz Jiménez) when this interview was conducted?

    (A) 93

    (B) 103

    (C) 101

    (D) 100

This is mentioned in the introduction to the interview.

55. Why didn't his father let him play the accordion?

    (A) Because he had a trauma from childhood

    (B) Because he wanted Beli to study

    (C) Because his didn't like the sound of the instrument

    (D) Because it was not a traditional Dominican instrument

Beli mentions that his father didn't want anything to distract Beli from his studies.

56. In addition to creating rhythms, Beli loves

    (A) dancing to the rhythm of the merengue

    (B) women who dance to the rhythm of the accordion

    (C) singing Dominican songs

    (D) learning how to play new instruments

Beli mentions that he liked to see how the women's dresses would move as they danced.

57. What is the only thing Beli asks God for?

    (A) More children

    (B) To die without pain

    (C) Health and to not die yet

    (D) Recognition from his admirers

Beli mentions that he asks God only for health and to not take him yet.

58. What does he most value in life nowadays?

    (A) The admiration of his family, health, a long life, and music

    (B) The admiration of the presidents, health, a long life and music

    (C) The love of his wife, health, a long life, and music

    (D) The opportunity to have met various presidents

Beli mentions this toward the end of the interview.

59. When Beli says "Yo estaba asfixiado de mi acordeón," that implies that

(A) he couldn't put up with the instrument anymore

(B) it consumed his life completely

(C) the cost of maintaining it was very expensive

(D) it was the cause of much conflict with his father

Normally **asfixiado** means *asphyxiated,* but in this case Beli is referring to his attachment to his accordion.

60. What does this interview show us?

(A) The effort of one person can make a difference in the lives of others.

(B) If you want something and go for it, everything is possible.

(C) Poverty is not an obstacle to success.

(D) Music is an international language that we all understand.

Beli always knew he wanted to make music and never gave up on it, eventually making a living from it, providing for his family, and becoming famous.

Selection 5: Translated Text and Questions, with Explanations

Introduction

The following recording is about the rich culture of Peru.

Peru relies on a rich history, native folklore, and also the European traditions that were imported many centuries ago. And as a result of this rich mixture, Peru enjoys one of the most diverse cultures in the entire continent of South America. In reality, Peru continues to be three countries in one, since the different geographic zones—the coast, the mountains, and the forest—are so distinct geographically and historically that each one has developed its own culture and lifestyle. For example, the Peruvian coast is known for its European influence: many families trace their roots back to Italy, Spain, Germany, France, and England. And, as is to be expected, in the large cities on the coast we find impressive European architecture, colonial touches in the churches and plazas, and also the European tradition of "siesta," a rest at lunchtime in which businesses close their doors for a couple of hours around midday. Even the English tradition of tea time in the afternoon continues in vigor with "lonche," a snack with coffee or tea at four o'clock in the afternoon. In the mountains, the majestic peaks of the Andes dominate the landscape and preserve the Incan culture—it is here where the indigenous heart of the country beats. Even though the real Inca no longer exist, their descendants still speak Quechua, the Incan language, and work the land in the same way, harvesting potatoes and raising llamas and alpacas for their wool. Finally, in the forest, the numerous tribes rooted there, because of geographic isolation, still avoid contact with the exterior world, and live primitively by hunting in the forest and living off the many natural resources that abound in the Amazon. In Peru, there is something that satisfies all tastes, and to experience it first-hand is the only way of capturing the unique spirit that is Peru.

61. Peru is a country that

(A) suffers isolation as a result of having so many geographical zones

(B) was colonized by Europeans and indigenous peoples

(C) enjoys a diversity that not all of the countries of the continent have

(D) lost much of its native flavor due to European influence

According to the selection, "Peru enjoys one of the most diverse cultures in the entire continent of South America."

62. European traditions are plentiful
    (A) both on the coast and in the jungle
    (B) mostly in the mountains
    (C) in all three zones
    (D) on the coast due to European immigration

The European descendants on the coast have influenced many facets of society.

63. Who probably is the author of this article?
    (A) A Peruvian politician
    (B) A promoter of Peruvian tourism
    (C) A Peruvian anthropologist
    (D) A Peruvian sociologist

The article invites a visitor, claiming that there is something for everyone in Peru and it is best experienced first-hand.

64. What relationship exists between geography and ethnicity in Peru?
    (A) Indigenous groups predominate in 2 of 3 main regions.
    (B) The decision of tribes to not assimilate makes the jungle the most backwards part of Peru.
    (C) Geography is the determining factor in the cultural and ethnic composition of the country.
    (D) Due to geographic isolation there is little contact between Peru's ethnic groups.

The Quechua-speaking peoples and the indigenous peoples of the jungle are both majorities in their regions, making (A) correct.

65. What is an example of assimilation in Peru?
    (A) The preservation of Quechua
    (B) The European diversity on the coast
    (C) La siesta y el lonche
    (D) The teaching of Spanish in the jungle

Both **lonche** and **siesta** are part of Peruvian culture, thanks to the British and Spanish traditions brought by settlers. These are examples of other customs assimilating into mainstream culture.

SECTION II

Interpersonal Writing: Email Reply (Page 301)

Translation of the Question

Introduction

This message is from the Let's Get to Work foundation. You have received this message because you recently had applied for work as a volunteer in Honduras. You will have 15 minutes to read the letter and write your response.

**LET'S GET TO WORK
CHARITABLE WORKS FOUNDATION
LA CEIBA, HONDURAS
www.manosalaobra.com**

Dear Student:

Thank you for your interest in working as a volunteer in Honduras. The following letter is to inform you of the opportunity to participate in a house-reconstruction program in Honduras this summer. The program lasts 4 weeks and you will live in the city of La Ceiba with a Honduran family who will be in charge of your lodging, meals, and personal necessities. Our program covers your flight to Honduras, transportation within the country, medical insurance, and volunteer training. You will receive that information soon.

As you already know, last year various hurricanes devastated the Atlantic coast of Honduras, and in their wake left destroyed the small fishing industry on which the residents depend to support their families. Honduras lacks a national infrastructure to help the thousands of people in need who reside in these costal areas.

Our agency accepts responsibility for placing volunteers in the areas best suited to their experience and talents. That's why we are offering you the opportunity to work in different areas:

EDUCATION: In Honduras more than half the population lives in poverty and more than 400,000 people are unemployed. It has one of the lowest literacy rates in Latin America. Volunteers need to be models: to teach basic skills, English, and Spanish to young people in rural towns.

HEALTH SERVICE: Although it is not necessary to have medical experience, volunteers can also help professionals in orphanages and primary schools, especially in the most remote areas.

COMMUNITY DEVELOPMENT: There are many areas in which a volunteer can help a community to sustain itself. You can work with organizations contributing to the employment rate and economic growth: these concentrate mainly on building textile shops, works of construction, reuse of recycled materials such as bicycles, and even more importantly, plowing.

CONSTRUCTION: Housing many times means hovels with straw or tin roofs. Often they have neither windows nor floors. These do not hold up against the destruction of earthquakes nor of hurricanes. As a construction volunteer, you would work with architects and carpenters to improve the quality of housing in only a couple of hours. It is an excellent opportunity to improve the quality of life and the level of hope among the residents of a town. Last year we built 7000 cement and brick houses in more than 45 Honduran towns.

Please include a reply indicating:

- in which area you would prefer to work and why
- what other skills you possess that might be useful during your stay
- any personal circumstances we should keep in mind in order to make your stay as agreeable as possible
- any questions you might have about the program

We eagerly await your reply. Always at your service,

Delfin Carrasquillo
Coordinator, Let's Get to Work, La Ceiba Honduras

Sample Student Response

Estimado Señor Carrasquillo:

Le agradezco su carta y su invitación para participar en el programa. La idea de ayudar a una comunidad tan necesitada como la de Honduras es algo que me motiva mucho. Sé que con la cooperación de muchos es posible hacer tener un gran impacto en las vidas de la gente que necesita ayuda.

He repasado las varias opciones de su programa, y creo que la que mejor me conviene es la construcción. El año pasado ayudé a mi familia a construir un garaje para mi casa y además he trabajado en los veranos en una compañía que instala techos en residencias, así que, el martillo y los clavos son amigos muy íntimos míos. La idea de mejorar las residencias para las personas me tiene un gran impacto ya que la felicidad empieza en el hogar, y si la gente tiene un bonito lugar donde vivir, su perspectiva hacia el futuro indudablemente mejora.

Tengo algunas habilidades que pueden beneficiar el programa. Soy músico, y toco la guitarra y los tambores, así que me encantaría tener la oportunidad de colaborar a enseñarles a los niños a tocar instrumentos y a cantar canciones en español. También he trabajado como socorrista por 2 años en mi comunidad, así que tengo entrenamiento en proveer los primeros auxilios a la gente.

Soy flexible y tranquilo—entonces lo único que necesito es buena comida y una cama para dormir. Quisiera saber si es necesario tener algunas vacunas antes de llegar a Honduras, y si tendremos algunas oportunidades de visitar las playas, ¡ya que me encanta correr tabla de vela!

Estoy muy emocionado de tener la oportunidad de trabajar con ustedes.

Atentamente,
Matthew Driscoll

Translation of the Sample Student Response

Dear Mr. Carrasquillo:

Thank you for your letter and invitation to participate in the program. The idea of helping a community in need such as that of Honduras is a great motivation to me. I know that, with cooperation among many, it is possible to have a large impact on the lives of people who need help.

I have reviewed the various options in your program, and I think that the best option for me is construction. Last year, I helped my family build a garage for my home, and I have also worked summers at a company that installs roofs on houses, so a hammer and nails are my best friends. The idea of improving residences for people has great meaning for me, because as we know, happiness begins at home and if people have a nice place to live, their perspective towards life will undoubtedly improve.

I have several talents that can benefit the program. I am a musician, and I play the guitar and drums, so I would love to have the chance to collaborate and teach children how to play instruments and sing songs in Spanish. I also have worked as a lifeguard for 2 years in my community, so I have training in providing first aid to people.

I am flexible and calm—so the only thing I really need is good food and a place to sleep. I would like to know if it is necessary to have any vaccinations before arriving in Honduras, and if we will have the chance to visit the beach, since I love to wind surf!

I am very excited to have the opportunity to work with you.

Sincerely,
Matthew Driscoll

Evaluation

This response fulfilled the requirements and did so in a concise and organized manner. He even asked additional questions, which is always good to get a higher score. He would have scored higher had there been higher-level grammar and tenses. There weren't a lot of past subjunctive or advanced transitional words either. The approach was safe and would net a 4. To get a 5, it would need more detail, sophistication, and depth of grammar. Try to always show this in your writing, by perhaps keeping a mental checklist of good transitional words, verb tenses, and vocabulary that you can incorporate into your responses.

Presentational Writing: Persuasive Essay (Page 304)

Translation for Source 1

Introduction

The following document was created by the Board of Supervisors for Educational District #242, Los Angeles, on the possibility of offering parents the option of reducing the school week from five days to four.

June 15, 2008

Re. Changing the routine: Reducing the school week from 5 days to 4

Dear Parents:

I understand how recent inflation and the rising cost of living have affected you and your families. This is a difficult time for all. Already affected by the rising costs of fuel for buses, for heating and cooling buildings, feeding students, and of almost all materials, school districts across the country are considering the idea of reducing the school week from five days to four. It's an option we should seriously consider.

More than 150 schools across the country have already adopted this option and seem to be happy with the results. A district in Topeka, Kansas has adopted a Tuesday to Friday schedule and has saved $248,000 of its $8.7 million budget. This money was used for refunds to district residents. They also reported improved student attendance and better results on standardized tests.

There are other benefits. A three-day weekend would provide more family time, something lacking in today's society. In addition, students could spend more time on school assignments without the pressure of a 5-day school week.

The costs associated with the maintenance of our buildings and the transportation of our students are staggering. As we are faced with an uncertain future in fuel costs, we have to act now. Obviously, reducing costs is the answer, and adding 1.5 hours to each school day, thus eliminating a full day, represents economic savings without the necessity of sacrificing jobs, academic instruction, or student programs. Without these savings, students living less than 2 miles from their schools will lose the free transportation provided by the district.

I invite you to attend a public forum at Fleetwood July 23, 2008, at 7 P.M. There, we can discuss this issue further.

Sincerely,

Luis Maldonado

Superintendent, District 242

Translation for Source 2

Introduction

The following article appeared in an American daily newspaper in August 2004.

5 – 1 = Success

It's a school day for most of the country, but not for Erica Bongiardina, a student in the fourth grade of the Betsy Ross School in Aspen, Colorado. Fridays are spent on the ski slopes with her family. "I love it. I have a three-day weekend. It's awesome!"

Her school debuted the 4-day week this year, mainly to reduce budget costs. According to school officials, the school reduced by 20% their transportation, food services, cleaning, and fuel costs. In all, they estimate they will enjoy a savings of $200,000.

Various states have experimented with the 4-day school week. What Betsy Ross has not done is reduce the academic curriculum: classes are longer, and an additional period of study has been added to the curriculum. School begins at 8:30 A.M. and ends at 4:15 P.M. for the students, "which represents a rather long day," explains Sophie Zbeig, director of the school.

"A reduced week means that the students have to apply themselves even more. They learn the importance of having discipline. They simply don't have time to get into trouble," explains Zbeig.

Results talk

A recent study in Colorado shows that there is no academic difference in the state exam results among students from four-day and five-day schools. "There are fewer absences; activities like sports are scheduled for Fridays, so students don't lose study time during the week. And parents tend to schedule appointments or family events on Fridays, and then they tend not to take them out of school from Monday to Thursday," offers Zbeig.

"The great thing is that it gives me a full day to spend with my kids. And when they are old enough, they can work a day more to get the things that they want, which helps me economically," says Carina Guichane, mother of three sons from 6 to 14 years old.

Another potential benefit with the longer day is that students will be arriving at home at the same time as their parents, which eliminates the need to look for child care help, another economic benefit. However, Friday presents a problem for some who must find someone to care for their children for a whole day.

Those who deny the benefit of the reduced school week indicate that the American students, who for years have been inferior to European and Asian students in science and math, are losing the chance to compete globally. Some fear that with a longer weekend, the students will not be able to retain the same amount of information.

Translation for Source 3 (Audio Track 19)

Introduction

Meeting of parents, School Management Board, July 23, 2008, Fleetwood School. The following residents of Los Angeles expressed their opinions on the proposal to change the school week from five to four days.

Myrta Morales	I'm not sure that there isn't a limit to what students can learn in a school day. And, I'm especially worried for children in the first grade and kindergarten possibly having to sit for an additional 90 minutes. It's about quality, not quantity.
Rene López	This would not save money. What's more, costs would rise. For those who think this is about saving fuel, they are mistaken. Many large buildings have to maintain a specific level of temperature for various reasons: From the economic perspective, it's more efficient keep a building at 65 degrees for 3 days instead of turning off the heat and

trying to heat up the building on Monday morning. In addition, we wouldn't save any money on salaries, as the teachers are still working the same number of hours. What's more, state financial aid is linked to the length of the school day, which has to equal 180 days of attendance. If we lower the attendance figures, we run the risk of losing state financial aid—and we would pay more taxes.

Roberto Méndez — Our children need more time in school, rather than less. Education is the basis of our society. Perhaps this would work with high school students, but not with grade school students. Some children will have problems getting used to school after the weekend. Three days off would be a disaster! As a country we need to find alternative ways to reduce energy costs. Reducing the time children spend in school will hold us back as a nation. We need to educate them and open their minds…they're our future!

Irene Ramos — We already have students who spend more than an hour on the bus to get to school. Adding more hours to this is simply too much for them.

Sample Student Response

Con los precios altos de energía, nos vemos comprometidos a encontrar nuevas maneras de ahorrar dinero y recursos. Ya no se puede dar por sentado todo lo que tenemos hoy, ya que puede que mañana no lo haya. Para tratar de ahorrar dinero, y controlar los gastos ascendientes, algunos distritos están considerando la opción de sólo operar 4 días por semana y extender cada día unos 90 minutos.

El superintendente explica que esto ahorraría dinero, mejoraría asistencia, y mejoraría rendimiento estudiantil en términos académicos. Sin embargo, la comunidad, demuestra que les importa más el éxito de sus niños que el ahorrar dinero. Además, señalan que es posible que no ahorren dinero. Cerrar las escuelas sin calefacción ni aire acondicionado podrá resultar más caro que simplemente mantenerlas a una temperatura estable. También, cuestionan la utilidad de extender el horario escolar. Sin embargo, un estudiante explica que el tiempo libre le permitiría dedicarle más tiempo a sus estudios, de acuerdo a lo que explica el Superintendente Maldonado.

Según la fuente 3, los padres insisten en que sus hijos pasen más tiempo en la escuela, no menos. Y la ayuda financiera del estado exige 180 días, no menos. La conservación durante el día escolar podrá ser una manera de ahorrar energía: no hace falta tener luces todo el tiempo, y tal vez otras tecnologías pudieran ayudar a ahorrar energía. En realidad no hay una solución al problema; hay que considerar las dos caras de la moneda. Tal vez si todos los miembros de la comunidad se sentaran a conversar, y así considerar las opiniones de muchos, podrían llegar a un acuerdo y ver como resolver el problema.

Pero hemos visto segun la fuente 2, que economicamente las escuelas ahorran dinero y tienen los mismos resultados. Las familias benefician pues pasan más tiempo juntas. Y lo que me convence que esta política si tiene sentido es que el comportamiento y la asistencia de los estudiantes mejoran en un horario de cuatro días. Siendo estudiante, puedo decir que esos dos factores son vinculados al éxito escolar.

Translation of the Sample Student Response

With the high prices of energy, we are obliged to find new ways of saving money and resources. We can no longer take for granted what we have today, because it may not be here tomorrow. In order to try to save money and control rising costs, some districts are considering the option of operating only 4 days a week and extending each school day by 90 minutes.

The superintendent explains that this would save money, improve attendance, and improve student academic performance. However, the community demonstrates that they are more interested in the success of their children than saving money. In addition, they show that it is possible that money would not be saved. Closing the schools without heat or air conditioning could be more expensive than simply maintaining them at a stable temperature. And they question the usefulness of extending the school schedule. However, one student explains that the free time would allow him to dedicate more time to his studies, in accordance with what Superintendent Maldonado explained.

According to Source 3, parents want their children to spend more, not less, time in school. And the financial aid from the state requires 180 days, nothing less. Conservation during the school day could be a way to save money; it's not necessary to have lights on all the time, and perhaps other technologies could help save energy. In reality, there isn't a solution to the problem; we have to consider both sides of the coin. Maybe if all of the members of the community sat down to speak and thus consider the many existing opinions, then they could come to an agreement and resolve the issue.

But we see that, according to Source 2, economically schools save money and have the same results. Families benefit because they spend more time together. And what convinces me that this policy does make sense is that student behavior and attendance improve in a four-day school week. Being a student, I can say that these two factors are extremely important to school success.

Evaluation

This response was adequate in addressing the three areas of topic development, task completion, and language usage. It was somewhat short and, rather than arguing for a point of view, mostly just summarized (although it did include some comparison and contrast). Make sure your essay includes a strong opinion. This student's opinion, when it finally appears, is weak and changes between the third and fourth paragraphs. This well-written but somewhat predictable and basic essay would merit a 3 on the exam.

Interpersonal Speaking: Conversation (Page 308)

Translation and Script for a Sample Student Response

Introduction

Your friend Laura calls you to talk to you about an experience you had last weekend when you went to the mountains for fun.

Laura: *Hola, ¿Qué tal? Oye, Cuéntame ¿cómo lo pasaste en tu excursión a las montañas?*

Hello, How are you? Tell me, how was your trip to the mountains?

MA: *Hola Laura, siempre me es muy grato hablarte. Claro está, me divertí mucho en la excursión; fue una experiencia inolvidable. Ojala estuvieras ahí.*

Hi Laura, it is always a pleasure to talk to you. Of course, I had a lot of fun on the trip; it was an unforgettable experience. I wish you had been there.

Laura: *¿Ah sí? Dime, ¿qué hiciste? ¿En qué actividades participaste?*

Oh, really? Tell me, what did you do? What activities did you participate in?

MA: *Pues, hicimos montañismo, esquiamos en la pista de esquí, exploramos la naturaleza y naturalmente hasta sacamos fotos de todos los animales y el lindo paisaje que vimos allá.*

Well, we went hiking, we skied on the ski slopes, we explored nature, and naturally we took pictures of the wildlife and the beautiful landscape that we saw there.

Laura: *Siempre me ha llamado la atención hacer una excursión a las montañas, pero tengo miedo. ¿Es peligroso, no?*

I have always wanted to take a trip to the mountains, but I'm afraid. It's dangerous, right?

MA: *De ninguna manera. No tengas miedo—es una experiencia muy placentera. Es muy seguro y bonito. No es necesario que uno vaya a la cima de las montañas, pues hay los áreas muy seguras para hacer campamento. Y fuimos un grupo grande de jóvenes.*

Not at all. Don't be afraid—it is a very pleasant experience. It is beautiful and safe. It's not necessary to go to the top of the mountains since there are safe areas to go camping. And a big group of young people went.

Laura: *Tienes razón, debería ir... pero me encantaría que me acompañaras. ¿Te gustaría ir el próximo viernes?*

You're right, I should go…but I would love for you to go with me. Would you like to go next Friday?

MA: *No, lamentablemente no puedo; tengo un compromiso el viernes. ¿Por qué no vamos el mes que viene?*

No, unfortunately I can't, I have an engagement on Friday. Why don't we go next month?

Laura: *Me parece una excelente idea. Pero en realidad no sé qué llevarme, ni como alistarlo todo. ¿Alguna recomendación?*

That sounds like an excellent idea. But I really don't know what to take with me, or how to get it all ready. Do you have any recommendations?

MA: *Por supuesto. Yo diría que necesitas llevar ropa abrigadora, una cámara para sacar fotos, botas, un saco de dormir si quieres hacer camping afuera, una linterna, comida, y por supuesto, una mente abierta.*

Of course. I would say you need to take warm clothes, a camera to take pictures, boots, a sleeping bag if you want to camp outside, food, a flashlight, and of course, an open mind.

Laura: *Ah perfecto, ya tengo una idea. Mil gracias por tu ayuda. ¿Entonces como lo haremos? ¿Dónde te encuentro? ¿Cómo vamos para allá?*

Oh, perfect, now I have an idea. Thanks for your help. So, how should we do this? Where should I meet you? How will we get there?

MA: *No te preocupes tanto. Puedo ir a tu casa a recogerte, metemos todo en mi auto y de allí manejamos a las montañas.*

Don't worry so much. I can pick you up at your house, we will put everything in my car, and from there we can drive to the mountains.

Laura: *Genial, listo. Nos vemos entonces. Cuídate. ¡Chau!*

Perfect. Done. I'll see you then. Take care, bye!

Evaluation

Notice how the student filled up the entire time allotted with meaningful conversation. He also made sure to use proper agreement and higher-level grammar (subjunctive, conditional, good transitional words, and commands). It would probably get a 5 due to its well-presented responses.

Presentational Speaking: Cultural Comparison (Page 309)

Translation of the Question

In our society, we see that cultural traditions define a people. However, what makes life interesting are the differences between cultures. In your experience, compare and contrast some cultural traditions that you have observed in your community with those of other countries in the Spanish-speaking world.

Sample Student Response

Las diferencias entre la cultura hispana e la estadounidense penetran cada nivel de la vida. Hay diferencias en las celebraciones y las costumbres asociadas con dichas celebraciones.

En los Estados Unidos muchas celebraciones tienen un valor recreativo y hasta económico, mientras que en América Latina, tiene un tono religioso. El día de los muertos, en México, las familias van al camposanto a honrar a sus seres queridos, y hay misas para recordar a la gente muerta. En los Estados Unidos, El día de los muertos es un día de disfraces y fiestas, y los niños van de casa en casa pidiendo dulces. Se dice que la gente gasta millones de dólares en fiestas y disfraces. En América Latina, la Navidad es una fiesta religiosa, y no se intercambian muchos regalos. Eso se hace el 6 de enero, el día de los Reyes Magos. En los Estados Unidos, la gente decora árboles, intercambian regalos, y aprovechan las tremendas rebajas en las tiendas. Los hispanos no hacen tantas compras para Navidad.

En Chile, el día de los Inocentes es el 28 de diciembre y todo el mundo gasta bromas. Hasta los periódicos publican información escandalosa y falsa para asustar a la gente. Pero en realidad la celebración conmemora un hecho de la Biblia, cuando Herodes ordeno la matanza de los niños inocentes de Belén. En los Estados Unidos tenemos algo similar, el primero de abril, pero en realidad no es un día importante ni tiene una base religiosa.

Es evidente que la religión en el mundo hispanohablante influencia profundamente las celebraciones y las actitudes de la gente. En los Estados Unidos, tal vez por la diversidad de religiones y grupos, las celebraciones tienen otro sabor.

Translation of the Sample Student Response

The differences between Hispanic and U.S. culture penetrate every level of life. There are differences in celebrations and in the customs associated with these celebrations.

In the United States, many celebrations have a recreational value and even an economic one, while in Latin America, they have a religious tone. On the Day of the Dead, in Mexico, families go to the cemetery to honor their dearly departed, and there are Masses to remember them. In the United States, the Day of the Dead is a day of costumes and parties, and children go door to door asking for candy. It is said that people spend millions of dollars on parties and costumes. In Latin America, Christmas is a religious celebration, and people don't exchange that many presents. That is done on the 6th of January, Three Kings Day. In the United States, people decorate trees, exchange gifts, and take advantage of the tremendous sales in the stores. Hispanics do not do as much shopping for Christmas.

In Chile, the Day of the Innocents is the 28th of December and everyone plays jokes. Even newspapers publish scandalous and fake information in order to scare people. But in reality, the celebration commemorates a story from the Bible, when Herod ordered the killing of the innocent children of Bethlehem. In the United States, we have something similar, April 1, but in reality it is not an important day, nor does it have a religious basis.

It is evident that religion in the Spanish-speaking world profoundly influences celebrations and the attitudes of the people. In the United States, perhaps because it is so diverse in terms of groups and religions, the celebrations have another flavor.

Evaluation

With only 4 minutes to prepare your presentation, it will be impossible to write it all out. So you will need to outline quickly. Get a clear introductory paragraph, a main point, and then details to illustrate that point. Notice how the student here touched upon several holidays and incorporated several countries into the presentation. It is obvious that they knew specifics about the target culture: religion and celebrations. The comparing and contrasting was strong because there were definite differences between the two cultures. This is the part of the exam where you will need to be able to speak without reading, which means you need to keep careful control of your grammar. This student played it a little safe by keeping the sentences simple, but under pressure, this is to be expected. It was a clean, well-thought-out sample, which showed command of the language and the topic and would score a 4 on the exam.

Completely darken bubbles with a No. 2 pencil. If you make a mistake, be sure to erase mark completely. Erase all stray marks.

1. YOUR NAME:
(Print) Last First M.I.

SIGNATURE: _____ DATE: __/__/__

HOME ADDRESS: _____
(Print) Number and Street

_____
City State Zip Code

PHONE NO. : _____
(Print)

5. YOUR NAME

First 4 letters of last name				FIRST INIT	MID INIT

IMPORTANT: Please fill in these boxes exactly as shown on the back cover of your test book.

2. TEST FORM

3. TEST CODE

4. REGISTRATION NUMBER

6. DATE OF BIRTH

Month	Day	Year
JAN		
FEB		
MAR		
APR		
MAY		
JUN		
JUL		
AUG		
SEP		
OCT		
NOV		
DEC		

7. SEX
MALE
FEMALE

The Princeton Review®

© TPR Education IP Holdings, LLC
FORM NO. 00001-PR

Section I Start with number 1 for each new section.
If a section has fewer questions than answer spaces, leave the extra answer spaces blank.

1. A B C D
2. A B C D
3. A B C D
4. A B C D
5. A B C D
6. A B C D
7. A B C D
8. A B C D
9. A B C D
10. A B C D
11. A B C D
12. A B C D
13. A B C D
14. A B C D
15. A B C D
16. A B C D
17. A B C D
18. A B C D
19. A B C D
20. A B C D
21. A B C D
22. A B C D
23. A B C D
24. A B C D
25. A B C D
26. A B C D
27. A B C D
28. A B C D
29. A B C D
30. A B C D

31. A B C D
32. A B C D
33. A B C D
34. A B C D
35. A B C D
36. A B C D
37. A B C D
38. A B C D
39. A B C D
40. A B C D
41. A B C D
42. A B C D
43. A B C D
44. A B C D
45. A B C D
46. A B C D
47. A B C D
48. A B C D
49. A B C D
50. A B C D
51. A B C D
52. A B C D
53. A B C D
54. A B C D
55. A B C D
56. A B C D
57. A B C D
58. A B C D
59. A B C D
60. A B C D

61. A B C D
62. A B C D
63. A B C D
64. A B C D
65. A B C D
66. A B C D
67. A B C D
68. A B C D
69. A B C D
70. A B C D
71. A B C D
72. A B C D
73. A B C D
74. A B C D
75. A B C D
76. A B C D
77. A B C D
78. A B C D
79. A B C D
80. A B C D
81. A B C D
82. A B C D
83. A B C D
84. A B C D
85. A B C D
86. A B C D
87. A B C D
88. A B C D
89. A B C D
90. A B C D

91. A B C D
92. A B C D
93. A B C D
94. A B C D
95. A B C D
96. A B C D
97. A B C D
98. A B C D
99. A B C D
100. A B C D
101. A B C D
102. A B C D
103. A B C D
104. A B C D
105. A B C D
106. A B C D
107. A B C D
108. A B C D
109. A B C D
110. A B C D
111. A B C D
112. A B C D
113. A B C D
114. A B C D
115. A B C D
116. A B C D
117. A B C D
118. A B C D
119. A B C D
120. A B C D

Completely darken bubbles with a No. 2 pencil. If you make a mistake, be sure to erase mark completely. Erase all stray marks.

1. YOUR NAME:
(Print)
Last   First   M.I.

SIGNATURE: _____ DATE: ___/___/___

HOME ADDRESS: _____
(Print)
Number and Street

_____
City   State   Zip Code

PHONE NO. : _____
(Print)

IMPORTANT: Please fill in these boxes exactly as shown on the back cover of your test book.

2. TEST FORM

3. TEST CODE

4. REGISTRATION NUMBER

6. DATE OF BIRTH

Month	Day	Year
○ JAN		
○ FEB		
○ MAR	⓪ ⓪	⓪ ⓪
○ APR	① ①	① ①
○ MAY	② ②	② ②
○ JUN	③ ③	③ ③
○ JUL		④ ④
○ AUG		⑤ ⑤
○ SEP		⑥ ⑥
○ OCT		⑦ ⑦
○ NOV		⑧ ⑧
○ DEC		⑨ ⑨

7. SEX
○ MALE
○ FEMALE

The **Princeton** Review®

© TPR Education IP Holdings, LLC
FORM NO. 00001-PR

5. YOUR NAME

First 4 letters of last name | FIRST INIT | MID INIT

Ⓐ Ⓑ Ⓒ Ⓓ Ⓔ Ⓕ Ⓖ Ⓗ Ⓘ Ⓙ Ⓚ Ⓛ Ⓜ Ⓝ Ⓞ Ⓟ Ⓠ Ⓡ Ⓢ Ⓣ Ⓤ Ⓥ Ⓦ Ⓧ Ⓨ Ⓩ

Section 1
Start with number 1 for each new section.
If a section has fewer questions than answer spaces, leave the extra answer spaces blank.

1. Ⓐ Ⓑ Ⓒ Ⓓ
2. Ⓐ Ⓑ Ⓒ Ⓓ
3. Ⓐ Ⓑ Ⓒ Ⓓ
4. Ⓐ Ⓑ Ⓒ Ⓓ
5. Ⓐ Ⓑ Ⓒ Ⓓ
6. Ⓐ Ⓑ Ⓒ Ⓓ
7. Ⓐ Ⓑ Ⓒ Ⓓ
8. Ⓐ Ⓑ Ⓒ Ⓓ
9. Ⓐ Ⓑ Ⓒ Ⓓ
10. Ⓐ Ⓑ Ⓒ Ⓓ
11. Ⓐ Ⓑ Ⓒ Ⓓ
12. Ⓐ Ⓑ Ⓒ Ⓓ
13. Ⓐ Ⓑ Ⓒ Ⓓ
14. Ⓐ Ⓑ Ⓒ Ⓓ
15. Ⓐ Ⓑ Ⓒ Ⓓ
16. Ⓐ Ⓑ Ⓒ Ⓓ
17. Ⓐ Ⓑ Ⓒ Ⓓ
18. Ⓐ Ⓑ Ⓒ Ⓓ
19. Ⓐ Ⓑ Ⓒ Ⓓ
20. Ⓐ Ⓑ Ⓒ Ⓓ
21. Ⓐ Ⓑ Ⓒ Ⓓ
22. Ⓐ Ⓑ Ⓒ Ⓓ
23. Ⓐ Ⓑ Ⓒ Ⓓ
24. Ⓐ Ⓑ Ⓒ Ⓓ
25. Ⓐ Ⓑ Ⓒ Ⓓ
26. Ⓐ Ⓑ Ⓒ Ⓓ
27. Ⓐ Ⓑ Ⓒ Ⓓ
28. Ⓐ Ⓑ Ⓒ Ⓓ
29. Ⓐ Ⓑ Ⓒ Ⓓ
30. Ⓐ Ⓑ Ⓒ Ⓓ

31. Ⓐ Ⓑ Ⓒ Ⓓ
32. Ⓐ Ⓑ Ⓒ Ⓓ
33. Ⓐ Ⓑ Ⓒ Ⓓ
34. Ⓐ Ⓑ Ⓒ Ⓓ
35. Ⓐ Ⓑ Ⓒ Ⓓ
36. Ⓐ Ⓑ Ⓒ Ⓓ
37. Ⓐ Ⓑ Ⓒ Ⓓ
38. Ⓐ Ⓑ Ⓒ Ⓓ
39. Ⓐ Ⓑ Ⓒ Ⓓ
40. Ⓐ Ⓑ Ⓒ Ⓓ
41. Ⓐ Ⓑ Ⓒ Ⓓ
42. Ⓐ Ⓑ Ⓒ Ⓓ
43. Ⓐ Ⓑ Ⓒ Ⓓ
44. Ⓐ Ⓑ Ⓒ Ⓓ
45. Ⓐ Ⓑ Ⓒ Ⓓ
46. Ⓐ Ⓑ Ⓒ Ⓓ
47. Ⓐ Ⓑ Ⓒ Ⓓ
48. Ⓐ Ⓑ Ⓒ Ⓓ
49. Ⓐ Ⓑ Ⓒ Ⓓ
50. Ⓐ Ⓑ Ⓒ Ⓓ
51. Ⓐ Ⓑ Ⓒ Ⓓ
52. Ⓐ Ⓑ Ⓒ Ⓓ
53. Ⓐ Ⓑ Ⓒ Ⓓ
54. Ⓐ Ⓑ Ⓒ Ⓓ
55. Ⓐ Ⓑ Ⓒ Ⓓ
56. Ⓐ Ⓑ Ⓒ Ⓓ
57. Ⓐ Ⓑ Ⓒ Ⓓ
58. Ⓐ Ⓑ Ⓒ Ⓓ
59. Ⓐ Ⓑ Ⓒ Ⓓ
60. Ⓐ Ⓑ Ⓒ Ⓓ

61. Ⓐ Ⓑ Ⓒ Ⓓ
62. Ⓐ Ⓑ Ⓒ Ⓓ
63. Ⓐ Ⓑ Ⓒ Ⓓ
64. Ⓐ Ⓑ Ⓒ Ⓓ
65. Ⓐ Ⓑ Ⓒ Ⓓ
66. Ⓐ Ⓑ Ⓒ Ⓓ
67. Ⓐ Ⓑ Ⓒ Ⓓ
68. Ⓐ Ⓑ Ⓒ Ⓓ
69. Ⓐ Ⓑ Ⓒ Ⓓ
70. Ⓐ Ⓑ Ⓒ Ⓓ
71. Ⓐ Ⓑ Ⓒ Ⓓ
72. Ⓐ Ⓑ Ⓒ Ⓓ
73. Ⓐ Ⓑ Ⓒ Ⓓ
74. Ⓐ Ⓑ Ⓒ Ⓓ
75. Ⓐ Ⓑ Ⓒ Ⓓ
76. Ⓐ Ⓑ Ⓒ Ⓓ
77. Ⓐ Ⓑ Ⓒ Ⓓ
78. Ⓐ Ⓑ Ⓒ Ⓓ
79. Ⓐ Ⓑ Ⓒ Ⓓ
80. Ⓐ Ⓑ Ⓒ Ⓓ
81. Ⓐ Ⓑ Ⓒ Ⓓ
82. Ⓐ Ⓑ Ⓒ Ⓓ
83. Ⓐ Ⓑ Ⓒ Ⓓ
84. Ⓐ Ⓑ Ⓒ Ⓓ
85. Ⓐ Ⓑ Ⓒ Ⓓ
86. Ⓐ Ⓑ Ⓒ Ⓓ
87. Ⓐ Ⓑ Ⓒ Ⓓ
88. Ⓐ Ⓑ Ⓒ Ⓓ
89. Ⓐ Ⓑ Ⓒ Ⓓ
90. Ⓐ Ⓑ Ⓒ Ⓓ

91. Ⓐ Ⓑ Ⓒ Ⓓ
92. Ⓐ Ⓑ Ⓒ Ⓓ
93. Ⓐ Ⓑ Ⓒ Ⓓ
94. Ⓐ Ⓑ Ⓒ Ⓓ
95. Ⓐ Ⓑ Ⓒ Ⓓ
96. Ⓐ Ⓑ Ⓒ Ⓓ
97. Ⓐ Ⓑ Ⓒ Ⓓ
98. Ⓐ Ⓑ Ⓒ Ⓓ
99. Ⓐ Ⓑ Ⓒ Ⓓ
100. Ⓐ Ⓑ Ⓒ Ⓓ
101. Ⓐ Ⓑ Ⓒ Ⓓ
102. Ⓐ Ⓑ Ⓒ Ⓓ
103. Ⓐ Ⓑ Ⓒ Ⓓ
104. Ⓐ Ⓑ Ⓒ Ⓓ
105. Ⓐ Ⓑ Ⓒ Ⓓ
106. Ⓐ Ⓑ Ⓒ Ⓓ
107. Ⓐ Ⓑ Ⓒ Ⓓ
108. Ⓐ Ⓑ Ⓒ Ⓓ
109. Ⓐ Ⓑ Ⓒ Ⓓ
110. Ⓐ Ⓑ Ⓒ Ⓓ
111. Ⓐ Ⓑ Ⓒ Ⓓ
112. Ⓐ Ⓑ Ⓒ Ⓓ
113. Ⓐ Ⓑ Ⓒ Ⓓ
114. Ⓐ Ⓑ Ⓒ Ⓓ
115. Ⓐ Ⓑ Ⓒ Ⓓ
116. Ⓐ Ⓑ Ⓒ Ⓓ
117. Ⓐ Ⓑ Ⓒ Ⓓ
118. Ⓐ Ⓑ Ⓒ Ⓓ
119. Ⓐ Ⓑ Ⓒ Ⓓ
120. Ⓐ Ⓑ Ⓒ Ⓓ

NOTES

NOTES

NOTES

NOTES

NOTES

NOTES

NOTES

NOTES

NOTES

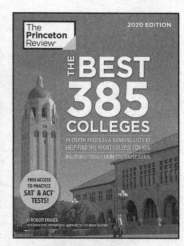

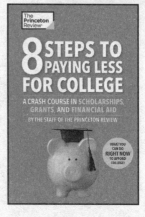